Gardens OF THE NATIONAL TRUST

Gardens OF THE NATIONAL TRUST

STEPHEN LACEY

THE NATIONAL TRUST

Distributed by Harry N. Abrams, Inc., Publishers

To the gardeners of the National Trust

First published in Great Britain in 1996 by
National Trust Enterprises Limited,
36 Queen Anne's Gate, London SW1H 9AS

Text copyright © Stephen Lacey 1996
Tabular information © The National Trust 1996

Distributed in North America in 1996 by
Harry N. Abrams, Incorporated, New York
A Times Mirror Company

Library of Congress Catalog Card Number: 96-67121
ISBN 0-8109-6321-3

Edited by Marilyn Inglis
Picture research by Gayle Mault
Designed by Newton Engert Partnership
Production management by Bob Towell

Phototypeset in Monotype Bembo Series 270
by Southern Positives and Negatives (SPAN), Lingfield, Surrey

Printed in Great Britain by Balding + Mansell

HALF TITLE: Martagon lilies against a brick wall at Acorn Bank, Cumbria.

FRONTISPIECE: Rose arches covered in blooms at Nymans, West Sussex.

Contents

Sponsor's Preface

Pull up outside the gates of any National Trust garden and you're sure to see a few Land Rover vehicles in the car park. Indeed, customer research tells us that visiting National Trust properties is a favourite pastime for Defenders, Discovery and Range Rover owners. But did you realise that our vehicles also play an important role *inside* those ornamental gates?

For many years, Land Rover Defenders have been seen as *the* means of transport for the Trust's estate wardens who help look after these beautiful gardens. In 1995 – the Trust's Centenary year – Land Rover began this association with a long-term sponsorship agreement including the supply of vehicles and driver training for vitally important conservation projects. It was a great day for two British institutions with so much in common – not least our shared pride in our national heritage and our joint commitment to protect the environment.

So, on behalf of everyone at Land Rover, from one national institution to another, let me extend our heartiest congratulations to the National Trust on this superb book which we are delighted to sponsor.

R.T.W. Ramsay
Marketing Director – Rover Group

LEFT: Cragside in Northumberland, viewed from Debdon Burn.

Foreword

The gardens of the National Trust make up the world's greatest collection under one ownership. This global claim is no idle boast – the Trust looks after the greatest in number, in diversity, in historic importance and in quality. Taken together, they contain the world's most important collections of cultivated plants, distinguished for their beauty, their rarity, their historic interest, their relevance to the gardens and their scientific value. In writing *Gardens of the National Trust*, Stephen Lacey took on a rich and large tapestry. The result is a celebration of gardening as art, craft and science, a repertory of expertise unmatched anywhere.

The impulse to preserve and restore other people's gardens arose early in the nineteenth century – until then, gardens reflected the fashions and needs of their time, and the personal whims of those who made them. Most still do, and it is right that new gardens should respond to the spirit of the age and the needs of those who own and use them. Today's extraordinary upsurge of interest in horticulture and design results in gardens that delight and satisfy their creators on various aesthetic and visual levels. Gardens and designers can learn much from examples from the past, not by slavish copying, but rather by analysing what made them successful and popular in their time.

It may take a century for a tree to mature, so that garden makers often cannot live to see the full outcome of their labours. Because gardens are constantly developing and changing, they can be fascinating documents of the past, if you know how to read them. They record, sometimes more vividly and indelibly than any archive, the ideals, interests and tastes of former owners, and the influences that affected their decisions. Perhaps because of the continuity of landowning families and the relative stability of British institutions, the main threads running through gardening traditions have been adaptation and addition. Although some features may have altered or been replaced, most old gardens contain a strong thread of continuity which is not difficult to detect. This has led to cumulative enrichment of style, ornament and planting, resulting in a complex and ever-changing relationship with the past. In conserving these gardens, the challenge for the Trust is to retain that thread of continuity and individuality while continuing to renew, restore and adapt to secure their survival.

The National Trust has just celebrated its centenary. At the outset gardens were not on the list of sites considered for preservation, although Sayes Court might have provided a very early example of a National Trust garden. This modest house in Deptford, South London had belonged in the seventeenth century to the great diarist and horticulturist, John Evelyn. In 1884 the property was offered by the Evelyn family to Octavia Hill and Robert Hunter with the proposal that the garden should become a public open space and the garden building a museum. Negotiations broke down because there was no public body with the necessary statutory powers for preserving it for these uses, and Sayes Court was lost. But the lesson was learnt and ten years later, Octavia Hill and Robert Hunter, together with Hardwicke Rawnsley, founded just such a body, the National Trust.

LEFT: The Terrace at Powis Castle, Powys, draped in wisteria.

9

Although several very important gardens were acquired with their houses and estates early on in the Trust's history, it was not until 1948 that the National Trust decided to accept gardens in their own right, quite independent of the quality of the remainder of the property. The first garden to come in this way was Hidcote in Gloucestershire, the life work of Lawrence Johnston and perhaps the most influential garden of the twentieth century. An appropriate choice but also a difficult challenge, for Hidcote represents an extremely complex combination of vegetable architecture, plantsmanship and artistry of planting, now much imitated. More gardens created in the twentieth century by great individualists followed: Mount Stewart, Rowallane, Nymans, Trelissick, Tintinhull, Knightshayes and Sissinghurst. Alongside these, the Trust acquired great historical gardens, products of an earlier era: Studley Royal, Biddulph Grange, Stowe and most recently, Prior Park.

With Hidcote the Trust began to learn some hard lessons about the realities of preserving gardens when the original genius had gone. It soon became apparent that gardening by committee was not the best way forward, and also that trusting to the whims of individuals, however talented, did not necessarily preserve the individuality of the original creation. In fact, gardens like Sissinghurst, Hidcote and Biddulph Grange were almost always the product of collaborative talents of two or three people working closely and consistently together. Bearing in mind the range of talents required – imaginative design, architectural skill, plants-manship, horticultural expertise and management ability – this is not surprising. The Trust has adapted this collaborative approach and evolved a system whereby all but the most far-reaching decisions can be made by a small group comprising the head gardener, property manager and adviser, with help from others when necessary. To avoid change in the character of the garden according to the personal prejudices of those most closely involved, all decisions are guided by long-term plans based upon the history and unique character of the place.

The astonishing growth in the popularity of garden visiting, impossible to predict half a century ago, has been the means of survival for many great gardens. But a garden of modest size which now accepts as many as 150,000 visitors a year cannot be the same as it was when used only by family and friends. Inevitably something is lost. Our job is to minimise this impact and to make it possible for as many visitors as possible to enjoy the Trust's gardens. Indeed, by producing his vivid word pictures and conveying the special significance of each garden, Stephen Lacey has helped us in this task. Many of you who enjoy this book cannot perforce visit National Trust gardens easily or often. Here you can savour the delights of a rose garden or the view across a lake in comfort, and with room for contemplation. For those who can visit, we hope this book will intensify your enjoyment of gardens familiar to you, and introduce you to other, new delights.

John Sales, Chief Gardens Adviser, The National Trust

Introduction

Unlike Graham Stuart Thomas, who wrote the first comprehensive guide to the Trust's gardens in the late 1970s and was closely involved with their management and restoration, I came to this project as an outsider. I had never been to Rowallane or Rievaulx Terrace; I had never even heard of Peckover House or The Courts, Holt. So it has been an adventure and an education, with a great many people from head gardeners to historic buildings representatives helping to illuminate each garden's evolution and idiosyncrasies.

The diversity of the Trust's gardens is immediately apparent from the photographs. They range from landscape park to walled town garden, box parterre to rhododendron woodland, Derbyshire hilltop to Cornish combe. Lakes, temples, herbaceous borders, Japanese gardens, conservatories, pinetums, collections of lawnmowers, daffodils, roses, regional apple varieties and eighteenth-century statues, views of sea, moor and motorway, yew trees clipped as pointed Welsh hats, even an artificial tree fern made from a length of clay pipe, it is all here.

The gardens engage you on many levels. There are the straightforward pleasures of seeing, smelling, touching, listening and exploring. For home gardeners, there are ideas and plant names to pick up. But go deeper and invariably you tap into a story, perhaps of great individuals and family successions, designers and plant hunters, period politics and pre-occupations, changing fashions, destructions and restorations.

Between them, the gardens chart some four hundred years of history. To medieval times, there are just momentary references, in the partnership of ancient building with flowery mead at Cotehele and Sizergh Castle, and in the presence of herb gardens at Acorn Bank and Buckland Abbey. Renaissance pleasure gardening is captured in the enclosures and mounts at Little Moreton Hall, the pavilion and bowling green at Melford Hall, the covered walks and knot garden at Moseley Old Hall, and, most imposingly, by the grand Elizabethan courts, gateways and finial-capped walls at Hardwick Hall and Montacute.

The landscape movement spelled destruction for many of the great formal gardens, but those at Ham House, Westbury Court, Powis Castle, Erddig and Hanbury Hall survived in large part, or have been resurrected by the Trust, and show the European-inspired styles of the late seventeenth and early eighteenth centuries. The story of the subsequent departure from these enclosed and geometric patterns and the evolution of the landscape style through its Arcadian, Brownian and romantically Picturesque phases is recounted, in whole or in part, at Claremont, Stowe, Fountains Abbey and Studley Royal, Wimpole Hall, Prior Park, West Wycombe Park and Stourhead, Kedleston, Petworth and Scotney Castle.

The early nineteenth century's renewed enthusiasm for formality and self-consciously artful gardening is marked at Ickworth, Calke Abbey and Peckover House, with grand revivals of earlier styles displayed at Oxburgh Hall, Montacute, Blickling and Belton. The innovation, ingenuity and daring-do that became the order of the day is revealed in the fantasy evocations at Biddulph Grange, the engineering feats at Cragside and the multi-coloured parkland and bedding schemes at Ascott, while Waddesdon Manor, Lyme Park,

Tatton Park and Polesden Lacey give a varied and luscious insight into country-house living and gardening in this Victorian and Edwardian heyday.

The influx of new trees and shrubs from the Americas, the Far East and Australasia through the nineteenth and early twentieth centuries fuelled the development of exotic woodlands, and at Killerton, Glendurgan, Nymans, Wakehurst Place, Bodnant, Rowallane, Trengwainton, Mount Stewart, Trelissick and Winkworth, we have supreme displays – equalled later at Knightshayes.

Simultaneously, architectural gardening was evolving, and in time became coupled with some dreamy and painterly herbaceous planting. Gertrude Jekyll's influence pervades the gardens at Barrington Court, Lutyens' at Castle Drogo and Coleton Fishacre, while in the crisp compartments and sophisticated colour schemes of Hidcote and Sissinghurst the marriage of plantsmanship and formal design reaches a new twentieth-century zenith.

It is a rich legacy, but also a dynamic one. For, as John Sales, the Trust's Chief Gardens Adviser, has written elsewhere, 'gardens are not only objects, they are also processes'. They come to the Trust already many-layered – often, as in the case of Cliveden, Dunham Massey, Kingston Lacy or Shugborough, shaped by activity (destructions as well as embellishments) over many generations. Restorations by the Trust – invariably based on fragmentary evidence, and with the degree of finish and style of upkeep modified to suit the available resources – add fresh layers.

And thereafter the gardens continue to change. Plants grow and die; Mother Nature unleashes her wood-boring beetles, honey fungus and storms. And then, year by year, there is change initiated from within – which, happily, the Trust recognises as essential if a garden is to be kept alive and pulsing. This may be a variation in bedding schemes or border planting, the continual enrichment of tree and shrub collections, or the sudden annexation of unemployed areas for new pursuits such as rose gardening, as at Mottisfont Abbey, or meadow wildflower gardening, as at Sheffield Park. Restoration always brings opportunities for innovation. And, particularly where the donor family is still in residence, the gardens may even be carried forward by bold new work from contemporary designers and artists, as at Ascott, Grey's Court and Dudmaston.

So there is much to contemplate on the garden tour. Since Graham Stuart Thomas wrote the last guide, major new gardens have come to the Trust – Stowe, Prior Park, Kedleston Hall, Kingston Lacy, Calke Abbey, Biddulph Grange, Coleton Fishacre, Hinton Ampner and the formal gardens at Cragside; almost everywhere, there have been significant embellishments and improvements, often major restorations – as at Osterley Park, Ham House, Hanbury Hall and Waddesdon Manor – and, in the wake of the great storms, major replantings – as at Nymans, Scotney Castle, Wakehurst Place and Sheffield Park.

Overall, the Trust's gardens are entering the new millennium in very good fettle and with ever-increasing visitor numbers. The tone of my descriptions will reveal which of them I have found particularly exciting and which have left me cool or puzzled; I hope there will be plenty of opportunity for you to see and judge them for yourself.

RIGHT: Flower borders along the south front of Moseley Old Hall, Staffordshire.

Gardens

Acorn Bank

Temple Sowerby, Cumbria

Just north of Temple Sowerby,
6 miles east of Penrith on A66

Area 2½ acres (1 ha)
Soil slightly alkaline/clay loam
Altitude 400 ft (122 m)
Average rainfall 36 in (914 mm)
Average winter climate very cold
Staff one

Pink opium poppies in the
borders at Acorn Bank.

Cumbria is a moody part of Britain and on a grey, wet, windswept afternoon, you may find Acorn Bank rather bleak. But on other days the sun draws out the red in the plum-coloured sandstone and reveals panoramic views across to the Lakeland fells, woodpeckers hammer the oak trees, newts rise in the well pond and the garden seems full of flowers.

The abundance of wildflowers and herbs at Acorn Bank carries you back to its medieval past, when it was home to the Knights Templar. Behind the house, where the oak-covered bank plunges steeply to the fast-flowing Crowdundle Beck, the former boundary line between Cumberland and Westmorland, the ground is studded with daffodils, primroses, cranesbills, Meadowsweet and Queen Anne's Lace. And in the orchard grow the wild yellow tulip, *Tulipa sylvestris*, the double white Wood Anemone, *A. nemorosa* 'Vestal', the Lent Lily, *Narcissus pseudonarcissus*, and the Pheasant's Eye Daffodil, *N. poeticus*.

The wildflower riches of Acorn Bank were considerably boosted by Dorothy Una Ratcliffe, the Yorkshire writer and traveller who, with her husband, Capt. Noel McGrigor Phillips, bought the property in 1934. She also restored the lawns and borders, and introduced the ironwork gates and statuary. And it is the balance she struck between picturesque effects and enhancing the habitats for wildlife that continues to set the tone for the garden today.

The garden is proof that a hostile climate need not preclude adventurous planting. Semi-evergreen *Rosa bracteata*, violet-flowered *Abutilon × suntense*, and crimson *Schisandra grandiflora* var. *rubriflora* all thrive unexpectedly against the sheltering walls. The shady

borders around the orchard contain various Turk's cap lilies (*Lilium martagon, L. pyrenaicum* and *L. pardalinum*), as well as that striking late-blooming perennial with yellow shuttlecock flowers, *Kirengeshoma palmata*. And growing in the lawn is a fine specimen of *Aesculus × mutabilis* '*Induta*', an unusual dwarf cousin of Horse Chestnut with pinky yellow 'candles'. The apple trees, however, are mainly old northern or local cooking varieties which avoid frost by flowering late and fruiting early. These include 'Dumelow's Seedling', 'Scotch Bridget', 'Keswick Codlin' and 'Carlisle Codlin'. And the avenue in the orchard is made of Sour Cherry, *Prunus cerasus* 'Rhexii', which gives a spectacular display of double white flowers, but at the end of the spring season in May.

Acorn Bank's most famous feature is also one of its most recent. In 1969, the long rectangular walled enclosure below the orchard was a redundant vegetable plot. Now it contains the most comprehensive collection of medicinal and culinary herbs in the north of England. The plants are assembled according to their preference for sun, part shade or shade, the first group being backed by an early example of a flued wall through which warm air used to be circulated; there is a record of apricots being grown here in the seventeenth century. With appropriate warnings about poisons and homespun pharmacy, the accompanying herb list indicates unlikely remedies for nose bleeds, bruises, toothache, heart palpitations and scrofulous swellings. In inclement weather, the place to contemplate all this is the glasshouse, which, though unheated, provides enough shelter to satisfy some tender plants.

BELOW LEFT: Angelica and cardoons in the herb garden.

BELOW RIGHT: White and pink foxgloves in front of *Rosa glauca*.

Anglesey Abbey

Lode, Cambridgeshire

In Lode village, 6 miles north-east of Cambridge on B1102

Area 98 acres (40 ha)
Soil good loam on clay base
Altitude 100 ft (30 m)
Average rainfall 21 in (533 mm)
Average winter climate cold
Staff six, plus one trainee

Looking through an archway into the Formal Garden.

What is one to make of this extraordinary twentieth-century garden? It is the product of one man's vision, Huttleston Broughton, the 1st Lord Fairhaven, who, with grand gestures and a breathtaking sense of scale, transformed an unpromising piece of fenland into a landscape which, as Arthur Bryant has described, 'can compare with the great masterpieces of the Georgian era'. It is a garden of broad avenues, immense vistas and 30 acres (12 ha) of mown lawn, decorated with extravagant flower gardens and classical statuary of the best quality, all maintained to the very highest standards.

When Lord Fairhaven bought this former Augustinian priory in 1926, he inherited a small garden, laid out by the Rev. John Hailstone in the 1860s, and some fine trees, including the cedars and Weeping Silver Lime. From this nucleus he gradually expanded into 90 acres (36 ha) of surrounding pasture-land. The network of avenues and grass walks do not radiate from the house, but are part of a series of surprises and enticements within an independent garden design. Walking west along Coronation Avenue, you come upon a dramatic cross-vista, culminating in a marble urn, framed at one end by a triple semi-circle of fastigiate Dawyck Beech, formerly Lombardy poplars, and, at the other, by Silver Birch. And as you emerge from the birch, you are then offered a view, between island beds of coloured-leaved shrubs, towards a circle of Corinthian columns that houses a replica of Bernini's David and is guarded by eighteenth-century lead lions.

Statuary is often the reward for exploration, for Lord Fairhaven was an energetic and discerning collector. Many pieces date from the eighteenth century; some are much older. The Emperors' Walk, on the eastern edge of the garden, is especially richly endowed. It takes its name from the twelve eighteenth-century marble busts of Roman emperors displayed along its 440-yard (401 m) length. But there are also lead figures within a central circle of Copper Beech, pairs of bronze and copper urns, a bronze version of the Versailles Diana and of Silenus holding the infant Bacchus, and an open temple sheltering a Roman urn made of Egyptian porphyry.

The displays of bulbs and border plants are as extravagant as the avenues and statues are impressive. Lord Fairhaven chose plants for their impact *en masse*, and several enclosures focus on individual species. Dutch Elm disease killed 4,000 trees here, and much of the garden has been replanted by the Trust. The new hornbeam avenue was underplanted with a ton of

LEFT: Temple Lawn, a circle of Corinthian columns enclosing a replica of Bernini's David, at Anglesey Abbey.

17

white poet's daffodils, *Narcissus poeticus* var. *recurvus* and *N.* 'Winifred van Graven'. And 10,000 summer snowflakes, *Leucojum aestivum*, grow in the grass of Warrior's Walk.

The rose garden beside the house was one of Lord Fairhaven's favourite areas, and contains a range of modern bush roses grown on imported Northamptonshire loam. The Hyacinth Garden beyond, one of the garden's most photographed features, is a sea of 4,000 scented white 'L'Innocence' and blue 'Ostara' hyacinths in spring, followed in summer by 1,500 red 'Madame Simone Stappers' and gold 'Ella Britton' dahlias. The Dahlia Garden is also filled with these potent performers. Delphiniums are a feature of the vast curved border in the Herbaceous Garden, but here not in solitary splendour but accompanied by a variety of other plants, including peonies, geraniums, campanulas and *Crambe cordifolia*, with its giant sprays of white blossom; heleniums, achillea, romneya and eupatorium help to carry the colour throughout the summer. At its peak, this is perhaps one of the most impressive herbaceous borders in the country.

Such spectacles contrast with the dark evergreen passages of yew, ruscus, box and ivy, and the open swathes of grass and trees, creating not only a stimulating pattern of light and shade, rest and drama, but also startling juxtapositions of style. In the end, Anglesey Abbey remains a triumphant anachronism; a garden to make you gasp.

Antony House

Torpoint, Cornwall	5 miles west of Plymouth via Torpoint car ferry, 2 miles north-west of Torpoint, north of A374	*Area* 28 acres (11 ha)
		Soil medium loam on shale
		Altitude 100 ft (30 m)
		Average rainfall 40 in (1,016 mm)
		Average winter climate mild
		Staff two, plus two trainees

As you turn into the approach drive at Antony, a prospect of Plymouth across the estuary is a final reminder of twentieth-century bustle and congestion. The limes now lead you into parkland and woods, back into a more elegant and spacious age. The silver-grey house was completed for Sir William Carew in 1724, though Antony had been home to his family for 250 years previously, and the garden and park radiate from it in a pattern of formal walks and enclosures and soft-edged avenues. The present design has evolved at a leisurely pace, but was much influenced by the great landscape gardener Humphry Repton, who was consulted by Reginald Pole-Carew in 1792. You can feel his hand in the uninterrupted, undulating sweeps of grass and trees, and in the gentle drama of the main views.

But other features pre-date Repton's involvement, including the terrace, the circular dovecote and the groves of Holm Oaks which frame the fine views from the house to the River Lynher; these were planted in the 1760s. By 1788, Reginald Pole-Carew had himself already embarked on an extensive programme of ornamental tree planting; the immense

FAR RIGHT: An eighteenth-century shepherd of painted lead in an alcove of yew at Antony House.

Wild garlic and bluebells in profusion in the woodlands at Antony House.

Black Walnut in front of the house and the Cork Oak at the end of the Yew Walk may date from this period.

The gravel terraces in front of the house and the formal walks and gardens to the west reveal layers of Victorian, Edwardian and more recent planting by subsequent members of the Carew family. The broad paths, high yew hedges and abundance of substantial trees continue the generous scale, but there are more intimate touches in the late Sir John Carew Pole's Japanese garden at the east end of the terrace and in the enclosed knot Summer Garden begun in 1983 by Mrs Richard Carew Pole.

The planting themes at Antony tend to be focused on favourite genera. Two of the avenues are of large, free-standing magnolias, the evergreen *M. grandiflora* and the deciduous *M. denudata*; at the end of the former, overhung by an old mulberry, is the splendid Mandalay Bell brought back as booty from the Second Burmese War by General Sir Reginald Pole-Carew in 1886. Hoherias and eucryphias, which provide a mass of white blossom in summer, set new themes for the west end of the garden. Around the walls, beneath tender climbing plants such as *Acacia pravissima*, *Senna corymbosa* (syn. *Cassia corymbosa*), *Sophora tetraptera* and various peaches, is an extensive collection of daylilies, including many new American varieties, assembled and hybridised by the late Lady Cynthia Carew Pole before 1977.

A romantic escape from order and elegance is offered by the 60 acres (24 ha) of woodland, wilderness and wildflowers between the house and the river. This is actually outside the Trust's domain, but open to the public by the Carew Pole Garden Trust which runs it. Paths take you past an eighteenth-century bathhouse (owned by the National Trust), mature rhododendrons and Asiatic magnolias, and, most memorably, a long bank of pink, red and white camellias, planted by Sir John Carew Pole, and now tumbling and frothing wildly.

Apprentice House

Quarry Bank Mill, Styal, Wilmslow, Cheshire

1½ miles north of Wilmslow off B5166, 1 mile from M56, junction 5, 10 miles south of Manchester

Area 1½ acres (0·607ha)
Soil loam with underlying clay
Altitude 250ft (76m)
Average rainfall 32in (813mm)
Average winter climate moderate
Staff two part-time

BELOW: Leeks and purple kale in the Apprentices' allotment at Styal.

Quarry Bank Mill and its Apprentice House provide a chastening glimpse of the hard life led by industrial workers some 150 years ago. The Mill, built in 1784 by Samuel Greg, an enterprising young textile merchant, is a vast expanse of russet-red brickwork, sitting in an unspoilt and well-wooded valley, beside the River Bollin, whose waters provided the necessary power to run the machines.

The apprentices were indentured child labourers who, from the age of nine or ten, were forced to work a twelve-hour day, six days a week, for a period of some seven years. The Apprentice House was home to these children who had been drawn from local workhouses, and later, from distant city slums. It housed up to 100 apprentices in a plain, whitewashed building, accompanied by a cluster of brick outhouses, a cobbled yard, and a productive garden, in which, under the supervision of the superintendents, the children grew food for themselves and for sale. Today, restored by the Quarry Bank Mill Trust, the site once again displays humble plots of fruit and vegetables, neatly divided by picket fences. And, with a few weeds between the cobbles, the grass a little shaggy, and poultry around the yard, the rural nineteenth-century flavour is slowly being recaptured.

One old apple and a few damson trees have survived; otherwise, the site has been planted afresh from sycamore scrub. But all the fruit and vegetable varieties are known to have been grown locally and date from before the end of the nineteenth century. The garden is managed traditionally, with no use of modern chemicals.

Among the apples are 'Irish Peach', 'Peasgood's Nonesuch', 'Lord Suffield' and the very

rare, locally bred 'Withington Welter'; among the plums, 'Jefferson' and 'Imperial Gage' (syn. 'Denniston's Superb'); among the pears, 'Williams' Bon Chrétien' and 'Jargonelle'; and the damson is 'Cheshire Damson'. The currants in the soft fruit compound include an interesting collection of gooseberries donated by Manchester University. 'London', 'Catherina', 'Blucher', 'King of Trumps' and 'Hero of the Nile' are among them; all were prizewinners in the gooseberry shows held in nearby Wilmslow.

The heavy clay soil, well-laced with manure, supports an extensive selection of vegetables, many grown from seed from the Henry Doubleday Research Association at Ryton-on-Dunsmore, near Coventry. These include the peas 'Champion of England' and 'Prince Albert'; the beans 'Black Canterbury' and 'Green Windsor'; the kale 'Ragged Jack'; the carrot 'Altrincham'; the turnip 'Manchester Market'; the onion 'Southport Red Globe'; and the rhubarb 'Timperley Early'. The potatoes used to be stored in special tunnels, which are due to be restored.

There are herbs, which would have been used to make food more palatable, for minor ailments and, in the case of alkanet and woad, as dye plants. To add some cheer to the scene, there is a bed of cottage flowers, including stocks, peonies, columbines and monkshoods, which succeed the snowdrops, daffodils and cowslips that appear on the scythed grass bank in spring. This is a memorable place to visit.

Ardress House

Portadown, Co. Armagh

7 miles from Portadown on Moy road (B28), 5 miles from Moy, 3 miles from Loughall junction 13 on M1, 9 miles from Armagh

Area 6¾ acres (2·7 ha)
Soil alkaline, clay
Altitude 100 ft (30 m)
Average rainfall 30 in (762 mm)
Average winter climate moderate
Staff none

The estate house of Ardress is washed rosy pink, the same colour as the apple blossom buds in the surrounding orchards. For this low-lying country is the garden of Ulster and Ardress sits on an eminence within it, commanding patchwork views of farmland, woods and acres of Bramleys. Poultry and pigs rummage in the cobbled yard. There is only a modest flower garden to accompany the farmhouse, gentrified by its architect-owner George Ensor, sometime after 1778. The rest of the land around the house is given over to grass, trees, apples and animals. As the ground drops away opposite the main, east front, the smooth lawn quickly turns into rough grass, grazed by tethered goats. A solitary Whitebeam makes a focal point here, a silver silhouette against the ploughed fields below, and the prospect is framed by belts of taller trees. In fact, this is the beginning of a woodland walk that leads down to the Ladies' Mile, a fringe of trees to the south of the house.

The garden opposite the south front offers a contrast in mood, and has been replanted by the Trust in recent years. Busts of the Four Seasons, placed in niches in the curved screen walls, together with young Irish Yews on the terraced lawn, strike a classical note. And as you descend the slope, past a mixed border of blue and yellow coloured flowers, a formal rose garden is gradually revealed, centred around an oval Coade urn, which is dated 1790 and decorated with leopards' heads and bunches of grapes.

The retaining wall in this part of the garden is hung with the slightly tender, trailing rosemary, *Rosmarinus officinalis* Prostratus Group, in partnership with a number of Irish-raised climbing roses, deep pink 'Bantry Bay', coppery orange 'Schoolgirl' and pink-tinged 'Handel'. And the bush roses are all early single Irish varieties, including silver-pink 'Dainty Bess' and orange-scarlet 'Irish Elegance'.

The Argory

Moy, Dungannon,
Co. Tyrone

4 miles from Moy, 3 miles
from M1, junction 13 or 14

Area 5 acres (2 ha)
Soil acid/clay and peat
Altitude 0–250 ft (0–76 m)
Average rainfall 33 in (838 mm)
Average winter climate very cold
Staff one

The setting here is perfect – the silver-grey house sits on a rise above the River Bracknell, amid lawns, woodland and a formal garden designed for the barrister Walter McGeogh by the Dublin architects John and Arthur Williamson, who also designed the house and its outbuildings. Wrought-iron gates lead into a small rose garden, known as the Sundial Garden, which has been replanted by the Trust using dwarf, pink and white, small-flowered Polyantha and China varieties. It is a delicate composition that contrasts briskly with the more solid shapes of the yew igloos and stone pavilions in the adjacent Pleasure Ground, where the ground slopes down to a curving rampart wall. Over this you can see the river and, sometimes, the herd of rare striped cattle, called moilies, grazing on the meadow.

The planting in the perimeter beds is young, but already contains Slieve Donard shrubs and perennials, including escallonias, brooms, rhododendrons and heathers, dieramas, kniphofias and agapanthus, as well as other Irish-raised varieties such as *Bergenia* 'Ballawley', *Cytisus* 'Moyclare Pink' and *Hypericum* 'Rowallane'. The sense of age, however, is conveyed by a few old shrubs and several good trees, including a cedar, a yew and a well-branched, knobbly-buttressed Tulip Tree, underplanted with Spotted Laurel.

Arlington Court

Barnstaple, Devon

7 miles north-east of
Barnstaple on A39

Area 30 acres (12 ha)
Soil acid/light, sand
    overlaying slate
Altitude 800 ft (243 m)
Average rainfall 60 in
    (1,524 mm)
Average winter climate
    moderate, occasional frost
Staff two

The green combes and woods of this 2,400-acre (971 ha) estate were conserved by Miss Rosalie Chichester as a wildlife sanctuary, with a lakeside nature reserve at its heart. Her domestic menagerie of dogs, canaries, budgerigars and parrots has gone, but peacocks still strut over the grass, and her beloved Shetland ponies and Jacob's sheep still graze the parkland on the garden's fringe.

The house, a sober Georgian mansion, stands among trees, lawns and shrubberies, looking out over the Yeo valley. In high summer, only hydrangeas – mostly an electrifying blue, but pink-tinged where they make contact with the limestone chippings of the curving carriage drives – interrupt the greens. Earlier in the year, the grass sprouts bluebells, primroses, violets, daffodils, Siberian claytonia and, beside the main drive, colonies of cerise-pink Japanese primulas. At the same time, the rhododendrons are in bloom: great banks of purple *Rhododendron ponticum*, supplemented by many other species, including those of the large-leaved Falconeri series, which, like the primulas, appreciate the high rainfall. Red, pink and white Hardy Hybrids reflect their colourful trusses in the atmospherically Victorian wilderness pond, hidden in the south-east corner of the garden, where they grow with ferns, gunnera and pampas grass, backed by the grey stone tower of the parish church.

The moist, clean air fosters the growth of mosses and lichens and, with ferns, which also colonise the branches and trunks, they give some of the trees a jungle flavour. The backdrop is ever-changing, with the native oaks, beeches and sycamores joined by Sweet Chestnut, Cut-leaved Beech, Tulip Tree, redwood, hemlock, fir, cypresses, a varied collection of ash and numerous others; the walk to the lake takes in an avenue of Monkey Puzzles. Miss Chichester could not bear to fell trees – neither would she interfere with the advance of the invasive Pontic rhododendron – with the result that the Trust inherited large tracts of derelict and senescent woodland. Much clearance and replanting has been required to rejuvenate these areas and to reopen the garden glades for wildflowers.

The chief surprise, as you stroll through the buxom plantings of these informal pleasure grounds, is suddenly to come upon the manicured terraces of the Victorian flower garden of 1865, neatly packaged in walls and grey railings. The Trust's restoration has included the rebuilding of part of the conservatory, the garden's centrepiece, which now displays plumbago, agapanthus, tibouchina, *Daphne odora* and potted azaleas and lilies, against crisp white woodwork and a slate- and tile-patterned floor.

Circular beds cut into one of the grass terraces have been enclosed in authentic, basket-weave ironwork frames, to re-create a quaint, early nineteenth-century feature, the basket bed. Cobaeas are encouraged to ascend the handles in summer, and the baskets are filled with colourful ephemera. The looped pattern is echoed by the arches of common honeysuckle – alternately, the Early Dutch cultivar, 'Belgica', and the redder-budded, Late Dutch cultivar, 'Serotina' – which stand either side of the goldfish pool on the platform below.

The upper borders are very delicate (too delicate to pass as Victorian creations) in their fresh blue, yellow, green and deep pink colour scheme – geraniums, alchemilla, irises, osteo-spermum, kniphofia, phlox and filipendula among the company. And with the conservatory as their centrepiece, and the bowed, whitewashed façade of the adjoining rectory to punctuate the view, they are expensively photogenic.

Ascott

Mauve asters at Ascott.

Wing, nr Leighton Buzzard, Buckinghamshire

½ mile east of Wing, 2 miles south-west of Leighton Buzzard, on south side of A418

Area 46 acres (18·5 ha)
Soil acid to neutral
Altitude 250 ft (76 m)
Average rainfall 26 in (660 mm)
Average winter climate moderate
Staff eight

Ascott is a spectacular illustration of the great reversal of gardening taste that took place during the nineteenth century, when, in response to technological innovation and a new celebration of the creative mind, art and artifice became the dominant forces, with colour, bedding, exotic foliage and formality replacing the predominantly green, naturalistic land-scapes of the Georgian era.

Leopold de Rothschild acquired the property from his brother, Baron Nathan Meyer, in 1876, and engaged the architect George Devey to transform the seventeenth-century farm-house into the present, rather surprising, black-and-white residence – strung together like a row of Tudor houses and cottages, and formerly romantically shrouded in ivy and other creepers. The task of setting out the garden was entrusted to the renowned Chelsea nurserymen, James Veitch & Sons, with Rothschild, himself an enthusiastic gardener, closely involved. The principal ingredients are presented immediately you walk down the curving entrance drive towards the house's north front: fine trees, neat lawns, pristine gravel, the splash of water from a fountain and patterns of clipped evergreens, in this case Portugal Laurels pruned into umbrella shapes.

Added to this are colourful and curious specimen plants: the autumnal flame of the large-leaved vine, *Vitis coignetiae*; and the seldom seen, female form of *Garrya elliptica*, producing its green and red fruits on one side of the house door, while its partner drips grey catkins on the other. A quirky contoured walk, featuring serpentine hedges of beech, leads to a skating and waterlily lake, fringed in weeping willows, bold-leaved gunnera and darmera, appointed with a thatched changing hut and home to a pair of whooper swans.

But all this is merely a taste of what awaits you, as you follow the meandering path down slopes and steps, through scented and shady shrubberies, to the main south garden. Here, the grounds open out into an extensive arboretum, the foreground to a sweeping panorama across the Vale of Aylesbury to the Chiltern Hills. Although there are acres of plain lawn and belts, groves and avenues of green trees (a number planted to commemorate royal events), it is the wealth of ornamental incident that immediately strikes you. Everywhere, there are trees of eccentric habit and hue: Weeping, Cut-leaved and Copper beeches, blue, golden and weeping cedars, variegated Sweet Chestnut (a superb specimen), Purple Maple, Cut-leaved Alder, yellow catalpa – the scene further enriched in autumn by the potent tints of Scarlet Oak, Red Maple, Tulip Tree and liquidambar. In spring, waves of yellow and white daffodils wash over the slopes, followed by colonies of Snakeshead Fritillaries and native wildflowers.

Most arresting of all are the clipped and coloured evergreens. Hedges, tumps and topiaries, including yews of an electrifying yellow, are strung through the landscape, contrasting abruptly with the relaxed mood of woodland and meadow, and signalling the presence of a series of impressive formal enclosures.

The Sundial Garden is one of the first you come upon, a splendid period piece made entirely out of topiary, with the gnomon in green and golden yew (the one grafted on to the other, and aptly described in an article by Arthur Hellyer as like a giant egg in an eggcup), the Roman numerals in green box, and the quotation – 'Light and shade by turn but love always' (with accompanying hearts) – again in golden yew.

In recent years, Sir Evelyn and Lady de Rothschild, the present tenants, have commissioned the garden designer Arabella Lennox-Boyd to add further features including, opposite the sundial, in the former fern garden, a sunken box parterre patterned with circles and squares and with a central bubble fountain. Further to the west, a garden of astrological topiary has sprung up, with the clipped specimens placed according to the conjunctions of the planets at the moment of birth of family members. To the north of the house, a maze formed of interlocking circles will shortly appear. These features are introducing a late twentieth-century flavour to parts of the garden, but the creativity and panache exactly echo that of Leopold de Rothschild's gardening a hundred years before, and they look well.

Below the house, a long, straight run of golden yew shelters double borders, again newly planted, of spring and summer bulbs and herbaceous plants, in a repeated pink, blue and silver

colour scheme (penstemons, sedums, delphiniums, eryngiums and artemisia among the cast) – a little soft and subtle for the garden, perhaps. The low wall behind is topped with a hedge of yellow holly and supports a range of frost-tender, winter-flowering and other shrubs and climbers – giving this garden its name of the Madeira Walk.

But it is when you enter the circular garden opposite that you receive your first taste of High Victorian flower gardening in all its shocking splendour. Here, a bronze Venus rises from the sea in a great marble shell-chariot, drawn by winged horses and with cherubs in attendance; this is a work by the American sculptor Waldo Story. Enclosing it is a radiant hedge of golden yew. In the box-edged borders is a changing display of rich seasonal bedding, the summer show being founded on a comprehensive range of tropical American cannas, flaunting luxuriant purple, yellow-variegated and emerald green leaves, and a glorious array of scarlet, flame-orange and golden-yellow flower spikes.

Passages of soothing grass and trees allow the optic nerves some respite, before a second, still more lavish scene is revealed. This is the Dutch Garden, a narrow strip of lawn presided over by Eros atop a slender fountain (also by Story), nestling below a high shrubbery ridge, and backed by a rock and tufa grotto, complete with mysterious dripping cavern and eruptions of Hart's Tongue and other ferns. The beds cut out of the grass, also filled twice yearly, are flamboyantly stocked with many of the great nineteenth-century favourites including coloured-leaved coleus and cabbages, cannas and Castor Oil plants all to provoke squeals of delight or horror, depending on your sensibilities.

Attingham Park

Shrewsbury, Shropshire	4 miles south-east of Shrewsbury, on north side of the Telford road (B4380, formerly A5)	*Area* 50 acres (20·2 ha) *Soil* sandy, clay *Altitude* 131–279 ft (40–85 m) *Average rainfall* 28 in (700 mm) *Average winter climate* moderate *Staff* two

Attingham, in an advanced stage of restoration by the Trust, is gradually regaining the elegant finish imposed by Humphry Repton. But in its overall design it has changed little since the 1820s, and offers much insight into Georgian landscaping. There is a fine view of the grand Neo-classical mansion from Tern Bridge on the A5, which was decorated at the 1st Lord Berwick's expense, and from the house is an important landscape feature; reverse views take in the Wrekin and the south Shropshire hills. But Repton was not the first landscape designer on the scene. A lesser known practitioner, Thomas Leggett, was employed here between 1769 and 1772, before the present mansion was built, and his tree planting was extensive; a single bill of 13 February 1770 reveals that 7,000 trees were bought from Messrs Williamson of London for £42 11 1d. Many of Repton's proposals, contained in his Red Book of 1798, consisted of alterations to this earlier work.

The tour centres principally on the mile-long ambulatory walk – a popular mid-eighteenth century garden feature. It begins above the cedar grove and leads off, between meadow and water, through a succession of stands and groves of different trees, shrubs and native daffodils. A number of species, notably rhododendrons and azaleas, were added early this century, but in its replanting programme the Trust is attempting to follow Leggett's original lists wherever this is possible.

A splendid Cedar of Lebanon presides over the north-east curve of the circle, behind which a secondary path meanders, through a willow carr and across the river, into the deer-park. And as you continue around the circumference, you pass a circle of Honey Locusts (gleditsia), and a sombre stretch of Giant Fir (*Abies grandis*) before the trees suddenly part and a broad expanse of mown grass, framed by a nuttery and a high, south-facing wall (part of the large, now unused, kitchen garden) clad in peaches, nectarines and apricots, carries the eye to the eighteenth-century Bee House. Beware, the skeps are occupied. There is further ornamental planting to the south-east of the hall, comprising rhododendrons (surrounding a brick ice-house), and a Spring Garden of trees and shrubs. But the remains of formal yew and knot gardens, made in the 1920s in front of the hall, were removed by the Trust in 1976. This is now restored to grass and Reptonian tranquillity, the only drama being provided in summer by the huge colony of resident house martins collecting mud from the riverbank.

Baddesley Clinton

Lapworth, Solihull, Warwickshire

¾ mile west of A41 Warwick–Birmingham road, at Chadwick End, 7½ miles north of Warwick, 15 miles south-east of central Birmingham

Area 11 acres (4·4 ha)
Soil neutral/clay and loam
Altitude 370ft (110m)
Average rainfall 27in (685mm)
Average winter climate moderate
Staff one, plus one trainee

The sight of this small, moated manor house, in its pastoral setting of oaks, wildflowers, grass and tail-flicking cows, cannot fail to bewitch. In spite of being a mere 16 miles (26km) from Birmingham, little appears to have ruffled the scene for centuries, its timeless air being preserved by the constant structure of moat, lake and stewponds, and the surrounding remnants of the ancient Forest of Arden. Paintings inside the house, dating from 1915, show the Walled Garden divided from the moat and south-east front by a high yew hedge and decorated elaborately with herbaceous borders, standard roses and pergolas. When it first came into the hands of the Trust, it was in a state of terrible decay, but plans are underway to reinstate the original arrangement.

Beyond the south wall an extensive 'flowery mead', important for its butterflies and moths, adds to this feeling of being in a rural time capsule. The grass is not mown until August to give the widest range of plants time to bloom and drop seed. Wildflowers are not confined to this area, however. Primroses spangle the grass around the stewponds, daffodils lay trails of yellow under the oaks and limes beside the drive and along the path to the adjacent church, while bluebells colonise under the oaks, sycamores and chestnuts behind the lake, which has been dredged and restored by the Trust.

One of the best prospects is through a stand of Scots Pine, over this tranquil stretch of water, complete with its two rushy islands and rafts of waterlilies. The perimeter offers a typical nineteenth-century wilderness walk, and the native trees and shrubs have been supplemented by rhododendrons. The invasive *R. ponticum* is gradually being replaced here with other colour forms, but on the north-west side of the moat its purple reflections in the water are a memorable sight in May.

Barrington Court

nr Ilminster, Somerset

Barrington village, 5 miles
north-east of Ilminster, 6 miles
south of Curry Rivel on A378

Area 11 acres (4·5 ha)
Soil neutral/lime, loam over
  clay
Altitude 65 ft (20 m)
Average rainfall 30 in (762 mm)
Average winter climate mild
Staff three

A sunflower in the garden at
Barrington Court.

Gertrude Jekyll was in her late seventies, and had very poor eyesight when she was approached by architects to the Trust's tenant, Colonel Arthur Lyle, to undertake the planting at Barrington Court. The plans were submitted to her with biscuit boxes of garden soil. Although only half her schemes were put into practice, those that were rank among her finest work. Their structure and style – familiar to all students of gardening from the black-and-white photographs in her many books – remain evocatively intact, as does the warm Arts and Crafts detailing of the different outdoor rooms. In fact, the garden at Barrington Court is one of the best preserved of her gardens.

The introduction is grand. Long avenues of Horse Chestnuts, into which generous, well-presented 1920s farm buildings are inserted, give way to closely mown lawn, high dark hedges (Lawson Cypress as well as yew), canal ponds and scrolled stonework. Ahead is the Tudor honey-coloured mansion, and beside it an equally large stable block, built in 1674 of red brick, and known as the Strode House. The two buildings are a curious pair, particularly on the south side, where they are in alignment in the midst of open lawn and park – the house here showing its Elizabethan E-shape, and skyline of gables, finials and twisted chimneys.

Away from the house, the grandeur quickly melts into the traditional and the rustic. Cider orchards, some grazed by sheep, fringe much of the garden. Clipped mushrooms of Portugal Laurel sprout in front of a line of thatched cottages, and runs of hurdle fencing provide makeshift pens. In spring, there are welcoming bursts of daffodils in the rough grass, and in summer, an assortment of wildflowers, including spotted and Twayblade orchids.

This blend of the grand and formal, homely and vernacular, the essence of the Arts and Crafts style, also characterises Gertrude Jekyll's flower gardens. The display begins to the west

29

LEFT: An oak bridge leads across part of the moat at Barrington Court and into the walled flower gardens; the doorway is hung with climbing hydrangea.

BELOW LEFT: The planting at Barrington Court is a blend of the grand and the vernacular; a close-up of physalis (Chinese Lantern), with cabbages in the background, adds a homely note to this part of the garden.

BELOW RIGHT: A circular window is draped with the climbing rose 'Iceberg'.

of the Strode House, with borders of predominantly pink and purplish shrubs and perennials – wisteria, buddleja, claret-leaved Smoke Bush and clove-scented *Daphne × burkwoodii*, with the glossy, evergreen leaves of her favourite bergenia and *Acanthus mollis* as punctuation marks – alongside one of the most beautiful paths to be seen in this country: a straight run of mellow Tudor brick, its pattern changing every few paces, from diamond to herringbone, circle to basketweave to square.

But it is in the adjacent Lily Garden that her influence is most keenly felt. Here, steps lead down from the Strode House's west terrace to a rectangular lawn and waterlily pool, surrounded by raised rectangular beds and, across the patterned paths, richly coloured mixed borders. These may shortly be replanted for, in the raised beds, only the crinums, with their bold strap-like foliage and pink trumpet flowers, remain from the original scheme. Miss Jekyll's hydrangeas have been replaced with salmon, apricot and flame-coloured azaleas (growing in imported lime-free soil) in partnership with the early yellow daylily, *Hemerocallis dumortieri*. The inner beds echo these tones and generous stands of orange alstroemeria, helenium and lilies, scarlet crocosmia and fuchsia, yellow hypericum and rudbeckia, are blended into powerful harmonies. Miss Jekyll's supreme legacy to modern gardening is, of course, her colour teaching and this is a wonderful demonstration of her principles.

The shrubs and perennials are also interwoven, as she advocated, with splashes of spring and summer bedding, including wallflowers, marigolds, snapdragons and dahlias, to disguise gaps and prolong the display. Bergenias mark the corners again, and the foliage of tropical

canna lilies helps the crinums and daylilies provide definition and contrasting structure. It is an appealing composition.

Beyond, through another of the garden's handsome, faded oak doors, is the Rose and Iris Garden, recently cleaned of perennial weed and due to be replanted along the lines of Miss Jekyll's original scheme. Following rose sickness, her Rose and Peony Garden changed more dramatically; it was redesigned by Col Lyle's grandson Andrew, in 1986 as a White Garden, such as Jekyll suggested in *Colour Schemes for the Flower Garden*. It is still strongly Edwardian in character, and the plantings of long-standing annual and perennial border favourites, such as phlox, crambe, alyssum, cineraria, cosmos and silver stachys, are marshalled within Jekyll's formal circular design.

The patterned brick paths run between and around these gardens, bordered by hedges of bulging boxwood and Munstead Lavender, fringed by beds of catmint and pink penstemons.

The White Garden at Barrington Court with antirrhinums, cosmos, gypsophila and *Eryngium giganteum*.

In one part, it is shaded by a long pergola (recently erected, but strongly Jekyllian in flavour), clad in vine, wisteria, jasmine, clematis and Golden Hop, and underplanted for early summer with geranium, alchemilla, aubrieta and Solomon's Seal. Until 1920, this was all a cow yard, and on the north side, the calf sheds, or bustalls, are still standing, picturesquely hung with climbing roses.

Further stretches of the canalised stream, which serves the Court as a moat, skirt the outer walls of the flower gardens, and you leave by way of an oak bridge, back into the cider orchard. A final surprise is sprung, another sudden change of scale: a long, deep, buxomly planted herbaceous border, designed by Col Lyle's wife, Ronnie, containing massive swathes of achilleas, hollyhocks, salvias, helianthus and other flowers for cutting, and, behind it, the huge walled kitchen garden with flower borders down its centre, and vegetables and soft fruit in rosy, Somerset abundance.

Basildon Park

Lower Basildon, Reading, Berkshire	Between Pangbourne and Streatley, 7 miles north-west of Reading, on west side of A329	*Area* 5½ acres (2.2 ha) *Soil* clay/sand, overlying chalk *Altitude* 250 ft (76 m) *Average rainfall* 27 in (686 mm) *Average winter climate* moderate *Staff* one

This fine Palladian house stands in one of those unspoilt, leafy pockets within the Thames Valley, with pastoral views of hills, beechwoods and river. It was built in the third quarter of the eighteenth century for Sir Francis Sykes, a Yorkshireman who had made his fortune in the service of the East India Company, and was set, according to the fashion of the time, in an open and elegant landscape park.

The gardens comprise parterre and pleasure grounds east and north-east of the house. The parterre, bounded by a handsome balustraded terrace and ha-ha, was carved from the park after 1838, but its present sympathetic planting and ornament reflect the taste of Lord and Lady Iliffe, who from 1952 rescued house and garden from an appalling state of dereliction. Roses and lavender feature prominently in the borders and do well in the free-draining soil. *Rosa* 'Sanders' White Rambler' scrambles over the stone balustrade and *Magnolia grandiflora* clothes the house walls. Nearby, *Viburnum × burkwoodii*, *Clematis montana* and other shrubs and climbers bring light and scent to the shady courtyard between the house and its north pavilion. Out of sight of the house, the pleasure grounds, which pre-date the parterre, roll down the hillside beside the drive. A concentration of yews and Holm Oaks, once clipped tightly into tumps, gives way to glades dappled by chestnuts, limes, beeches, Japanese cherries and specimens of Tulip Tree and catalpa. Daffodils, primroses, anemones and vast carpets of bluebells accompany them in spring. Currently, these grounds are undergoing restoration to their eighteenth-century form.

Bateman's

Burwash, Etchingham, East Sussex	*Area* 10 acres (4 ha)
	Soil acid/clay
½ mile south of Burwash on A265	*Altitude* 250 ft (76 m)
	Average rainfall 30 in (762 mm)
	Average winter climate mild–moderate
	Staff two

ABOVE: The Pear Arch with clematis trained through the fruit trees.

BELOW: *Clematis viticella* 'Kermesina'.

'It is a good and peaceable place, standing in terraced lawns nigh to a walled garden of old, red brick, and two fat-headed oast houses with red brick stomachs, and an aged silver grey dovecote on top … We entered and felt her spirit – her *Feng Shui* – to be good.' This was Rudyard Kipling's first impression of Bateman's, which was to be his home from 1902 until his death in 1936.

The Jacobean house is a solid squire's residence, set in undulating wooded countryside, 'alive with ghosts and shadows', and with rooms dark, comfortable and creaky. The garden is a spacious accompaniment to it, a blend of firm, traditional design and soft-edged planting, and, with the surrounding landscape, is rich in associations with Kipling's stories and poems, especially *Puck of Pook's Hill* and its sequel *Rewards and Fairies* which were set here. The mill that features in these stories is a short walk from the house, through the Wild Garden.

Visitors enter the property through the old kitchen garden, passing alongside a herb border heavy with suitable spicy and eastern odours – the curry scent comes from *Helichrysum italicum* – and then arriving at the mouth of the Pear Alley at the bottom of the slope. The pears – 'Conference', 'Superfine' and 'Winter Nelis' – share their supports with clematis and are underplanted with a range of intermingling ground-cover plants including periwinkle, bluebells, cyclamen and Corsican hellebore.

Wrought-iron gates, displaying the initials RK, now lead into the Mulberry Garden opposite. The original mulberry died some time ago, but there is a fine Chinese Snakebark Maple, *Acer davidii*, in the south-west corner. The chief interest here, however, is in the herbaceous borders. A succession of hardy plants – this is a frosty garden, with a retentive clay soil – ensures colour all summer. Peonies, phlox, asters, Japanese anemones, tulips and geraniums are among the cast, which also includes unusual items such as honey-coloured *Crocosmia* 'Citronella' and the thistle-like *Morina longifolia*. These are bolstered by yellow and blood-red tree peonies and shrub roses.

To the south of the house, the gardens are broad, open and flat, the expanse of lawn broken by some very good trees, a pleached wall lime avenue pre-dating Kipling, and by other vertical and horizontal features in neat geometric shapes. Apparently, I am not the first to remark on the strange alignment of some of these – in particular the procession of stone steps, Irish Yews and symmetrical pairs of *Aesculus flava* – which seem to have a life independent of the house and landscape. Other visitors have noted the absence of anticipated focal points and quirkiness of 'paths leading nowhere'. The main lawn is separated from the upper part, the Quarter Deck, by a low retaining wall, and as you descend, it is worth scrutinising it for its collection of lichens and rock plants. A raised platform is necessary protection from the River Dudwell, which is apt to burst its banks and submerge the lower garden.

The lily pond was constructed by Kipling so that his children could use it for swimming and boating. But it had its accidental users, too; a number of names in the family visitor's book are followed by the initials F.I.P., meaning 'fell in pond'. The formal Rose Garden beyond it was also added by Kipling, and contains three varieties of Polyantha rose – pale pink 'Inge Poulsen', mid-pink 'Betty Prior', and scarlet 'Frensham' – underplanted, for spring, with a yellow and blue bulb scheme comprising *Narcissus* 'Hawera' and *Muscari* 'Blue Spike'. And behind it is a sundial bearing an inscription that will have a familiar ring to all who absorb themselves in the gardening, 'It is later than you think'.

Pear trees laden with fruit at Bateman's.

The Italian Garden at Belton House, with clipped yews and carved stone vases and urns.

Belton House

Grantham, Lincolnshire

3 miles north-east of Grantham on the A607 Grantham–Lincoln road, signposted from the A1

Area 33 acres (13·3 ha)
Soil neutral/sandy loam
Altitude 170 ft (52 m)
Average rainfall 27 in (686 mm)
Average winter climate cold
Staff four

Looking across the Italian Garden towards Belton House, the foreground urn containing variegated periwinkle, *Vinca major* 'Variegata'.

This elegant composition of green and gold takes its cue from the honey-coloured mansion, which presides over its level acres with the serenity of a French château. Built for Sir John Brownlow in the 1680s, its architect is thought to be William Winde, who may also have been responsible for the elaborate geometric gardens that once accompanied it; Winde designed the grand terraces at Cliveden and, probably, Powis Castle. Most of this early formality has gone, a victim not only of the dramatic change in gardening taste that occurred in Britain during the eighteenth century, but also of flooding caused by the accidental and disastrous breach of Belton's canal in 1751, which was the garden's most important feature and acclaimed as 'one of the noblest sights in England'. It was filled in as a consequence.

Avenues, however, continue to radiate from the house: a spectacular lime avenue to the east, sweeping up to the Bellmount Tower, constructed *c*.1750 to provide a prospect of the park; another of Turkey Oak, leading south to the Lion Gates; and a lime avenue leading west, recently reinstated by the Trust. A canal pond, north-east of the house, also remains, as does a small Palladian temple.

The linear framework therefore survived the 1740s, when the picturesque Wilderness, with its Gothic ruin, cascades, shrubberies and flower-rich meadows, was added, and the late 1770s, when the parkland planting suggested by William Emes – engaged on the advice of the 1st Baron Brownlow's brother-in-law, Philip Yorke I of Erddig – was pursued. The resulting blend of styles is one of extreme beauty, and in the late nineteenth century, when red-blooded formality returned to accompany flowing lawns studded with specimen beech and oak, cedar and Wellingtonia, the harmony merely deepened.

The Dutch Garden, a reproduction of the earlier Georgian layout, was created by the 3rd Earl Brownlow in the 1870s. Its theme of green and gold is taken up by alternating green yew pillars and golden yew globes, and the pattern is infilled with honey-coloured gravel, urns and statuary, and complex bedding schemes comprising yellow tulips, pansies, marguerites and *Allium moly*. 'Iceberg' roses, lavenders, catmint and sea-green cedars provide cool contrast.

The sunken Italian Garden, on the site of the former kitchen garden, is a larger scale composition dating from the early nineteenth century, with a lavish structure of golden stone part-supplied by the house. Its central axis consists of the handsome Orangery, Lion Exedra, and large circular fountain, all designed by Jeffry Wyatville. There is further ornamental planting behind the Orangery, where pastel borders, coloured by roses, geraniums, peonies and Madonna Lilies, lap the ancient garden walls. The medlars in the lawns are the variety 'Nottingham'. The Orangery itself, recently restored and replanted by the Trust, was, in Edwardian times, used to house a large flock of free-flying budgerigars, but unfortunately plants and parrots are not compatible.

Beningbrough Hall

Shipton-by-Beningbrough,
York, Yorkshire

8 miles north-west of York,
2 miles west of Shipton,
2 miles south-east of Linton-on-Ouse (A19)

Area 7 acres (2.8 ha)
Soil neutral/silty loam
Altitude 50 ft (15 m)
Average rainfall 30 in (762 mm)
Average winter climate cold
Staff two

FAR RIGHT: The West Formal Garden at Beningbrough with box-edged beds of pansies and roses with *Heuchera* 'Palace Purple'.

By the time restoration of this handsome Baroque house, standing among water meadows in the Vale of York, began in 1977, the gardens, too, were moving silently towards dereliction. The estate records were lost and there were no clear historical guidelines for the Trust, but there had been especially active passages in the evolution, and it was decided to anchor the garden in these periods, layering each over the other to create a homogenous composition. The hall itself seems to cry out for a simple, uncluttered setting that conveys a flavour of eighteenth-century elegance. Early maps show it at the centre of a formal landscape of radiating avenues, typical of the period. But the eighteenth-century tide of opinion against formal landscaping gathered momentum, and at Beningbrough a more natural landscape of open parkland and irregular clumps of trees replaced the avenues. Today the south front of the hall, flanked by trees, including an unusual variegated oak, surveys a pristine gravel walk and velvet lawn and, across the ha-ha, a relaxed prospect of the water meadows bordering the River Ouse.

The first Ordnance Survey map of 1852 shows the two wings of the garden, the Wilderness and the American Garden, well furnished with trees. The latter takes the form of an open glade encircled by a shady walk of trees and shrubs. Spring is its high season, when the ground is buried in daffodils and there is blossom on cherry and amelanchier. Rhododendrons tolerant of a little lime take over in early summer – 'Cunningham's White', 'Cunningham's Blush' and *R. catawbiense*.

From 1827, Beningbrough benefited from the presence of an outstanding Head Gardener, Thomas Foster, and during his time the Walled Garden must have been a model kitchen garden. Sadly, financial considerations have forced the Trust to opt for a more labour-saving treatment here, but the walls continue to shelter a range of pears, apples and figs, and the original pear alley has been retained as a centrepiece, with the varieties 'Black Worcester', 'Beurré Hardy' and 'Pitmaston Duchess' underplanted with herbs. Foster's home-raised grape varieties, 'Lady Downe's Seedling' (still rated one of the finest, late-keeping grapes) and 'Foster's Seedling' (one of the best early-fruiting vines) have been returned to the vinery.

The Victorian pleasure grounds at Beningbrough contained their share of formal touches, and formality returned to the Park with the installation of the Lime Avenue sometime after

The East Formal Garden at Beningbrough with its lily pond, box, lavender and pots of *Lilium candidum*.

1913. Although this feature is being retained, the Broad-leaved Limes (*Tilia platyphyllos*) are gradually being replaced with Common Limes (*T. × europaea*) which are more tolerant of the high water table.

After 1916, when the estate was bought by the 10th Earl and Countess of Chesterfield, the gardens were treated to a further period of formal ornamental gardening. The Chesterfields' main interest was racing and their main enterprise their stud, so they orchestrated the long South Border, below the Walled Garden, to peak during the week of the Doncaster St Leger meeting in late September. Today the swathes of colour are produced by shrubs, including hebes, lavatera, senecio and hardy fuchsias. To the west of the Walled Garden are more intricate planting schemes. The double borders have been redesigned on an Edwardian theme of cool midsummer tints. 'Iceberg' roses, purple berberis, philadelphus and deutzias are repeated down their length, along with standard wisteria and varieties of clematis. In front are waves of catmint, Purple Sage, salvia, alchemilla and *Geranium* 'Russell Prichard', with pink and white Japanese anemones to take over later, and tulips and anemones as an appetiser for spring. They are extremely photogenic.

At right angles to the double borders there is a graduation of hot to cool colours, and, in front of the hall, hidden from the lawn by hedges, a pair of small formal enclosures. The East Formal Garden has a ground cover of cobbles and Yorkstone flags, and also a rectangular pond surrounded by clipped box and lavender, while the West Formal Garden, adjacent to the newly restored nineteenth-century conservatory, has a pattern of box hedging filled with miniature roses and other richly coloured plants. Altogether, this now adds up to a garden of great charm.

Benthall Hall

Broseley, Shropshire

1 mile north-west of Broseley
(B4375), 4 miles north-east of
Much Wenlock, 6 miles south
of Wellington

Area 3 acres (1·2 ha)
Soil alkaline/clay
Altitude 620 ft (189 m)
Average rainfall 27 in (686 mm)
Average winter climate cold
Staff two, plus one trainee

Benthall Hall is tucked into well-wooded countryside close to the Severn Gorge. The approach is unassuming, along a lime-edged lane and past a whitewashed church, and suddenly the sandstone hall is revealed, flanked by topiary, and softened by a sweep of flowers.

In gardening history, Benthall is most famous as the home of George Maw, the bulb and alpine specialist, who lived here for a period of 35 years from 1853. Maw, a manufacturer of ornamental tiles, travelled extensively, especially in the Alps, Pyrenees and Mediterranean region, and brought a great many plants back to Shropshire, including the familiar glory of the snow, *Chionodoxa luciliae*, which bloomed for the first time in Britain at Benthall in 1877. He researched his great work, *A Monograph of the Genus Crocus*, here, and the garden's self-sowing carpets of spring-flowering *Crocus tommasinianus* and *C. vernus*, and autumn-flowering *C. speciosus*, *C. pulchellus* and *C. nudiflorus* are another of his legacies.

In the June 1872 issue of *The Garden*, the thunderous Victorian gardening writer William Robinson stated that '. . . for the culture and introduction of valuable new and hardy plants, there is not a more noteworthy garden'. Robinson was particularly impressed by Maw's collection of saxifrages and by his method, now commonplace, of displaying alpines in broad, shallow pans instead of small pots. Sadly, the only remaining evidence of the rockery are some large rocks beneath hollies and beech trees to the east of the lower lawn, and a strange hollow in the grass, which was once an extensive run of cold frames.

In the hands of his successor, Robert Bateman – son of James Bateman of Biddulph Grange (qv) – the nucleus of the garden shifted to the west side of the house. Bateman, a sculptor and painter, built the dovecote here and, with his wife, Octavia Caroline, laid out the Rock Garden beneath it. It is a romantic Arts and Crafts composition with a fountain, pond and symmetrical rosebeds sheltered by walls, dissected by narrow paths and foaming with mixed beds of choice plants, many inherited from George Maw. Against the walls are the late-flowering *Clematis aethusifolia* and *C. tibetana*, growing beside roses such as 'Easlea's Golden Rambler' and 'Dr W. Van Fleet'. Hybrid Musk, Modern Shrub and Polyantha roses share the beds with lavenders, potentillas, halimiocistus and perovskias. And scillas, narcissi, sisyrinchium, hardy geraniums and dianthus are part of the varied carpet beneath them. Homage is paid to George Maw through the inclusion of a scree bed, which is home to a number of alpine plants, including a collection of saxifrages.

There is a flavour of Biddulph Grange in the shady rockery behind this formal area, where you must squeeze along stone paths, mount stone steps, and duck under cherry branches. Hellebores, pulmonarias, comfreys and arums make a leafy contrast to the garden below. The plantsman's theme is also carried on to the rock banks and shrubberies that frame the sweep of terraced lawn to the front of the house. Roses and brooms are here interspersed with stands of Devil's Walking Stick, *Aralia elata*, mats of mouse plant, *Arisarum proboscideum*, and drifts of an unusual form of bear's breeches, *Acanthus balcanicus*.

The present high standard of labour-intensive gardening at Benthall is due in large part to members of the Benthall family, who reclaimed their ancestral home in 1934 after a gap of nearly a hundred years. Their continuing presence as tenants, enthusiasm for plants (which includes drying them for indoor decoration) and sensitivity to Benthall's pastoral setting, ensure a relaxed and homely mood in the garden. Brash blocks of plants and excessive neatness are eschewed, and a liberal view is taken over the colonising activities of ferns, campanulas, Welsh Poppies and the ubiquitous *Geranium nodosum*.

Berrington Hall

nr Leominster, Hereford and
Worcester

3 miles north of Leominster,
on west side of A49

Area 11½ acres (4·6ha)
Soil clay/silty loam
Altitude 250–450ft (76–137m)
Average rainfall 25in (635mm)
Average winter climate cold
Staff two

The diarist Viscount Torrington, visiting in 1784, refers to Berrington as 'just finish'd and furnish'd in all the modern elegance, commanding beautiful views, a fine piece of water, and . . . throughout a scene of elegance and refinement.' Although they are now accompanied by the rumble of the Hereford road, the views remain pastoral. A circuit walk, recently opened up by the Trust, takes you across the park, fashioned by 'Capability' Brown sometime after 1775, to the 14-acre (6-ha) pool with its 4-acre (1.6-ha) island and, once again, allows the visitor the equally fine reverse views, back between the oaks, limes, beech and ash, to the portico and pediments of the red sandstone hall.

The garden sits within an important Georgian framework, complete with ha-ha (recently reconstructed by the Trust), elegant stable block and office pavilions, and a grand triumphal archway as the entrance lodge. Around the west front of the hall, the open lawn rolls away into the park, and to the north, there is a shady shrubbery walk (the shrubbery expanded into a protective wood in 1906), offering views out over Bircher Common. But elsewhere, the Brownian scheme has been subjected to a more ornamental overlay, applied from the mid-1840s onwards.

South-east of the hall, a medley of flowering trees and shrubs now border the curving entrance drive. Bladder Nut (*Staphylea colchica*), Persian Lilac, Chinese Tulip Tree, *Lonicera involucrata*, *Magnolia wilsonii*, and several ginkgo trees are among the company, many of which have been introduced by the present Lord Cawley. An avenue of clipped golden yews, planted in 1901, processes from the triumphal arch. And an assortment of shrubs and climbers flank the wisteria pergola on the south-facing wall of the Walled Garden, including yellow Banksian Rose, red *Buddleja colvilei*, white-flowered *Crinodendon patagua*, and the very unusual (and invasive) yellow-flowered climbing marrow, *Thladiantha oliveri*, found by Lord Cawley in a Surrey garden. Until recently, a further 36 flower-beds adorned the east lawns and their departure has rather stranded the remaining stone fountain. All this jollity certainly counters the rather sombre look of the hall, but, of course, it also confuses one's initial taste of the eighteenth-century composition. The colour is much more readily appreciated in the replanted Walled Garden.

The Trust has now replanted the Walled Garden around patterns of fruit trees: medlars, mulberries, figs and, in the main grass plots, a large collection of pre-1900 apple varieties, either raised in Herefordshire (such as 'King's Acre Bountiful', 'Downton Pippin' and 'Lady's Finger of Hereford') or widely grown here (such as 'Doctor Hare's', 'Warner's King' and 'Tom Putt'). These are accompanied by a lavender-edged sundial lawn, cutting beds, a herb garden, double herbaceous borders of mixed colours and the camellias and climbing plants in the adjacent laundry drying ground. There is a further concentration of flowers behind the curtain of Weeping Ash to the north-east of the hall, where the woodland path meanders between Handkerchief Trees, maples, and a large collection of azaleas and rhododendrons, including hybrids raised by Lord Cawley. Hydrangeas give a later wash of summer colour, together with daylilies, crocosmias, and, back along the north front of the hall, past the clipped tumps of holly, rhododendron and laurel, a pool of pink and white cyclamen in the grass.

Biddulph Grange

The long, stepped Dahlia Walk at Biddulph Grange. Various dahlias provide a pattern of contrasting colour in the walled and yew-hedged borders.

Biddulph, Stoke-on-Trent, Staffordshire

½ mile north of Biddulph, 5 miles east of Congleton, 7 miles north of Stoke-on-Trent

Area 15 acres (6ha)
Soil acid/loamy clay
Altitude 475–640ft (145–195m)
Average rainfall 36in (914mm)
Average winter climate cold
Staff four

Gardens do not come more ingenious or entertaining than Biddulph. The meandering paths have you squeezing between rock faces, crossing water by stepping stones and plunging down dark tunnels; you enter a half-timbered cottage and suddenly find yourself in an Egyptian tomb, clamber through a Scottish glen and come out in a Chinese water garden; at every turn, there are strange beasts, flamboyant flowers, eruptions of rock, or soaring exotic conifers in ambush. The genius behind it all was Victorian plantsman James Bateman, aided by his wife Maria and their friend, the marine artist Edward Cooke. The estate, at the edge of the town, in cold hilly country below Biddulph Moor, was originally bought by Bateman's grandfather for its coal-mining potential, with the family living at nearby Knypersley Hall. James and Maria Bateman moved here in 1840, two years after their marriage, and soon began transforming the existing vicarage into an Italianate mansion, and working on the grounds some mind-boggling feats of earth-moving, contouring and stonework.

When the garden came to the Trust in 1988, it was in serious decline. However, the superstructure remained and, thanks to good documentation and on-site archaeology, a very precise reconstruction was possible. An appeal was launched and the immense and labour-intensive programme of work began, which is now well advanced.

From the south-west corner of the house, the starting point of the tour, the view is of an intimate garden, with foreground terraces, a small lake below and a heavy fringe of yews, hollies, rhododendrons and evergreen trees. There are lively splashes of colour, as you would expect, but no jarring contrasts of style. Bateman avoided falling into the trap set by Victorian

LEFT: *Acer palmatum* 'Rubrum', one of the first specimens of this superb wild form of Japanese maple, introduced into cultivation by Robert Fortune in the 1850s.

ABOVE LEFT: A huge stone frog, based on a model by Waterhouse Hopkins.

ABOVE RIGHT: A water buffalo, restored and gilded, under a newly painted canopy at Biddulph.

eclecticism by subdividing the garden into different compartments, each with its own theme and screened from one another by a unifying framework of hedges and walls, trees and rocky mounds. It was an innovative and influential approach. The terraces extend the width of the house. At the west end, the door opens on to an Italian garden of stone platforms, stairways and balustraded walls. To the east, within a framework of yew hedges, a range of nineteenth-century plant novelties and artful styles of cultivation is displayed. There are parterres devoted to verbenas, hybrid China roses and the quirky Monkey Puzzle tree (reintroduced to gardening by William Lobb in 1844). An ornamental orchard features clipped, double Morello cherries, planted on raised mounds and associated with *Cotoneaster horizontalis*, pruned as bells, and various clematis, grown up posts and trained along chains. Hardy herbaceous plants, in the form of peonies, *Iris pallida*, phlox and delphiniums – favourites of Maria Bateman – also appear. And, running almost the full length of the terrace, is a kaleidoscopic walk of hybrid dahlias, whose tropical colours and appearance were enthusiastically embraced by many a Victorian gardener.

Earlier in the year, it is the shrubberies around the lake that steal the show, for they are stocked with rhododendrons of every hue. At the head of the lime avenue marking the garden's western boundary, Bateman arranged them in rainbow bands around a stone seat. Beside the water, they are loosely dispersed – flashes of yellow from the scented yellow azalea *R. luteum*, and mounds of pink, purple, white and cherry-red from the Hardy Hybrids.

Rhododendrons also once filled the adjacent stream-fed glen. These were the new species collected by Joseph Hooker on his expeditions to Sikkim, Nepal and Bhutan in 1849–51. But

45

their reluctance to bloom here, in spite of the provision of moist, shady pockets of peaty soil, persuaded Bateman to move them under glass, and instead, the glen was stocked with ferns, another fashionable tribe of plants of which both Bateman and Edward Cooke were devotees.

Cooke's major contribution to the garden was the architectural features, both ornamental buildings and rockwork. Here in the glen you see the results of his careful study of rock formation for his paintings: spectacular outcrops and massive boulders of locally quarried gritstone, with every crack and cascade geologically justified. Wild heather and bilberries, collected on the Moor, contribute to the realism, with weeping holly added for picturesque effect, and native and foreign water plants strung along the stream.

From the lakeside shrubberies, you pop down a tunnel to emerge in the Pinetum, among high redwoods, hemlocks, cedars and pines. The range of impressive conifer species had been considerably boosted by David Douglas's plant-hunting on the west coast of America in the 1820s and '30s, and here Bateman prepared ideal conditions for them; many are planted on mounds to give improved drainage and a better display. In late spring, bluebells lap the long, curving walk between the grassy banks and there is carefully contrived contrast from variegated oak, golden yews and a collection of hollies – many added by Robert Heath, who bought Biddulph from the Bateman family in 1871.

The focal point of the walk is the half-timbered façade of a Cheshire cottage, sporting the date 1856 and the intertwined initials 'J & MB', but as you enter there is no cosy welcome. Instead, you are met by a squat, subhuman creature (the Ape of Thoth, an associate of the Egyptian god of botany) bathed in bloody light by a pane of red glass in the roof. You are inside an ancient pyramid, and you emerge from the dark into its open court to see a heavy stone arch set into a giant slab of clipped yew, guarded by two pairs of sphinxes. This stands at the opposite end of the terraces from where you began, and the main path continues east behind it, through a rough arboretum, planted with autumn-colouring North American red maples and liquidambar, gorse and other heathland shrubs, and pampas grass and osmunda fern set beside a small pool, then on to a long avenue.

The principal tree here was intended to be the most majestic of the newly introduced conifers, the Wellingtonia (brought in by William Lobb in 1853, and immediately obtained by Bateman through Messrs Veitch). He interplanted his specimens with Deodar Cedars for quick effect – and gave them an interesting backing formed by lines of white briar rose, Red Horse Chestnut and Austrian Pine – but unfortunately, when it came time to thin, his successor Robert Heath decided to retain the cedars instead. The Trust has returned to Bateman's original plan and, in time, the Wellingtonias will assume their rightful dominance. From here, the sandy path leads upwards to the moor through heath and woodland, gradually narrowing as it rises to give the appearance of a natural obelisk; this land is now a country park, belonging to the local district council.

Where is China? So well concealed is the prize exhibit that it is quite possible to complete the circuit without encountering it. Yet it is a large compartment at the garden's very heart. There are two points of entry. One is via a cleft in the Scottish glen and along a dark tunnel and grotto; the other is below Egypt. This latter route takes you through one of the most curious of Victorian garden features, the Stumpery. This involved excavating tree stumps and upturning them to create a rustic framework for woodland perennials like ferns, ivies, hellebores and epimediums.

FAR RIGHT: The Wellingtonia Avenue at Biddulph. The original Wellingtonia were replaced by Deodar Cedars, as shown here. Now the Trust is planting Wellingtonia once more.

The path descends between rocks and shrubs and suddenly you are inside the Great Wall. There is a watch tower high on the north-east bank and a joss house to the south, above a winding flight of steps. The flora of the Far East is all about: Japanese maples, bamboos, cryptomeria, paulownia, tree peonies, hostas and a splendid golden larch – once again, many of these were collected by contemporary plant-hunters, in particular Robert Fortune who explored China and Japan in the 1840s and 1850s. Irish Yews, weeping trees and coloured foliage strike contrasting notes.

Behind a stone doorway you come upon the gilded head of a water buffalo – a Chinese idol, sculpted by Waterhouse Hawkins – and further along, an enormous stone frog. Dragons are carved out of the lawn, and more dragons and grebes perch on the corners of the temple's upturned eaves. The central water scene will look familiar, for it is based on the willow pattern featured on countless household plates, with its hump-backed footbridge joined to a zig-zag railing, and waterside rocks and plants. The pagoda is the predominant structure, a glorious flight of fancy but, as always, with its surprises: one tunnel leading to the Scottish glen and the other to an ice-house. These buildings were among the last expressions of the fashion for Chinoiserie, and, painstakingly restored and freshly painted in their original livery of scarlet, buff and blue-green, are once again a sparkling contrast to the black waters and coniferous backdrop.

Blickling Hall

Blickling, Norwich, Norfolk

On north side of B1354, 1½ miles north-west of Aylsham on A140

Area 43 acres (17·4 ha)
Soil acid/loam
Altitude 100 ft (30 m)
Average rainfall 25 in (635 mm)
Average winter climate cold
Staff six, plus one trainee

The sudden prospect of this beautiful Jacobean mansion, with its turrets and gables and salmon-red brickwork, is arresting. It sits square to the road, separated by simple railings, backed by trees and flanked by ornate, Dutch-style service ranges and ancient hedges of yew. It is a complete picture, with which decorative horticulture does not interfere. Only as you walk up to the house do you take in the creamy globes of *Magnolia grandiflora* either side of the stone bridge, and the unusual shrubs and climbers in the dry moat below. These are an hors d'oeuvre to the gardens awaiting you through the arch in the east wall.

Of the early seventeenth-century design to accompany Sir Henry Hobart's house, there is only an outline. Before you is the product of the three subsequent centuries, each layer building on the bones of its predecessor. The central axis, the vista uphill to the Doric Temple, is the work of the 1st Earl of Buckinghamshire, who swept away his great-grandfather's garden in the early part of the eighteenth century. The present grid pattern is a Victorian evolution and was carried out between 1861 and 1864 by the 8th Marquis of Lothian. It is a much grander and more intricate design than was here previously, with radial walks, each of a single tree species – Turkey Oak, beech and lime – infilled with mixed deciduous trees with their shrubby understorey of evergreens, and leading to circular clearings. The hurricane of October 1987 wreaked havoc here and it will be some years before the area regains its maturity.

In front of the hall is the 2-acre (0·8-ha), flower-filled parterre, its rich colours playing against the shadowy topiary. It, too, is Lord Lothian's creation and part of the garden's momentous return to Jacobean formality. Interestingly, it was excavated for him from the sloping lawn by Markham Nesfield, son of the garden designer William Andrews Nesfield,

Stone sphinxes and herms overlooking the parterre at Blickling with lythrum and *Campanula lactiflora* in the foreground.

the great champion of parterres, though the interior planting of the parterre was designed and planted by Lady Lothian.

But the inspired planting that colours it today is the work of Norah Lindsay, whose theatrical influence pervaded many country gardens in the 1920s and '30s. She was commissioned by the 11th Marquis to simplify the elaborate pattern of beds and ribbon borders, which she achieved by clearing the centre of all but its seventeenth-century fountain, and joining the corner flower-beds into four large squares. She retained the yew topiary, including the famous Blickling grand pianos.

49

To each square she gave a two-tone fringe of roses – pink and crimson Floribundas 'Else Poulsen' and 'Kirsten Poulsen', or red and orange 'Locarno' and Polyantha 'Gloria Mundi' – and underplanted them with catmint. She then filled two with herbaceous plants in tints of pink, white, violet and blue, including monkshoods, bellflowers, globe thistles and delphiniums; and the remaining two with glowing yellows, oranges and reds in the form of achilleas, heleniums, rudbeckias and the apricot Nankeen Lily, *Lilium × testaceum*. Since the gardener's palette becomes hotter as the summer advances, it is inevitable that the cooler beds should peak slightly earlier than their neighbours, soon after midsummer; nevertheless, it is a triumphant composition.

The subterranean world of the dry moat must certainly have appealed to Norah Lindsay's romantic temperament. It is a world of old walls and arched bridges, and she caught its spirit well in her plantings of dripping fuchsias, ferns and ghostly Japanese anemones. The shelter has since been exploited to grow a range of wall shrubs and climbers that you might not expect to see in this hostile Norfolk climate of dry summers and cold, windy winters. These include spring-flowering *Buddleja farreri* and autumn-flowering *B. auriculata*, ceanothus, camellia and variegated *Trachelospermum jasminoides* with flowers scented of orange blossom.

Penetrate the formal woods above the parterre, or turn the corner towards the north front of the hall, and suddenly you see a further layer of the garden's history. For here is the parkland landscape moulded in the late eighteenth century by the 2nd Earl of Buckinghamshire. Living through the golden era of the English Landscape Garden, he set his father's classical ornaments in this more natural setting of rolling pasture, broken by groves and stands of oak, beech and Sweet Chestnut. There are fine elevated views of the park behind the Temple, where the remnant of an earlier fortification serves as a broad terrace and provided the 2nd Earl with a ready-made ha-ha. At one end of it he built the handsome Orangery. Probably designed by Samuel Wyatt, it was completed in 1782. It no longer contains oranges, for it is unheated and the light is poor, but instead is filled with cool, shade-tolerant greenery including *Fatsia japonica*.

On the other side of the woods, tucked under the oaks, hollies and Sweet Chestnut, is the Secret Garden. With its 'profusion of Minionet Roses, mirtles and honeysuckles', this was the principal flower garden in the late eighteenth century and the domain of Lady Buckinghamshire. The great landscape designer Humphry Repton offered suggestions on its improvement, and his son John was employed extensively at Blickling after 1823 designing trellis, arbours and furniture.

The garden took on its present shape and reduced size in the 1860s, and is now a quiet green retreat of grass and beech hedge, brick paths and sundial. The cool shrubbery, fronted with hostas and daylilies, by which it is approached, is the work of Norah Lindsay (although largely supplemented by the Trust), and is quite a contrast to her plantings near the house. The soil is more acidic here and joining the laurel, philadelphus, bamboo and dogwood are rhododendrons and blue-flowered hydrangeas.

The centrepiece for the 2nd Earl's park was the great lake which comes into view suddenly as you walk from the parterre to the north front. It makes a dramatic moment, linked in my mind to the scent of the vast Oriental Plane trees growing on this corner, and whose leaves, on the right day, infuse the air with sweet resin. The ancient Turkey Oak is also a major feature, and in spring both it and the plane trees are knee-deep in bulbs and wildflowers.

PREVIOUS PAGE: Blickling Hall

FAR RIGHT: A view of the fountain in the parterre surrounded by Norah Lindsay's plantings.

Bodnant

Tal-y-Cafn, Colwyn Bay,
Clwyd

8 miles south of Llandudno
and Colwyn Bay on A470,
entrance ⅓ mile along the
Eglwysbach road

Area 80 acres (32 ha)
Soil acid/clay
Altitude 170 ft (52 m)
Average rainfall 40 in
   (1,016 mm)
Average winter climate moderate
Staff eighteen

The famous Laburnum Arch at
Bodnant.

The scale, grandeur and scenic beauty of this garden are nothing short of stupendous. Set on a west-facing slope, 170 feet (52 m) above the tidal River Conway, the massive granite house commands panoramic views of the eastern edge of the Snowdonia range. Below, a series of five gigantic Italianate terraces anchor the house majestically in its mountainous setting. To the south, the precipitous-sided valley of the River Hiraethlyn is embraced, manipulated and coloured to make a woodland garden of epic proportions. And furnishing and overlaying each part of the composition is a plant collection to excite expert and layman alike.

The estate was bought by Henry Pochin, the present Lord Aberconway's great-grandfather, in 1874. There was little garden here then, apart from lawns and shrubberies, but when the house was built in 1792, a large number of native trees, in particular beech, oak and chestnut, were planted. With the help of landscape architect Edward Milner, Pochin began laying out a 'reposeful garden' comprising a spacious terrace, grass banks and spreading trees. On the valley floor, he planted the conifers, which are now one of Bodnant's chief delights, and in succeeding years continued to expand the bounds, adding features such as the Mausoleum and the Laburnum Arch in 1878.

The leap of imagination that transformed Bodnant into the garden we see today was made by his grandson Henry Duncan, the 2nd Lord Aberconway. It was he who, in 1902, with his mother's encouragement, conceived and constructed the great terraces and supervised their execution, and who, in 1908, encouraged a sceptical head gardener to try his hand with Chinese rhododendrons. Subsequently, he subscribed to many plant-hunting expeditions and engaged Bodnant in an extensive programme of rhododendron hybridisation. The evolution

continues today under the stewardship of the 3rd Lord Aberconway, who, like his father, is a former President of the Royal Horticultural Society and holder of its highest award, the Victoria Medal of Honour. The garden has also benefited from a remarkable partnership between the family and their head gardeners, since the post has been handed down through three generations of Puddles. Frederick Puddle was appointed in 1920, followed by his son Charles in 1947 and his grandson Martin in 1982. Both Frederick Puddle and Charles Puddle have also been awarded the Victoria Medal of Honour.

A tour of Bodnant traditionally begins with the East Garden and terraces, where the emphasis is on a summer show to succeed the woodland shrubs. Sheaves of *Phormium tenax* among the herbaceous plants of the broad entrance border hold the eye before it is carried off, across the gentian bed, by the sweep of smooth lawns. Among the many trees and shrubs to admire in this area are some fine Paperbark Maples, *Acer griseum*, one of which has its flaking chestnut trunk memorably backlit by orange azaleas.

The drama of the view greets you as you approach the front of the house, though the scale and contents of the terraces below are cleverly concealed. Each is intended as a revelation. You descend alternately by the sides and the centre to savour the full size of the composition, and each set of steps opens on to a vast empty stage of grass or water, edged and flanked by plants and architectural ornament.

The staircase from the Rose Terrace to the Croquet Terrace, hung with white *Wisteria venusta* and *W. floribunda* 'Alba', curves around a Baroque sandstone fountain, and water flows underground and through basin and rill into each of the platforms below. The high

BELOW LEFT: The River Hiraethlyn in spring, with Japanese azaleas.

BELOW RIGHT: Azaleas tumbling down the steep banks of the valley at Bodnant.

grey-blue retaining walls are home to many slightly tender shrubs including *Crinodendron hookerianum, Eucryphia lucida, Buddleja colvilei, Ceanothus × lobbianus* 'Russellianus' and scented white rhododendrons. Carpenterias, blue hydrangeas and wall-trained *Magnolia grandiflora* 'Goliath' and *M. delavayi* ensure later colour. The great cedars on the Lily Terrace are a legacy of Henry Pochin and account for the asymmetry of the terraces in relation to the house. To adorn the Canal Terrace, Lord Aberconway had parts of an eighteenth-century mill, once used for the manufacture of pins, dismantled and transported from Gloucestershire. The rebuilding was completed in 1939 and makes a romantic reflection between the rafts of waterlilies.

The tree and shrub borders to the north and west of the terraces provide the first hints of the spectacle awaiting you in the Dell. Here are camellias and tree magnolias, including *M. robusta, M. × veitchii, M. campbellii* 'Charles Raffill' and *M. sprengeri* var. *diva*; and a host of rhododendrons, including cream 'Penjerrick', blue *R. augustinii*, the deciduous *R. albrechtii*, *R. quinquefolium* and *R. schlippenbachii*, and some of the famous blood-red Bodnant hybrids. In August, the large group of *Eucryphia glutinosa* in the North Garden is a vision of white.

Behind the Pin Mill a path leads past further banks of camellias and rhododendrons and through a stream-fed rockery before arriving at the famous vantage point over the Dell. Well over 50 feet (15 m) beneath you is the Hiraethlyn, lushly edged by ferns, hydrangeas and large-leaved bog plants, studded by moss-covered boulders and the haunt of dippers and wagtails; to your right is the old stone mill; and ahead, a long linear prospect of woodland shrubs, speared by rocket-shaped conifers and bare-trunked pines. In spring, it is a riot of colour, in summer, a valley of cool greens.

The conifers on the east side of the river were planted ten years before those on the west, in 1876. They include immense specimens of fir, cedar, hemlock and redwood, and from the shrub borders above the valley you get the rare opportunity of viewing their cone-studded tops. The rich, alluvial soil and moist atmosphere of the Dell suit the larger-leaved rhododendrons well, though frost can be trapped here and many plants were lost in the severe winter of 1981–2. Accompanying them are belts of Japanese and deciduous azaleas, the fruity scent of the latter flooding the valley in early June. Magnolias, including the Bodnant-raised 'Claret Cup' and the potently fragrant *M. hypoleuca*, are also a feature.

The shrub borders provide an additional tier of entertainment. Japanese cherries, viburnums and shrubby magnolias are succeeded in May, in spectacular fashion, by the suckering stands of Chilean fire bush, *Embothrium coccineum lanceolatum* 'Norquinco'. The hardiest form, this was collected in the wild by Harold Comber in an expedition organised and part-financed by the 2nd Lord Aberconway (*see Nymans entry*). The flame red of the flowers has few rivals among woody plants. Later performers here include *Cornus kousa* var. *chinensis* and the Handkerchief Tree, *Davidia involucrata*. At the end of the year there is a panoply of autumn colour from birches, rowans, liquidambar and Japanese maples.

Visitors to Bodnant at the beginning of June have an additional treat, the Laburnum Arch, where saplings of *L. × watereri* 'Vossii' – which have, incidentally, been replaced many times since the arch was first planted – are forged into a long, glowing tunnel of brilliant yellow. As a feature it epitomises the spirit of Bodnant: generous in concept, stunning in decoration, and, with its raised sides and twisted passage, ingenious in design. In case I have left you in any doubt, this garden is a masterpiece.

Looking down to the Lily Terrace and the Pin Mill below, with clumps of pampas grass lit by the winter sun.

Buckland Abbey

Yelverton, Devon

6 miles south of Tavistock,
11 miles north of Plymouth:
turn off A386 ¼ mile south of
Yelverton

Area 3 acres (1·2 ha)
Soil acid/heterogeneous
 mixture, shale
Altitude 250 ft (76 m)
Average rainfall 40 in
 (1,016 mm)
Average winter climate moderate
Staff one

A view of the Herb Garden with
yellow elecampane in the
foreground.

The approach to Buckland is across the edge of Dartmoor National Park, through a landscape of gorse and bracken, wind-shaped thorn trees and damp sheep and ponies. From this you descend into a green pocket of the Tavy Valley, watered by one of its tributaries and presided over by the great, golden-grey Cistercian Abbey, which was the home of Sir Francis Drake.

A vast and cavernous thirteenth-century barn is the gateway into the garden and the intimate tracery of the herb enclosure beyond is a surprise. The idea of a herb garden was suggested by Vita Sackville-West, a member of the Trust's Gardens Committee, after a visit in 1953. She disapproved of the serpentine path already in place, convinced that 'everything at Buckland should be as straight and geometrical as possible, to conform with the severity of the house'. But, in fact, the wavy theme was expanded into an irregular web of 52 box-edged compartments, each containing a different herb, and the resulting pattern is a great success.

A rather sad Venus at Buckland Abbey.

This informal mood extends into the main abbey gardens over the wall, where specimen trees, evergreens and groups of flowering shrubs edge the sloping lawns and frame the views of the Devon hills. Rhododendrons, azaleas, camellias and magnolias are the main providers of colour, and they are punctuated by curiosities including a Handkerchief Tree, a stand of Devil's Walking Sticks and a splendid old mulberry that has collapsed, as mulberries are wont to do, and now rests one giant limb on the ground and another on the wall behind.

In spite of being exposed to wind and frost, the south front of the abbey hosts huge plants of *Magnolia grandiflora* and the larger-leaved *M. delavayi*, while the adjacent wall shelters *Callistemon citrinus* 'Splendens', a half-hardy Australian shrub with curious red bottlebrushes in summer. The Chilean *Berberidopsis corallina*, with red cherry flowers late in the season, is also here, trained against the wall of the barn. The chief talking point, however, is invariably *Aristolochia macrophylla*. A hefty specimen of this hardy North American climber scrambles over a giant box bush near the north-west corner of the garden. Its large leaves are impressive enough, but in summer they are accompanied by bizarre brownish flowers, bent like an ear trumpet and flared at the mouth, which give it its common name of Dutchman's Pipe.

The ferocious gale of January 1990 took its toll on Buckland, ripping through the ancient Yew Walk to the north of the abbey. It will be many years before the yews recover their composure and overhang the path once again, but this remains a tranquil and picturesque garden and they can take their time.

Buscot Park

Faringdon, Oxfordshire	Between Lechlade and Faringdon, on A417	*Area* 62 acres (25 ha) *Soil* acid, alkaline/clay, sandy, loam *Altitude* 328 ft (100 m) *Average rainfall* 30 in (762 mm) *Average winter climate* cold *Staff* four, plus one trainee

Towards the end of the nineteenth century, the great gardens of Renaissance Italy began once again to exert their influence on garden designers. Buscot boasts one of the finest designs from this period, by one of its leading exponents, Harold Peto. He was commissioned in 1904 by the financier and connoisseur Alexander Henderson, later the 1st Baron Faringdon, to create a water garden that would connect his Neo-classical house to the 20-acre (8-ha) lake below. It was meant to appear suddenly between two elm trees to the north-east of the house, but sadly one of the elms fell almost immediately and the other died some years later.

Nevertheless, the drama of first seeing the long, narrow vista cut through the tall, dense woods framed by box hedges and terminating in the temple on the other side of the lake, remains intense. The stone steps lead first to a circular pool containing a statue of a dolphin embracing (or strangling) a boy, and the water then flows off, via canals, rills, still pools and

LEFT: Harold Peto's Italianate Water Garden at Buscot with its pools, fountains and statuary, and the lake beyond.

rushing cascades until it reaches the lake. Much of this is revealed only as you descend, which you must do on a serpentine line, skirting the different shapes of the basins, with the invitation to cross sides by means of a small hump-backed bridge. Roman herms and other statues embellish the design, and Irish Junipers and yews furnish sharp verticals.

The theme of dynamic formal avenues slicing through the woods below the house was pursued further by the 2nd Lord Faringdon. A *patte d'oie*, or goose foot, of avenues, constructed of fastigiate oak and beech, cherry and poplar, is centred on the Theatre Pavilion arch. Along one of these rides is a sunken garden planted entirely with a low juniper called 'Grey Owl', which can give the impression of mist hanging in a frost hollow.

Always there is the backdrop of the park. It was presumably the first owner of the house, Edward Loveden Townsend, who landscaped the grounds with two lakes and dense belts of trees, but many more trees were planted subsequently. A long period of neglect, coupled with the ravages of Dutch Elm disease, necessitated an extensive programme of replanting and thinning by the present Lord Faringdon, and many young oaks and beeches are now swelling into position for the future.

A second, distinct portion of garden lies to the west of the house. This centres upon Townsend's walled kitchen gardens, which have been redesigned and replanted over recent years as formal flower and fruit gardens. The powerful contrasts of the Parent's Walk borders were devised by Peter Coats in 1986. The path, like the avenues on the other side of the garden, plunges and ascends dramatically. It leads to the orchard, where many old varieties of apple and pear are assembled, some espaliered on the walls. The main section of walled garden has a formal groundplan, revolving around a central fountain and quartered by alleys of Judas Tree and hop hornbeam. The walls are concentric, to take full advantage of the sun's warmth, but although fruit and vegetables are still grown here, the emphasis is now on flowers. Statues of the Four Seasons, sculpted in fibreglass, set the theme, and the planting of each corner, designed by Tim Rees, is anchored in winter, spring, summer or autumn flowers, with roses, potentillas, hellebores and rosemary acting as unifying links.

Calke Abbey

Ticknall, Derbyshire

9 miles south of Derby, on A514 at Ticknall between Swadlincote and Melbourne

Area 10 acres (4 ha)
Soil acid, alkaline/clay
Altitude 300 ft (91 m)
Average rainfall 25 in (635 mm)
Average winter climate cold
Staff two

In 1985, the Trust lifted Calke's veil and exposed an estate that had hardly been disturbed for a hundred years. The grey Baroque house is well sited for seclusion, concealed between deep folds of a large and hilly park, and a succession of idiosyncratic and reclusive members of the Harpur Crewe family, owners of the estate since 1622, ensured it remained a private, self-contained world. The Trust's restoration has been unusual, for the temptation to spruce up the house and garden has been vigorously resisted. Rough grass and the colonising activities of wild yellow mimulus between paving and walls preserve the air of a house lost in time and shrouded in mystery.

The flower and kitchen gardens are hidden. They were moved up the hill from the house in the late eighteenth century, following the conversion of the park to a more natural landscape. You can still see vestiges of the earlier formal layout, such as sections of avenues that used to carry the geometry of the house into the park and fragments of the former walled orchard. But the house's present tranquil setting of trees, pasture and lakes is one of curves and

The Auricula Theatre at Calke featuring a summer display of pelargoniums.

undulations. The heart of the woods is ancient, confirmed by the rich population of beetles, associated with an unbroken continuity of decaying trees stretching back many centuries.

A shady Pleasure Ground of trees and evergreen shrubs is currently being renovated after years of damage by Calke's herds of red and fallow deer; these have now been fenced into the north-east section of the park. The plantation is lightened by wildflowers and bulbs, and in one of its secret hollows there is a mineral-lined grotto.

The invisible rebuilding of the gate-piers that lead into the walled gardens has left the old rust stains on the brickwork. Between the piers, the path leads past summer borders of sweet peas and dahlias, to the fruit store and gardener's bothy, still with its old tools and seed cabinet leaning against walls washed a surprisingly opulent blue.

Lady Crewe's Garden to the west has been reconstructed as a rare example of an early nineteenth-century villa flower garden and given the same polish as the best-kept rooms in the house. The basketweave ironwork that encircles the fountain pond is a typical feature of the period, as is the elaborate, labour-intensive and, to modern eyes, rather eccentric pattern of small beds cut out of the lawn. There are 22 of these, and each is bedded out brightly with wallflowers in spring and a mixture of annuals and exotic feature plants, such as cordylines, Chusan Palms and abutilons in summer. The herbaceous planting that laps the surrounding walls is in Loudon's 'mingled style' and includes the double, richly fragrant,

A scarecrow above the brussels sprouts in the Physic Garden, now a working kitchen garden. In the background are the frames for growing delicate fruit and vegetables.

yellow wallflower *Cheiranthus* 'Harpur Crewe', named after the respected gardener and plant collector, the Rev. Henry Harpur Crewe, rector of Drayton Beauchamp in Buckinghamshire, who died in 1883.

But the most exciting feature, for garden historians and plant enthusiasts alike, is in the north-west corner. Here, along from the stove house and aviary, is a theatre for displaying auriculas and summer pot plants, possibly the last structure of its kind in existence. Auriculas, cousins of the primrose, have enjoyed waves of popularity since Elizabethan times, and the idea of showing them off on covered staging, which exposes them to the air but protects them from rain and midday sun, was being recommended as far back as 1717. Calke volunteers have now built up a large and fascinating collection.

To the east of the bothy is the Physic Garden, which has been restored as a working kitchen garden. As far as possible, old varieties are grown here, and its 1½ acres (0·6ha) are divided into rotating beds for potatoes, brassicas, legumes and root crops; permanent beds for asparagus and globe artichokes; a herb border; cages for soft fruit; strips for cut flowers; and an orchard. In addition, there are frames and hot beds, and glasshouses for tomatoes and cucumbers. A vinery is currently being restored. The 4-acre (1·6-ha) Upper Kitchen Garden over the wall, once a model Victorian working kitchen garden, is now largely a sheep-grazed paddock, and the glass-domed conservatory moulders elegantly.

Canons Ashby

Canons Ashby, Daventry,
Northamptonshire

14 miles south-west of
Northampton, off the A361
Daventry–Banbury road; easy
access from either M40,
junction 11, or M1, junction 16

Area 3⅓ acres (1·3 ha)
Soil neutral/loam over clay
Altitude 459 ft (140 m)
Average rainfall 22 in (559 mm)
Average winter climate cold
Staff one

A view, taken in 1921, of the
garden at Canons Ashby looking
towards the Lion Gate. Old
photographs like this provided
the Trust with guidelines for
restoring the garden's design,
albeit in a simplified form.

In the decaying house, derelict gardens and priory church of Canons Ashby, the Trust
acquired a rare unspoilt piece of early eighteenth-century rural England. The house looks
much as it did in 1710, when Edward Dryden replaced the Tudor brickwork of the south
front with golden-brown ironstone. It is neither grand nor ornate, but a solid, masculine
residence, with a squat, square pele tower commanding views over the chilly Northamptonshire countryside. The structure of the garden dates from 1708, and the 'extreme simplicity of
its design' with its sheltering walls and humble terraces, delighted H. Inigo Triggs, who
included it in his book *The Formal Gardens of England and Scotland*, published in 1902.
Formality was then back in fashion and the garden had been invigorated by topiary and
detailed planting in the Victorian 'Old English' style. Indeed, it is thanks to the plans
and photographs that appear in Triggs' book, Alicia Amherst's *History of Gardening* (1895),
and *Country Life* articles of 1901 and 1921 that the Trust has such clear guidelines for restoring
the garden's design, though the intricacy of some of the planting has had to be simplified.

By grubbing out tree stumps, brambles and ivy, and carefully lifting areas of turf, the
gravel paths in front of the house were uncovered and the walls exposed. Now the main vista
down the grass terraces, concluding in the Lion Gates and the finest of the impressive series of
Baroque gate-piers, is once again revealed, though, sadly, the four great cedars which used to
flank the steps leading to the second terrace are gone – three in a gale in 1947 – and it will be
some years before their replacements make their presence felt.

Otherwise, the terraces are fast regaining their character. Fruit bushes, including red-
currants, blackcurrants and standard gooseberries share ground with flowers in the traditional
cottage style. And there are grapevines and various early French varieties of apple, including
'Nonpareil' and 'Calville Blanc d'Hiver'. The apple scent of sweetbriar roses flavours the

descent to the lowest terrace where the mown path is freshly bordered by lines of *Rosa × alba* varieties, plums, pears, Irish Yews, mock orange and lilac; this is extended beyond the Lion Gates into the former park by means of a lime avenue. This avenue is one of several that carries the garden's axes into the landscape, connecting it to the church, the former approach road and the lake. This last, which begins beside the summer-house on the south-west corner of the garden, is an unusual zig-zag design, switching trees from lime to hornbeam to oak as it runs into the countryside, possibly following old field boundaries.

Visitors to Canons Ashby have often remarked on its romantic character, and this relaxed, slightly unkempt country spirit is being nurtured in the rough grass and areas of wildflowers between trees and shrubs, and in the preponderance of grass rather than gravel paths.

Eight topiary yews, restored by the Trust, form the centrepiece of the west Green Court. This modestly sized enclosure was once the main entrance for the house, but now closed gates, a sweep of lawn and a lead statue of a shepherd boy seal it from the park. Against the surrounding walls old varieties of pear have been espaliered, including 'Catillac', 'Beurré Alexandre Lucas' and 'Louise Bonne of Jersey'. It is a complete and perfect example of a small, early eighteenth-century formal garden, and cannot fail to impress upon even the most horticulturally minded visitor the virtues of restraint and symmetry in garden design.

Castle Drogo

Drewsteignton, Devon

4 miles south of A30 Exeter–Okehampton road via Crockernwell

Area 12 acres (5 ha)
Soil lime-free/clay, variable
Altitude 1,000 ft (304 m)
Average rainfall 45 in (1,143 mm)
Average winter climate cold, wet
Staff two

Castle Drogo – the name sounds a bass note of foreboding, which reverberates when, from the road, you first catch sight of the granite fortress sprouting from its rocky spur, high above the bleak expanses of Dartmoor. Even as you climb towards it, it stretches out no welcoming hand; the long drive has no entrance lodges or banks of flowers, only dark clumps of ever-green oak and belts of beech trees framing dramatic views of the wild moorland. And when you finally arrive, you are confronted by hostile, defensive walls, with battlements and few windows, silhouetted starkly against the sky. Edwin Lutyens entered fully into the spirit of his unusual brief when he designed this Norman fantasy for Julius Drewe, founder of the Home and Colonial Stores.

The contrast with the wilderness behind is intentionally abrupt. Drewe wanted his castle to appear to rise directly out of the moors and the suggestion by Gertrude Jekyll for elaborate terraced gardens directly below the house was rejected in favour of untamed vegetation lapping the precipice.

The only garden connected to the house is the small, draughty Chapel Garden, planted with patio roses and wall shrubs, including red-flowered *Camellia* 'Adolphe Audusson' and a cordon-trained *Viburnum plicatum*. Julius Drewe decided to locate his main flower gardens beyond the drive, to the north-east. Echoing the castle, they are potently architectural, generous in scale and solidly walled in yew, but it is likely that they owe more to George Dillistone, a garden designer from Tunbridge Wells, than to Lutyens. The Trust replanted them in the early 1980s. The centrepiece is the Rose Garden, planned as a series of square and rectangular beds chequered into a velvet lawn. The soil being naturally poor, hungry and stony, rose cultivation is a labour-intensive business, but Hybrid Teas and Floribundas are here in a variety of colours.

65

ABOVE: The 'Bunty House' by the formal gardens.

LEFT: View of the formal rose beds from the herbaceous border.

The highlight of the composition is on the terrace above, where the contributions of both Dillistone and Lutyens are clearly defined. The paths follow an intricate Indian motif that Lutyens, then at the height of his international career, imported from Delhi, and conclude in yew pavilions, roofed originally in weeping elm but now in Persian Ironwood, *Parrotia persica* 'Pendula'. Into this crisp pattern Dillistone wove gorgeously hued and textured plantings of tree peonies, agapanthus, crinums, daylilies, phlox, delphiniums, bearded irises and the glaucous-leaved *Kniphofia caulescens*. The result is as imaginative a herbaceous garden as you are likely to see. In the centre of the terrace, steps rise between spiky yuccas and dripping wisterias to a formal herb garden, and thence via a gravel corridor between shrub borders, foaming with azaleas, cherries and magnolias in spring, and hoherias, eucryphias and lilies in summer, to a further flight of steps guarded by erect cypresses. Here is the greatest surprise of all, for you enter into a huge circle of yew, empty of all but a smooth expanse of shaven grass – a silent (but for the sound of water crashing over the weir below the house) counterweight to the bulk of the castle and busy detail of the flower gardens below.

The ever-present backdrop to all this is the trees: beeches marshalled into avenues and flooded in spring by blue anemones and daffodils; and woods of oaks, beeches, Scots Pines, tree magnolias and birches, with their understorey of ferns and bluebells. Among these, on the steep slope north-west of the house, meandering paths entice you down into a rhododendron garden, created by Basil Drewe, second son of Julius Drewe. Blue *R. augustinii* 'Electra', pale yellow 'Lionel's Triumph', pink *R. racemosum* and rose-magenta *R. albrechtii* pull the eye this way and that, while tactile Snakebark Maples draw the fingers and heavy lily scents of Loderi rhododendrons excite the nose. Like the rest of the grounds, it simultaneously defies its raw, windswept terrain and merges scenically with it, and makes a comfortable addition to what is one of the most extraordinary flights of fancy of this century.

Castle Ward

Strangford, Downpatrick, Co. Down

7 miles north-east of Downpatrick, 1½ miles west of Strangford village on A25, on south shore of Strangford Lough, entrance by Ballyculter Lodge

Area 40 acres (16ha)
Soil acid
Altitude 80ft (24m)
Average rainfall 34in (863mm)
Average winter climate frost-free
Staff one, plus one trainee

The setting for this, one of the most eccentric houses in the British Isles, is exceptional, with broad, soft views down over Strangford Lough, a glistening stretch of sea water fringed by misty and lush woods. Into this scene, Bernard Ward, later 1st Viscount Bangor, placed what seems, at first, to be a straightforward Palladian residence, but at its north and east fronts, suddenly it transforms itself into an ornate Gothic structure. The gardens also betray sharp changes in style, through the evolving fashions of several centuries.

Lord Bangor set his new house in an informal, parkland landscape, in the style that was capturing the imagination across the Irish Sea. His planting was considerably enriched after 1841 and the slopes are now well-wooded with oak, beech and sycamore, and with numerous exotics featured in the undulating lawns around the house. The mild, damp climate seems not only to promote tremendous growth but also to encourage trees to develop a multi-stemmed habit, the most extraordinary example here being *Thuja plicata*. But there are many notable conifers here, including firs, Wellingtonias and *Fitzroya cupressoides* from South America, supplemented by massive evergreen shrubs of *Griselinia littoralis*, yew, and, most dramatically, scarlet-flowered *Embothrium coccineum*.

The nucleus of the Victorian gardens is the formal sunken lawn and terraces, studded with tall Cabbage Palms and sheltered by walls, a young hedge of Chilean Yew, *Prumnopitys andina* (syn. *Podocarpus andinus*) and a screen of fastigiate Irish Yews. In the flower-beds, the Trust has taken advantage of the climate to pursue the subtropical theme to the full, and the beds now bristle with exotics, including glaucous-leaved *Melianthus major* and *Kniphofia caulescens*, red-flowered *Lobelia tupa* and *Acca sellowiana* (syn. *Feijoa sellowiana*), *Sophora macrocarpa*, watsonias, cordylines, phormiums and spiky-leaved *Beschorneria yuccoides* and *Fascicularia bicolor*. As complete and absorbing as this upper garden is, it is only half the story. For as you crunch down the shady paths below the house, between the banks of laurel and walls of moss and Hart's Tongue Fern, towards the farmyard and Elizabethan tower-house, the parkland begins to reveal further formal touches: a three-tier terrace of ancient yews; a lime avenue, recently replanted (and including, according to tradition, one odd oak for good luck); and, the biggest surprise of all, a great rectangular lake, fringed by trees and shrubs.

Neptune and cabbage palms presiding over the Sunken Garden at Castle Ward.

These are the legacy of the early eighteenth century, and accompanied the family's second residence which once stood on the rise above the lime avenue (it was demolished two centuries later). It is a picturesque composition that absorbs, as its focal point, Audley's Castle, the fifteenth-century fortification guarding the entrance to Strangford Lough, and signals the coming of more civilised times by answering the castle with the serenity of a Doric Temple, erected in about 1750 on top of the lakeside hill.

The Trust has restored the formal shape of Temple Water, but the scene remains soft-edged, with long grass peppered with wildflowers, clumps of gorse and dogwood, and the edge of the lake broken by weeping ash and giant-leaved *Gunnera manicata*. It has long been a favourite haunt of wildfowl, and swans and dabchicks nest on the small island near the west side. Dragonflies abound, and on my first visit, I remember being unable to take a step without the air blackening with clouds of mayfly.

Charlecote Park

Wellesbourne, Warwick

1 mile west of Wellesbourne, 5 miles east of Stratford-upon-Avon, 6 miles south of Warwick

Area 5 acres (2 ha)
Soil acid/light well-drained gravel
Altitude 170 ft (52 m)
Average rainfall 25 in (635 mm)
Average winter climate moderate–cold
Staff one

A weathered, palisade of split oak runs around most of the park, and you look across from the Warwick road to see an expanse of low-lying meadow, furnished with oaks and other trees and grazed by groups of red and fallow deer and Jacob sheep. The entrance drive carves a straight channel to an Elizabethan gatehouse, and then across a balustraded court to the east façade of a red-brick house, appointed with gables, cupolas and dressed white stone.

Stately and sleepy though it seems, Charlecote – the seat of the Lucy family since 1247 – has passed through tremendous swings of fashion. A painting hanging in the Great Hall shows the house in a seventeenth-century setting of splendid parterres, formal water gardens and great avenues. Little of this, except the gatehouse and the long procession of limes that comes in from the south-west, survived beyond 1760, when George Lucy engaged 'Capability' Brown to landscape the grounds in the new style. Even the River Avon, curving beside the house's west front, was remoulded, its channel widened and its banks given a 'natural and easy level', while the River Dene (formerly the Hele), joining just to the south, was brought closer and made to enter the Avon via a cascade. The eye wanders freely over the open meadowland, the only architectural eyecatcher being the church tower and adjacent rectory of Hampton Lucy village. In winter, the flooding can be comprehensive.

The nineteenth-century Elizabethan revival brought a return to formal order in the garden. The terrace giving on to the river was re-created, together with its flower parterre; grassed over in the 1950s, this is soon to be remade, for a third time, by the Trust. A croquet lawn was laid opposite the house's north front. And the entrance court was set out with elaborately patterned flower-beds; in their place, the lawns and gravel are now fringed with borders, featuring an assortment of flowering shrubs, climbers and perennials, including wisteria, buddleja, catmint and lavender, and structural greenery in the form of yucca, euphorbia and clipped tumps of yew.

North of the entrance court, steps lead to the cedar lawn, part of the raised section of garden that rides ship-like above the park. A small Victorian orangery, a replacement for George Lucy's 'frightful' Grecian temple, and a thatched garden house stand under the trees, the latter inspired by a visit by Mary Lucy to the Ladies of Llangollen.

PREVIOUS PAGE: The steps and forecourt statues at Charlecote Park, leading to the Cedar Lawn.

Beyond, Brown's Ladies' Walk offers a gentle circuit around the prow of the garden, which opens on to lawn shaded by gnarled and ancient mulberries and a fine prospect of park and river. The centre ground was planted as a contrasting Wilderness, and you plunge through gaps in the hedge into a small labyrinth of dark passages, shaded by Scots Pine and chestnut, thick with yew, box, ivy, evergreen honeysuckle, Butcher's Broom and periwinkle, and in spring coloured by snowdrops, aconites and, later, daffodils. Close by, a new border has been made using plants – roses, herbs, fruit trees and cottage perennials – mentioned in Shakespeare's plays. The story goes that, in about 1583, the young William was caught stealing a fallow deer from the park, and was brought before Sir Thomas Lucy, the resident magistrate, to be fined or flogged. He took revenge by immortalising Sir Thomas as the pompous Justice Shallow in *Henry IV (Part II)* and *The Merry Wives of Windsor*. How Sir Thomas would now react to seeing Shakespeare's flowers in Charlecote's garden, and his bust in the Great Hall, we can only guess.

Chartwell

Westerham, Kent

2 miles south of Westerham, fork left off B2026 after 1½ miles

Area 82 acres (33·1 ha)
Soil acid-neutral/sand, loam
Altitude 450–550 ft (137–168 m)
Average rainfall 29 in (736 mm)
Average winter climate moderate–cold
Staff five

From November 1922 until his death in January 1965, this was the family home of Sir Winston Churchill. The great man lived here as Chancellor of the Exchequer, Leader of the Opposition and as Prime Minister. It is hard to view the house and garden today without straining to hear his voice and to smell the smoke of Havana cigars. The house is packed with paintings and mementoes, uniforms and letters, while in the garden, his chair stays as he left it, empty beside the goldfish pond.

'I bought Chartwell for that view', he once declared. Blasted as the old beechwoods were in the hurricane of October 1987, the prospect remains beautiful. The ground falls away steeply below the house into a quiet combe; a series of rock pools and channels, fed from the seven springs of the Chart Well, carry water around the northern edge of the garden down into a pond-like swimming pool and on into the first of two lakes. Beyond, the land climbs to woodland and on towards the Weald of Kent. There is a panorama from nearly every window of the house, and six doors connect the airy rooms with the garden. The series of terraces and walls, anchoring the house on its hillside, was elaborated for the Churchills by their architect, Philip Tilden, who was responsible for transforming and modernising the gloomy residence into the bright and comfortable family home we see today.

The planting and overall design of the garden were the province of Lady Churchill, ably assisted by Victor Vincent, head gardener from 1947 until 1979. Although inevitably much replanted, the walled rose garden beneath the north front of the house, awash with pink and while Floribunda and Hybrid Tea roses, indicates immediately her penchant for simple soft, eye-catching effects. In the water garden, the combination of white foxgloves grown from seed in summer, and royal blue anchusa propagated from root cuttings in April, is repeated each year.

On Churchill's death, Chartwell passed to the Trust; Lanning Roper, then a gardens consultant to the Trust, suggested improvements to the structure and planting in consultation with Mary Soames, Sir Winston's youngest daughter. To cope with the large numbers of visitors, many of the grass paths had to be surfaced in stone, gravel or tarmac. Borders had

their flowering season extended and other areas of the garden were altered to allow for plant growth and the shaping of views for the future. The walled gardens to the south-east of the house acquired much of their present character from Roper, who enlivened the walls with flowering shrubs and climbers, and planted a number of specimen trees in the grass, including crab apples, rowans, thorns and robinias.

The centrepiece for this area is the Golden Rose Walk, part of the present given to the Churchills on their golden wedding anniversary by their children. Backed by a beech hedge and lapped by catmint and *Stachys byzantina*, it is a dazzling sight from the terrace above throughout the summer and early autumn, when the tones of the 32 yellow and golden roses are taken up by the fruits of *Malus* 'Golden Hornet'.

The adjacent Wendy house, built for Mary Soames, and much of the lower wall, were constructed by Churchill himself, and in 1928, at the invitation of the General Secretary, he became an adult apprentice of the Amalgamated Union of Building Trade Workers. In this corner of the garden is also his artist's studio.

73

Chirk Castle

Chirk, Clwyd

½ mile west of Chirk village
off A5; 1½ miles of private
driveway to castle

Area 5½ acres (2 ha)
Soil neutral-acid/sandy loam
Altitude 700 ft (213 m)
Average rainfall 40–45 in
  (1,016–1,143 mm)
Average winter climate cold
Staff three

The gilded wrought-iron gates at the entrance to the park, and the gentle folds of oak-studded pasture through which you climb, lull you back into the luscious decades of the eighteenth century. It comes as quite a shock when a massive medieval fortress rears up on the horizon, its high walls joined to heavy drum towers and topped with battlements. For Chirk, completed by 1310, is one of the chain of great border castles built at the command of Edward I to survey the defeated Welsh tribes. It is the transition from military stronghold into a comfortable and splendid home, and the fact that the changes – sometimes subtle, sometimes dramatically abrupt – have been effected since 1595 by a single family that give Chirk such powerful character. Add to this its stupendous hilltop views, topiary and richly planted shrub borders, and you have one of the Trust's most exciting little-known gardens.

It is an exposed site and the great oaks help to filter the wind through the gardens. As Lady Margaret Myddelton explained to me, 'Without them it would be impossible to stand up'. The yew hedges and shrubberies provide further barricades. But a hilltop has many advantages. The panorama from the Terrace, looking out over the Ceiriog Valley towards the hills of Shropshire, is said to encompass fourteen counties; there is a pavilion by William Emes, who landscaped the park after 1764, from which to savour it.

The falling ground also accentuates shapes. This is a garden of spectacular silhouettes, cast against a broad sky. Among the most striking is the long topiary hedge beneath the castle, whose black-green battlements create a further defensive courtyard beyond the grey walls. On the terraced lawns within them are many more yew specimens, a double row of large cones and 'Welsh hats', and a magnificent giant crown resting on a cushion. These were all planted in the late nineteenth century, but allowing them to grow to their present size and plumpness was the suggestion of the celebrated garden designer Norah Lindsay, a close friend of Lord and Lady Howard de Walden, who leased the castle from 1911 until 1946. The task of pruning the Chirk yews takes two gardeners from mid-August until the end of October.

The sunken Rose Garden, filled with old Hybrid Tea and Floribunda varieties, is a softening influence on the scene, as is the lavish assortment of shrubs and climbers against the castle walls, including *Lonicera tragophylla* and *L. × brownii*, roses, clematis, and, for its autumn colour, *Celastrus orbiculatus*. The climate being relatively mild here, half-hardy plants such as *Luma apiculata* can also be risked in the more sheltered niches.

Pass between two hefty yew buttresses and their accompanying graceful bronze nymphs – yet another disarming juxtaposition – and you step on to a long, linear sweep of lawn, flanked by fine trees and flowering shrubs. In summer, the large weeping Silver Lime will be wafting its intoxicating scent; earlier it will be the scarlet flowers of *Embothrium coccineum*, backed by

LEFT: Chirk Castle and its castellated yew hedges.

75

the purple leaves of beech, that catch your eye; and in spring, sheets of daffodils swirl towards the great larch and cedar in the rough grass.

The undulating, 300-yard (274-m) border on the north side was originally designed for herbaceous plants, but it fell derelict during the war and was replanted along more labour-saving lines, with azaleas, lilacs, shrub roses and flowering cherries, by Lady Margaret Myddelton. The luxurious planting of the rock bank, flanking Lord Howard de Walden's thatched Hawk House and the Shrub Garden opposite, is also by Lady Margaret. In late spring, the fiery trusses of rhododendrons and azaleas blaze against the whites and pinks of pieris, magnolias, dogwoods and the Handkerchief Tree, *Davidia involucrata*. Later, near the newly extended waterlily pool, white-flowered *Eucryphia glutinosa* glows above pools of blue hydrangeas. The conclusion of this long walk is the Terrace and the views; as the land drops away, a high Lombardy Poplar makes a final dramatic silhouette against the eastern sky.

Clandon Park

West Clandon, Guildford, Surrey

3 miles east of Guildford at West Clandon on A247

Area 7½ acres (3 ha)
Soil alkaline to neutral/loamy
Altitude 250 ft (76 m)
Average rainfall 27 in (686 mm)
Average winter climate moderate
Staff one

The Dutch garden at Clandon in its Edwardian heyday.

The park and pleasure grounds at Clandon have been subjected to abrupt swings in taste over the years, resulting in a green landscape of contrasting features. At its heart is the imposing Palladian mansion, with its high red-brick walls, dressed in white stone. It was built in 1731 for Thomas, 2nd Baron Onslow, and originally stood within a grand geometric pattern of avenues, parterres, formal walks and canal. By the 1750s a new, naturalistic landscape in the style of 'Capability' Brown was already replacing it. And in the late nineteenth century the tide again turned. The 4th Earl Onslow divided the flowing composition into fields, re-instated a double avenue of trees west of the house and laid out extensive ornamental gardens.

The shrubberies that lap the lawns, and furnish the Wilderness behind the house, recall some of its Victorian past. Plants that would have adorned the early eighteenth-century garden, such as yew, laurel, holly and mock orange, are supplemented by kerria, snowberry, mahonia, *Osmanthus armatus* and fine stands of Japanese maples. Purple Beech, hazel and Smoke Bush, golden philadelphus and variegated dogwood interrupt the green backdrop. And among the specimen trees are a Wellingtonia and a splendid *Magnolia acuminata*, known as the cucumber tree because of the shape and colour of its young fruits. In spring, large areas of rough grass are stained yellow with primulas.

In addition, there are several architectural surprises. An eighteenth-century shell grotto stands opposite the south front, and three Corinthian capitals, flanked originally by a double row of Lawson Cypress, sit deposed on low brick plinths in the grass. Even more disarming is the sight of a Maori meeting-house among the trees and shrubs, obtained by the 4th Earl while Governor of New Zealand. And some distance to the north-east is a sunken Dutch garden, created after 1897 and based on the Pond Garden at Hampton Court.

Some of the grandeur of the earlier Georgian garden was restored to the property in 1976, when the Trust remodelled the parterre beside the south front. Forget-me-nots in spring and a summer scheme of verbenas, petunias and ageratum colour the box-edged beds. And at the side, palissades *à l'Italienne* – stilt hedges of hornbeam – pay homage to the mansion and its architect, the Venetian Giacomo Leoni.

Claremont

Esher, Surrey

At west Clandon on A247, 3 miles east of Guildford; if using A3, follow signposts to Ripley to join A247 via B2215

Area 49 acres (19·8 ha)
Soil acid/sandy loam
Altitude 100 ft (30 m)
Average rainfall 25 in (635 mm)
Average winter climate moderate
Staff three, one part-time

The restoration of this landscape garden, once praised as 'the noblest of any in Europe', began in 1975, thanks largely to a generous grant from the Slater Foundation. The task facing the Trust was monumental. Twenty years of neglect had turned the entire site into an impenetrable evergreen jungle.

Today, you can see just how much the clearance revealed: contributions by a succession of the eighteenth-century's greatest gardeners, each building on (and only occasionally destroying) the work of his predecessor; the whole encapsulating the early evolution of the English landscape movement. A place of varied beauty was awoken, a composition of framed views, dramatic eye-catchers, open arenas and meandering lakeside and woodland walks; the greens complemented by the changing trees and seasonal surges of colour from bluebells, daffodils, purple rhododendrons and yellow azaleas.

The Belvedere Tower, crowning the ridge above the garden, is the obvious place from which to embark on the historical tour, though it stands just a few feet outside the Trust's boundary; the adjoining part of the estate still belongs to the house, now a school, with limited opening in 1995 for the first time in conjunction with the Trust.

Equipped with a banqueting room and viewing platform, the Belvedere (designed by Vanbrugh) was the place from which the landscape was to be surveyed, and was the first building erected by the garden's creator, the Duke of Newcastle (then Lord Clare: hence, Clare Mount) in 1715. From this battlemented pavilion, a long grass corridor channels the eye downhill, over Vanbrugh's accompanying bastions (reconstructed by the Trust) and between beech hedges, to a rectangular bowling green. The corridor extends into a lime avenue

Charles Bridgeman's grass amphitheatre at Claremont is seen across the lake on a frosty winter day.

introduced in the 1730s, and replanted by the Trust; following this around to the left, you suddenly arrive at the vantage point over the next feature to be installed by the Duke, the 3-acre (1·2ha), grass amphitheatre – Claremont's masterpiece.

The designer of this stupendous earthwork, a reference to ancient Rome and, perhaps, an idea borrowed from the gardens of Renaissance Italy, was Charles Bridgeman, the foremost landscape gardener of the time, and a colleague of Vanbrugh at Stowe (qv). The Duke had been consulting him since 1716, and he is thought to have built the amphitheatre not long after the Vitruvius Britannicus plan of 1725 was drawn.

Scenic rather than thespian drama was the amphitheatre's purpose, and from the vantage point, you have a fine panorama of trees and water. The view below, however, is not of circular pond and plantations, but of informal lake and woods. This change took place in the early 1730s, under the supervision of a second celebrated gardener, William Kent, who would now use the natural contours to create scenes evocative of landscape painting, complete with curving lines and architectural eye-catchers.

The next architectural structure you come upon, as you round the south-west corner of the lake, is the grotto. Constructed of sandstone and chalk conglomerate, it is probably the work of Joseph and Josiah Lane, the builders of the splendid grotto at Painshill. Behind the lake, the path entices you up a mound, thickly covered in beech, chestnut and oak, and carpeted with bracken. This piece of land, formerly severed from the garden by the main Portsmouth road, was landscaped and brought into the composition after 1768, when, on the Duke of Newcastle's death, the estate was bought by Lord Clive of India.

The bold, sweeping style of 'Capability' Brown was now the prevailing fashion, and Lord Clive turned to Brown both to build him a crisp new Neo-classical house in place of Vanbrugh's low-lying, castellated palace, and to expand and further deformalise the garden. Part of this work involved the smothering of Bridgeman's amphitheatre (which had become far too artificial a feature for current taste) with cedars, deciduous trees and evergreen shrubs. Skirting the north side of the lake, past the laurel shrubberies, through the rhododendron tunnels, and following the line of Brown's brick ha-ha, you come to open meadow, sheeted with native Lent Lilies (*Narcissus pseudonarcissus*) in spring and spangled with other wildflowers in summer, and then back up the ridge to the sites of the nineteenth-century's architectural additions.

In 1816, the estate was purchased as a home for Princess Charlotte, the only daughter of the Prince Regent, and her husband Prince Leopold of Saxe-Coburg, and it remained a royal residence until 1922. Several buildings were put up in this period, but apart from the Thatched House (a replacement for the thatched building put up by William Kent, and now a dovecote), they survive only as foundations. Above the amphitheatre, you can see the vestiges of Princess Charlotte's Gothic tea-house, which became a mausoleum after her death in childbirth. And just below the Belvedere, framed by an ironwork balustrade, are the remains of the camellia house, built in 1824. The bushes of *Camellia japonica*, hardier than the Victorians suspected, now grow in the open.

Clevedon Court

Clevedon, Avon

1½ miles east of Clevedon, on Bristol road (B3130), signposted from exit 20 M5

Area 8 acres (3·2 ha)
Soil alkaline
Altitude 100 ft (30 m)
Average rainfall 32 in (813 mm)
Average winter climate moderate
Staff one

This is an ancient habitation. Remains of a Roman dwelling have been uncovered here, and the Great Hall and Tower were already standing when Sir John de Clevedon built the present manor house with its erratic roofline and thick, buttressed walls *c*.1320. It is a snug and sheltered spot, gaining some protection from the west wind whipping across the Bristol Channel and the high water table of Clevedon Moor from its south-facing position on the side of Court Hill. Well-wooded and with broad pastoral views, the ancient scene remained tranquil until the construction of the M5 a short distance away.

Trees are one of the garden's main features. About the house, a dense canopy of Evergreen Oak, planted in the 1820s, lends a southern European air to the backdrop, while the many specimen trees added to the sloping lawns later that century set the manor between layers of its own small arboretum. Pines and beeches, and a massive London Plane beside the short drive, rise high above the roofline. There are also good Tulip Trees and robinias, a splendid catalpa, and a Black Mulberry, recorded as being ancient as far back as 1822. They are at their most beautiful in spring, when daffodils and wildflowers filter through the grass.

More intricate gardening is concentrated on the slope between the house and the oak woods above. Here Sir Abraham Elton, the second in the 250-year succession of Eltons to own Clevedon Court, constructed two retaining walls to replace what may have been early fortifications. A painting outside the State Bedroom, shows the new Pretty Terrace complete and espaliered fruit trees against the wall. The upper terrace, an ancient fosse way, had its retaining wall constructed after 1815, possibly to give work to soldiers returning from the Napoleonic Wars; it was subsequently named the Esmond Terrace to commemorate William Makepeace Thackeray who wrote part of *Henry Esmond* during one of his frequent visits here as a guest of Sir Charles Elton.

The terraces offer fine views down over the house and out across the moor to the Mendip Hills, and the mild climate and sunny, well-drained ground allow adventurous planting. The Pretty Terrace was adorned with a Gothick Octagon and balancing Summer House in the late eighteenth century, and these, together with the steps, half-landings and series of central pools, give the composition an emphatic architectural structure.

The style of its planting has swung dramatically with the pendulum of fashion. In the late nineteenth century, Dame Agnes Elton replaced her forebears' work with the elaborate formal patterns of small beds, annuals and subtropical perennials, popular at the time. The schemes were praised by *Country Life Illustrated* in 1899, but not Getrude Jekyll, who lamented, in *Wall and Water Gardens*, published in 1901, that 'one of the noblest ranges of terrace walls in England' should be 'given over to the most commonplace forms of bedding'.

Today a relaxed, more natural style prevails, with simple, bold associations of shrubs, climbers and perennials and 'the noblest plants', for which Miss Jekyll pleaded. *Magnolia grandiflora* and yuccas, osmanthus, pittosporums, *Photinia serratifolia* (syn. *P. serrulata*), *Mahonia lomariifolia*, hardy palms and self-sowing arbutus furnish the varied and exotic evergreen backbone into which *Buddleja colvilei* 'Kewensis', *Solanum crispum* 'Glasnevin', ceanothus, azara, passionflower, crinums and agapanthus have been inserted.

Cliveden

Taplow, Maidenhead, Berkshire

3 miles upstream from Maidenhead, 2 miles north of Taplow

Area 180 acres (73 ha)
Soil neutral-alkaline gravel
   overlying chalk
Altitude 246 ft (75 m)
Average rainfall 27 in (686 mm)
Average winter climate moderate
Staff nine

An opulent marble fountain by Thomas Waldo Story, which has water pouring from a giant shell between female figures intoxicated by the elixir of love, meets you in the drive; you turn to the south to find yourself looking down a long, broad lime avenue at an ornate Italianate palace. It is a grand and theatrical opening scene. The house, one of the masterworks of Sir Charles Barry, was built in 1850-1 for the 2nd Duke and Duchess of Sutherland. As you approach, you pass between two forecourt borders of herbaceous plants laid out by the Trust. Planned primarily for seasonal flower colour rather than for textural contrast, they reach a climax in high summer – after displays of tulips, geraniums and early daylilies – with massed phlox, Japanese anemones, macleaya, achillea, rudbeckia and much else. The scale is suitably impressive and the colours are founded in one border on the yellow end of the spectrum and the other on the pink.

Cliveden's two earlier houses were both destroyed by fire, but when you emerge beside the garden front – having passed further planting in the Edwardian fashion, of roses and fuchsias – you discover the first has left a magnificent legacy, a brick terrace in the French Baroque style with arcades, balustrades and central double stairway. It stands as a podium below the house,

A moss-covered statue in the Long Garden at Cliveden, with patterns of box and clipped variegated euonymus.

and from it you look out over a sweeping platform of lawn and a landscape of plunging beechwoods and still largely pastoral valley, centred on a glistening stretch of the Thames. There are miles of hill and riverside walks to explore in this panorama, the eastern route taking you through a landscaped valley, much admired by the influential Victorian garden writer William Robinson, and offering superb views back to the house.

The first house and the terrace, both designed by William Winde for the 2nd Duke of Buckingham, were built in the 1660s and 1670s. The plateau of lawn, levelled for the Duke, was extended and given its terminating raised circle after 1695 by his successor, the Earl of Orkney, and then, in the early 1850s, decorated with the present pattern of wedge-shaped parterre beds. Although now filled with labour-saving grey-leaved santolina, senecio and catmint, they used to contain a colourful array of flowering shrubs, perennials and, not least, bedding. The gardener at the time, John Fleming, is credited with being the first to use spring-flowering bulbs and other plants, bedded out in the autumn, to follow up the summer annuals and tender exotics (earlier gardeners relied upon evergreen bushes), and he wrote an account of his experiments in *Spring and Winter Flower Gardening*, published in 1870.

LEFT: The Fountain of Love by Thomas Waldo Story on the approach drive to Cliveden.

The Japanese Pagoda in the Water Garden in autumn.

The other notable feature directly beneath the terrace is the Baroque balustrade brought from the Villa Borghese in Rome. This was installed by William Waldorf (later 1st Viscount) Astor, who bought Cliveden in 1893. This introduction to the south garden indicates that the composition was shaped over many years and involved a succession of owners, not least the Trust. Much of the framework, however, is due to Lord Orkney, and the early eighteenth-century mood becomes strong as you turn to the north-west and exchange the open plateau for the shady, wooded bank that runs high above the river. Here, you come to an octagon temple with a copper-domed roof, designed for Orkney by Giacomo Leoni – later transformed into a chapel and mausoleum by Lord Astor – and pick up traces of the earlier landscape. Orkney's garden designer, probably recommended by their mutual friend Alexander Pope, was Charles Bridgeman, the leading practitioner of the day and a key figure in the transition towards the more naturalistic gardening style shortly to come into fashion.

The combination of straight walks, many bordered by large yew trees, and prospects of the countryside beyond, give the flavour of his work, even if much of it has evolved subsequently. And in the north-west corner, you come upon the most remarkable remnant, a turf amphitheatre (c.1723), a miniature version of that at Claremont (qv), carved into the slope. Further straight drives cut through the woods, one leading to a triumphal pedimented pavilion, also by Leoni, commemorating the Battle of Blenheim (Lord Orkney was one of Marlborough's brigade commanders), and another leading to a stone urn, said to have been presented to Orkney by Queen Anne.

These enclosed spaces play against the views out over the countryside – the most celebrated being the picturesque prospect of the river from Canning's Oak, named after the statesman

83

who often sat here – and the open glades. In one of these, you are suddenly surrounded by swirling lawns and clouds of Evergreen Oak, *Quercus ilex*, probably planted by Lord Orkney. In another, you enter a circular garden of sinuous beds of roses and other plants, gravel paths, and arches – a secret and soothing refuge recently restored by the Trust to an original design by Sir Geoffrey Jellicoe.

The Astors have contributed two further gardens. To the north of the woodland, the 1st Viscount set out a formal garden, echoing the parterre below the house. A great collector of classical and Renaissance art, he introduced the many urns, well-heads, statues and sarcophagi you encounter in various parts of the grounds, and here you find a group of eighteenth-century figures, placed within a linear composition of box-edged beds.

Topiary adds additional verticals, and originally the beds contained herbaceous plants arranged by the designer Norah Lindsay. Now, as in the parterre, there is a simplified scheme, this time of grass and clipped variegated euonymus. The flowers are confined to the south-facing brick wall behind, and come from a range of half-hardy shrubs and climbers, including *Umbellularia californica*, *Azara microphylla*, *Drimys winteri* and the narrow-leaved bay.

The other Astor garden is in complete contrast. It is an informal water garden, begun by the 1st Viscount and developed by his son and latterly the Trust, into a rather magical landscape with an oriental flavour. The centrepiece is a painted pagoda, made for the Paris Exhibition of 1867 but bought later from Bagatelle. This is set on an island amid a pool of waterlilies and Golden Orfe, and reached by stepping stones. The marginal plants and ornamental trees and shrubs are also mainly from the East, and include primulas and water irises, azaleas and rhododendrons, witch hazel and wintersweet, white cherries above white daffodils, and wisteria grown as shrubs. Behind, among newly developed shrub beds, there are more cherries, sophora, cercidiphyllum, Japanese maples, Chinese thujas, bamboos and weeping birches. There are scenes at Cliveden for every taste.

Clumber Park

Worksop, Nottinghamshire

4½ miles south-east of Worksop, 6½ miles south-west of Retford, 1 mile from A1/A57, 11 miles from M1 junction 30

Area 26 acres (10·5 ha)
Soil acid/sandy
Altitude 100 ft (30 m)
Average rainfall 24 in (609 mm)
Average winter climate cold
Staff two

Enter the park under the Apleyhead arch, and you will drive through one of the most impressive lime avenues in England, over 2 miles (3·2 km) in length; the bands on the trunks are to fend off egg-laying moths, whose caterpillars have ravaged the foliage in the past. The avenue is purely a landscape feature, planted in the 1830s by W. S. Gilpin, the pioneer of picturesque gardening, to enliven an otherwise featureless stretch of approach road and to indicate the magnitude of the domain through which it leads.

At its heart is the great serpentine lake, created in the mid-eighteenth century by damming the River Poulter. This provides the setting for a long terrace walk, adorned with specimen trees and shrubberies, urns and a temple. The transformation of the site was effected from about 1760 by successive Dukes of Newcastle, to whom the estate, then adjacent to Sherwood Forest, had been granted some 50 years earlier. Although 'Capability' Brown was working nearby and may have contributed, it seems most likely that the principal influence on the landscape was Joseph Spence, a tutor and 'man of letters' widely consulted on garden matters by northern landowners.

The surprise is that there is no great mansion to give the park its *raison d'être*. The first house

burned down in 1879, and its replacement, by Sir Charles Barry, was demolished in 1938 as a drastic tax-saving measure. Adjoining estate buildings, including the stable block and clock-tower, however, remain. The treatment of the ground fronting the vanished house poses rather a dilemma for the Trust, since evocation of the earlier formal garden by intricate horticulture only emphasises the void. But as you move away from the buildings, along the lakeside walk, this sense of absence gradually wanes. The entire scene is framed in oaks, limes and other broadleaved trees, sheltering the garden from the north wind, shading the lawns, furnishing the distant banks and reflecting in the water.

The paths meander through stands of willows, past dense island beds of conifers and *Rhododendron ponticum*, and under some impressive specimen trees. Mediterranean species, in particular cedars, Sweet Chestnuts, Turkey and Algerian oaks, prove themselves well suited to Clumber's poor sandy soil. Quite a diverse collection of rowans (Sorbus) is also growing here. The mood is strongly Victorian, and the design is likely to be the work of Gilpin. In the late 1880s, the ornate Gothic chapel, by G. F. Bodley, was added to the Pleasure Ground, and in the absence of the house, now serves as the core of the garden.

The formal path leads to the Lincoln Terrace, also thought to be by Gilpin, a promenade ornamented with splendid stone seats, and concluding in a narrow dock where a pleasure boat was once moored. North of the chapel, an avenue of cedars leads to a 7-acre (2·8-ha) walled garden. Now given over to grass and local varieties of fruit trees, its prize feature is a splendid range of glasshouses, in which vines and figs share space with a recent collection of early garden implements.

Coleton Fishacre

Coleton, Kingswear,
Dartmouth, Devon

2 miles from Kingswear; take
Lower Ferry road, turn off at
toll house

Area 20 acres (8ha)
Soil acid/silty-clay
Altitude 330ft (100m)
Average rainfall 36in (914mm)
Average winter climate frost-
    free, mild
Staff two

A fine rock rose, *Cistus*.

The plunging sides and deep bowl of this south-facing valley garden offer near perfect growing conditions. Cold air flows away quickly through the combe, and the shelter belts of Monterey Pine and Holm Oak limit the impact of the salt-laden winds. Humidity is high, thanks to the proximity of the sea, while the abundance of underground springs, coupled with the shaly soil and precipitous terrain, provide that ideal but elusive combination of constant moisture and sharp drainage.

Rich and extensive as its collection of rare and tender plants may be, the mood at Coleton Fishacre is not, however, exotic. Rather, true to the spirit of the Arts and Crafts Movement, house and garden maintain a strong bond with their Devon setting. Walls and terraces are of stone quarried on site, and their vernacular construction, incorporating steeply pitched roofs and curved walls, enables them to blend easily with the contours of the land. The spirit of Edwin Lutyens is pervasive, though this is the work of his pupil Oswald Milne, commissioned by Rupert D'Oyly Carte, son of Gilbert and Sullivan's business partner, and his wife Lady Dorothy, soon after they purchased the estate in 1924.

A generous leavening of native and traditional plants also helps to mellow the impact of rarified horticulture. But between the cherries and chestnuts, rosemary and wisteria, banks of daffodils and wild garlic, there is rich fare indeed. Following a long period of inactivity during the ownership of Rowland Smith, the golden opportunities the site offers have again been seized as the Trust advances its programme of restoration and improvement.

As you walk into the garden past suede-trunked *Luma apiculata* and *Acacia pravissima*, foaming in spring with yellow blossom, you are immediately diverted by the Seemly Terrace. Earlier in the year it will be hellebores, euphorbias and scented daphnes, such as *D. bholua* and *D. acutiloba*, that catch your eye and draw your nose, as you pass the polished mahogany trunks of *Prunus serrula*; later, perhaps, it may be brightly hued crocosmias and hedychiums.

LEFT: Spring wildflowers, including bluebells and wild garlic, flow down the wooded sides of the combe at Coleton Fishacre.

The Rill Garden below, with its canalised stream and horizontal patterns of stone, is strongly redolent of the great formal gardens of the Lutyens-Jekyll partnership. Originally planted with roses, which struggle in the humid maritime atmosphere, it is now filled with half-hardy perennials, including osteospermums, salvias, argyranthemums, cannas and kniphofias. Unusual climbers, including fiery *Acca sellowiana* (syn. *Feijoa sellowiana*), *Berberidopsis corallina*, *Clianthus puniceus* and *Mitraria coccinea* decorate the walls, their trunks lapped by autumn-flowering Belladonna Lilies. Beds near the house, and along the walk to the Gazebo, shimmer with half-hardy shrubs from the hotter and drier parts of the world. *Ceratostigma willmottianum*, *Lithodora diffusa* (syn. *Lithospermum diffusum*) and prostrate rosemary contribute washes of blue; *Buddleja officinalis*, *B. nivea* and *B. farreri* and numerous forms of olearia, phlomis, cistus and brachyglottis, give mounds of silver. Strong highlights are supplied by *Crinodendron hookerianum*, cytisus, callistemon, leptospermum, sophora and *Grevillea* 'Canberra Gem'; while accompanying perennials, such as libertia, dierama and *Fascicularia pitcairniifolia*, introduce contrasting notes of spiky foliage.

The views from the Gazebo out towards the jagged outcrop of the Blackstone rocks and the wide expanse of sea allow a brief pause from this intensive horticulture. But then, taking a deep breath, you must choose your descent into the combe. The open sunny terraces now give way to the dappled shade of woodland, and formal stone-edged rill and basins become burbling stream and natural pools. In spring and early summer you are submerged in colour from camellias, magnolias, rhododendrons, embothriums and dogwoods, with azaleas and tender, white-flowered rhododendrons, including *RR. maddenii* ssp. *crassum*, *burmanicum*, *johnstoneanum* and *lindleyi*, providing pools of scent. Hydrangeas, eucryphias, orange-

BELOW LEFT: Formal terraces below the house at Coleton Fishacre, with watsonia, dierama, lavender and erigeron.

BELOW RIGHT: A stone urn containing astelia and helichrysum, accompanied by crocosmia, dark-leaved dahlias and penstemon.

flowered *Lomatia ferruginea*, melon-scented *Magnolia × wieseneri* and self-sowing *Cornus capitata* extend the season through the summer. And providing the backdrop, and a host of subtle green delights, are bamboos and tree ferns, nothofagus and *Pinus radiata*, glossy-leaved *Gevuina avellana*, a large Tree of Heaven, and a magnificent Tulip Tree.

A multitude of paths snake their way between the shrubs and trees, and as you swing sideways up the combe's high flanks, the scale and drama of the terrain become thrillingly apparent. The reward for this slow descent is the sheltered, rocky inlet of Pudcombe Cove, and in late spring your arrival is sweetened by thickets of scented *Elaeagnus umbellata*. No lover of plants will be disappointed by this garden.

Cotehele

St Dominick, nr Saltash	1 mile west of Calstock, 8 miles south-west of Tavistock	*Area* 19 acres (7·6ha) *Soil* acid/loam *Altitude* 250ft (76m) *Average rainfall* 45in (1,143mm) *Average winter climate* mild *Staff* three

Here is an estate full of Cornish character. The approach is along narrow, plunging, high-banked lanes, affording sudden views across the Tamar Valley over the hilly expanse of Dartmoor. Below is the tidal river itself, punctuated by Cotehele quay, once busy with traffic transporting copper and other minerals downstream to Plymouth, but now the tranquil mooring for the last of the Tamar barges, the *Shamrock*. Cream teas are served in the former hostelry, the Edgcumbe Arms.

The house and its outbuildings are at the head of the wooded combe high above. In spite of the towers and battlements, they are a snug and welcoming collection of buildings, low-lying and warmly constructed of brown and grey slate. Of medieval origin, the property was remodelled and enlarged in Tudor times by Sir Richard and Sir Piers Edgcumbe, whose family were to own Cotehele for nearly six centuries. But, thanks to the decision of Sir Piers's son, Richard, to build a new house at Mount Edgcumbe in 1553 as the family's principal seat, the property saw little further alteration.

The gardens, divided into a series of intimate enclosures and sheltered walks, are equally inviting. Splendid sycamores opposite the old barn take up the colour of the walls in their clean grey trunks, and in spring this opening scene is cheered by a swathe of daffodils growing on the bank. Later in the year, there will be colchicums and autumn crocuses, and cyclamen flowering under the sycamores. Beyond the two cobbled courtyards, one with walls hung with wisterias and *Rosa bracteata* and lapped with Algerian Iris, and the other flaunting myrtle, camellias and *Crinodendron patagua*, we find a gateway leading into an enclosed acre of sloping meadow. Here daffodils grow in their hundreds between the well-spaced trees; simple, old

The lattice gate leading into the Upper Garden at Cotehele with old narcissus in the foreground.

varieties, in clumps that are seldom disturbed. The grass is not cut until the middle of June, by which time orchids and other wildflowers have completed their cycle. It is a timeless picture.

A white-painted gate leads into the Upper Garden, a large enclosure of sloping lawns with, as its centrepiece, a pool of pink and white waterlilies. Scattered trees, including Tree of Heaven, a superb Tulip Tree and a fine yellow-twigged ash, *Fraxinus excelsior* 'Jaspidea', preserve an informal character, while on the south side, a border of tall shrubs screens the garden from the estate cottages and the old cider orchard. A rill burbles softly. The surrounding borders, and the Cutting Garden beyond, are at their most colourful in summer. On the west side, a striking Victorian colour scheme of orange and gold designed to counteract the many overcast Cornish days, consists of cardoons, acanthus and *Stipa gigantea*, daylilies, kniphofias and an assortment of daisy-flowered perennials. On the north side, tulips and peonies are succeeded by fuchsias and agapanthus, *Eucomis bicolor* and autumn-flowering *Amaryllis belladonna*. Early in the year, as you walk back into the daffodil meadow along the top path, you will catch the scent of *Acacia pravissima*, foaming with bright yellow flowers. It vies for attention with one of the garden's young Cork Oaks, standing in the grass above the squat grey tower of the house. While to the left, another path beckons, leading over a stile to the three-sided Prospect Tower and its panorama of Plymouth and the rolling fields, woods and moors of the Cornish-Devon border.

The top path now descends between laurel and aucuba, through a bowl of Japanese maples, under the drooping branches of *Erica arborea* var. *alpina*, also casting vanilla scent in spring, and across the gravel drive, past crimson *Rhododendron russellianum* and a weeping Silver Lime, to bring you out on to the stone terraces below the east front of the house. This is the most formal part of the garden, constructed in 1862 to complement the house's rebuilt façade. But even here the character is modest and mellow, the walls and self-conscious beds of yellow and red Floribunda roses softened by generous, informal planting. Aubrieta, silver *Stachys byzantina* and hardy geraniums tumble over the paving, while magnolias, white wisterias, green-tasselled *Itea ilicifolia*, a bower of *Robinia hispida* and a spectacular pink *Clematis montana* scrambling up a laurel, provide part of the varied backdrop.

The views over the stone balustrade, down into the combe and across to Calstock village and the railway viaduct, were opened up by the severe gales of January 1990. This is not the first time a storm has blasted the woods; Calstock and Cotehele were also rudely revealed to each other in 1891. But although privacy has been lost from the terraces, the gales did not disturb the sense of secrecy within the combe itself, a feeling heightened by having a dark stone tunnel as its entrance.

The slopes and fringe woodland, boosted by the Trust, provide the shelter required to exploit Cornwall's mild maritime climate to the full. The tree and shrub planting is exciting and diverse, but so interwoven with the native trees as to appear natural and homely. Self-sowing bluebells, primroses, foxgloves and red campions form an unpretentious carpet, and on the shady slopes, ferns, especially Lady Ferns, grow in abundance.

Presiding over the valley is the handsome domed dovecote and stewpond, relics of medieval days when they would have provided meat and fish for the house. From this pond, water splashes down the combe in a series of pools and runnels, increasing the humidity and supplying damp ground for primulas, marsh marigolds, wild mimulus, *Darmera peltata* (formerly *Peltiphyllum peltatum*) and giant-leaved *Gunnera manicata*. The ornamental tree and shrub planting appears to have begun at the head of the valley in 1867, while the building of the viaduct in 1905 prompted the addition of screening conifers. Much of the present planting, however, is the work of the Trust, including the establishment of a new arboretum on the land known as Nellson's Piece.

Early in the year, rhododendrons are prominent, including large stands of *Rhododendron arboreum* and *R.* 'Cornish Red' as it is known in Cornwall, Devon Pink over the border) and an extensive range of azaleas. But they are not grown to the exclusion of other shrubs. Camellias, enkianthus, kalmias, embothriums and magnolias are also well represented, with eucryphias, hoherias, hydrangeas and Japanese maples providing later colour. Hemlocks, firs and the unusual *Sciadopitys verticillata* are among the comparatively modest conifer population. And striking an exotic note is the Chusan Palm, *Trachycarpus fortunei*, which produces panicles of yellow flowers in early summer, followed by great bunches of black fruits that persist throughout the winter and spring. Towards the bottom of the combe, the vegetation reverts to native woodland and a footpath leads to Sir Richard Edgcumbe's chapel and the Tamar.

The Courts

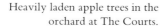

Holt, nr Trowbridge, Wiltshire

3 miles south-west of Melksham, 2½ miles east of Bradford-on-Avon on south side of B3107

Area 7 acres (2·8 ha)
Soil alkaline/loam
Altitude 200 ft (61 m)
Average rainfall 30 in (762 mm)
Average winter climate moderate
Staff two

Heavily laden apple trees in the orchard at The Courts.

This is a garden in the Hidcote tradition, full of charm and variety, and deserving to be far better known. The house, described by Christopher Hussey as 'an early Georgian gem', was built for one of the area's prosperous cloth manufacturers, and had a mill adjacent, powered by the stream that flows from Great Chalfield Manor (qv); it is believed to have acquired its name from being the former law courts, where the weavers brought their disputes for arbitration. The mill was demolished in the third quarter of the nineteenth century, however,

the stone pillars still stand, from which the chains that supported the drying wool were strung, and, at the bottom of the garden, there is the pond where the wool was dyed.

The bones of the present garden were set out by the architect Sir George Hastings, who owned The Courts between 1900 and 1910, and the design was elaborated and given its rich overlay of plants by Lady Cecilie Goff after 1921. It is a compartmented garden, not as severely delineated as Hidcote, but each section has a formal structure and its own rather imaginative blend of colours. Generally, it is a quirkier composition: Lady Cecilie loved springing surprises. You enter from the village along a walk of pleached limes (formerly of pollarded poplars), emerging opposite the east front of the house on to wide lawns, framed by assorted hedges and topiaries. Though planted symmetrically, each seems to have its own idiosyncratic bulging or lop-sided shape, immediately setting the relaxed mood. Pillars and cones of Common Yew, fringes and slabs of green box, umbrellas of holly and giant buns of golden yew are part of the scene, supported by an old acacia and a backdrop of a good many other fine trees.

Into this are inserted the self-contained planting schemes. There are hedged semi-circles of pink, lilac and white (lavender, limonium, galtonia and pink Hybrid Musk roses, among them); a pair of blue and yellow borders (featuring thalictrum, asters, achillea and the sun-tolerant form of golden cutleaf elder, 'Sutherland Gold'); a long fuchsia border, brightened with white Japanese anemones; and a small fernery, screened by bamboos. The most exciting colouring is in the Mediterranean-style walk, flanked by sentinel yews, down which scarlet, orange and pale yellow flowers (zauschneria, crocosmia, cephalaria and others) crackle among the silver mounds of santolina, artemisia and French and Spanish Lavenders, *Lavandula stoechas* and its subspecies *pedunculata*, with their curious topknots of purple and magenta. A superb piece of planting.

All is in contrast to the pale stone of the house and its loggia, the terraces and paths (the slabs gleaned by Lady Cecilie from the demolished Devizes gaol), and the various ornaments – a large dog, a column surmounted by a heraldic lion, pillars hung in vines and much else – many of the grander pieces being brought here by Sir George Hastings from Ranelagh House, Barnes.

The greenhouse, kept frost-free and stocked with exotics like strelitzia and honey-scented *Hoya bella*, grown in a hanging basket, is similar to the pastiche Georgian orangery he created at Ranelagh. And at the head of a long, straight grass walk below the house, now flanked by borders on a pink and yellow colour scheme (phlox, crinums, pink achilleas and Japanese anemones, partnered with golden-leaved *Cornus alba* 'Spaethii' and physocarpus, and the curious evening-opening daylily, *Hemerocallis citrina*), he installed a classical temple.

We are now in the lower garden. Water sets the theme here, and at various points you cross the trickling stream by little bridges. A large rectangular pool, created by Lady Cecilie and restored by the Trust, is framed by beds of Siberian iris, lavender and salmon-pink roses, and covered by vast rafts of pink, crimson, yellow and white waterlilies. It lies parallel to the temple walk, and below it is the informally shaped dyeing pool, fringed with giant gunnera and other bog plants. Everywhere, there are thickets of trees and shrubs. The range should inspire all visitors who share a heavy, limy soil, especially in autumn, when the leaf colours are quite as brilliant as those to be seen in acid woodlands. Paperbark and Nikko maples, *Acer griseum* and *A. maximowiczianum* (syn. *nikoense*), *Viburnum carlesii*, cotinus and Sargent's

LEFT: A painted timber seat with the red foliage of the purple form of *Cotinus coggygria*.

93

Early morning mist and frost on the topiary at The Courts.

Cherry are among those contributing reds and oranges, and there are major displays from the various cultivars of Guelder Rose, *Viburnum opulus*, the native Wayfaring Tree, *V. lantana*, and the thorn, *Crataegus persimilis* 'Prunifolia', all of which partner their tinted leaves with coloured fruits.

There is more drama in the arboretum, an extensive area of pasture planted by Moyra Goff in 1952, and a welcome change from the intimacy and formality of the rest of the garden. Pink-candled Horse Chestnuts, limes, walnuts, a fine Cut-leaved Beech, Turkey Oak and catalpa are among the contents, with daffodils appearing beneath them in spring, followed by Snakeshead Fritillaries – a native plant that once carpeted many an English water meadow.

Cragside House

Rothbury, Morpeth,
Northumberland

At Rothbury, 13 miles south-
west of Alnwick (B6341) and
15 miles north and west of
Morpeth (B6334)

Area 1,000 acres (404·7 ha)
Soil acid/sandy moorland
Altitude 500 ft (152 m)
Average rainfall 32 in (813 mm)
Average winter climate cold
Staff four

Rock falls punctuate the burn
that runs below the house at
Cragside. Ferns and wildflowers
colonise the banks.

Here is the rugged and mystical landscape of the Gothic novel and Wagnerian opera, a landscape of dark conifer forests, boulder-strewn hillsides, lakes and waterfalls. It encompasses 1,700 acres (688 ha), 1,000 (404·7 ha) of which are owned by the Trust, and in its midst, on a site blasted from the cliff face, stands the massive frame of the Victorian schloss. It is all the work of the 1st Lord Armstrong, inventor and armaments manufacturer, who, from 1864 began harnessing in earnest his great wealth, ingenuity and engineering skill to create an extensive picturesque retreat out of the empty moorland. The transformation involved much of the male population of Rothbury and included the planting of seven million trees and shrubs, the laying of 31 miles (50 km) of road and pathway and the digging of four large lakes. The hydraulic schemes were revolutionary. The house was the first in the world to be lit by water-powered electricity and in the grounds water was piped and pumped to supply cascades and pools, and to operate machinery.

There is no tame garden around the house. The stupendous rockery that anchors it to the steep, west-facing slope running down to Debdon Burn looks as if it has been created by an avalanche. Before the Trust began its restoration, there was hardly a rock showing; gaultheria had run rampant, and *Rhododendron ponticum* swept in from the surrounding woods. Now, thanks partly to the help of volunteers, the giant stones are again revealed. Alpine and moorland plants, including saxifrages, sedums, *Hypericum olympicum*, heathers and edelweiss, have been reintroduced into the crevices and bays, with cistus and herbs in the hotter spots. And a gentle transition from wilderness into garden has been allowed by planting a range of shrubs and trees that furnish splashes of contrasting colour without being overly ornamental.

A detail of carpet bedding in the Flower Garden at Cragside.

These include a wide range of hardy hybrid rhododendrons, evergreen and deciduous azaleas, brooms, berberis, species roses and some beautiful Asian rowans, including orange-berried *Sorbus sargentiana*, pink-berried *S. hupehensis* and that seldom-seen whitebeam *S. cuspidata*.

This same transition takes place rather more dramatically nearer the burn. Here, on the lower banks and floor of the valley, the black woods of pines and firs break into an open arboretum of conifers. The cool, moist atmosphere promotes tremendous growth, especially in North American species and many trees have reached champion size. There are soaring specimens of Douglas, Caucasian, Noble and Colorado White Fir, Western Hemlock and Nootka Cypress, and, as at Bodnant (qv), the terrain allows you both to stand among their trunks and view their crowns from above. Dippers and grey wagtails can often be seen braving the fast-flowing water, and beyond the arched steel footbridge, the paths entice you into many more acres of wooded pleasure ground, past drifts of foxgloves and rustic bridges, towards Tumbleton Lake.

In 1991, the Trust acquired the missing part of the picture, the terraced formal gardens, half a mile from the house. The restoration is proceeding apace. The Orchard House, complete with its quirky system of turntables for rotating the pots in order to promote balanced growth, has survived intact and is once again filled with cherries, peaches, citrus and other fruits. Other houses remain as roofless shells, but hardy plants and summer bedding are being cleverly used to convey their former character. *Lobelia tupa* is a feature in what was once the Display House; hardy cordylines grow in the Palm House; and an assortment of selaginellas and crested and fancy ferns filter between the boulders in the Temperate Ferneries.

A display of Victorian carpet bedding – the most intricate example in the Trust's gardens – is part of the colourful fringe to the lawns, which also includes a walk of double-flowered dahlias. The lowest terrace once included open-topped, glass-sided rooms and beds as protection from the wind, and in time these will be restored. It is all in striking contrast to the rest of this wild estate.

Croft Castle

nr Leominster, Hereford and Worcester

5 miles north-west of Leominster, 9 miles south-west of Ludlow

Area 5 acres (2 ha)
Soil lime-free/light loam
Altitude 550ft (167m)
Average rainfall 25in (635mm)
Average winter climate cold
Staff one

Far-reaching views over unspoilt border countryside, ancient trees and a rare taste of the Picturesque phase of English landscaping are the principal draws to this remote property. The fortress of grey-brown limestone was built sometime around the fifteenth century, and it stands on a ridge above parkland and woods, with a prospect south to the Black Mountains. You climb to the castle under avenues of great oaks and young beeches, and there are further avenues off to the west, which you can trudge to across the park – passing more venerable oaks on your way, including one with reputedly the largest girth in the country. The avenue is in alignment with the house and is composed of limes.

The other, of Sweet Chestnuts, is some distance away and something of a mystery. Some of the trees are huge, gnarled and with characteristic fissured, twisted trunks. They are arranged in one and then three ranks over a distance of half a mile, and, according to legend, represent battle lines for the Spanish Armada. Otherwise, the avenues are presumed to be part of the larger formal composition of garden and park which, as in so many properties, was swept away in the eighteenth century. However, at Croft the landscape that replaced it was not flowing parkland adorned with Neo-classical temples, but a more rugged, romantic style as championed by Richard Payne Knight, who may have tendered advice here.

You taste it at the head of the oak avenue, where you are met by a Neo-medieval curtain wall; around the castle, Gothicised inside and out, and fringed by a battlemented terrace wall; and in the narrow Fish Pool Valley that runs beside the approach drive. This is a steep-sided glen, heavily wooded with ash, oak, birch, alder, poplar and willow, its stream dammed to form a chain of nine ponds (most now silted up and engulfed in vegetation), and appointed with a rough stone pump house and grotto. It is a mysterious and tranquil place, echoing to the sounds of songbirds and woodpeckers; goshawks are also seen here.

Over the centuries, the fortress has evolved into a welcoming home, and there are many eruptions of flowers to soften the impact. The giant white Rambler roses, *Rosa filipes* 'Kiftsgate' and *R. brunonii* 'La Mortola', cloak the curtain wall, and as you continue down the curving drive, you pass between a border of rhododendrons and other shrubs, and a lawn where primroses and daffodils appear around the boles of the trees in spring, followed by cyclamen in late summer.

The castle walls shelter roses, clematis and a variety of flowering foliage and flowering shrubs, including aralia, *Itea ilicifolia* and purple Smoke Bush (strikingly partnered with blue-leaved *Kniphofia caulescens*). The small-flowered pink nerine, *N. flexuosa*, is among the bulbs and perennials in the small secret garden below the west wall; given protection from the wind, this is a fairly benign climate, with good frost drainage. There are also beds of roses in front of the adjacent St Michael's church, which predates the castle, and a 3-acre (1·2-ha) walled flower garden and vineyard, owned and developed by the Croft family, who are still in residence. Myriad house martins swoop about the turrets and battlements in summer.

Dudmaston

Quatt, nr Bridgnorth,
Shropshire

4 miles south-east of
Bridgnorth on A442

Area 8 acres (3·2 ha)
Soil acid/sand
Altitude 250 ft (76 m)
Average rainfall 35 in (889 mm)
Average winter climate cold–
   very cold
Staff two

A short walk across the park from Dudmaston Hall, the sheep-grazed pasture drops into a wooded dell. It is a dark place, cool, green and silent but for the birdsong and the splash of water at the bottom of the high-sided banks. You descend, cross the stream and climb, your nose treated to the damp scents of ferns and moss, and your eyes to the beauty of the trees and the drama of the rock, and finally you emerge into daylight to be greeted by a long sheet of still water, edged by trees, wildflowers and rafts of waterlilies.

The valley wilderness, known as the Dingle, is a romantic piece of late eighteenth-century landscaping, and of considerable interest to garden historians as the best surviving example of the Picturesque style of William Shenstone. It is the creation of one of his former gardeners, Walter Wood, in collaboration with his employers at Dudmaston, William and Frances Whitmore, and it reflects closely Shenstone's influential ideas that a landscape should offer 'scenes of grandeur, beauty or variety' and that, to paraphrase his friend Dr Johnson, its walks should be entangled and its water winding.

By contrast, the William and Mary hall has a deliciously lush setting of grass, woods, hills and water. The terraces connecting the house to the Big Pool, the largest of the string of lakes, were constructed soon after 1816 by Whitmore's son, William Wolryche Whitmore, and marked the arrival of more formal gardening at Dudmaston. His gravel paths and island beds were later grassed over, but the flowers are preserved around the brewhouse and the small paved terrace beside the house, added in the 1920s. Three of the most eye-catching plants here have been introduced recently by Lady Labouchère: the daisy-like *Erigeron karvinskianus*, which has now extensively colonised the cracks between paving slabs and steps, and two opulent roses, the cream 'Lorenzo Pahissa' and the bright pink 'Gava', brought from Spain where Sir George Labouchère was the British Ambassador.

The prominent outcrop of red sandstone nearby – a rugged feature that must have delighted his parents – William Wolryche Whitmore tamed with walls and steps. Topped by big cedars and a stand of amelanchiers, it is now home to a variety of rock plants including helianthemums, brooms and heathers. The American garden to the east of the house, a popular feature in gardens of the time, was also his creation, though its design has since been made less formal and the planting extended. *Kalmia latifolia* and *K. angustifolia* thrive on the sandy soil here, together with magnolias, Japanese cherries, azaleas and old hybrid rhododendrons.

Of especial interest in the house is the large collection of botanical art, ranging from the work by P. J. Redouté to John Nash, collected by Lady Labouchère. Outdoors, Sir George introduced some fine modern sculpture, including the abstract *Watcher* beside the Big Pool, and the dynamic steel gates near the stable block. Thus Dudmaston enriches itself from yet another passing century.

Dunham Massey

Altrincham, Cheshire

3 miles south-west of Altrincham off A56

Area 30 acres (12 ha)
Soil severely acid/loamy sand
Altitude 82 ft (25 m)
Average rainfall 35 in (889 mm)
Average winter climate mild–moderate
Staff five

Thanks to the bequest of the 10th Earl of Stamford, one of the most generous in the Trust's history, these 3,000 acres (1,214 ha) of farmland and woods will be a permanent green oasis between the conurbations of Manchester and Liverpool. At their heart is a predominantly early eighteenth-century brick mansion, tactfully described by the landscape architect Dame Sylvia Crowe as one of 'beautifully proportioned austerity', richly planted gardens and a wooded park of great historic and scientific interest.

Dating back to medieval times and still roamed by a large herd of fallow deer, the park was formalised by George Booth, 2nd Earl of Warrington, in the fashionable French style. The first avenues were already installed by 1697, and the final, all-embracing landscape of radiating rides, *allées*, circular, triangular and oval plantations, canals, formal ponds and architectural eye-catchers (the whole bounded by brick wall) is depicted in the series of fine bird's-eye paintings by John Harris the Younger hanging in the Great Gallery; they date from about 1750. Very few such landscapes survived the change in eighteenth-century taste towards a more flowing, naturalistic composition. But at Dunham this informal style was practised in a new park to the east, leaving much of the old framework intact. The Trust has now repaired and replanted a number of these tree lines, so that from the south front of the house you have the rare prospect of a triple row of lime trees either side of the forecourt, leading to a grand *patte d'oie* (goose foot) of six long avenues centred on a grass semi-circle.

An obelisk, dating from 1717, survives as a focal point for one of these. It is the only ornamental monument to remain, but as you explore the park, you come upon other handsome functional buildings, notably a two-tiered, brick deer barn. The garden also has its ancient features. Your first view of the house is across the moat belonging to the previous

The north front and parterre at Dunham Massey seen across the moat.

Elizabethan house. It appears as a broad, lake-like swathe of water, curving around the north and west walls, and in spring there are contrasting reflections, surprisingly good, between the red brick and the mauve fringe of *Rhododendron ponticum*. A new planting of autumn-tinted trees is growing up to boost the garden's contribution. In one direction, the water runs from the garden as a narrow canal, while in the other, a channel leads past the cupola of the stables and coach-house to a seventeenth-century saw-mill.

Just to the side of the house, a semi-circle of ground extends into the lake, and here, behind the trees, are the remains of a mount. The core may be Norman, but it was built up in the Elizabethan period to form a garden vantage point, a favourite feature, complete with circling terraces and a crowning pavilion; the garden then extended to the west of the house, where the service range now stands. The mound survives today as a mysterious hummock of grass under a grove of robinias, planted by the Trust to create a shady copse within a walk of laburnum, ivy, fern and climbing hydrangea. The remainder of the garden is, likewise, many-layered, thoroughly restored after years of gradual and almost terminal decline to convey the pristine flavour of a Victorian pleasure ground, but one founded on a late eighteenth-century layout of meandering lawns and shrubberies, and including some formal Edwardian touches and inspired contemporary planting.

You enter through a slice of woodland, brought into the garden in the last century and bordered by a stream. This area was totally overgrown in 1976, but clearance revealed some good trees including two forms of sycamore, the rare *Acer pseudoplatanus* 'Corstorphinense', and 'Brilliantissimum' with eye-catching shrimp-pink leaves in spring. Cream-flowered *Holodiscus discolor* and the elegant, rosemary-like grey willow, *Salix elaeagnos* var. *angustifolia*, are among the shrubs drawing you into the plantation, while moisture-loving perennials such as persicaria, Shuttlecock Fern and a mesmerising display of the blue Himalayan Poppy, *Meconopsis × sheldonii*, in an intense turquoise form, appear in drifts above the water.

LEFT: The east border in early summer, with white *Eremurus himalaicus*, rhododendrons and bergenia.

The acid sandy soil and high water table make good azalea ground, and those in the wood belong to a notable strain, being seedlings raised by an amateur Cheshire-born plantsman, Denny Pratt. His main purpose was to carry the colour and scent of the tribe into mid-summer, by crossing various Knap Hill azaleas with the late-flowering American species, *RR. viscosum, arborescens, prunifolium* and *bakeri*; seedlings were also produced from *R. atlanticum*, and from crossing *R. occidentale* with the common yellow azalea, *R. luteum*. So far, only a few have been named and widely propagated – 'Summer Fragrance' and 'Anneke' being the best known. But a June visit to Dunham is a revelation.

Hardy hydrangeas are also well represented here, with various forms of white-flowered *H. heteromalla* and *H. arborescens*, and the large, felted-leaved *H. aspera*, growing on the wood's fringe with the contrasting foliage of bamboos and grasses. Others, forms of *H. serrata* – more tolerant than the common lacecaps of the late frosts to which the garden is prone – grow in the dappled shrubbery along the wall, with lilies, *Rhododendron yakushimanum* and a collection of skimmias.

You are now in spacious open lawn, in the company of large specimen trees – beside the house, a tall Swamp Cypress; away to the east, mature Lucombe, Cork and Red Oaks; and elsewhere, rarities such as ferny-leaved *Tetradium (Euodia) daniellii* and tropical-looking (though bone hardy) *Magnolia tripetala*.

Further plant riches are revealed as you break through the shrubbery, following a meandering grass path between birch and Purple Beech, north to the canal. First you pass low beds of *Geranium macrorrhizum*, bergenia, tiarella, evergreen iris, brunnera and other ground-cover subjects – the pastel schemes finely tuned for textural contrast – and then, on the sunny banks by the canal itself (cleared and rebuilt by the Trust), there are lush waterside plantings; the Panther Lily, *Lilium pardalinum*, does especially well here, the orange Turk's cap flowers leaping out of the borders in high summer, and there is a memorable leaf partnership between

The canal bordered with a deep purple form of *Iris kaempferi*.

Hosta sieboldiana 'Elegans' growing in a tub in the courtyard at Dunham Massey.

two invasive colonisers, the purplish hearts of pink *Clerodendrum bungei* and the grey, feathery foliage of the Californian Tree Poppy, *Romneya coulteri*.

The main lawn, however, also has architectural attractions. Tucked into the shrubbery is an early nineteenth-century rustic arbour, made of robinia bark, and a fine eighteenth-century orangery. In the Edwardian era, the orangery was incorporated into elaborate formal gardens, set out when the house was restored. These had mostly fallen into disrepair during the Second World War and were removed afterwards. But traces do remain. The grove of Purple Beeches evolved from hedges that once enclosed the rose garden and a moss garden. Other more manicured examples can be found about the house.

A small parterre of 1905 lies between the north front and the lake, contained by hedges of golden yew and coloured with spring- and summer-bedding schemes on a yellow and blue theme. Permanent structure comes from spiky clumps of yucca and short, clipped evergreen domes – not of box, but, interestingly, of an unusual bushy oak, *Quercus phillyreoides*. Iron railings give an open view across the water down the north avenue into the park, and if you penetrate it, you will find a long line of dog's graves, beginning with that of a pug, Old Vertue, dated 1702; his portrait, by Knyff, hangs in the house.

Below the east front, there are blowsy borders, planted in dark rich shades to combat the strength of the red brick – including peonies, dahlias, delphiniums and *Anchusa azurea* 'Loddon Royalist', with the grey-bloomed Dusty Miller Vine as a backing. Within the house, you come upon a courtyard where shrubs and perennials with yellow and cream flowers, including choisya, eucryphia and kirengeshoma, are set around a central fountain.

Dunster Castle

Dunster, nr Minehead, Somerset	3 miles east of Minehead on A396, just off A39	*Area* 17 acres (6·8 ha) within parkland
		Soil acid to alkaline/sandy loam
		Altitude 0–280 ft (0–85 m)
		Average rainfall 33 in (838 mm)
		Average winter climate mild–moderate
		Staff three

The picturesque vision that greets you from the Taunton–Minehead road is, in large part, a Victorian fantasy. There has been a castle on this precipitous outcrop of rock since Saxon times, when the sea, now a mile away, lapped the base of the hill. But in 1617 a mansion was built within the fortifications, and by the end of the Civil War, when Dunster was besieged for 160 days, little of the castle, though a surprising amount of the house, remained. The present assembly of warm sandstone towers, turrets and battlements was grafted on to the Jacobean mansion by Anthony Salvin between 1868 and 1872.

The slopes that link the water meadows to the castle shelter a wealth of plants. They were already thickly wooded by 1733, and by 1830 evergreens and flowering shrubs had joined the company. This planting has been considerably enriched both by the Luttrell family and latterly by the Trust. The climate here is windy but exceptionally mild, offering scope for adventurous gardening. Furthermore, the hill provides slopes facing in every direction, encompassing a range of habitats from sun-baked terrace to moist, shady dell.

This potential has long been exploited on the South Terrace beside the castle, where a row of tall Chusan Palms strike the subtropical note much enjoyed by the Victorians. Even more exotic is the mix of mimosa, *Beschorneria yuccoides*, and bottle brush (*Justicia brandegeeana*) that provide the supporting cast; and, to cap them all, a lemon tree grows by the castle wall. This celebrated plant, guaranteed to astonish all who see it, is protected in winter by a cold frame, and was already well established by 1830. Although it has suffered some dieback recently, its lower portions appear as vigorous as ever.

A small, bow-fronted conservatory, refurbished and replanted by the Trust, connects with the Drawing Room and Library. This building, with its cool green and Indian red colours, is as redolent of the Victorian age as anything at Dunster. A variety of pot plants jostle on wirework stands, others spill from hanging baskets, while scented jasmine and geraniums, begonias and parlour palms pack the deep box containers.

Out on the slopes, the mild climate has promoted some very bold effects, and as you walk along the labyrinth of paths and drives that spiral their way steeply up the hill, your eyes will frequently be on stalks. This is not from encountering exotic plants of giant height, for the tree cover is essentially native, but from meeting shrubs that you are used to seeing in ones and twos luxuriating in monstrous drifts. Laurustinus has colonised freely to envelop huge chunks of shady slope; philadelphus, Spurge Laurel and Common Laurel, periwinkle and *Rubus tricolor* have spread likewise. On the sunnier banks, hypericum, buddleja, and crimson-tasselled leycesteria have taken control of sizeable areas, together with self-sowing Holm Oaks. Accompanying these are massive groupings of, among many others, *Brachyglottis* (formerly *Senecio*) 'Sunshine', hydrangeas, escallonias, deutzias, *Lonicera syringantha*, yew and fuchsia; ivy and Virginia Creeper; carpets of woodrush, *Luzula maxima*, a handy substitute for grass on banks; and on the southern side, an entire wood of strawberry trees, of which Dunster holds a National Collection. This is ground-cover planting on the largest scale.

At the bottom of the hill, the River Avill, a winding walk, an old mill, a rustic Lover's Bridge and a rocky cascade, provide the picturesque setting for a more intricate garden. Here there is moisture and shelter enough for a full-blooded plantsman's paradise, in which *Bupleurum fruticosum*, rhododendrons, azaleas, camellias, eucryphias and large-leaved hydrangeas grow in the company of Shuttlecock Ferns, hostas and giant-leaved *Gunnera manicata*. Specimen trees, including Wellingtonias, cryptomerias, magnolias, styrax and a large Handkerchief Tree, add to the scene, and a *Celastrus orbiculatus*, spectacular in autumn, scrambles to quite a height up into the canopy of its host.

I have not mentioned the views out over the countryside, which are among the chief rewards for making the ascent to the castle. They encompass moorland, hills, deer-park and sea, and, at the foot of the hill, the cluster of Dunster village. From the keep they are panoramic, vying for attention with the myrtles, pittosporums, nandinas, *Acca sellowiana*, aralias, abelias and romneyas that grow on the tor's dry, windy summit.

Dyrham Park

Dyrham, nr Chippenham,
Avon

8 miles north of Bath, 12 miles
east of Bristol on A46

Area 6 acres (2·4 ha) within
parkland
Soil alkaline/sand, loam
Altitude 450 ft (137 m)
Average rainfall 30 in (762 mm)
Average winter climate
moderate–cold
Staff one

Neptune looking down on the
east front at Dyrham Park.

Neptune, landlocked in Dyrham's deer-park, now gestures down at the mansion like a
madman. Armed with a trident, he once presided over a spectacular cascade of 224 steps and
one of the grandest Dutch-style gardens of the late seventeenth century, extending from both
sides of the house, complete with fountains and a canal, and an elaborate and extensive pattern
of terraces and parterres, avenues and formal walks. But fashion changed, the cost of upkeep
was too great, and the Bath–Gloucester road was improved behind his back. He was left, as it
were, high and dry.

I find it hard to regret the garden's passing. The present setting is nothing short of stupendous. From the entrance, you plummet down the Cotswold escarpment and suddenly,
between muscular folds of green hillside and splendid beeches, Horse Chestnuts and cedars,
the handsome Baroque house is revealed in the valley. If the sun is drawing out the gold
in the Bath stone and illuminating the distant mountains of Wales, so much the better. But
the scene will only be marred if you have left your arrival late, and rows of cars are parked
on the grass; a new car-park is being planned.

The Tudor manor house was transformed into the present mansion by William Blathwayt, Secretary of State to William III, between 1692 and 1704. George London, the most
celebrated contemporary designer of formal gardens, was consulted on the landscaping. The
garden, though not wholly complete, was already impressing visitors by 1700. At that time,
the main entrance was opposite the west front of the house, and you can still see the ridge of
the old carriageway leading from the west gate to the Italianate double stairway adjoining the
terrace. The rectangular ponds on the west side, now edged in lawn and flanked by natural
plantings of Weeping Silver Pear, grey-green Rosemary-leaved Willow *Salix elaeagnos* var.
angustifolia, dogwoods and Guelder Rose, were part of the original formal design, fed by
water channelled under the stable block.

The long terrace above the church still exists, and the old limes are possibly those shown in
Kip's engraving of 1712. In the park, radiating avenues of elms were also spared, only to
succumb, ironically, to Dutch Elm disease. They have been replaced mainly with limes by the
Trust. Little else remains of the formal garden which had fallen into disrepair by 1779.

William Blathwayt IV engaged a Bath surveyor, Charles Harcourt-Masters, to 'mark out
plantations' and 'dispose and plant trees' and Humphry Repton visited in 1780 and made

some further additions, probably rebuilding the niched wall below the ponds. In turning the east garden into a deer-park, Blathwayt reasserted again an ancient role, for the name Dyrham is derived from the Saxon 'deor hamm', meaning 'deer enclosure'. The pale-coloured strain of fallow deer that graze the slopes is of great antiquity.

Today, the only detailed horticulture to be found on the east side of the house is pursued inside the Orangery. Built in 1701, this is one of the earliest greenhouses in the country to be given architectural importance, and was used to overwinter the pots of oranges, bay trees and aloes that adorned the formal walks and parterres. Now its walls cascade with blue and white *Plumbago auriculata* (syn. *P. capensis*), passionflower and scented *Jasminum polyanthum*, and shelter citrus fruits and oleander.

In spite of the hard climate at Dyrham, some quite adventurous planting has succeeded on the west front of the house and the adjoining south walls. Myrtles, Loquat, *Solanum crispum* 'Glasnevin', *Magnolia delavayi* and the double red pomegranate are among the cast.

The chief horticultural glory of Dyrham is its trees. Holm Oak, Purple Beech, Manna Ash, mulberry and parrotia billow above the grass and water, in defiance of honey fungus, while numerous North American species such as Tulip Trees, catalpas, *Pinus strobus*, Red Oak and Black Walnut, pay homage to the first William Blathwayt's position as administrator of the American Colonies. Many plants were sent from Virginia in 1694. Daffodils fringing the perry pear orchard, beyond the cobnut walk, add to the springtime beauty.

East Riddlesden Hall

Bradford Road, Keighley, West Yorkshire

1 mile north-east of Keighley

Area 12 acres (4·8 ha)
Soil slightly acid loam
Altitude 250 ft (76 m)
Average rainfall 37·5 in (952 mm)
Average winter climate cold
Staff one

Standing on the north-western edge of the Bradford/Leeds conurbation, this mid-seventeenth-century property preserves a small pocket of rural calm. The soot-darkened walls of the hall, part-framed by a fine stand of beech trees, are revealed immediately you turn off the A650. But dividing you from it is the large stewpond, fished in ancient times by the monks of Bolton Abbey. Reeds and willows soften its sides, and mallard and farmyard ducks ripple the still water. In spring, the grass is studded with wildflowers and bulbs, including primroses, campions and the native Lent Lily, *Narcissus pseudonarcissus*. And in late summer you will see rare white-berried elders on the rough banks leading down towards the River Aire.

The walled, formal garden, reached through the house, was designed by the Trust in the early 1970s. It is not a period piece, but plays on traditional themes to provide an appropriate and colourful accompaniment to the house. Box hedges and avenues reinforce the linear framework. From the rose window on the south front, there is a procession of pyramidal fruit trees, including the apples 'James Grieve' and 'Lane's Prince Albert' and the pears 'Winter Nelis' and 'Doyenné du Comice'. And beside the relics of the gabled façade of the Starkie wing, demolished in 1905, runs a double line of Mophead Acacia, *Robinia pseudoacacia* 'Umbraculifera' (syn. *R. pseudoacacia* 'Inermis'), so compact in growth that it needs to be clipped only every other year.

A new double border of herbs and soft fruit also helps establish a link with the past. Woad, camphor, the prostrate borage *Borago pygmala* (syn. *B. laxiflora*) and alecost (*Tanacetum balsamita* syn. *Balsamita major*), used to flavour ale in the Middle Ages, are some of the curiosities, together with liquorice, whose cultivation in Britain is closely associated with nearby Pontefract. The garden also boasts a large number of varieties of sweet violet, a plant that has been cultivated for many centuries. The nucleus of the collection was donated by a Lancashire enthusiast, and includes singles and doubles, pinks, reds, whites, blues and purples. They form an intricate and absorbing cast. Brighter splashes of colour come from beds of 'Marlena', a bushy, long-flowering, if rather mildew-prone, crimson Patio rose, in the sunken garden, and the frothing array of shrubs, climbers and herbaceous plants that fringe the lawn. Improved with generous quantities of organic matter, the light soil produces good displays of hardy geraniums, including magenta *Geranium psilostemon* and the tireless and exquisite *G. pratense* 'Plenum Violaceum'. Shrub roses, sweet-scented philadelphus, lavender and clematis are also here, accompanied by daylilies, irises, peonies and bellflowers.

The view across the valley over the low east wall is rather marred by the proximity of the gasworks. But this will be screened in time by the young hedge of *Ilex × altaclerensis* 'Hodginsii', a handsome green holly valued in the Midlands from the nineteenth century for its tolerance to industrial pollution.

Emmetts Garden

Ide Hill, Sevenoaks, Kent	1½ miles south of A25 on Sundridge–Ide Hill road, 1½ miles north of Ide Hill off B2042	*Area* 6 acres (2·4 ha) *Soil* acid/greensand ridge over stone *Altitude* 600 ft (182 m) *Average rainfall* 35 in (889 mm) *Average winter climate* cold *Staff* two, plus trainee

Emmetts is one of Kent's highest gardens. After the 1987 storm, the views are now panoramic; north to the North Downs, east towards Ide Hill village, and south and west over the great sweep of trees that lead towards Crowborough Ridge and Chartwell. And in this new, more open setting, old and young plantings look well.

The garden is largely the creation of Frederick Lubbock, a banker who bought the property in 1893. But in its design and planting it owes much to the influence and advice of his friend, the garden writer William Robinson, who lived not far away at Gravetye. Part of the former rock garden was illustrated in Robinson's *Alpine Flowers for the Garden* (1903). The only touch of formality now is the Italianate rose garden, in which purple 'Cardinal Hume', pink 'Escapade' and white 'Iceberg' roses, Hybrid Musk roses and catmint are arranged around a central pond. This was embellished by Mr and Mrs Charles Boise who bought the estate in 1928, two years after Lubbock's death. They are also responsible for the present rock garden, with its cascade and lily pond and outcrops of Westmorland limestone.

Otherwise, the garden follows a relaxed pattern of lawns, glades and meandering paths; an informal design that evolved in response to a straightforward enthusiasm for plants, displayed in a natural way. The conditions are not perfect for a collection of trees and shrubs, the

George Fillis, the head gardener, at work in the Rock Garden at Emmetts.

soil being light and fast-draining, but the altitude provides a cool, moist atmosphere in which many Asian and American species flourish. Among the notable plants in the upper garden are *Eucryphia glutinosa*, showered in white blossom in August, *Magnolia denudata* and the heavily scented summer-flowering *M. × wieseneri*, *Chionanthus virginicus* and Vine Maple, *Acer circinatum*. These are accompanied by generous plantings of azaleas, including the white-flowered *Rhododendron quinquefolium*, and seed-raised *Berberis wilsoniae*, which give a panoply of berry and leaf colour in autumn.

Lower down the slope, across the former drive, the collection takes on the flavour of an arboretum, with individual trees and stands of shrubs displayed in grass. The tall Dawyck Beech withstood the 1987 storm, and there are still good examples of *Cercidiphyllum japonicum*, *Davidia involucrata* var. *vilmoriniana* and *Stewartia pseudocamellia*, together with an enormous clump of *Pieris japonica* and a number of good rhododendrons including *R.* 'Mrs John Clutton', *R. ferrugineum* and *R. smirnowii*. In spring, the grass here is patched yellow with daffodils and, below the South Garden, the path leads off enticingly into bluebell woods.

Erddig

nr Wrexham, Clwyd

2 miles south of Wrexham, signposted A525 Whitchurch road, or A483/A5152

Area 13 acres (5·2 ha)
Soil slightly acid/loam and clay
Altitude 200 ft (61 m)
Average rainfall 35 in (889 mm)
Average winter climate moderate
Staff two, plus one part-time

'We call this the State Bedroom', announced Philip Yorke III as he showed his television audience around Erddig, 'because it is always in such a state.' It is hard for me to maintain a proper perspective on this property, whose wooded park and minnow-filled brook was my childhood playground, and whose squire, frequently seen cycling around Wrexham on his penny-farthing, was the stuff of local legend. The bedroom was not the only part of Erddig to have fallen into disrepair. The garden was all but lost in a jungle of nettles, brambles, overgrown shrubs and seedling sycamores, with sheep as the only gardeners. After what has been described as 'a heroic holding operation', Philip Yorke eventually passed his beloved estate, tenaciously held by his family at least since 1718 and comprising nearly 2,000 acres (809 ha), to the Trust in 1973.

There is no hint today of the monumental task of restoration that was faced in 1973. Spread out before the east front of the hall is a crisp pattern of straight paths and mown grass, avenues of pleached limes, groves of pyramid fruit trees, yews and variegated hollies, lines of Portugal Laurels clipped to mimic orange trees in white Versailles tubs and a broad, smooth-edged canal. Remarkably, the bones of the design had been unaltered since the early eighteenth century, and thanks to the bird's-eye view drawn in 1739 by Thomas Badeslade, the Trust was given the opportunity to reconstruct fairly accurately this rare example of a formal garden in the Dutch style.

Fruit trees, marshalled into quincunxes and espaliered on walls, were then especially valued as part of the formal structure. Lists were made in 1718 detailing Erddig's wall fruits, and varieties still in existence have been reintroduced. Apples, now the most numerous wall fruit, were not, in fact, mentioned, suggesting they were grown only as free-standing trees. Today the collection includes a number of ancient varieties including 'Nonpareil' and 'Fenouillet Rouge', supplemented by pears such as 'Bon Chrétien d'Hiver' and 'Windsor', and plums 'Blue Perdrigon' and 'Red Magnum Bonum'. All these were in cultivation before 1700.

The borders are strewn with climbing and herbaceous plants, and beneath each fruit tree

107

The Edwardian parterre at Erddig bedded out with spring forget-me-nots and edged with festuca grass.

there are bulbs: in the orchard are strips of Pheasant's Eye Narcissus, and in the borders, a number of old varieties of daffodil dating from before the First World War. 'Lord Kitchener', 'Will Scarlett', 'Saint Olaf' and 'Bonfire' are among the many unfamiliar names. The banks of the canal are also colonised by the wild Welsh Lent Lily. It is a fascinating collection.

Fruit trees were not merely decorative; their crops were an important part of the garden's utilitarian function. The pond, north of the canal, would also have been stocked with fish for the table, and it seems likely that the strange yew niches beyond were designed for bee skeps and honey production. This same productive theme is evoked by the squadron of plump, egg-laying farmyard ducks waddling across the lawns, and the new border of culinary, medicinal and strewing herbs against the south-facing wall of the former vegetable garden.

Powerfully rooted in the early eighteenth century though they remain, Erddig's formal gardens continued to be embellished by the Yorkes, most notably in the late nineteenth century. The parterre is decorated with mossy, stalagmitic fountains, and the Trust's bedding schemes of cheerful pink annuals reinforces the Victorian flavour. The adjacent walled rose garden is being developed in the Gardenesque style; and it houses, apart from Shrub roses, a large Black Mulberry – once a single stick in the undergrowth – a young *Cornus controversa* 'Variegata', pampas grass in the lawn, and a Silver Birch, whose trunk was at one time tapped for sweet sap to be used in wine-making.

The nineteenth-century mood is even stronger in the small Flower Garden, which was described in detail in the *Journal of Horticulture* of 1909. Here pink 'Dorothy Perkins' roses and deep violet *Clematis × jackmanii* are strung along swags of rope, around specimens of variegated *Acer negundo* against geometric pattern planting of bush roses and annuals. Specimen trees, including a magnificent Swamp Cypress, date from the mid-1800s. *Taxodium distichum*, at the head of the fish-pond, and the avenue of Wellingtonias beyond the south wall of the garden also date from this period. And against the shadiest walls is a National Collection of varieties of that popular Victorian plant, the ivy.

The west front offers a quite different prospect – an abrupt drop into woods and undulating parkland. The landscape was moulded by William Emes, a contemporary of 'Capability' Brown who also worked at nearby Chirk Castle (qv) and Powis Castle (qv) in the dominant naturalistic style of the late eighteenth century. But the pastoral scene is now interrupted by the looming silhouettes of Hafod and Bersham collieries in the middle distance, binding Erddig firmly to its locality. Emes' most wonderful feature can be seen between trees to the north-west: an extraordinary circular weir, known as the Cup and Saucer, into which the waters of the Black Brook – no longer darkened by passing through coal seams – are flushed; at times of flood, it becomes a whirlpool in the meadow and, to an impressionable child, a vision that stamps itself forever on my mind.

Farnborough Hall

Banbury, Warwickshire	6 miles north of Banbury, ½ mile west of A423	*Area* 8 acres (3·2 ha) *Soil* neutral *Altitude* 250 ft (76 m) *Average rainfall* 27 in (686 mm) *Average winter climate* cold–very cold *Staff* one

A Grand Tour to complete his education, followed by much travelling to and from Italy, turned William Holbech into a connoisseur of Italian art and architecture, and in about 1745 he set about reconstructing the manorhouse inherited from his father. The result is an elegant Palladian-style villa of golden ironstone, which stands among trees at the edge of the village, slightly elevated above the patchwork of meadows in the Warmington valley.

The broad, grass terrace walk, ascending the ridge to the south-east of the hall, is Holbech's other great legacy. Beginning steeply, it follows a leisurely S-shaped line to terminate in a soaring obelisk, three-quarters of a mile distant. *En route* are his 'viewpoints' – an Ionic temple and an unusual oval pavilion with open loggia and an upper-storey Prospect Room, its ornate blue and white interior recently restored to full Rococo glory. There was a third temple in the park but it was demolished about 1820. Probably completed in 1751 and pre-dating the great Rievaulx Terrace by a few years, it thus gives an insight into eighteenth-century landscape gardening at a period when the last touches of formal design were giving way to the Picturesque. Holbech's friend, the amateur architect and landscape gardener Sanderson Miller, almost certainly assisted in the remodelling of Farnborough and was probably the designer of the temples.

The walk is flanked on one side by a dense belt of trees and evergreen shrubs, and on the other by a curving laurel hedge, broken by 33 projecting bastions along its length which provide views out over the surrounding countryside. The views between these trees and those on the bank below are panoramic, looking out over the Warwickshire plain and across to Edgehill and the Malvern Hills, with the glistening stretch of Holbech's river pool directly below. Sadly, the scene has now been disturbed by the arrival of the M40 in the middle distance. Broken belts of trees are being planted in the valley to lessen its impact but the former tranquillity will never quite be regained.

The return walk takes you through the wood behind the terrace to the Game Larder, a handsome hexagonal building which looks back towards the village across seventeenth-century stewponds. These feed into the large Sourland Pool over the road from the hall and then into the river pool. This last, topped by a cascade, is reached by a path leading from the spacious, cedar-shaded lawns, and as you skirt the field, a flowery surprise is sprung in the form of a parterre of bush roses, framed by box and cubes of golden yew. The site of the old eighteenth-century orangery (pulled down in 1960) is threaded with thyme and backed by wisterias, its alcove seat (the terracotta-pink wall well matched by 'The Fairy' roses foaming over the stones) offers another green prospect for quiet contemplation.

Felbrigg Hall

Cromer, Norfolk

2 miles south-west of Cromer, off B1436

Area 6½ acres (2·6 ha)
Soil neutral/light loam
Altitude 200 ft (61 m)
Average rainfall 25 in (635 mm)
Average winter climate cold
Staff two

A short walk from the hall, across the donkey paddock, is one of the Trust's best preserved potagers. Walled kitchen gardens have been a prime casualty of increased labour costs, and even Felbrigg's 2¾-acre (1-ha) enclosure has been greatly simplified.

But the economies have enabled the restoration and tending of the gravel paths and half mile of dwarf box edging, and the reintroduction of fan-trained and espaliered fruit trees against the 12-foot (3·7-m) high brick walls. Dahlias are still grown and grapes still hang in the greenhouse. In their spare time the gardeners still cultivate an array of vegetables and soft fruits, the rows punctuated by lantern cloches, rhubarb forcers and pea and bean tents; a local bee-keeper tends the orchard's hives. The essential elements are thus present to conjure up again the luscious atmosphere of the potager in its country-house heyday.

The south-facing slope is divided into three compartments, with a handsome octagonal dovecote, probably dating from the eighteenth century, crowning the central axis. Today, the birds are purely decorative; in the past they would have been a source of meat and manure.

Myrtle flanks a stone archway into the walled Kitchen Garden at Felbrigg Hall, showing the two vinery greenhouses and the dovecote beyond.

Sunlight on the herb garden at Felbrigg Hall.

Borders of herbs fringe this northerly path, accompanied by espalier pears, ancient fig trees, and grapevines grown on timber pyramids.

The pyramid apple trees lined in front of the dovecote are 'Norfolk Royal Russet', one of the many varieties growing here associated with East Anglia; 'Norfolk Beefing', 'Wyken Pippen', 'D'Arcy Spice' and 'Braddick's Nonpareil' are among the other evocative names. Everywhere, the ornamental qualities of the fruits are contrasted with those of flowers. The old orchard plots are carpeted with spring bulbs and wildflowers. Along the east-facing wall, the plums, apples and pears are joined in one compartment by phlox, in another by peonies and lilies (an excellent partnership), and in another by old Shrub roses; and along the west-facing wall, by dahlias and herbaceous perennials. Opposite and adjacent to the fruit cage is a plot housing the National Collection of colchicums.

In early autumn, there are some spectacular runs of these goblet-flowered bulbs. The uncommon *Colchicum tenorei* grows *en masse* along the central cross-walk, and its presence and obvious liking for the compacted sandy soil prompted the Trust to build up the collection. This now comprises more than 60 varieties in all shades of lilac, mauve, carmine and white, single and double, plain and chequered. *Amaryllis belladonna*, another autumn-flowering bulb, is also long established, producing its pink funnels beneath the apricots and peaches on the central compartment's south-facing wall. Equally arresting is the sight of great bushes of half-hardy *Buddleja crispa* close by; their success in the open borders, in the company of hardier buddlejas, lilacs, potentillas, Jerusalem Sage and other shrubs, is an indication of the maritime influence – the North Sea is only 2 miles (3·2 km) away.

The presence of a flourishing old grapefruit, cropping with the 'Black Hamburgh' grapevine in one of the unheated, lean-to glasshouses, is similarly telling. The second house is occupied by scented mimosa and ginger lilies, abutilon, vallota, and other exotics. Plantations of medlars and many different species of thorn tree giving fine autumn tints, lead to the lowest compartment, which is open to the south, grassed and sparingly studded with mulberries, rowans, thorns and a Pyrennean Oak.

The Walled Garden has always been Felbrigg's main flower garden, but there is a small garden of Polyantha and Rugosa roses beside the hall and, on the rising ground below the Great Wood, a Victorian collection of ornamental trees and shrubs. Many of the woody plants available in the nineteenth century originated from North America, and like other contemporary collections, this is known as the American Garden. Azaleas, liquidambar, *Robinia viscosa*, Tulip Tree and various conifers are among the cast. The centrepiece is the early eighteenth-century Orangery, filled with camellias, scented rhododendron and Woodwardia fern.

The hall's Jacobean south front looks on to open parkland receding towards Norwich. William Windham III, the great-great-grandson of the hall's builder Thomas Windham, was landlord and patron to the young Humphry Repton from the mid-1770s, and it is likely that the Felbrigg landscape was the first sizeable project to which this great designer contributed. The woods and stands of oak, Sweet Chestnut, beech and sycamore are welcome breaks to the bleak horizontals of the Norfolk countryside, and give vital shelter to the hall and gardens from the bitter North Sea winds. The many trees felled for timber during the First World War were replaced in subsequent decades by Robert Windham Ketton-Cremer, who bequeathed the estate to the Trust; it was he who added the Coronation group of beeches and the Victory V rides to commemorate VE Day. And in turn, the Trust has done much replanting in the wake of the 1987 storm.

Fenton House

Windmill Hill, Hampstead,
London NW3

West side of Hampstead
Grove, NW3

Area 1½ acres (0·6 ha)
Soil neutral/sandy loam
Altitude 400 ft (122 m)
Average rainfall 25 in (635 mm)
Average winter climate moderate
Staff one

It was the discovery of mineral springs on the slopes of the hill at the turn of the eighteenth century that began the transformation of the little village of Hampstead into a fashionable place of residence, eventually to be annexed as another London suburb. Standing a short distance from the busy arterial roads and shopping streets, the warm brick merchant's house, built in 1693, and its gardens are now a reminder of the village's quiet past.

The narrow walk that leads from the ornate ironwork entrance gates to the south front is now a redolent, though not slavish, period piece, with an avenue of false acacias (a tree that became popular soon after its introduction from the eastern part of North America in the early seventeenth century) shading the gravel path. The fresh green of its foliage, and of the lawn, is set off by a heavy backdrop of ivy, holly, arbutus, bay, aucuba, Holm Oak, evergreen viburnum and acanthus – the last echoing the gates' motif.

Behind the house, the garden opens out into a series of sunny terrace walks. Lines of clipped holly and tubs of Portugal Laurel, grown as standards to mimic citrus bushes, now help to strike the late seventeenth-century note. A crisp box hedge divides the long west-facing border from the gravel. And across the lawn, a new yew hedge and a broken line of Irish Yews (a plant not, in fact, in cultivation until the end of the eighteenth century), accompanied by a riot of spring bulbs, perennials and shrubs, complete the formal frame.

The Trust has re-created a garden in the Old English style. The borders are lively and the

The orchard at Fenton House in spring, with apple and cherry blossom, euphorbia, daffodils, narcissi and white Spanish bluebells.

changing levels and visual blocks allow many surprises. Hollyhocks, grown among lavender and other cool-coloured plants, lean over the upper path, while pink and white Japanese anemones froth below. As you walk along the path, sunken cross borders are suddenly revealed, the blue and yellow scheme fuelled through the summer by geraniums, violas, daylilies, coreopsis, eryngium and *Aster × frikartii*. Beyond is a brick-paved sunken garden with pastel-coloured Shrub and Floribunda roses and a statue of a shepherd as its centrepiece. At the end of a long walk above that is a wisteria bower, a border of asters partnered with vines and a fine *Magnolia grandiflora*.

The greatest surprise is the sight of the lower garden, a relaxed country orchard and vegetable garden. 'It's like a supermarket down there', London children have been heard to exclaim. In spring the scene is more poetic, as you look over the primroses, anemones and Crown Imperials in flower between the Irish Yews above, at trees in blossom and grass sheeted with daffodils. At the southern end of the orchard, where the greenhouse once stood, runs a herb border spiked with impact plants such as euphorbia and *Melianthus major*, and backed by honeysuckle, vine, jasmine and ceanothus. The vegetable and cut-flower garden is to the north, behind espaliered apples, including the old varieties 'Pitmaston Pine Apple', 'Beauty of Bath' and 'Devonshire Quarrenden'. A fig tree hangs over the wall of the yard.

Florence Court

Enniskillen, Co. Fermanagh

1 mile west of Florence Court
village, 8 miles south-west of
Enniskillen via A4 and A32

Area 21 acres (8·4 ha)
Soil acid/clay
Altitude 300 ft (91 m)
Average rainfall 24 in (610 mm)
Average winter climate moderate
Staff one

'The Situation has a Majestic Wildness', wrote the Rev. William Henry in 1739, and though many acres have since been tamed by park and pleasure grounds, the encircling hills, mountains, peat bogs and lough continue to instil a sense of remoteness. The first view of the Palladian house is across open, rising pasture, speared by rushes and grazed by sheep, with the mass of the Cuilcagh range looming behind. Mixed woodlands, managed by the Forest Service from whom the Trust lease the park, provide a lush frame. The house was built in the mid-eighteenth century for John Cole, Governor of Enniskillen, and the park was landscaped for his son around 1778 by a Mr King, who also worked at Castle Coole, in the smooth 'Capability' Brown manner.

The Copper Beech beside one of the flanking octagonal pavilions indicates the start of the Pleasure Grounds, and after the house's simple parkland setting, the panorama of exotic trees and shrubs that confronts you is electrifying. Beeches and maples, silver pears and White-beams, rhododendrons and conifers are clumped or scattered between the glades and paths.

In spring, the sharp tints of the new leaves add to the contrasts, none more impressively than those of the celebrated weeping beeches, represented here in a tall rather than wide-spreading form. The lime green stands out crisply against the dark woodland belts and the brooding bulk of Benaughlin behind. After the massed display of 'Cornish Red' rhodo-dendron, flowering highlights are furnished by azaleas, dogwoods, *Rosa rugosa*, eucryphias, hydrangeas and naturalised drifts of the giant montbretia, *Crocosmia paniculata*.

The dark Irish Yews punctuating the planting have a very special association, for it was on the slopes of Cuilcagh Mountain that the original plant, one of two seedlings of markedly erect habit, was found. Mr George Willis, a farmer from Aghatirourke, made the discovery while coursing hares, but in exactly which decade of the mid- to late eighteenth century is disputed. One seedling he took to his own garden, and the other, a free-berrying female type, was transplanted here and propagated. The mother of all the millions of Irish Yews around the world, it grows near the bank of the Largeness River, west of Kerrshill Wood, and is passed on one of the woodland trails.

The Pleasure Grounds were laid out for the 3rd Earl and Countess of Enniskillen sometime after 1844, probably under the direction of the landscape gardener James Frazer. The saw-mill and hydraulic ram below were built in the same period and, now restored by the Trust, accompany the birdsong with trundling and splashing sounds. The air down here is infused with the grapefruit scent of giant firs, and you can follow the course of the little stream, past stands of large-leaved gunnera and darmera, and pockets of meadows grasses, rich with orchids and other wildflowers, to Lady Kathleen's Garden, where hostas, daylilies and astilbes fringe the shrub beds.

From the late eighteenth century, fruit and vegetables were grown in the Walled Garden beside the entrance drive. Overgrown when the Trust leased it in the mid-1970s, this has now been cleared and restored to a simplified plan including a rose garden. Like the Pleasure Grounds, it is bordered by water in the form of two narrow ponds, and the accompanying trees and waterside plants provide a relaxed wilderness setting; in spring, there is a fine show of Irish daffodil cultivars on the grass banks. Groups of cherries, amelanchiers and cercidiphyllum contribute to spring and autumn colour, but most remarkable of all to many visitors from across the sea is the luxuriant growth of mosses and lichens growing on the branches – evidence of the sweetness of Fermanagh's air and an extremely high rainfall.

Fountains Abbey and Studley Royal

Fountains, Ripon,
North Yorkshire

4 miles west of Ripon off
B6265, signposted from A1

Area 202 acres (82 ha)
Soil alkaline–neutral/
   limestone, boulder clay
Altitude 262–328 ft (80–100 m)
Average rainfall 20 in (508 mm)
Average winter climate cold
Staff six

This remarkable landscape garden, now in the process of being restored, has become one of the Trust's most popular properties. Nature's gift was a narrow, wooded gorge and the tumbling water of the River Skell. In the early eighteenth century, these features were seized upon and manipulated to create a sinuous garden of formal pools, canals and shady walks, adorned with classical temples, Gothic eye-catchers, grottoes and rustic bridges, and later, annexed as its climax, was the stupendous prospect of the great Cistercian abbey itself, its massive tower surprisingly intact and its ruined walls still standing high and pale against the hanging woods.

Excavated and planted over a period of some 65 years from 1716, the garden unfolds the early chapters in the story of Georgian landscaping, though none of the famous names of landscape gardening were involved here. The designer was its owner John Aislabie, who immersed himself in the project after his expulsion from Parliament for his role, as Chancellor of the Exchequer, in the South Sea Company scandal. After Aislabie's death in 1742, his son William completed the garden by acquiring the abbey. The nucleus of John Aislabie's design, and the oldest section, is the formal water garden, a serene composition of lawn-lapped moon- and crescent-shaped ponds, in which the golden Temple of Piety and statues of Bacchus, Neptune and Endymion are reflected as in a mirror. Beside them, the canal channels the river over a cascade between two fishing pavilions into the lake.

In this spot is most memorably captured the turn from French- and Continental-inspired gardening to the new classical English landscape. The symmetry and order of the water garden is set against the billowing curves of the wooded hillsides, where meandering paths

FAR RIGHT: The Temple of Piety seen across the Moon and Half Crescent ponds at Studley Royal.

A view from the Octagon across Studley Royal Water Garden towards the Banqueting House.

lead you to discover a series of garden buildings and prospects down across the valley. On the west is the Banqueting House, at the head of a coffin-shaped lawn; on the east, the Octagon Tower, Temple of Fame, and Anne Boleyn's Seat, from which you obtain that famous surprise view, across the Half Moon Pond and up the river, to Fountains Abbey.

The layers of trees and shrubs on the slopes are full of interest, with the beeches, oaks and limes capped with larch and Scots Pine, and underplanted with predominently native shrubs, with a generous complement of yews to furnish winter colour and permanent frames for views. The area is noted for its limestone flora.

Below the lake is the sharpest contrast to the formal water garden. Here, William Aislabie indulged in the new taste for the wildest landscapes. Instead of taming this stretch of gorge, he emphasised its plunging contours and exposed rocks by judicious tree planting and a zig-zag series of rustic bridges to highlight the twists of the river. It is one of the earliest examples of the Picturesque style in England.

A final surprise awaits you if you leave the property by the east entrance. Enter by this gate and the sweeping avenue of limes carries your eye to St Mary's church, the Victorian masterpiece by William Burges. Now, as you leave, you find the great abbey on the opposite edge of the garden has its counterbalance, for, framed in the gateway, are the distant towers of Ripon Minster. To have two such noble medieval structures on his doorstep was an extraordinary stroke of good fortune for John Aislabie: for his landscape, they are borrowed eyecatchers which few other gardens can match.

Gawthorpe Hall

Padiham, nr Burnley, Lancashire

On east outskirts of Padiham, entrance north of A671

Area 30 acres (12 ha)
Soil acid
Altitude 250 ft (76 m)
Average rainfall 45 in
  (1,143 mm)
Average winter climate cold
Staff none

The Burnley–Padiham conurbation has advanced on Gawthorpe, but at the end of the drive you find yourself in an amphitheatre of greenery, enclosed by layers of beech, oak, lime, chestnut and sycamore, and presided over by a high, square house of yellow sandstone. Above the hall, an avenue of young limes carries the eye up to the woods; below, the ground plunges into the meadows of the Calder Valley. The Victorian mood is pervasive. In the early 1850s, Sir James Kay-Shuttleworth engaged the architect Sir Charles Barry to restore and embellish the hall, built for the Shuttleworths at the turn of the seventeenth century. The tower, parapets and opulent interior, the last recently refurbished, are the result.

You must walk around to the north front in order to see Barry's reinterpretation of Elizabethan garden design reproduced in full. Here, using the waste from the excavation for the South Parterre, he extended the ground to make a broad semi-circular bastion, fringed with a parapet wall. Obelisks and, at the end of the terrace walk, armorial seats, designed by Barry's son Edward, reinforce the Elizabethan flavour. And filling the composition is a geometric pattern of radial flower-beds, edged in stone and separated by gravel paths. All Barry's work is in sympathy with early seventeenth-century style. The strong Victorian mood comes from the planting. In the North Parterre, the present scheme, installed in 1978, is a simplified, labour-saving version of the original. But the colour scheme of purple and gold – for modern eyes, a spectacular affront to the optic nerve – and the use of exuberantly hued and exotically shaped foliage, sets the composition squarely in the nineteenth century. Berberis, privet, yucca and the shrub honeysuckle 'Baggesen's Gold' are the plants employed.

Other parts of the garden display the Victorian fashion for sombre evergreens, which at the time were flooding into Britain from the Americas and the Far East. Rhododendrons filter through the woods, their purple and pink trusses of flower in sharp contrast to the yellows of laburnum, azalea, spotted aucuba and golden privet. The hall is fringed with mahonias, berberis, laurels, bergenias and *Yucca recurvifolia*. By contrast, the small rose garden, opposite the east front and on the site of another of Barry's parterres, has a lighter, Edwardian air. It was planted in 1987 using pink 'Petit Four', 'White Pet' and 'Sanders' White Rambler' as standards among bushes of purple 'Cardinal Hume', white 'Yvonne Rabier' and pink 'Petit Four'. The design was taken from a photograph in the hall, dated around 1900.

In winter, the church spire of Habergham is visible between the limes that rise above the South Parterre. The path leads to the pond, sited on high ground, with its banks raised. It is a tranquil spot, with oaks and birches furnishing shade, ferns and bluebells colonising the ground, and pheasants calling; buttercup fields provide the backdrop.

Glendurgan

Helford River, Mawnan
Smith, nr Falmouth, Cornwall

4 miles south-west of
Falmouth, ⅓ mile south-west
of Mawnan Smith, on road
to Helford Passage

Area 25 acres (10ha)
Soil acid/sandy loam
Altitude 33–230ft (10–70m)
Average rainfall 40in
  (1,016mm)
Average winter climate mild
Staff three

The Cherry Laurel maze at
Glendurgan, before restoration.

The woodland gardens of Cornwall's southern coast are a world apart. Glendurgan, wedged between folds of hillside, with grassy, stream-fed banks rolling down to the Helford estuary, has a site as snug as any to be found in this mild corner of Britain. Gales are the main enemy, and as soon as Alfred Fox, a Quaker businessman from Falmouth, bought the property in 1823, he set about erecting shelterbelts of native deciduous trees, strengthened with Scots and Maritime pines, Silver Fir, Norway Spruce and Holm Oak. In the three valleys, the early emphasis on fruit trees began to wane as the possibilities for growing the more flamboyant and tender trees and shrubs were exploited by successive members of this prominent Cornish gardening family and, latterly, by the Trust with the family's continued involvement. As shipping agents, the family were well placed to request seed and plants from abroad, and there was much exchange of material between their own gardens and those of friends.

Rhododendrons luxuriate in the warmth and humidity. *R. smithii*, *R. arboreum* and the Loderi hybrids create huge domes of scarlet, pink and white, supplemented by the blue of *R. augustinii*, the sulphur of 'Saffron Queen', and the fiery tints of Exbury azaleas. Additional lily fragrance comes from the white-flowered Maddenii clan, including *R. crassum* and *R.* 'Countess of Haddington'.

In the Camellia Walk there is a concentration of camellia blossom from numerous hybrids of *C. japonica*, including 'Lavinia Maggi', *Grandiflora* 'Alba', 'Tricolor' and 'Ville de Nantes', complemented by 'Captain Rawes' and other of the more tender variants of the Chinese *C. reticulata*. Elsewhere, drama comes from a stand of white-tiered *Viburnum plicatum* 'Mariesii', a glade of white magnolias and cherries, Chilean fire bushes (*Embothrium*), and a Handkerchief Tree. But in spite of the luxury of such scenes, the flavour of Cornwall is pervasive. There are the views of woods, estuary and fields; the rough paths that saunter gently down the slopes; the open sweeps of meadow that bring light and warmth into the garden, providing a simple backdrop to so many of the exotic displays; and there are the wildflowers. Primroses, violets and native Lent Lilies (*Narcissus pseudonarcissus*) spangle the meadows and woodland fringe in early spring; further on there are bluebells, campions and naturalised columbines, and, in the damper sites, Ragged Robin, Early Purple Orchids and the scented, yellow bells of naturalised *Primula prolifera* (syn. *helodoxa*).

Rhododendrons, azaleas, viburnums and bluebells on the west side of the valley that rolls down to the Helford River at Glendurgan.

Half-way through the tour, having descended into the lower, wilder portion of the valley, by paths dark with yew and Portugal Laurel and banks mossy and ivy-covered, you take a deeper draught of rural Cornwall by stepping out of the garden altogether. Crossing the old cattle rush, through which the animals were brought to the stream to drink, you find yourself in the hamlet of Durgan, consisting of some twenty cottages clustered around the cove. Refreshed by the sound of the lapping water and the tang of seaweed, you re-enter the garden by the kissing gate up the lane.

As the spring tide of colour ebbs away, a patchwork of greens is left in the valley. Many belong to evergreen plants: *Michelia doltsopa*, *Drimys winteri*, ferny-leaved *Lomatia ferruginea*, bamboos, and self-sowing myrtles and *Cornus capitata*, with clotted cream bracts in early summer, are among the broad-leaved cast. Further contrasts of shape and texture come from conifers, including *Cunninghamia konishii* and *C. lanceolata*, *Cupressus macrocarpa* 'Lutea', *C. lusitanica* 'Glauca Pendula' and a massive *Thuja plicata*. The collection has recently been boosted by a gift from the Royal Botanic Garden, Edinburgh, of tender conifer species, seldom seen in British gardens. In spring, these are joined by the ephemeral greens of beech, Sweet Chestnut and oak and a host of other species, among which the two fine Tulip Trees, planted by Fox, and the weeping *Taxodium distichum*, with its exposed knuckle-shaped roots, lodge in my mind.

Following the line of pools and streams down the centre of the valley is some of the most startling greenery of all. On the shallow, well-drained banks near the house, the sight of gigantic, spine-tipped succulents, *Agave americana*, has everyone rubbing their eyes; the flower spikes rise over 20 feet (6m). This unreal theme is continued by tall Chusan Palms, and, in the deeper, damper ground, by Japanese Bananas, *Musa basjoo*, giant-leaved *Gunnera manicata*, and self-sowing tree ferns, *Dicksonia* and *Cyathea*. Hydrangeas, eucryphias, hoherias, streamside plantings of pink *Persicaria campanulata* and white *Zantedeschia aethiopica*, and an impressive specimen of Rhododendron 'Polar Bear' add summer flower.

Generally, this is a lush valley of woods and meadows with natural plantings and pastoral views, rather than expressions of self-conscious design. However, in the middle of the garden, on the west-facing slope, is an entirely unexpected leap into formal gardening: an asymmetrical Cherry Laurel maze. It was laid out by Alfred Fox in 1833. The entrance and exit routes are $\frac{3}{4}$ mile (1·2km) in length, and the hedges take two gardeners a full week to prune; Glendurgan's long growing season means the job must be done five times a year. The maze is currently undergoing major restoration and there are plans to move back a thatched summer-house which once stood in the centre. The Christian symbolism of mazes may be contemplated on the Holy Bank above, where plants with biblical associations are assembled, among them Tree of Heaven (*Ailanthus altissima*), Christ's Thorn (*Paliurus spina-christi*) and Judas Tree (*Cercis siliquastrum*).

Great Chalfield Manor

Melksham, Wiltshire

3 miles south-west of Melksham via Broughton Gifford Common (sign for Atworth, drive on left)

Area 7 acres (2·8ha)
Soil alkaline, neutral/limestone
Altitude 150ft (46m)
Average rainfall 28in (711mm)
Average winter climate cold
Staff one

The collection of honey-coloured buildings sit secluded in low-lying pasture at the end of an oak avenue. The manor, rebuilt in the second half of the fifteenth century, was restored between 1905 and 1912 for the engineer Robert Fuller, who had purchased the property from his father and whose family continues to live here. With gables, oriel windows, gargoyles and other figures, it is splendidly decorative. Architecturally, the north front is the finest, for which the fourteenth-century parish church and the defensive moat, fed by a medieval leat 900 yards (823m) long, provide picturesque accompaniments.

But the south front and adjacent half-timbered wing, clad with wall shrubs and climbing plants, including Moroccan Broom and yellow Banksian Rose, enjoy the most romantic views of the garden. From here you look out over the sunny and sheltered Inner Court, where scented bush roses surround a well and *Campanula pyramidalis* self-sows between stone paving slabs, down to the lower moat or fish-pond. It is a timeless scene. Meadowsweet, rushes and scarlet-stemmed dogwood (a striking partnership in winter, when the rushes turn parchment-tan) soften the division between grass and water, and in spring the far bank, backed by a copse of tall trees, is a ribbon of daffodils. Moorhens and dragonflies enliven the picture, and the fortunate will catch sight of kingfishers.

South-east of the house, a rough orchard slopes down to the fish-pond. The grass is cut once a year for hay, and in spring it too is stained yellow with daffodils. Wildflowers, including Snakeshead Fritillaries, anemones, cowslips, primroses and wild asparagus, are in abundance here, as elsewhere in the grounds. And roses, including 'Rambling Rector', 'Wedding Day' and 'Sanders' White Rambler', scramble up the apple trees.

It is this combination of old, mellow architecture, meadows and wildflowers, trees and water, that sets the mood at Great Chalfield. And it is respected in the simple, unpretentious treatment of the more formal parts of the garden. The grounds were renovated by Robert Fuller at the same time as the house, with advice from a Mr Partridge and the watercolourist Alfred Parsons. East of the house are a lily pond, a fine mulberry tree, yew topiaries, and a huge sweep of enclosed lawn concluding in a handsome gazebo. Along the retaining wall below the lawn are softly coloured herbaceous borders.

Greys Court

Rotherfield Greys, Henley-on-Thames, Oxfordshire	3 miles west of Henley-on-Thames	*Area* 3 acres (1·2 ha) *Soil* limy soil *Altitude* 250 ft (76 m) *Average rainfall* 27 in (686 mm) *Average winter climate* moderate *Staff* one

An arch covered with Rose-Acacia and *Robinia hispiola* framing a view of the Great Tower at Greys Court.

This garden has an almost mystical atmosphere. Cut off from the outside world by folds of Chiltern downland and hills capped with beechwoods, the gabled Elizabethan house and its accompanying medieval towers present their own picturesque vision of reality. To this has been added the flair and sensitive touch of Sir Felix and Lady Brunner, who bought the property in 1937. And the result is a blend of ancient flint walls, dappled walks, fountains, scents and mellow colours, that transports the mind and engulfs the senses. The house stands on the western edge of the fourteenth-century courtyard, surveying the Great Tower and its adjoining ruined walls across an expanse of lawn. Scots Pines add their craggy shapes to the scene, and north of the house a venerable European Larch rests its branches on the grass.

On both sides of the house, the grass merges quietly with the park, assisted by the encircling ha-ha, but to the north, the view is partly interrupted by a grove of strawberry trees, planted on the bank at the suggestion of the Brunners' friend Humphrey Waterfield, a painter and gardener. The Killarney strawberry tree, *Arbutus unedo*, carries bountiful crops of white pitcher-shaped flowers and red fruits simultaneously in late summer and autumn; while *A.* × *andrachnoides* contributes peeling branches of cinnamon and chestnut-red.

Slip through the gateway beneath the Great Tower, past the warm aromas of sun-loving Mediterranean cistuses and rosemaries growing in the rubble, and you find yourself surrounded by white flowers and grey foliage, in the first of a disorienting series of irregular-shaped enclosures.

A silver-leaved pear, *Pyrus elaeagrifolia*, stands beside the heart-shaped lily pond in the

123

The great Wisteria Arbour at Greys Court.

centre of the lawn, and against the flint walls is an impressive Japanese Bitter Orange, *Poncirus trifoliata*, flaunting vicious spines. In spring, it bears fragrant white flowers. Later, there are heady scents from roses, choisyas and the delicious pineapple-flavoured *Philadelphus microphyllus*. Variegated ivy climbs the tower, and the verandah in the corner is home to a number of swallows and bats.

The rosarian Hilda Murrell advised the Brunners on the planting of the Rose Garden, reached through the next gateway. Here, the central lawn is shaded by a spreading foxglove tree, *Paulownia tomentosa*, and at midsummer the surrounding borders are awash with old-fashioned roses, fringed with pinks.

The principle that, if a plant is worth growing, it is worth having a decent show of it, is followed happily at Greys Court. In the Wisteria Arbour, which connects the Rose Garden to the Kitchen Garden, there is a display of *Wisteria sinensis* such as you will never have seen. You duck right under it, weaving between the gnarled and part-rotten stems, under an enormous canopy of twisted branches and, in spring, dripping flowers. The gardeners refer to it as The

Monster. In the Kitchen Garden, designed as a matrix of straight paths infilled with fruit trees, vegetables, and flowers for cutting, there is a hedge of striped *Rosa* 'Mundi', an avenue of 'Ballerina' crab apples, and a circle of fastigiate Irish Yews and *Prunus × hillieri* 'Spire', arranged around a Roman-style fountain.

Still more striking, is the tunnel of pink and white blossom in the adjacent Cherry Garden, through which a rustic path of stone and cobbles curves enticingly past another fountain, found on a farm in Switzerland and installed to mark the Brunners' 40th wedding anniversary. This grove was another of Humphrey Waterfield's inspirations, and, like the other cherry highlights, comes into its own again in autumn when the leaves turn orange and russet. A soaring Tulip Tree and ancient weeping ash over the wall enhance this scene, and provide part of the backdrop for the little knot garden, redesigned by the Trust, beside the Cromwellian stables; the building was reputedly commandeered by soldiers during the Civil War.

The garden has not been anchored in any single historical period, and modern additions compatible with its character have been welcomed. Furniture, fountains, ironwork and statuary have all been commissioned from contemporary artists. And in 1980, inspired by the enthronement sermon of the Archbishop of Canterbury, in which Dr Robert Runcie drew an analogy between people searching for life's secret and being lost in a maze, Lady Brunner conceived the idea of a pavement maze at Greys Court. It has been realised in brick and grass by Adrian Fisher, and, with its wealth of Christian symbolism and allegory, adds yet another contemplative layer to a timeless and tranquil garden.

Gunby Hall

Gunby, nr Spilsby,
Lincolnshire

7 miles west of Skegness on
south side of A158

Area 7 acres (2·8 ha)
Soil alkaline/clay, loam
Altitude 100 ft (30 m)
Average rainfall 25 in (635 mm)
Average winter climate cold
Staff two

Eryngium alpinum at Gunby Hall.

Roses galore; that will be your lasting impression of Gunby if you visit during the summer months. They foam against walls, scramble up trees, spill into water, fling themselves across pergolas and billow from flower-beds, creating welcoming scenes of carefree opulence that defy the inhospitable climate and featureless landscape.

The unreal quality is set by the William and Mary house, built in 1700 for Sir William Massingberd, from a Saxon family long established in the neighbourhood. An impossibly

125

pretty building of orange brick with limestone dressings, it is entirely unexpected in the midst of this Lincolnshire farmland, eight miles from the North Sea. Numerous handsome outbuildings accompany the house, including coach-houses, a clock-tower, and a pigeon house, pre-dating the present hall and surmounted by an ornate weather-vane. Succeeding generations of Massingberds have left their mark on the garden, but its present character can be attributed largely to Margaret Massingberd, who undertook a thorough overhaul in the early years of the twentieth century, and to the present tenants Mr and Mrs John Wrisdale, who, in collaboration with the Trust, have restored the garden with imagination and gusto.

Lawn sweeps around three sides of the house, interrupted by ornamental trees and some formal planting beside the tennis court and in front of the house. The grass is peppered with early spring bulbs and roses make their first appearance. Against the hall are 'Alister Stella Gray', 'Climbing Lady Hillingdon', the richly scented 'Climbing Madame Butterfly', 'Breeze Hill' and the extremely rare Rambler 'Elisa Robichon'. On the east side, crimson 'Etoile de Hollande' and in box-edged beds, the unusual Hybrid Tea 'Mrs Oakley Fisher' which, with its coppery flowers and plum-tipped foliage, is particularly associated with Gunby Hall.

The older trees on the lawns, including the great cedar, were planted by Peregrine Massingberd, a friend of Sir Joseph Banks, the naturalist and traveller, in the early nineteenth century. He is also responsible for considerable park and woodland planting, as recorded in the Gunby Tree Book which has been kept since 1670.

At the eastern edge of the garden, the vista from the house is terminated by rose shrubberies where, on my first visit to Gunby, I recall watching a family of stoats playing in the midday shadows. Yellow-flowered *Rosa × cantabrigensis*, white 'Nevada', pink 'Constance Spry' and ferny-leaved *R. multibracteata* are part of the cast, underplanted with hardy geraniums. At midsummer, a cascade of white roses of 'Wedding Day' illuminates the sombre evergreens behind; and a second cascade, in pink, is furnished later by 'Minnehaha'.

The ghost of one Miss Massingberd, searching for her lover, is said to haunt the walk beside the rectangular pond, possibly a stewpond for the earlier manorhouse. The planting of slim, swaying Irish Junipers and luminous white flowers, including those of *Rosa × paulii* tumbling down the bank, is intended to spook those foolish enough to stroll at or after dusk.

Mellow brick walls and arched entrances beckon you towards the walled garden. Even the herbaceous borders that front them, lavish with a succession of plants from anchusas to asters, fail to prepare you for the sight ahead: massed displays of dazzling and extrovert flowers assembled in great belts and blocks beside long, straight paths. Here is a colony of yellow Floribunda roses, including 'Chinatown' and 'Arthur Bell'; there, the bright reds of 'Frensham' and 'National Trust', and 'Orange Triumph'. Lavender, dianthus and bearded irises stream beside them; while hefty climbing roses such as pink 'Léontine Gervais' and 'Madame Isaac Pereire' furnish spectacular backdrops.

It is the same story in the adjacent Kitchen Garden. Here there are hydrangeas, rivers of catmint and creamy *Sisyrinchium striatum*, and further extravagant plantings of Bush roses such as pink 'Madame Caroline Testout' and scented Hybrid Musks. For me, the most entrancing performance is by the Rambler *R. multiflora* 'Grevillei', the Seven Sisters rose, which presents its huge trusses of flowers, comprising every shade from white and soft pink to lilac and crimson-red, against the pigeon-house wall. Experts are also quick to spot 'Reine Marie Henriette', a rare Victorian climbing rose with highly fragrant blooms in cherry-red.

Both gardens offer a varied diet. The Walled Garden also contains a very fine herb garden, a temple summer-house, cutting borders, a sundial lawn and jam-packed greenhouses. The Kitchen Garden has vegetable borders, a fruit cage and a croquet lawn. I have not mentioned fruit trees. A survey of 1944 listed 228 varieties, probably planted by Margaret Massingberd. There are still nearly half that number remaining, lining paths and espaliered on walls, and in spring and autumn they are a memorable sight. The produce is stored in the handsome apple house over the wall.

Ham House

Ham, Richmond, London

On south bank of Thames, west of A307, at Petersham

Area 18 acres (7·2 ha)
Soil lime-free/sandy
Altitude 50 ft (15 m)
Average rainfall 25 in (635 mm)
Average winter climate cold
Staff three

'. . . to see the House and Garden of the Duke of Lauderdale, which is indeed inferior to a few of the best Villas in Italy itself; the House furnished like a great Prince's; the Parterres, Flower Gardens, Orangeries, Groves, Avenues, Courts, Statues, Perspectives, Fountains, Aviaries, & all this at the banks of the Sweetest River in the World, must needs be surprising', wrote the diarist John Evelyn, after walking to Ham on a summer's evening in 1678.

What strikes the visitor as most remarkable today is that so much of it is still here, little ruffled by centuries of change and the burgeoning of London. Its avenues of trees still stretch out towards Ham Common and the Thames – the most comfortable and convenient means of getting to the city in the seventeenth century. The house itself is still almost exactly as it looked in the 1670s when it was enlarged: a tall, compact building of reddish-brown Jacobean brick dressed in white stone, and its rooms still with their original furnishings. Even better, the architectural bones of the formal, seventeenth-century garden have also survived, making

Cotton Lavender and box cones in the East Garden at Ham House. Once called the Cherry Garden, this part of the garden was redesigned by the Trust after a plan devised in 1671.

this one of the earliest and rarest garden layouts in the Trust's hands. The inspiration at the time came from the Baroque gardens of Europe, and Ham's style is a simple form of the typical Dutch garden, referred to by contemporaries as the New Mode. Sadly, the identity of the designer is unknown.

The clipped greens and statuary of the entrance forecourt set the mood. The topiary planted by the Trust comes as hefty drums of bay and, against the flanking walls, umbrellas of Portugal Laurel, cones of yew and bedding squares of box. All these are kept sharp-edged and tight, the dark colours contrasting with the central oval of closely mown lawn, in which the large frame of a River God reclines. Thirty-eight busts, representing Charles I and Charles II, Roman emperors and their wives, look over the scene from niches in the house and garden walls. Originally, the court was completely enclosed, with a straight path leading to the front door, but alterations were carried out at the end of the eighteenth century, and now the park is separated only by an ironwork screen.

The adjacent East Garden, redesigned by the Trust after a plan of 1671, is the most intimate part of the composition. Fruit was integral to the formal Dutch garden, and the cherries may have been either trained *in situ*, or grown in containers. Now, the garden is purely ornamental, with the central diamond-pattern box parterre – filled with Dutch Lavender and dwarf Cotton Lavender, clipped as silver knots within an embroidery – held in a *berceau*, or cradle, of hornbeam tunnels. It is a simple but striking treatment. Likewise, figs,

The Hornbeam Berceau at Ham, underplanted with box hedges.

vines and other espaliered fruits adorn the walls of the main enclosure, part of the green, expansive scene surveyed from the broad gravel terrace. In the foreground are the plats – eight large squares of close-mown grass, separated by paths – which were re-made out of the existing lawn in 1975. To convey more of the flavour of the Lauderdales' garden, which would have been filled with ornament and tender orangery plants, a statue is being placed in the centre of each plat and the corners marked by plants in white box containers. Beyond, an avenue of limes carries the eye past the garden gates, deep into Ham Common.

Occupying the middle ground is the Wilderness, a fashionable contemporary adjunct to the formal garden offering a taste of mystery and solitude. The Trust has reimposed its geometric pattern with hedges of hornbeam, speared by field maples, and the grass paths once again radiate, as in the 1671 plan, in a *patte d'oie* (or, more recognisably, a Union Flag design) from a central circle. Within the layout, the detail is presently being altered. Each compartment is being planted as a thicket of deciduous and evergreen trees and shrubs – with scented plants next to the grass paths – and further statues on plinths, together with bush oranges, displayed in white box containers, will provide centrepieces.

Rosemaries flower below the lower terrace wall. The borders have been filled with shrubs of the period, mainly from the Mediterranean region, which enjoy the heat and shelter of the south-facing walls. Sages, cistus, myrtle, Scorpion Senna (*Hippocrepis emerus*, syn. *Coronilla emerus*) are among the company, together with later introductions from North America and

Tulips, yellow wallflowers and forget-me-nots under the wisterias on the seventeenth-century Orangery at Ham in a photograph taken in 1994. These beds have since been removed.

the Far East, such as *Magnolia grandiflora*. On the main terrace there is the Chaste Tree (*Vitex agnuscastus*), which produces panicles of lavender and white flowers in early autumn.

An avenue of evergreen oak, *Quercus ilex*, brings you into the farthest compartment. Once the formal kitchen garden in front of the Orangery, this has now been left as lawn and rose beds. A cut-flower border, using period plants, is being established along the east side. Research may provide sufficient information to enable at least a partial restoration of the seventeenth-century kitchen garden. The Orangery itself, one of the oldest to survive in Britain, is draped in eleven wisterias and shaded by some ancient and unusual trees, among them a Christ's Thorn, *Paliurus spina-christi* and a Judas Tree, *Cercis silaquasrum*.

Hanbury Hall

Droitwich, Hereford and
Worcester

4½ miles east of Droitwich,
1 mile north of B4090, 6 miles
south of Bromsgrove, 1½ miles
west of B4091

Area 20 acres (8 ha)
Soil neutral/clay
Altitude 216 ft (66 m)
Average rainfall 25 in (635 mm)
Average winter climate moderate
Staff one

Before 1993, you would have found this decorative William and Mary squire's house – built in red brick, with hipped roof, cupola and pavilions – somewhat stranded in well-treed but flat parkland. Now, one of the rarest and most curious forms of English garden has sprung up beside it, a flower parterre, topiary fruit garden and formal Wilderness in the style of 1700.

The restoration, financed by two generous private legacies and a heritage award from the EU, is based on the original scheme installed by the celebrated lawyer Thomas Vernon to accompany his remodelled mansion. The designer appears to have been the leading garden advisor of the day, George London, since the plans are endorsed 'Mr London's Draughts'. This is exciting, for London's elaborate, labour-intensive gardens were immediate victims of the abrupt swing in eighteenth-century taste in favour of naturalistic landscapes, and not one has survived to the present day. At Hanbury, this destruction happened in the 1770s. No one knows if 'Capability' Brown himself was the vandal responsible, but since his portrait was hanging in the house at the time of the 1790 sale, it seems likely.

In the Victorian era, formality was back in fashion, and the small forecourt beside the house's south front was remade, even using copies of the original ironwork gates, which had been sold in 1790 to the owners of nearby Mere Hall. It is a lively composition with little Moorish pavilions, climbers on the walls and an array of bulbs, perennials and potted exotics.

Had its creator, another Thomas Vernon, not died at the age of 27, he might well have set to work re-creating a parterre on the lawn to the west. But this was left to the Trust. Other than a dip in the lawn, there was not a trace remaining, so the starting point was the existing plans and illustrations, especially the bird's-eye drawing of 1732 by James Dougharty. The exact layout and dimensions were then established by archaeology. There are some peculiarities: the garden is not properly aligned with the house; the sunken parterre is not a true square, and the twin pavilions at the northern end are not at right angles to the garden, but set at what the *Garden Guide* calls 'a jaunty angle'.

The Wilderness behind – to modern eyes, already an eccentric piece of design – has its oddities, too. Shaped like one segment of the Union Flag, it seems to have no central focus, the grass paths leading you on expectantly, but simply converging on an empty piece of lawn. The main path also suddenly narrows by 6 feet (1·8 m) for no apparent reason. It all adds up to an idiosyncratic composition. Happily, the Trust has decided to preserve the quirkiness. For its plants, it has turned to the lists drawn up by the Royal gardener Henry Wise, with whom London ran the celebrated Brompton Nursery; other information has been gleaned from *The Retir'd Gard'ner*, the French work translated and published by London and Wise in 1706.

In the flower and fruit gardens, the planting is colourful but of unfamiliarly strict regimentation, with repeating sequences of plants arranged in straight rows – tulips, auriculas, hyacinths and other spring flowers, backed by taller bulbs and annuals, and then by perennials such as valerian, tradescantia, Feverfew and hollyhock. In the sunken garden four giant box-edged grids, each with a topiary centrepiece, display perennials such as asphodel, columbine and Madonna Lily, and Mediterranean shrubs such as cistus, lavender and old roses are among the cast. A central oval bed has ranunculus, carnation and other florist's flowers. Shaped Morello cherry, 'Gold Pippin' apple and 'Black Worcester' pear trees alternate with topiary yews in the adjacent fruit garden surrounded by herbs, clipped red and white currants, and gooseberries, grown as bushes and standards. Behind, two trellis pavilions evoke the brick summer-houses of the original scheme.

These gardens are divided from the formal Wilderness by an avenue of *Juniperus virginiana*. Here, one of the wedge-shaped portions has its sections planted as a dense thicket of beech, which will be evenly clipped in due course; the other has centres of open grass and a mixed fringe of shrubs and trees, including ash, viburnum, laurel and wild roses. A similar feature was designed by George London for the park, a semi-circle of trees spliced by radiating vistas towards the distant hills. This will also be reinstated soon.

The potted lemons that stand in the fruit garden in summer come from a handsome brick Orangery to be discovered west of the Wilderness, thought to have been built soon after 1732. Wisterias are trained between each high window, with lavender lapping the base of the wall. Oranges in Versailles tubs are stood outside, and within you meet Loquat, lapageria, abutilons and tender, scented rhododendrons.

Beyond, the pockets of wood, spinney and orchard contrast with formal elements – an oak avenue; the colourful Primrose Walk, a straight ride between yew and holly hedge, leading to the old walled kitchen garden; and a cedar walk, edged in white and yellow daffodils. This last was the only surviving feature from London's garden, and one original cedar still stands; it leads to an exceptionally fine eighteenth-century ice-house.

Hardwick Hall

Doe Lea, Chesterfield,
Derbyshire

6½ miles west of Mansfield,
9½ miles south-east of
Chesterfield; approach from
M1 (junction 29) via A6175

Area 17½ acres (7 ha)
Soil alkaline/light sandy loam
Altitude 584 ft (178 m)
Average rainfall 26 in (660 mm)
Average winter climate
    moderate–cold
Staff four

A view of Hardwick Hall from the herb garden, one of the largest in Britain. Substantially redesigned by the Trust in the mid-1970s, the herb garden displays a splendid array of plants, many of which would have been familiar to Elizabethan gardeners and cooks.

'A woman of masculine understanding and conduct, proud, furious, selfish and unfeeling. She was a builder, a buyer and seller of estates, a moneylender, a farmer and a merchant of coals and timber; when disengaged from those employments, she intrigued alternately with Elizabeth [Tudor] and Mary [Stuart], always to the prejudice and terror of her husband.' So wrote Edmund Lodge in 1790 describing Bess of Hardwick, Countess of Shrewsbury. It was she who, in the 1590s, built this awe-inspiring house; the initials ES, carved above the high, square towers and topped by a coronet, proclaim her name and status across the estate; and the entire property pulsates with her personality.

The Old Hall, now a ruin, was once her childhood home and was extensively rebuilt by Bess in about 1585; but on the death of her estranged fourth husband, Lord Shrewsbury, she had control of fabulous wealth, and, although in her early sixties, embarked on a second, grander residence a short distance away. There have been gardens around the New Hall since its completion, and the spacious courts that we see today, with their decorative gateways and garden houses, finial-capped walls and banqueting house, were set out at that time. But the smart hedges and colourful plantings within them are the creation of the last two centuries.

Colour is concentrated in the surrounding borders, and what triumphant colour schemes they are. The Trust redesigned them in the mid-1980s, basing the planting on a Jekyllian sequence of lively harmonies. Variegated aralias, flowering grasses and cimicifugas furnish creamy highlights, while dahlias, argyranthemums, penstemons, crocosmias, purple heuchera and cotinus progress through the hottest shades, and sedums, verbenas, asters, caryopteris, buddleja and *Clerodendrum trichotomum* through the warmer pinks, blues and purples. There is a generous complement of half-hardy perennials. I would recommend a trip to Hardwick in late summer purely to savour them.

Running along the other side of the south wall is a long border of cooler, pastel colours, at its brightest in spring and early summer when tree peonies, old Shrub roses and philadelphus hold sway, in the company of a variety of perennials, including pulmonarias, and an unusual and robust form of Lily of the Valley with pale edges to its leaves, which was discovered here and called 'Hardwick Hall'. This border is part of the largest court, the South Court, which covers an area of $7\frac{1}{4}$ acres (3 ha) and was laid out in its present pattern of four quarters, divided by *allées* of yew and hornbeam, by Lady Louisa Egerton, daughter of the 7th Duke of Devonshire, in 1861. The Devonshires are direct descendants of Bess, and the fact that Hardwick has changed so little over the centuries is due in large part to its being owned by a family whose principal seat was elsewhere. The statues in the central *rond-point* are from Chatsworth. At one time, this entire court was given over to fruit and, probably, vegetable production. Today two of the quarters are orchards replanted by the Trust, and in the third, *Magnolia × soulangeana* and other specimen trees grow in the grass.

The fourth quarter contains the *pièce de résistance*, one of the largest herb gardens in Britain, accompanied by a nuttery. Redesigned by the Trust in the mid-1970s, this is no green and wispy affair, but a breathtaking array of vibrant colours, in which slabs of blue rue and pink soapwort are set against a procession of golden and green hops trained up wigwams. These echo the gilded posts that were a favoured ornament in Elizabethan gardens. The great array of culinary plants on show here would all have been familiar to gardeners of the time, and in constant demand for the house.

The scale and crispness of this court can be appreciated fully from the upper landing of the house, where you can see it set out against a broad backdrop of Turkey and Pedunculate Oaks, sycamores, limes, estate buildings and farmland. And from the adjacent long gallery, there is a fine view out over the East Court, with its lawn, roses and central pond, across the ha-ha, and down the lime avenue, planted in the 1920s. The limes curve to embrace the field opposite the house, giving the effect of an upturned wine glass with a $\frac{1}{2}$-mile stem.

Among the many fine tapestries in the house is a series of 32 octagonal panels embroidered with botanical subjects, with accompanying aphorisms. They are a further reminder of the delight the Elizabethans took in flowers and another happy link between house and garden. Many carry Bess's monogram. The initials ES are likely to haunt you long after you have departed this extraordinary place.

Hardy's Cottage

Higher Bockhampton, nr
Dorchester

3 miles north-east of
Dorchester

Area 2 acres (0·8 ha)
Soil poor soil, heathland
Altitude 350 ft (106 m)
Average rainfall 24 in (609 m)
Average winter climate cold
Staff family concern

'So wild it was when first we settled here', Thomas Hardy quotes his grandmother in his poem *Domicilium*, written when he was sixteen. The thatch and cob cottage, where the novelist and poet was born in 1840 and spent most of the first 34 years of his life, is still secluded, framed by Thorncombe Wood and looking east towards what was 'untamed and untameable' Egdon Heath, now a forestry plantation. But cottage and garden are a chocolate-box picture, with roses and honeysuckle around the windows and door, and a profusion of traditional shrubs and perennials spilling on to the grit paths and daisy-covered lawn. Lupins, columbines, Solomon's Seal, peonies, foxgloves, Japanese anemones and asters – 'such hardy flowers / As flourish best untrained' – rise above the primroses, Lily of the Valley and pinks. Lilac and mock orange add their scents, and the formal pattern of beds and paths is reinforced by clipped box and bay, and a modest knot garden. Old varieties of apple tree grow in the orchard, while the wood is peppered with bluebells and other wildflowers.

Lupins and Jacob's Ladder among a medley of summer flowers at Hardy's Cottage.

Hare Hill Garden

Over Alderley,
nr Macclesfield, Cheshire

Between Alderley Edge and
Prestbury, turn off north at
B5087 at Greyhound Road

Area 10 acres (4 ha)
Soil slowly permeable fine
    clayey loams subject to
    seasonal waterlogging
Altitude 394–492 ft (120–150 m)
Average rainfall 32–39 in (813–
    991 mm)
Average winter climate moderate
Staff one

Ilex aquifolium 'Golden Queen',
part of the large collection of
hollies at Hare Hill.

There is the option of walking to this estate along the 2-mile (3·2-km) path from the red
sandstone ridge of Alderley Edge. The rolling dairy farmland makes Manchester and its
conurbation seem a world away. You arrive to find a garden set into a wood, a walled
enclosure surrounded by a web of meandering pathways and glades of exotic shrubs. There
is no house visible. The planting is centred on the detached former kitchen garden, and
the Georgian mansion was sold off by the Trust in 1978 to help finance the running of the
remainder of the estate. Thus, there is some sense of a garden stranded, and of exploration and
discovery. The whole garden is quiet, wrapped in its oaks, beech and conifers, with dappled
light, mossy scents and the sounds of woodpeckers and other forest birds. There is an especially mysterious area to the north, where the trees open on to an old marl pit, filled with peaty
water, which you cross by bridge and grass causeway, between dark evergreens and bamboo.

From midsummer onwards, the greens predominate. In spring, the wood is a quite different place. The moist, acid loam and westerly location make this prime rhododendron land.
Colonel Charles Brocklehurst, the Trust's benefactor, was a great enthusiast and, with advice
from the plantsman James Russell, introduced them steadily from the 1960s until shortly
before his death in 1981. There are no colour schemes or specialisations. You pass from
colourful banks of Hardy Hybrids and richly scented Knap Hill and Exbury azaleas to drifts of
white, red and pink *R. williamsianum* and specimens of yellow *R. wardii*, purple *R. edgarianum*,
orange *R. cinnabarinum*, pink *R. Loderi* and white *R.* 'Polar Bear'. The foliage colours, shapes
and sizes are equally magnificent, ranging from glaucous-blue *RR. lepidostylum* and
cinnabarinum subsp. *xanthocodon* to elephantine *R. macabeanum* and the staggeringly beautiful
cinnamon growths and soft, rust-red undersides of *RR. rex.* subsp. *fictolacteum* and *bureavii*.

Accompanying them are *Pieris formosa* var. *forrestii*, viburnums, *Magnolia sprengeri* var.
elongata, hostas, bluebells, Himalayan poppies and a notable carpet of the creeping, white-
flowered *Cornus canadensis*. The Trust continues to enrich the scene, progressively replacing
the thickets of old purple *R. ponticum* with fresh assortments of colour. The season is also being
extended. The early colour was already provided by snowdrops, daffodils, a massive *Clematis
montana*, yellow-flared Skunk Cabbage and by the pink chalices of *Magnolia campbellii*. The
later interest came principally from roses, most impressively a huge pink Rambler 'Paul's
Himalayan Musk'. Now, there is a boost from lacecap and other hydrangeas, and from the
white-flowered Nymans eucryphia, grouped in a line outside the Walled Garden.

Vitis coignetiae over an arch leading into the walled garden at Hare Hill.

The garden inside is a curiosity: at its head, a white trellis pergola draped in clematis; a flanking pair of equestrian wirework sculptures set in beds of 'Pearl Drift' roses; surrounding orange brick walls cloaked in an array of blue and yellow shrubs and climbers; and, at its heart, an empty lawn of such vastness that it throws everything out of scale. The contrast of light and scale is exciting, but the absence of an impressive centrepiece, such as a sweep of waterlily pool or an imaginative modern sculpture, is sorely felt.

There is one further feature to mention: the hollies. The wood is home to an extensive collection, from rare forms of the green Highclere holly, *Ilex × altaclerensis*, like large-leaved 'Atkinsii' and dark 'Nigrescens', to curious forms of the common holly, *Ilex aquifolium*, like the delicate 'Ovata' and the spineless, twisted-leaved 'Scotica'. With them come an assortment of silver and golden, yellow- and orange-berried varieties, providing the material for an absorbing visit. The garden is closed in winter to preserve the woodland paths.

Hatchlands Park

East Clandon, Guildford,
Surrey

East of East Clandon, on north
side of A246 Guildford–
Leatherhead road

Area 12 acres (4·8 ha)
Soil alkaline–acid/heavy soil
Altitude 300 ft (91 m)
Average rainfall 27 in (686 mm)
Average winter climate cold
Staff two

The curving path from the old orchard, now the car-park, brings the eighteenth-century mansion into view at an oblique angle between the trees. In its restored state, it is a striking block of red brick and white paintwork, contrasting sharply with the parkland grass that sweeps almost to the door. The Reptonian flavour of the scene is intensifying as the Trust's new plantings mature. Humphry Repton was at the height of his career when engaged by the estate's owner, George Sumner, to improve the park and garden, and his recommendations of 1800 alterations seem to have been carried out. The London road was diverted, a new carriage drive and gravel walks were constructed, and an area of lawn was set out around the house, complementing features already planted by Fanny Boscawen, the wife of Admiral Edward Boscawen, who built Hatchlands in the 1750s.

These lawns are endowed with some fine trees and shrubs, notably cedars, arbutus, a huge Monterey Pine and a magnificent Oriental Plane, which casts its resinous scent far and wide. New shrubberies frame the stone temple, brought here in 1953 from nearby Busbridge Hall, and in spring, snowdrops, daffodils and bluebells abound. Fanny Boscawen's Walk, edged in lilac, laburnum, philadelphus and iris is presently being restored.

In 1900, Gertrude Jekyll submitted plans for a south and west parterre garden. Only the first was executed, and this has now been reinstated, the pattern of beds planted with Shrub and old Bush roses, in the company of peonies, geraniums and irises. It is a pretty scheme at its summer peak, but does sit somewhat oddly in the flowing parkland. Reconciling the conflicting styles and contours is one of the Trust's tasks, together with elevating the overall standard after the decline seen between 1959 and 1980, when the property was let as a finishing school. But slowly the garden is becoming a fitting accompaniment to the house.

Hidcote Manor

Hidcote Bartrim, nr Chipping
Campden, Gloucestershire

4 miles north-east of Chipping
Campden, 1 mile east of B4632

Area 10 acres (4 ha)
Soil alkaline
Altitude 600 ft (182 m)
Average rainfall 25 in (635 mm)
Average winter climate cold–
   very cold
Staff six

An encounter with England's most influential twentieth-century garden begins softly. The high, twisting lanes of the Cotswold countryside lead into a courtyard only slightly grander than those accompanying the other large houses that pepper the hilltops. It takes an eagle-eyed plantsman to notice that the sober plantings against the golden walls are a little out of the ordinary – *Schizophragma hydrangeoides*, *Magnolia delavayi*, *Schisandra rubrifolia* and *Mahonia lomariifolia* are among the cast.

The enclosure beyond, framed by humble stone outbuildings and sparsely decorated with Handkerchief Tree, wisteria and a Noisette rose 'Rêve d'Or', maintains the suspense. You turn through a narrow gateway, and the Theatre Lawn is revealed. It is vast, incomparably bigger than you would expect to find in such a garden. Rather – with its immaculate sward, crisp surround of dark yew, and elevated stage containing a solitary beech tree – it seems to have strayed from an early eighteenth-century landscape park. The first surprise has been sprung, and you have hardly recovered before you step into the second, the Circle, an enclosure so intimate in scale that there is scarcely room to pass the other visitors.

Suddenly, there is the sense of standing in somebody's private garden or, rather, in a network of private gardens. For Hidcote is now revealed as a patchwork of passages, open spaces and flower-filled enclosures, each gaining impact from the garden before it. At each turn there are changes in scale, design, colour and atmosphere. There is a tiny White Garden,

LEFT: The White Garden at Hidcote, with topiary birds, *Rosa* 'Grüss an Aachen' and scarlet *Tropaeolum speciosum* filtering through yew and holly hedges.

surveyed by a thatched cottage, animated by topiary doves and contained by yew hedges dripping in early summer with blood-red Flame Flower. There is the garden beside the house, with its Cedar of Lebanon, clematis-hung walls, pastel borders of Hybrid Musk and Floribunda roses, bulbs and hardy and half-hardy perennials.

From the Circle, you walk into a succession of green gardens: a brick and box parterre with a permanent bedding scheme of spring scillas and summer fuchsias; a dark garden filled with a huge, circular, stone basin; and then a small empty circle of lawn. Rough, meandering paths lead on into the Stream Garden, a large loose, shady area of ditches and spinneys. Here, the sticky banks and gulleys are furnished with fat clumps of leafy perennials, including comfreys, darmera, *Rodgersia pinnata* 'Superba' – splendidly partnered with blue-leaved hostas – and colonies of *Lysichiton americanus*, which illuminate the garden in spring with yellow, sour-smelling flares. These grow among a choice collection of trees and shrubs, including magnolias, hydrangeas, daphnes and *Osmanthus forrestii*.

Now, another *coup de théatre*. From the wooded wilderness, you step directly into the grand, open sweep of the Long Walk. Really, it needs to be viewed from the gazebo above to savour the full drama of the plunging and ascending hornbeam hedges. But from this intermediate point, the climb to the empty horizon is thrilling enough.

And so the garden goes on, varied and enticing, through 10 acres (4 ha) of compartments. Hidcote's linear patterns recall earlier, grander, Continental styles of gardening. The Theatre Lawn, Fuchsia Garden and Bathing Pool Garden are part of this, as are the pillars of yew in the Pillar Garden, the umbrellas of Portugal Laurel in the Pine Garden, the avenue of Irish Yews in the Old Rose Walk, and, famously, the stilt hedges of hornbeam, or *palissades à l'Italienne*,

Waterlilies in the Pine Garden at Hidcote.

The Red Borders at Hidcote
with *Tulipa* 'Red Shine'
and *Rheum palmatum*
'Atrosanguineum' and the
hornbeam palissade behind.

that flank the last section of the main east–west axis. The abundance of evergreen oaks also add to the Continental flavour.

It was an American-born Englishman, brought up in France, who had the vision to pull these disparate threads together. When Lawrence Johnston and his mother, Mrs Winthrop, came to live at Hidcote in 1907, the present garden was exposed farmland. It does not appear that Johnston ever had a masterplan; rather, land for the garden was snatched piecemeal from the farm over a number of years. The design draws on many contemporary themes, but he moulded and fused together with triumphant originality. The sequence of terraces, lawns and flower gardens seen in larger country houses he reduced to a chain of intimate rooms. And Gertrude Jekyll's art of arranging plants with one eye on nature and the other on associations of texture, form and colour, he carried to new levels of romantic informality, with shrubs, climbers, self-sowing perennials and bulbs spilling into one another in carefree style. A large debt for this was owed to his close friend Norah Lindsay, a gifted gardener who designed and

The lower Pillar Garden with *Allium rosenbachianum*, *A. aflatunense* and double red peonies.

planted with great panache. Johnston had intended to give Hidcote to Mrs Lindsay after he had moved permanently to Serre de la Madonne, his winter home in France, where he had another celebrated garden. But she died prematurely, in 1945.

Plants at Hidcote are assembled principally by colour, texture and flowering season. At midsummer, old Shrub roses strew the borders in the Kitchen Garden with pink and crimson, their tints picked up by drifts and pools of penstemon, lupin, dianthus and purple sage. Mrs Winthrop's Garden blends yellow daylilies, acid green euphorbias, blue cynoglossum and copper cordyline. And in high summer, the Red Borders swelter with salvias, dahlias, verbenas and Floribunda roses, supplemented by the sombre leaves of purple berberis, heuchera, plum and sloe.

Vita Sackville-West believed Johnston would want to be remembered principally as a botanist and plant-hunter, and at heart Hidcote is, of course, a plantsman's garden. The plant collection is huge; at every turn there are choice and rare subjects, and the garden offers the 143 maximum diversity of planting sites, including, in the Old Garden, raised beds filled with lime-free soil for the cultivation of fastidious woodlanders. Johnston participated in two notable plant-hunting expeditions; to China with George Forrest, and to South Africa with 'Cherry' Ingram. To the former, we owe *Mahonia lomariifolia* and the pot jasmine, *Jasminum polyanthum*. Johnston's sharp eye for a superior garden variant is evident in the number of excellent plants bearing his or Hidcote's name, including a lavender, hypericum, verbena, campanula, penstemon and rose.

Indeed, it is Hidcote's preoccupation with plants and the art of planting that explains why it strikes such a deep chord with so many visiting gardeners. And it is the fact that it reconciles, on a scale to which we can all relate, the demands of good design with the urge to grow every beautiful plant that comes our way, which explains why it has had such an influence on the course of British gardening, from Sissinghurst and Tintinhull to the suburban backyard.

Hill Top

Near Sawrey, Hawkshead, Ambleside, Cumbria

In village of Near Sawrey 2 miles south-east of Hawkshead

Area ½ acre (0·2 ha)
Soil acid/loam
Altitude 295 ft (90 m)
Average rainfall 60 in (1,524 mm)
Average winter climate moderate
Staff one, part-time

FAR RIGHT: Beatrix Potter's vegetable patch at Hill Top.

144

Anyone familiar with Beatrix Potter's stories will feel immediately at home in her village farmhouse and cottage garden. The scenes are just as she painted them. We have seen Mrs Tabitha Twitchit brandishing her toasting fork in this same rose-covered porch, and watched Jemima Puddle-Duck try to hide her eggs in this same rhubarb patch. Indeed, it was the royalties from *The Tale of Peter Rabbit* and other early works that enabled her, at nearly 40, to escape the stifling atmosphere of her parents' home in London and buy Hill Top.

Recently restored by the Trust, the garden is planted and maintained in the neat but muddled style of an old-fashioned cottage plot, its contents and arrangement loosely based on old photographs, Beatrix Potter's paintings and journal notes. The long borders accompanying the sloping path up to the front door undergo an imperceptible transition from currant bushes and herbs to traditional annuals, perennials and flowering shrubs, and generous quantities of farmyard manure give the hungry, slaty soil good heart.

Spikes of lupins, mulleins and hollyhocks rise between clumps of Lady's Mantle, Lamb's Lugs and Sweet William, while lilac and sorbaria foam, and violets, snapdragons and Poached-egg Plants self-sow merrily. Sweet peas are trained up a tripod of canes, and the trellis that screens the apple-tree paddock is festooned with Rambler roses, clematis and honeysuckle. Scent wafts from *Rosa rugosa*, *Lilium regale* and summer jasmine. And a white Chinese wisteria on the house and a *Eucryphia glutinosa* in the border add unexpected notes of sophistication. Gooseberry 'Wynham's Industry', which entangled Peter Rabbit in its protective net, still occupies the right-hand side of the border. Opposite the front door, over the dry-stone wall, is the small vegetable garden, its businesslike rows of potatoes, carrots, cabbages and sprouts complemented by colourful bursts of ruby chard, runner beans and raspberries.

Beatrix Potter was a great supporter and benefactor of the National Trust, and a close friend of its co-founder, Canon Hardwicke Rawnsley. Concerned by the growing threat to the Lake District of insensitive development, she began buying farms and tracts of land, with the ultimate aim of giving them to the Trust. By the time of her death in 1943, she had ensured the preservation of over 4,000 acres (1,618 ha) of pasture and fell.

Hinton Ampner

Bramdean, nr Alresford,
Hampshire

On A272, 1 mile west of
Bramdean village, 8 miles east
of Winchester; leave M3 at
junction 9 and follow signs to
Petersfield

Area 13 acres (5·2 ha)
Soil alkaline/clay, chalk
Altitude 400 ft (122 m)
Average rainfall 33 in (838 mm)
Average winter climate moderate
Staff three

Magnolia grandiflora against the
south wall of Hinton Ampner.

Ralph Dutton, the 8th and last Lord Sherborne, inherited this estate in 1935 at the age of
37, and devoted the following 50 years to improving and embellishing it. A deeply cultured
man, a connoisseur of art and architecture, author of *The English Garden*, and with the wealth
and leisure to indulge his tastes, he produced as elegant a composition of house, park and
garden as this century can show.

The Georgian house stands on a ridge of chalk above well-treed farmland. You pass
through a series of gentle transitions as you climb to it, curving through parkland, and then,
across a cattle grid, through ornamental shrubberies speared by conifers and specimen trees.
There is a pocket of deep acid greensand here on the northern fringe, which allows rhododendrons, azaleas, camellias, blue hydrangeas, *Magnolia × soulangeana* and various Japanese
maples to accompany the more chalk-tolerant species like *Magnolia wilsonii* and parrotia, but
the colour scheme is kept soft, as it is throughout the grounds, with the richer tints of yellow
and orange confined to highlights.

As the house looms between the trees, the drive straightens and the grounds become more
formal. On one side is the walled kitchen garden (not open) belonging to the original house,
demolished in 1793, and, on the other side, a Norman church beyond. Ralph Dutton extended the kitchen garden's path-line to turn this area into a formal cherry orchard, in which
the trees – pink- and white-blossomed, and in a meadowy carpet of early bulbs, daffodils, and
then cow parsley – stand inside four box-edged enclosures: an unusual and very effective
combination of the natural and the ordered. This pattern of simply designed, rectangular
compartments and strong long axes connecting them, provides the framework for the many
flower-filled scenes to the south, in classic mid-twentieth-century style. A lily pond, partnered by a bed of 'Iceberg' roses and pink *Diascia rigescens*, aligns with the east front of the
house, while the main, sunny façade looks on to a sweeping grass terrace, inherited by Dutton
and retained as the necessary quiet counterbalance to the surrounding colours.

Before the Second World War, he created further terraces below, using the lines and
proportions of the Georgian façade to set the parameters of the central space and carrying the
cross path east and west to form another long axis, running one way through an avenue of
Irish Yews and the other between ornamental shrubberies; both views conclude in a classical
ornament, one backed by trees and the other by open park. It is a beautiful passage of design,
further enhanced by a flight of steps providing a graceful change of level *en route*. Later, he
cleverly connected the lime avenue, dating from the eighteenth century and cutting across the
park in alignment with the original house, by extending and connecting it, via a straight
walk, to this axis, and erecting a temple at the intersection.

But as well as valuable lessons for the design student, there is also much to absorb the plant-
lover. Shrubs are the principal source of colour. Evergreens, including *Magnolia grandiflora*,
pittosporums, bay and *Hoheria sexstylosa* grow against the house's south wall, and, below the
stone terrace, they are joined by lower-growing subjects, including lavender, caryopteris,
perovskia, escallonia and the short, indigo-blue, summer-flowering *Ceanothus* 'Henri Des-
fossé' (together with seams of Headbourne Hybrid Agapanthus), all appreciative of the hot,
dry conditions. Crisply partnered for foliage contrast, larger shrubs also flank the many grass
walks fringing the terraces, especially those to the east, around the tennis court lawn. The
Smoke Bush, *Cotinus coggygria*, is prominent in its purple and green-leaved cultivars, together
with lilacs, various viburnums (especially evergreen *V. davidii*, *V. rhytidophyllum* and the

Wayfaring Tree, *V. lantana*), scented philadelphus, berberis, cotoneasters, buddlejas, Weeping Silver Pear and many different Shrub roses.

At one point, the ground suddenly plunges into the basin of a chalk pit – giving the garden a strong sense of locality – and you find yourself looking up at steep banks clad in yew, rampaging Rambler roses and Russian vine. They are joined, in the damper pockets, by foliage plants such as spotted lungwort, hostas, rheum and giant hogweed, and in the drier parts by euphorbias and Corsican hellebore. It is a peaceful and atmospheric place to linger.

Around the house, the shrubs also give way here and there to other plants. Delicately blended bedding plants fill the small, yew-hedged room, east of the main lawn terrace, while to the south, you descend to a lawn appointed with topiary figures, where dahlias traditionally follow a spring show of bulbs, to the accompaniment of a border of pastel perennials and silvery foliage. I remember striking partnerships here between Regale Lilies and blue shrubby euphorbia, pink helianthemum and the trailing *Convolvulus altheoïdes* (hardy here), and, best of all, magenta *Allium cernuum* and *Artemisia schmidtiana* 'Nana', the former's magenta heads sprouting through the rug of grey leaves. But schemes like this are being tended creatively, with new plants and combinations of plants allowed to play variations on the themes, and they do not remain static.

An opening in the hedge, directly opposite the house, gives an interlude in the garden tour, bringing you out above the ha-ha and on to a grass bastion. Ahead, the park rolls away into the Hampshire countryside, past the stands and belts of trees, rigorously thinned by Dutton to ensure the development of good, spreading specimens. Trees were his favourite plants, and the large specimens of beech, lime, oak, pine and Wellingtonia shading the garden's drives and neat lawns contribute to the sense of history, spaciousness and tranquillity he so valued, as well as supplying the much-needed shelter against the wind.

Hughenden Manor

High Wycombe,
Buckinghamshire

1½ miles north of High Wycombe; on west side of Great Missenden road (A4128)

Area 4¾ acres (1·9 ha)
Soil alkaline
Altitude 500 ft (152 m)
Average rainfall 28 in (711 mm)
Average winter climate cold
Staff one

The Gothic house, sitting on its chalky hilltop among the steep-sided combes and beech-woods of Buckinghamshire, today cuts as exotic a figure in the landscape as did its former owner in the Tory establishment. For Hughenden was the country home, from 1848 until his death in 1881, of Benjamin Disraeli, statesman, novelist and prime minister.

The trees were among Disraeli's chief delights. Singly and in groups, they soften the lower reaches of the park and shade parts of the curving drive and churchyard, where Disraeli is buried; on the hillside, they thicken to screen and shelter the house, and on the escarpment and hills beyond, they unite into full-blown woods. Whitebeam, ash, oak, lime and horn-beam accompany the beeches, and Old Man's Beard (*Clematis vitalba*), snowdrops, Wood Anemones and bluebells enliven the picture; here and there are patches of Disraeli's favourite flower, the primrose. The scene was already set when the Disraelis came to Hughenden, but over the years they undertook much new planting. Mary Anne Disraeli developed part of the wood as a 'German Forest', adorned with rustic seats, and with rides edged in laurel and yew. And on the banks and lawns around the house, numerous conifers were installed.

The sight greeting you as you walk into the forecourt is triumphantly Victorian, with an assortment of dark and decorative cedars, firs and spruces set against the pinnacles and red

147

Pink Japanese anemones at Hughenden.

and blue brick of the Gothic façade. This area, in common with much of the rest of the garden, has been restored and replanted by the Trust over recent years, following contemporary photographs. The trees in the oval lawn make an interesting assembly of lime-tolerant species, and include the Chilean Yew, *Prumnopitys andina* (syn. *Podocarpus andinus*), Brewer's Weeping Spruce, *Picea breweriana*, and the Cyprus Cedar, *Cedrus brevifolia*. The main garden is reached by skirting the east wall of the house. From here you step out on to a wide terrace fringed with trees and with broad views over the valley, neighbouring hills and an advancing High Wycombe.

'We have made a garden of terraces, in which cavaliers might roam and saunter with their ladye-loves,' wrote Disraeli to his friend Mrs Brydges Williams. Today the main terrace comprises an expanse of lawn, edged in gravel paths and statuary, with the original lawn bedding schemes restored. Wisteria, *Solanum crispum* 'Glasnevin', ceanothus and jasmines flower against the house, fronted by a herbaceous border of sedums, asters, Japanese anemones and other perennials contemporary with the period. The row of stone Florentine urns that flank the flight of steps is filled each spring and summer with annuals in gaudy Victorian colours, as is the large cast-iron basket below. And at the southern extremity of the plateau is a small formal rose garden with a central fountain. This is a windy site, and plants have to be chosen with care. The only missing element is peacocks. 'You cannot have a terrace without peacocks', was Disraeli's dictum. But peacocks and flowers do not go happily together.

The Kitchen Garden has also been partially restored recently and is planted mainly with old varieties of apple, including the local variety 'Arthur Turner', grown on semi-dwarfing rootstocks. Vines, figs and Morello cherries are trained against the walls. In the last five years the orchard has also been renovated.

Ickworth

The Rotunda, Horringer,
Bury St Edmunds, Suffolk

3 miles south-west of Bury St
Edmunds on west side of A143

Area 70 acres (28 ha)
Soil very alkaline/clay
Altitude 250 ft (76 m)
Average rainfall 21 in (533 mm)
Average winter climate cold–
    very cold
Staff three

A fairly cold climate, level ground and heavy clay soil are not an ideal combination for an Italian garden. But the light is good and the rainfall low, and here, in the gently undulating Suffolk countryside, there is one of the finest examples in Britain, a garden of evergreen plantations, where Mediterranean scents hang in the air and slim conifers cast pointed shadows across the grass. It was laid out by the 1st Marquess of Bristol in the 1820s, as an accompaniment to the astonishing Italianate house begun by his father, the 4th Earl of Bristol and Bishop of Derry, in 1795. And it is thus one of the first properties to have re-embraced geometry and the plants and patterns of European gardens, after the long supremacy of 'Capability' Brown and the English landscape garden.

The proportions of the house demand large-scale effects, and generous stands and belts of trees set the mood of the garden. You approach the vast rotunda, the centrepiece of the entire composition, past towering evergreens, including redwood, Crimean and Pyrenean pines (*Pinus nigra* var. *caramanica* and *P.n.* var. *cebennensis*), Lucombe Oaks and a young grove of cedars, planted at 15-yard (14-m) spacing. Many of the original cedars were nearing the end of their lives when the hurricane of October 1987 struck, enabling the Trust to undertake comprehensive replanting. Eighteen varieties of Deodar, Lebanon, Atlas and Cyprus Cedar have been installed, using an interesting technique, widely favoured on poorly drained soil in

An ornate cast-iron bench, backed by Portugal laurel and buddleja at Ickworth.

the nineteenth century. Instead of being planted in a hole, the trees were placed on the surface and earth mounded over their roots. Fast-growing cypress and hemlock have been employed as a nurse crop and will be removed in time. In spring and early summer, this plantation is spangled with bulbs and wildflowers. The herbaceous border on this north side of the house is very generously proportioned, but the bulk of the rotunda behind does it no favours.

The main part of the garden is to the south, reached through a gateway beside the Orangery. Here, a pair of large, wing-shaped lawns, echoing the architecture of the house, meet on the central axis of the rotunda. A procession of young *Phillyrea angustifolia*, a bushy Mediterranean evergreen with sweetly-scented flowers in early summer, reinforces the symmetry. And framing the scene are two plantations of majestic Holm Oaks, supplemented by a wealth of evergreen shrubs and contained by box hedges.

The assortment of outlines and leaf shapes is fascinating. The slim verticals, so characteristic of the Italian landscape, were originally authentically furnished by extensive plantings of Italian Cypress, *Cupressus sempervirens* 'Stricta'. But the majority were badly damaged in a series of severe winters around the turn of the century, and over the years they have been generally replaced with hardier species which have a similar outline, in particular *Chamaecyparis lawsoniana* 'Erecta', 'Wissellii' and 'Kilmacurragh'. Textural contrasts are provided by

149

LEFT: An African agapanthus, stood out in summer, on the Orangery terrace at Ickworth.

shrubs such as *Phillyrea latifolia*, mahonias, photinias, osmanthus, hollies, *Viburnum tinus* and large-leaved *V. cinnamomifolium*, choisyas, privets, *Arbutus unedo* and a National Collection of box, which includes bushes in all shapes and colour variants, from gold and fresh green to deep green and blue. Olives have been successfully tried in the more sheltered spots, but in the open garden, the hardier Sea Buckthorn, *Hippophaë rhamnoides*, serves as a silvery substitute; the females bear heavy crops of orange berries.

The overall formality belies the variety of detail in this part of the garden. There is a secret glade of bluebells and silver leaves; a sinister Victorian 'stumpery', where ferns grow on upturned roots; a glade of golden foliage, boasting a fine specimen of half-hardy *Olearia solandri* with heliotrope-scented flowers in late summer, and a little garden of Floribunda roses presided over by a temple. The trees include two large Cucumber Magnolias, *M. acuminata*, a range of evergreen oaks and a spectacular Golden Rain Tree, *Koelreuteria paniculata*. Further colour is provided by the rich blues of *Agapanthus africanus* set out in tubs on the Orangery steps. The Orangery is unheated, and hardy fatsia, ivy and their hybrid fatshedera have been planted inside to mimic tropical foliage, echoing the mimicry of half-hardy cypresses and olives outside.

The southern boundary of the garden is marked by a raised gravel terrace, 350 yards (320 m) long and separated from the lawns and plantations by a tapestry hedge of seedling box; this, and the fact that it seeds freely in the woods, was the inspiration for the box collection. From here, there are broad views over the park, encompassing Ickworth church and, in the distance, the Obelisk, erected in memory of the Earl Bishop by the people of Derry. 'Capability' Brown advised on the park in the mid-eighteenth century, when the family were living in Ickworth Lodge. And he may well have suggested the idea of a walk encircling the present deer-park, to the west of the existing house, though it was not laid out until the early nineteenth century. The path leads you through alternating areas of dappled sunlight, created by groves of oak, beech, ash and maple, and deeper shade, created by yew, pines and evergreen oaks. The woods are a haven for wildlife.

Ightham Mote

Ivy Hatch, Sevenoaks, Kent

6 miles east of Sevenoaks, off A25, and 2½ miles south of Ightham, off A227

Area 14 acres (5·7 ha)
Soil acid–neutral
Altitude 279–377 ft (85–115 m)
Average rainfall 23 in (584 mm)
Average winter climate moderate
Staff two

'On entering . . . you seem at once transported into the home of some powerful landowner of the sixteenth century . . . and when you enter the courtyard you quite expect some of the grand dames of the period to be seen at the windows.' So the *Gardeners Chronicle* reported in 1889. Even today, when part-clad in scaffolding which it will be for some years to come, the house is a dreamy sight, a varied assortment of russet stone and half-timbered walls, tiled roofs, gables, high chimneys and gatehouse, guarded by a moat and reached by stone bridges. With additions and restorations dating from every century, it has been woven together by its various owners with remarkable sensitivity to its medieval origins. And this respect for the past has also encompassed the garden, whose linear medieval design has been little altered.

Much of the tranquillity and sense of mystery is owed to water. The low-lying position, in a cleft between woods, makes Ightham a damp and misty place, and in nearly all parts of the garden there is the sight or sound of a pool, fountain or rivulet. Indeed, water features occupy much of the main north-south axis. At the upper end of the garden, a stream flowing through

Pink and white valerian colonising the old stone moat wall at Ightham Mote.

the Victorian Wilderness collects in a recently dredged small lake. From here, the water drops into two catchment pools and is carried, via culverts under the lawn, into the moat around the house, and down into a second lake below.

In contrast to the moat's mellow formality, the two lakes are edged in rough grass, wildflowers and trees, principally ash, poplar, alder and birch, and the walks around them are shady and green. Shrub planting is being developed for a late summer effect. The south lake, divided from the house by a country lane, is also accompanied by two cobnut coppices and a London Plane of enormous dimensions. This was happily spared by the 1987 hurricane, which tore down so many of the garden's best trees, and in spring, it is the backdrop for a sheet of daffodils; in autumn, its own leaves deliver another spectacle of yellow. Adding to the romance is the knowledge that, buried under part of the lawn, are the remains of a medieval stewpond. The outline, smaller than previously supposed, has recently been traced by dowsing. But at some unknown time it was converted into a bowling green and became the green foil for a more ornamental garden.

The red berries of *Cotoneaster horizontalis* against the clock-tower wall.

The magazine articles of the late nineteenth and early twentieth century revelled in Ightham's 'quaint old-world look' and relaxed plantings, in stark contrast to self-conscious Victorian bedding. This new nineteenth-century taste for evocative design and poetic planting is clearly expressed in the Trust's restoration of the more ornamental areas on the west side of the lawn and house. The long border running beside the lawn has the swaying heads of plume poppies (Macleaya) and tall grasses (*Miscanthus sinensis* 'Silberfeder' and *Stipa gigantea* among them) repeated down its length. And *Gypsophila paniculata* and varieties of *Aster ericoides*, geranium and veronica froth between them, in the company of a range of other soft-toned shrubs and perennials to carry colour through the summer.

Beside the picturesque group of Scots Pines at the north-west corner of the house, a circular water basin, surrounded by clipped box domes, herbs and dwarf phloxes, makes a striking feature. Hereabouts, the ragstone walls are clothed with various shrubs, climbing roses and *Vitis coignetiae*, and a gateway leads into a small walled and paved garden, where a lily pond, scented philadelphus and tobacco flowers, and a host of silvery plants are set against the beautiful Elizabethan stable range. As the entry in *Gardens Old and New* (*Country Life*, 1900) relates, 'There seems to be no jarring note here, and Ightham is a place where the sweetness of the garden and the country reigns.'

Kedleston Hall

Derby, Derbyshire	5 miles north-west of Derby, signposted from roundabout where A38 crosses A52 close to Markeaton Park	*Area* 12 acres (5 ha) *Soil* acid/sandy loam *Altitude* 330 ft (100 m) *Average rainfall* 27 in (686 mm) *Average winter climate* cold *Staff* two

Pass through the arched gateway at North Lodge and you enter one of the great eighteenth-century arcadias, a serene and sweeping composition of trees, lake and pavilions, presided over by Robert Adam's Neo-classical palace. The 'swelling and sinking' contours of the land are nature's gift; the rest is art. Adam was commissioned from 1758 by Sir Nathaniel Curzon, 1st Lord Scarsdale, and the composition offers an insight into his skill as a landscape gardener, for as well as being given sole responsibility for the hall by Lord Scarsdale, Adam had, as he wrote to his brother James, 'the intire Manadgement of his Grounds ... with full powers as to Temples Bridges Seats and Cascades', although William Emes also worked here from 1756–60.

The open pasture in front of the house is framed by generous belts of trees, which fill the hilltop horizon and embrace the furthest stretches of lake. The eye-catcher in the middle distance is the bridge, somewhat grander than Adam envisaged, with three arches spanning the cascade. His finest piece of garden architecture, the Fishing Boat house, is just upstream.

The garden, or Pleasure Ground, is on the south side of the house. Bounded by a ha-ha, the

153

expanse of lawn and accompanying trees carry the eye across the rising parkland to the woods above. But to the west, the informal shrubberies, adorned with a fine urn and Medici lion installed by the 1st Lord Scarsdale, soon give way to more formal gardens. In spring and early summer, the scene is filled with colour and fragrance from naturalised daffodils, azaleas and Hardy Hybrid rhododendrons, accompanied by philadelphus, Portugal Laurel, roses and a scattering of more unusual shrubs such as the yellow-flowered currant, *Ribes odoratum*, and *Weigela middendorffiana*. Hydrangeas and sweet-scented *Osmanthus heterophyllus* perform later. Spearing through the shrubberies and standing sentinel in the open glades are some fine trees, including Wellingtonias, Swamp Cypress, Corsican Pine, Turkey Oak, and, near the Orangery, a superb Fern-leaved Beech, *Fagus sylvatica* 'Aspleniifolia', a variant worth planting in large gardens purely for the hiss of its leaves in the wind.

Behind this beech, you turn, through wrought-iron gates, back into Adam's landscape. You are now at the start of the Long Walk, a 3-mile (4·8-km) circuit that takes you up into Vicarwood, directly opposite the south front of the hall, and back down to the lakes on the other side of the house. Such belt walks were a popular feature of eighteenth-century gardens, and the changing moods instilled by alternating evergreens and deciduous trees and flowering shrubs, by heavy shade and dappled sunlight, and by tunnels of foliage and breaks in the canopy, are gradually being restored by the Trust. Adam proposed a series of buildings along the path, but the tiny Hermitage seems to have been the only one constructed.

Killerton

Broadclyst, Exeter, Devon

On west side of Exeter–
Cullompton road (B3181)
entrance off B3185

Area 21 acres (8·5 ha)
Soil acid/sandy loam
Altitude 164–351 ft (50–107 m)
Average rainfall 36 in (914 mm)
Average winter climate mild
Staff four

FAR RIGHT: *Paeonia* 'Bowl of
Beauty' at Killerton.

It takes little effort to imagine the excitement of gardening in those decades of the nineteenth and early twentieth century when exotic and untried woody plants, collected in far-flung corners of the world, were flooding into Britain. Killerton was one of the first gardens to indulge, and for a period of over 130 years the enthusiasm only briefly waned. Today it offers an arboretum of the highest calibre and a springtime spectacle that few gardens can equal.

The garden lies on the slopes of Killerton Clump, a volcanic outcrop that rises several hundred feet above the flood plain of the River Exe. The soil is free-draining, deep, fertile, acidic and a rich, Devon red; coupled with the southerly aspect and comparatively mild climate, it provides excellent growing conditions. The foundations for the collection were laid in the 1770s, when Sir Thomas Dyke Acland decided to create a landscape park to accompany his new house; the present flat-topped, pink-washed building was originally intended as a temporary residence, but a grander mansion was never built.

Acland chose as his gardener and land steward John Veitch, who soon proved an exceptional landscaper. With Acland's help, he also started a nursery at nearby Budlake. It was to become the most celebrated of its day, and in 1840, under the direction of his son James, was the first to dispatch plant-hunters into the wild. The association between the Acland and Veitch families held until 1939, and, apart from a 30-year period following Sir Thomas's death in 1871, Killerton was receiving batches of new plants with regularity. Old specimens of *Thuja plicata* and *Sequoiadendron giganteum* in the garden are almost certainly from seed brought back from the west coast of America by Veitch's collector, William Lobb, in the 1850s. And a great many other trees and shrubs are either original plantings or direct

Stone steps leading up the rock garden at Killerton, colonised by soleirolia (helxine or Mind-Your-Own-Business).

descendants from seed collected in South America, China, Japan and the Himalayas during the nineteenth and early twentieth centuries.

From the house, the view up the hillside is of mown grass, specimen trees and flowing shrub beds, capped by an exotic woodland of mixed conifers and broad-leaved trees. Fine specimens of Californian Chestnut, *Aesculus californica*, the erect Japanese Walnut, *Juglans ailanthifolia* var. *cordiformis*, and the wide-spreading *Zelkova serrata*, are some of the highlights among a cast that includes *Nothofagus obliqua*, Indian Horse Chestnut, blue Atlas and Incense Cedars, golden Monterey Cypress, Wellingtonias and redwoods. Early in the year, the banks are peppered with daffodils, magnolias, rhododendrons and Japanese cherry blossom.

The hillside paths reveal countless treasures: a stand of Cork Oak, with thick, rugged bark; the evergreen, acid-loving *Quercus acuta*; a magnificent *Stewartia pseudocamellia*, with patterned trunk and fiery autumn colour; *Ehretia dicksonii*, with fragrant flowers in June, and *Taiwania cryptomerioides*, a rare and tender conifer, both from seed gathered in China by Ernest Wilson from 1899–1905; a soaring *Liquidambar formosana*; *Cornus kousa*, producing a cascade of white flowers in June; and *Cryptomeria japonica* and its variant 'Lobbii', grown from William Lobb's Javanese seed.

This is only scratching the surface. Drifts of scented azaleas and further hummocks of *Rhododendron arboreum*, in red, pink and white, colour the glades between trees. Early in the year, crocuses and *Cyclamen coum* create pools of lilac and carmine; later come *Cyclamen repandum*, primroses, violets and bluebells; later still, campions and Queen Anne's Lace; and finally, *Cyclamen hederifolium*. At every turn, there are fresh surprises and framed vistas.

In the early part of the twentieth century, two significant features were added to the garden, enabling the vast plant collection to expand still further. In about 1900, the great garden writer William Robinson was asked to advise on the garden, which over the previous 30 years had fallen into a sorry state. His legacy is the great terrace, west of the house. Originally planted with roses, which did not succeed, the generously proportioned beds here now contain an assortment of low-growing Mediterranean shrubs and other plants in soft, pastel tones, their shapes contrasting with stands of *Yucca gloriosa* and the heavy verticals of Coade stone vases. Over the terrace wall, there are broad views of the gently undulating park. The herbaceous border that runs alongside the parterre was originally planted by John Coutts, who became head gardener as the garden was being completed. The present Jekyllian colour schemes of pastel tints, blending into a hotter core of reds and oranges, is more recent. It has a long season, beginning with tulips and Crown Imperials in spring, reaching its climax at mid-summer with peonies, irises and Shrub roses, and continuing into autumn with buddlejas, dahlias and other late perennials.

The second significant new feature, also installed by Coutts, is the rock garden, sited beyond the thatched summer-house, known as the Bear's Hut (it once housed a Canadian black bear). This precipitous composition, recently restored, is a superb period piece, busily intricate in rockwork and planting, and capped by a stand of Chusan Palm, *Trachycarpus fortunei*. A cool and private part of the garden, the silence is broken only by the recently created stream that trickles softly into the rock pool, edged in ferns, primulas and astilbes. Following exposure to all this colour and variety, there is refreshment to be had in the green shadows around the Victorian chapel, where you can walk among oaks, chestnuts, box and conifers, and search for the lime-yellow flowers on the two Tulip Trees planted by Veitch.

FAR RIGHT: *Acer palmatum* 'Osakazuki' in autumn colours.

156

Kingston Lacy

Wimborne Minster, Dorset

1½ miles west of Wimborne,
on B3082 Blandford road

Area 20 acres (8 ha)
Soil alkaline, some acid, varied
Altitude 200 ft (61 m)
Average rainfall 32 in (813 mm)
Average winter climate moderate
Staff three

The high-chimneyed Italianate mansion, remodelled in the 1830s by Sir Charles Barry for William John Bankes, stands pale and elegant in the midst of an open park. Oaks, beeches and other venerable trees, survivors of the ferocious gale of January 1990, are dispersed, singly and in clumps, over the level terrain. And animating the scene is a herd of what seems, from a distance, to be bison; at closer range, they reveal themselves as horned Red Devon cattle.

This pastoral scene was set in the late eighteenth century as the original linear landscape laid out by Sir Roger Pratt, the builder of the house, was dismantled, and it is somewhat deceptive. For, as in so many of the great country seats, the pendulum of fashion continued to swing, and as you walk around the house, you find a strict Victorian and Edwardian formality ordering the immediate surroundings in the form of terrace and parterre gardens, with accompanying 'balls and skittles' of golden yew and gaudy spring and summer bedding schemes, a strong central axis path and avenues of trees. As you move away from the house, an alternating pattern of straight vistas and curving walks begins to register on the mind.

The individual flavour comes from the architectural ornaments, enthusiastically assembled by Bankes. Veronese lions, well-heads and vases – some endearingly supported by tortoises – decorate the terrace, while, in line with the door, a soaring pink obelisk, brought from a temple beside the Nile, casts a crisp shadow across the broad expanse of grass,

The gardens were in a sorry state when the Trust took possession of the property in 1982, and the large, box-hedged fernery, collapsed and buried under seedling sycamores, was one of the first features to be tackled. For me, it is now the most bewitching part of the garden, a strange and shady world of meandering gravel paths, horizontally trained yews, stone walls and raised beds, in which countless varieties of ferns, so appealing to the Victorians for their eccentricities and Gothic habitats, hold court.

There are collections of Wood Anemones and Lily of the Valley, and snowdrops carpet the ground in late winter, as they do so much of the garden; the property opens in February especially for their display. They are a memorable sight along Lady Walk and in the Lime Avenue, where they are complemented by the glowing red twigs of the limes; and there is a warm glow also from the base of the trees, where, unusually and rather pleasingly, the epicormic growth has been allowed to remain. This avenue, extended by Walter Ralph Bankes in the 1870s, is, in fact, a vestige of the seventeenth-century formal layout.

On breezy days, you will hear the distinctive hiss of the Cut-leaved Beech, *Fagus sylvatica* 'Aspleniifolia', as you enter the Blind Walk, so-called because it is hidden by evergreens from view. Here the Victorian taste for coloured leaves is fully indulged, the thickets of purple and gold shrubs and small trees leading to a monument erected to celebrate Queen Victoria's Jubilee. Maples, plums, privets, berberis and elders add to the indigestion. There is a further assembly of ornamental trees and shrubs in Nursery Wood, part of the loop walk that takes you out along the Lime Avenue and back through the Cedar Avenue beyond the parterre. A pocket of greensand allows a colourful run of lime-hating azaleas and rhododendrons here, which would not thrive on the chalk and clay elsewhere in the garden. The trees include Hungarian Oak, Black Walnut, ginkgo, Tulip Tree, a tremendous old Black Pine and some striking young *Prunus serrula*, with polished chestnut trunks. The Bankes family were meticulous in recording tree planting, and at one time all the trees in the Cedar Walk carried commemorative plaques. Sadly, the cedar planted by King Edward VII fell in a recent gale, but that planted in 1907 by the Kaiser remains, though somewhat battered.

Knightshayes

Bolham, Tiverton, Devon

2 miles north of Tiverton
(A396), 8 miles from M5
junction 27

Area 250 acres (101 ha)
Soil acid–neutral/heavy from a
    base of the old red Devon
Altitude 400–500 ft (122–152 m)
Average rainfall 36 in (914 mm)
Average winter climate moderate
Staff six

A lead tank in the formal garden
at Knightshayes flanked by
standard wisterias, with scarlet
zauschneria, helianthemum and
verbena.

This garden, developed by Sir John and Lady Heathcoat-Amory, the former champion golfer Joyce Wethered, is one of the best displayed plant collections in the country, comprising formal gardens, conservatory, alpine beds, naturalised bulbs and acre upon acre of exotic woodland and glade, stocked with the choicest trees, shrubs and perennials. Neither had any experience of gardening when they began married life here in 1937, but Sir John became a dedicated collector, Lady Amory a gifted plant arranger, and they worked with a small staff of gardeners, turning for outside help to some of the best contemporary designers and landscapers: Lanning Roper and Sir Eric Savill; and plantsmen, including Graham Stuart Thomas, Norman Haddon and Miss Nellie Britton, who ran a well-known alpine nursery near Tiverton.

The setting is potently Victorian. The red sandstone house, standing high on the eastern flank of the Exe Valley with open views across the Devon countryside towards Tiverton, was designed by William Burges and built between 1869 and 1874. The long, curving entrance drive through the park takes you past its western flank, uphill between Burges's stable block with its fairytale tower and the 4-acre (1·6-ha) walled garden, which used to supply the household with vegetables and fruit, and onwards to the car-park. Favourite Victorian trees, including Scots Pine, cedar, Wellingtonia and Purple Beech join the parkland oaks (English and Turkey), and beyond the walled garden is a suitably gloomy plantation of Douglas Firs, offering a hushed, cool walk through the box and bracken understorey.

In front of the house, the scene becomes cheerier. The terraces here were set out by the garden designer and writer Edward Kemp in the 1870s, but they are no longer the scene of swashbuckling bedding schemes. Instead, you look down upon clean patterns of lawn, clipped yew, paving and stone ornament, fringed by pastel schemes of rosemary, cistus, lavender, iris, agapanthus and other sun-lovers, backed by evergreen magnolia and, at midsummer, a curtain of white from the Himalayan rambler, *Rosa brunonii*.

Restraint and profusion: these two themes interplay throughout the garden, the contrast heightened here by the tension between the crisp, formal groundplan and the curves and spill of the flowers and foliage. It is felt still more intensely in the yew-hedged compartments, up the short flight of steps to the east. Here, you come to a small paved garden, patterned with low silver and ice-blue perennials, a lead cistern and flanking pair of standard wisterias; and formal terraces of alpine (in a lowland setting, far more harmonious a feature than an eruption of rock), including scented daphnes, dianthus, dwarf iris and pink Dwarf Russian Almond, *Prunus tenella*.

These are placed in contrast with an empty lawn, around which topiary hounds chase a topiary fox – a much celebrated touch of whimsy added by Sir Ian Heathcoat-Amory, a keen huntsman, in the 1920s; and a larger space (formerly the bowling green) framed by Victorian battlemented hedges and backlit by *Acer* 'Brilliantissimum', where a circular pool, the solitary statue of a bather and a Weeping Silver Pear are the only ingredients: a charming piece of modernist composition, simple and complete.

Another few steps and you are inside Knightshayes' most famous planting, the Garden in the Wood. This area was annexed from about 1950 at the rate of 2 acres (0·8 ha) a year and now encompasses some 30 acres (12 ha) of ornamental walks and glades, under the canopy of the thinned and high-pruned nineteenth-century oaks, beeches, limes and conifers. It begins with a straight grass walk, bordered by Shrub roses and rhododendrons (not a partnership often encountered in gardens), underplanted with geraniums, pulmonarias and electric blue omphalodes. As the walk breaks into curves and glades, you came upon raised beds edged in peat-block walls – an idea gleaned from Branklyn Garden in Scotland – colonised by mosses, ferns, Wood Anemones, violets and much else.

Larger grass glades open up, speared by the trunks of the tall pines and native trees. At the edges are herbaceous schemes – perhaps shrubby euphorbias, their lime-yellow cylinders of flower matched with tellima, alchemilla, white-veined arum, purple-leaved violet and Bowles's Golden Grass, or, later in summer, a flush of yellow, apricot and orange crocosmias. Sword-leaved phormiums and silver astelia punctuate views, and in one spot, a purple thundercloud looms, created by massed *Rhododendron augustinii* hybrids – 'Electra' providing blossoms of the deepest colour.

Gravel paths meander through a grove of larches and lead into an area of distinctive character where grass has been replaced by moss, and waves of creamy-white and pink erythroniums break against outcrops of bronze Polystichum ferns; later, white Excelsior foxgloves filter between the pines. Naturally, spring and early summer see the main flowering of the wood – the former a magical time when the chalices of tree magnolias are lighting a largely leafless canopy, and hellebores are blooming in thick carpets under their shrubby cousins – but hypericums, hydrangeas, clethras, gentians, clerodendrums and Japanese anemones keep the colour flowing into high summer and autumn, when the large colonies of

The pool, enclosed by castellated yew hedges and overhung by a Weeping Silver Pear.

cyclamen, growing on the dry banks and around the boles of trees, are performing their pink and white butterfly dance.

In one area, prostrate junipers fall as a cascade between mounds of broad-leaved rhododendrons, while blue-leaved spruce interplay with Japanese maples (an especially fine partnership in autumn, when the maples catch alight). Mahonias are a favourite tribe, and ferns are ubiquitous – delicate Maidenhair Ferns beside the discs of *Cyclamen repandum*, and the creeping, rust-coloured *Blechnum penna-marina* picking up the suede undersides of *Rhododendron falconeri*, among the many memorable associations. Knightshayes cannot support the more tender trees and shrubs encountered on the Cornish peninsula, but the soil is rich and the climate is still warm and wet enough for some of the early-flowering and more exotic-looking trees and shrubs denied to many inland gardens. There is a concentration of them on the grass slope below the wood. These 3 acres (1·2 ha) also support a collection of southern beeches (Nothofagus), flowering dogwoods and birches, as well as cherries and ever more hardy rhododendrons; crimson-red 'Queen of Hearts' blooming in front of white-trunked birches is an amazing sight.

Knole

Sevenoaks, Kent

At the Tonbridge end of Sevenoaks on A21

Area 22 acres (8·9ha)
Soil lime-free
Altitude 250ft (76m)
Average rainfall 30in (762mm)
Average winter climate moderate
Staff The Sackville family is responsible for the garden

This vast and ancient house was the childhood home of Vita Sackville-West and compared by her to an Oxford college, 'though more palatial and less studious'. It stands on a plateau within a 1,000-acre (405-ha) park of undulating ridges, valleys and woods, with fallow and Japanese deer grazing up to its battlements.

The gardens, to the south-east of the house, are completely enclosed by walls of Kentish ragstone, dating from the second half of the sixteenth century, with grilles and gates giving you views out into the park. The layout within remains substantially unaltered since the early eighteenth century. As well as formal lawns, flower and herb gardens, it incorporates a large Wilderness or woodland garden, being redeveloped by the Sackville family in the wake of the 1987 storm – which also devastated the park. Bluebells and azaleas are a feature, while the garden walls display many fine climbing plants, including dozens of old wisterias.

A photograph taken in the early years of this century shows a formal sunken garden at Knole, with the great house behind.

Lacock Abbey

nr Chippenham, Wiltshire

3 miles south of Chippenham, just east of A350

Area 9 acres (3·6ha)
Soil alkaline/loam
Altitude 100ft (30m)
Average rainfall 25in (635mm)
Average winter climate cold
Staff one

The vaulted chapter house and cloisters of the former Augustinian nunnery are preserved behind the mellow walls of this great house, a cool and silent refuge from the outside world. Of the formal medieval and later gardens, there is now little trace. The setting is of open water meadows, belts of trees, rough shady lawns and a series of crumbling walled enclosures given over to fruit and allotments.

For the richest display of flowers, early spring is the time to visit, when snowdrops, Winter Aconites, Sweet Violets and spectacular sheets of wild *Crocus vernus* are covering the ground, soon to be followed by drifts of daffodils, Dog's Tooth Violets and Snakeshead Fritillaries. But for much of the year, there are scattered plants in bloom. Roses, mock orange, wild cranesbills and Martagon Lilies give summer colour in the grassy glades, while the abbey walls lend a golden backdrop to a range of shrubs and climbers. A new rose garden has recently been re-created following a photograph of 1841, incorporating old Shrub roses and Climbers growing up wrought-iron arches.

The hot, dry conditions of the south and west façades suit yellow Banksian Rose, Judas Tree, figs, rosemary and lavender, together with abelia, ceratostigma and *Geranium renardii*. *Rosa primula* stands beside the door to the cloisters, appropriately casting the scent of incense from its ferny leaves whenever there is moisture in the air. Against the east wall grow hydrangeas, Alba roses and Virginia creeper, a fine sight in its autumnal scarlet.

But these can only be incidents in the large-scale scene of abbey and meadow. Behind the house, the mood is more intimate, set by the canopy and fringe of trees. Beeches hang over the old stewpond, with its rushes and Sweet Flag, newts and dragonflies. Nearby there are tall oaks and limes, a group of huge London Planes and a suckering wing-nut tree, *Pterocarya fraxinifolia*, with fissured bark; elsewhere, fine specimens of Black Walnut, Tulip Tree, Swamp Cypress and catalpa, with late trusses of highly scented, white flowers. Sadly, the old nettle tree, *Celtis australis*, growing in the orchard, fell in the severe gale of January 1990; a young plant stands beside the drive.

Lamb House

West Street, Rye, East Sussex

In West Street, facing west end of church

Area 1 acre (0·4ha)
Soil neutral/loam
Altitude 50ft (15m)
Average rainfall 30in (762mm)
Average winter climate moderate
Staff part-time only

'The quite essential amiability of Lamb House only deepens with age', wrote Henry James, who lived and worked here from 1898 until his death in 1916. The Georgian house, built of russet-red brick, stands at the turn of one of Rye's cobbled streets, and behind it is a mellow, walled garden with a central expanse of grass, gravel and stone paths, cherry trees and box-studded borders packed with plants. The American novelist was not a gardener, but as his last secretary, Theodora Bosanquet, noted: 'It never failed to give (him) pleasure to look out . . . at his English garden where he could watch his English gardener digging the flower-beds or mowing the lawn or sweeping the fallen leaves.'

Soon after his arrival, James was advised by Alfred Parsons, the painter and garden designer, on a new layout for the garden. No plan exists, however, and the garden's present appearance reflects a continuing evolution. Periodic gales, invariably a hazard in coastal gardens, have also brought changes. But on most days, the garden is kept snug by its walls and trees and by the upper storeys of the surrounding houses; the principal view is over the spikes of acanthus flowers to the spire of St Peter's church at the end of West Street.

The borders that flank the perimeter paths are narrow and full of surprises. Flame-coloured *Campsis radicans*, an ancient specimen here in James's time, and variegated trachelospermum grow against the south wall of the house, where once there stood a lean-to greenhouse. In the sunny beds, among violets, lavenders and irises, you will come across stands of eucomis and scented hybrid lilies; in the shady corners, camellias, hellebores, montbretia and white impatiens. In spring, bluebells and grape hyacinths are ubiquitous; in autumn, Japanese anemones, nerines and hardy plumbago create pools of pink and blue between the amber curtains of the cherry branches. There are no sophisticated planting themes here. The borders are the product of the straightforward English delight in growing plants for their own sake; and the mood is homely and relaxed. A trellis, hung with roses, conceals the kitchen garden. There are more roses beyond – bushes of 'Paul Shirville', 'Peace' and others – for cutting, with alyssum and, in spring, chionodoxa and jonquils growing beneath them. The vegetable plots are also accompanied by a herb garden and greenhouse.

Lamb House's literary association did not end with James's death: the property also became the home of E. F. Benson. His Mapp and Lucia novels were written and set in Rye, and the house and garden feature prominently.

Lanhydrock

Bodmin, Cornwall

2½ miles south-east of Bodmin

Area 30 acres (12·1 ha)
Soil acid/good loam
Altitude 400 ft (122 m)
Average rainfall 45 in
  (1,143 mm)
Average winter climate moderate
Staff four, plus one part-time
  and one trainee

Hanging beechwoods, plunging entrance drives and tree-studded parkland rolling down to the River Fowey, provide a dynamic setting for this low, labyrinthine house of silver-grey granite, with its accompanying church and ornate, obelisk-capped gatehouse. The buildings, part seventeenth-century and part late-Victorian, are tucked close into the wooded ridge and face east, down the valley and away from the prevailing wind. For although this is Cornwall, the house stands at 400 feet (122 m), 7 miles (11 km) from the sea and with the south-western edge of windswept Bodmin Moor only 2½ miles (4 km) away.

This chillier climate and shadier aspect distinguishes Lanhydrock from the balmy coastal gardens, depriving it of the more tender and earliest-flowering exotics. But the spring display is every bit as spectacular and, as the season advances, colour surges through the woods. Thickets of camellias and enormous specimens of Rhododendron Smithii group become beacons in the landscape, while above, various forms and hybrids of *Magnolia campbellii*, the first in a long succession of tree magnolias, hold their pink and white chalices to the sky. By late April, countless other shrubs are in bloom, together with waves of daffodils and bluebells.

Most of the other great Cornish woodland gardens are made on slopes below their houses, but here the main garden is above, and the flower-framed views down across the rooftops, gatehouse and accompanying lines of Irish Yew trees are one of the property's most memorable features. The yews are part of a very different style of garden set out around the house by the 1st Baron Robartes and the architect George Gilbert Scott in 1857. The design was simplified in the 1920s and '30s and is now a crisp formal composition of lawns, yews, urns, rose and bedding schemes, enclosed and partitioned by Scott's low, battlement walls.

Floribunda and Polyantha roses – pink 'Else Poulsen' and 'The Fairy', yellow 'Bright Smile' and the well-scented, rosy-violet 'Escapade' and white 'Margaret Merril' – give a long display of colour opposite the east front, while in the parterre, the schemes are usually

based on tulips, pansies and forget-me-nots for spring, with begonias and impatiens later. Fine trees fringe these formal lawns, including Cork Oak, chestnuts, a towering Monterey Pine, and two Copper Beeches planted by the Prime Ministers William Gladstone and Lord Rosebery. Behind the Croquet Lawn stands a remarkable Field Maple, its limbs caked in lichens, mosses and polypody ferns, which flourish in the clean, moist air. It was not until after 1930, when the 7th Viscount Clifden inherited, that the more flamboyant species of trees and shrubs – for decades, the sensation of other Cornish gardens – began to be sampled at Lanhydrock.

As you walk towards the Higher Garden, you get an inkling of the displays to come. In spring the shrubby *Magnolia loebneri* and its hybrids, 'Leonard Messel' and the exquisitely scented 'Merrill', will be in bloom and beyond, the first of the show-stopping trees: among them forms of *M.* × *veitchii* and *M. dawsoniana*. Rhododendrons, including the crimson-flecked, creamy 'Dr Stocker', pink 'Mrs C.B. van Nes' and *R. arboreum* var. *roseum*, add to the scene. Later, there will be scented Occidentale azaleas, *Magnolia tripetala*, and, in high summer, 'Rostrevor' eucryphias.

The winding paths lead through ever richer banks of blossom, on and on, past a stream up to the Holy Well and thatched gardener's cottage. Everywhere, the magnolias billow and 165

the rhododendrons and camellias surge. *Magnolia sargentiana* var. *robusta*, *M. sprengeri* var. *diva* and hybrids of *M. cylindrica* make spectacular trees, while the shrubby *M.* × *soulangeana* and its many selections are ubiquitous; at one point, lines of *M.* × *soulangeana* 'Lennei' form a tunnel of blossom. In late spring, *M. sieboldii* and its relatives, with pendant flowers, enter the stage, followed by *M. ashei*, fragrant *M. thompsoniana*, and *M. hypoleuca* and *M.* × *wiesneri* (syn. *M.* × *watsonii*), both carrying the pervasive scent of ripe melons.

Hardy hybrids make up a large proportion of Lanhydrock's rhododendron collection and they are here in all colours. One of the most notable is the old, crimson-trussed variety 'Lord Roberts', a stand of which covers an area the size of a tennis court. Massed lacecap and mophead hydrangeas reproduce for summer some of this springtime spectacle, but now attention shifts to the great circle of clipped yew below the woodland banks. Here, beside a barn, is a distinctively designed circular garden of herbaceous plants, the southern half of which was set out by Lady Clifden before 1914. The Trust completed the hedge and added matching perimeter flower-beds in 1971. The foliage of *Yucca recurvifolia*, yellow tree peony, *Melianthus major*, fascicularias, rodgersias, hostas and ligularias set a lush, exotic theme, against which the flowers of agapanthus, penstemons, *Canna iridiflora*, *Cautleya* 'Robusta', and other perennials appreciative of the long, warm, moist summers, are displayed. A National Collection of crocosmias, relatives of the familiar orange montbretia, is held here, the spectrum of colours encompassing lemons, apricots and scarlets.

In April, the Higher Garden's Top Walk is bordered by a notable colony of white Pheasant's Eye Narcissi, the bulbs having naturalised luxuriantly since their introduction in the mid-1970s. A new summer-house has been installed here and a gate leads into the wilder Woodland Garden, where ferns and bluebells invade the steep banks, beneath oak and beech. The finest views of the house and park are now revealed, complemented by the dazzling blood-reds of the rhododendrons 'Tally Ho', 'Matador' and 'Cornish Red', and the elephantine leaves of *R. macabeanum*, *R. grande* and other giants.

Little Moreton Hall

Congleton, Cheshire	4 miles south-west of Congleton, on east side of A34	*Area* 1 acre (0·4 ha) *Soil* lime-free/sandy loam *Altitude* 250 ft (76 m) *Average rainfall* 25 in (635 mm) *Average winter climate* moderate *Staff* one

When the Trust acquired this startling timber-framed house, built for the Moreton family in the fifteenth and sixteenth centuries, the moated garden was neglected and overgrown. There were no records of the early design, nor many significant features remaining, other than the two grass-covered mounts – one within and one without the garden – so it was decided to reinvent a garden, which, though without the support of direct historical evidence, would be an appropriate setting for the house and would reinforce its domestic Elizabethan flavour. The design of the knot, happily echoing the timber pattern on the house, was taken from Leonard Meager's *The Complete English Gardener* of 1670.

Now, twenty or so years later, the new plantings are well established, and the garden has acquired much charm, the only jarring note being the proximity of the busy A34. From the small cobbled courtyard, you are drawn into the orchard, where the older trees have been supplemented by traditional varieties. Quinces, apples and medlars are among them, with one of the mature pears supporting a Rambler rose.

The Elizabethan pattern of formal enclosures has been restored through the planting of hedges. A mixed screen of hornbeam, holly, sweetbriar and honeysuckle surrounds the orchard, and the adjacent knot garden and tunnel have sides of yew. The knot itself is made of dwarf edging box (*Buxus sempervirens* 'Suffruticosa'), with gravel, grass and yew topiaries filling the spaces within. In the sixteenth century, the spaces were often planted with flowers, but to keep the design crisp and uncluttered, these have been confined to side beds. Here, long-grown herbaceous plants such as tradescantia, iris, peony and astrantia are cultivated in neat, rectangular blocks, with standard gooseberries (replacements for lavenders, which succumbed to the prevalent cold, damp winters) rising from square mats of Sweet Woodruff, golden marjoram, thrift, camomile, wild strawberry, bugle and other low perennials.

The narrow walk around the moat brings you to other beds. One pair contains old varieties of vegetable, including 'Dwarf Green Curloo Kale', 'Brown Trout' bean, ruby chard, 'James Long Keeping' onion and the runner bean 'Painted Lady'; another contains culinary and medicinal herbs such as bergamot, sorrel, yarrow and leopard's bane. The ornamental beds within the house's projecting wings are, alarmingly, wet enough to support fat clumps of umbrella plant, *Darmera peltata* (formerly *Peltiphyllum peltatum*). But these outlying plantings are simply details beside the tranquil fringe of trees, sweeps of meadow and expanse of dark water. The perch and Golden Orfe that break the surface are further reminders of the varied produce an Elizabethan household would have expected from its domain.

Lyme Park

Disley, Stockport, Cheshire

On south side of A6; 6½ miles south-east of Stockport

Area 15 acres (6·1 ha)
Soil acid/clay
Altitude 500 ft (152 m)
Average rainfall 40 in
  (1,016 mm)
Average winter climate cold
Staff four

The contrasts between the formal elegance of Lyme Hall and its gardens, and the wild landscape in which they sit, gives the spice to this property. High and remote on the edge of the Peak District, the hall, originally a hunting-lodge, surveys wooded slopes and rolling moorland, still grazed by ancient herds of red deer. The climate is harsh, with high rainfall, a cool, late spring and a short summer – conditions which have prompted complaints from many of the gardeners at Lyme Hall since the late seventeenth century when the first records of the garden appear.

The Elizabethan house was given its Italianate grandeur by Giacomo Leoni in the early eighteenth century. The gardens had their heyday in the late nineteenth century, and their present planting and patterns, like the interiors of the hall, are reminders of that sumptuous era of gracious country-house living. But by 1947, when Lyme Park was transferred to the Trust, the property had suffered the inevitable decline due to high taxation and shortage of staff. Until 1994 Stockport Metropolitan Council was responsible for its upkeep but funds

The Sunken Dutch garden at Lyme Park before restoration. The planting has since been revised.

were not available for the full restoration of the hall until the early 1970s and attention was turned to the garden after that.

The starting point was the most spectacular feature, the huge sunken Dutch Garden to the west of the hall, created in the early eighteenth century. In 1973 disaster struck the garden in the form of a violent summer storm which caused a torrent of water to flow into the lake above, to which the ancient sluice system proved unequal. The south-east corner of the wall could not support the pressure from the floodwaters, and cracked, and the result was a devastating cascade of mud, water and stones across the parterre. Today, however, you look down once more on the pristine scheme as installed by the 1st Lord Newton. Surrounding the central fountain, the intricate patterns of beds, edged in ivy, are filled with seasonal schemes with a strong period flavour. Tulips and forget-me-nots are the mainstay of the spring display, and scarlet *Lobelia* 'Queen Victoria' with splashes of golden yew are highlights of the summer show. And from the heavy evergreen and variegated shrubberies that clothe the banks come further bursts of colour from rhododendrons, osmanthus, philadelphus and hydrangeas.

The smaller sunken garden to the north is set out with trees and shrubs mainly given by or commemorating the Hon. Vicary Gibbs, a renowned gardener and friend of the 2nd Lord Newton. *Malus × purpurea* 'Aldenhamensis', 'Gibbs' Golden Gage' and *Ligustrum* 'Vicaryi' are among the plants carrying Gibbs's name or that of his garden in Hertfordshire.

In the nineteenth century, no fashionable country house was complete without its conservatory, and here, in a cold and wet climate, such an indoor garden would have been especially appreciated. Lyme's grand Orangery was designed by Lewis Wyatt in about 1815, but the interior, with its central fountain and floors in Minton patterned tiles, was remodelled some fifty years later by Alfred Derbyshire who also added the glazed cupola. Once warmed by the excess heat from the laundry and brewhouse behind, the Orangery is no longer heated. But the fig tree and two great camellias survive from Victorian times, and, together with acacia, choisya, pittosporum, *Cestrum elegans*, ferns and scented *Lilium regale*, continue to project the exotic mood.

Terrace beds in front of the Orangery, in summer often displaying the half-hardy, white-throated *Penstemon* 'Rubicundus' raised at Lyme in 1906, and the Rose Garden to the east, planted with standard 'Sanders' White Rambler' and various Floribunda roses, are further expressions of formality. Beyond, the garden's lines become more flowing, the eye following first the sweep up to the Lanthorn Tower, erected as a folly in the early eighteenth century and framed by woods, and then turning to trace the curving path between hedged herbaceous borders.

From Hamper's Bridge, you follow the stream through still more meandering and naturalistic plantings, installed in more recent times. The area known to the gardeners as Killtime is sufficiently moist and sheltered to suit a good collection of rhododendrons and azaleas, accompanied by ferns and other pondside plants. Swiss Arolla Pine, Bhutan Pine and Small-leaved Lime are among the many good trees. Behind the lake, you walk through more rhododendron shrubberies until you are in line once more with the centre of Leoni's south façade. The Lime Avenue, rising to the south is, together with the lake, is one of the four remaining vestiges of the seventeenth-century garden. It was planted originally by Richard Legh, whose family was associated with Lyme for nearly 600 years.

Lytes Cary Manor

Charlton Mackrell, Somerton, Somerset

1 mile north of Ilchester bypass A303

Area 4 acres (1·6 ha)
Soil alkaline/clay
Altitude 200 ft (61 m)
Average rainfall 30 in (762 mm)
Average winter climate cold
Staff one, plus tenant

In 1907, the medieval and Tudor manor of Lytes Cary, home of the Lyte family for five centuries from 1286, found its champion in Sir Walter Jenner, son of Sir William Jenner, the eminent physician. As well as restoring and sympathetically enlarging the decaying house, Jenner set out a series of simply furnished, grassed and paved formal enclosures, aptly described by Christopher Hussey as 'a necklace of garden rooms strung on green corridors'. Like the house, Jenner's garden is broad and low-slung, crouching for shelter in its flat, exposed farmland. The yards of yew are important buffers, in addition to giving the garden its patterns and secrets.

Although the bones of the gardens are largely unaltered since Sir Walter's day, a programme of renovation and improvements was begun by the Trust in 1963. This included the replanning and enrichment of the main flower border, which runs along a corridor opposite a buttressed yew hedge. The planting is mixed and follows a deliberate colour sequence, in the Jekyllian manner, warming from the blues and yellows of potentilla, caryopteris, *Hibiscus*

RIGHT: The White Garden at Lytes Cary with 'Iceberg' roses and argyranthemums.

LEFT: A view through the yew topiary to the east front of Lytes Cary.

'Blue Bird', achillea, polemonium and *Aster × frikartii*, into the purples and rich crimsons of Smoke Bush, berberis, self-sowing *Atriplex hortensis* and mats of Purple Sage. Floribunda roses, including 'Magenta', 'Lavender Lassie', 'Rosemary Rose' and 'Yellow Holstein', help to ensure a good succession of flowers, and the wall behind is hung with a range of climbers, including clematis. Beyond is a white garden with 'Iceberg' roses, hebe, philadelphus and silver foliage.

Other parts of the garden have their bursts of colour too. The ornamental orchard, planted with crossing avenues and symmetrical pairs of medlars, quinces, crab apples, walnuts and corners of weeping ash, is spangled with daffodils, cowslips, fritillaries and other wildflowers in spring and early summer. Clumps of pink and white Rugosa roses, and a stream of *Hypericum calycinum* between the Irish Yews on the raised walk above, contribute flowers and fruits later in the year. The house walls are clad in evergreen magnolia, clematis, *Campsis radicans* and 'Paul's Lemon Pillar' and yellow Banksian roses, and the south façade, with its handsome oriel window, is lapped with cistuses, rosemary, myrtle, *Teucrium fruticans* and other Mediterranean herbs, many of which appear in the 1578 translation by Henry Lyte of Dodoen's Flemish text, the *Cruedeboek* (1569). A copy of this translation, *A New Herbal or Historie of Plants*, is on display in the Great Hall.

But the predominant colours of this garden are the greens of trees, lawns, yew hedges and countryside, and the mellow tints of the golden stone walls and dovecote (in reality, a disguised water-tower). From the raised walk above the orchard, from which there are wide views towards Yeovilton and Camel Hill, you descend through a long grass alley into a series of restrained enclosures: a tranquil pool garden; an oval of evergreen and variegated shrubs, reached through a hornbeam tunnel; a grass arena empty but for a stone seat and flanking pair of strawberry trees; and a wide sweep of open lawn. They are reminders that the simplest treatments make for some of the most satisfying garden pictures.

Melford Hall

Long Melford, Suffolk

In Long Melford on the east side of A134, 14 miles south of Bury St Edmunds

Area 9 acres (3·6 ha)
Soil limy
Altitude 100 ft (30 m)
Average rainfall 23 in (584 mm)
Average winter climate cold
Staff Sir Richard Hyde-Parker employs one gardener

A turreted gatehouse beside Long Melford village green is the entrance to this Elizabethan mansion. It stands across a dry moat, a sweep of warm red brickwork bristling with onion-domed towers and chimneystacks. Built by Sir William Cordell, a distinguished lawyer who rose to become Speaker of the House of Commons and Master of the Rolls, it was erected on the site of a monastic manorhouse sometime before 1578, for in that year Sir William received

The Octagon pavilion at Melford Hall.

his sovereign here. According to one observer, Queen Elizabeth was waited upon by '200 young gentlemen cladde all in whyte velvet, and 300 of the graver sort apparrelled in black ... with 1,500 servyng men all on horsebacke ... and there was in Suffolke suche sumptuous feastinges and bankets as seldom in anie parte of the worlde there hath been seen afore.'

The gardens, contained within the walls and moat, are no longer grand or extensive, but have evolved over the centuries in response to changing tastes and reductions in staff. Two fine features, however, remain from Sir William's day. One is a narrow, raised bowling green running between the drive and the house, emphasised by the Trust with the addition of flanking pairs of Irish Yews along its length. The second is the handsome, and rare, octagonal Tudor garden pavilion that stands at its head. Though its purpose was probably as a look-out tower, it was built both as an ornament and for comfort, with gables and finials and a heating system worked by a furnace and flues in the wall. The panelled upper room, found on restoration to have been sumptuously decorated in green and gold, is reached by two stairways, one from the terrace and the other from the flower-filled sunken garden to the south.

Here, in the most sheltered part of this exposed property, a tree-studded Victorian pleasure ground replaces the intricate patterns of flower-beds and trained fruits that would have existed in Sir William's time, the trees interspersed with topiary domes of green and vari-egated box. Aconites and daffodils flood the grass in spring, with pink cyclamen succeeding them in late summer. Sir William Hyde Parker, father of the present baronet, was a keen hybridiser of daffodils and a number of his bulbs are growing here; the hall contains many display vases, and daffodil parties were held each April. Melford is also noted for its snow-drops and limestone wildflowers, among them the Meadow Saxifrage, *Saxifraga granulata*. Herbaceous borders run below the high west wall, against which are trained wisteria and Moroccan Broom, a Maidenhair Tree (an unusual use of this plant), and, as an echo of the past, a rich array of ornamental vines. The Victorian Rambler rose 'Blush Boursault' was reintroduced into cultivation from the Melford specimen, which still grows on the west wall of the house.

To the south, fronted by a belt of flowering shrubs and small trees, including sucker-ing *Xanthoceras sorbifolium*, a seldom-seen Chinese species with panicles of white flowers resembling those of Horse Chestnut, is the most quirky ingredient – a serpentine, or crinkle-crankle, wall. Designed to take maximum advantage of sunshine in order to ripen fruit, such walls were an eighteenth-century innovation and are more commonly encoun-tered in Suffolk than elsewhere. This example dates from 1793, but was rebuilt in 1990.

In 1937, to give the garden more of an Elizabethan flavour, Ulla, Lady Hyde Parker, set out a small enclosure of yew in the centre of the lawn, and arranged a crisp pattern of herbs including blue rue, purple sage, lavender and germander around a circular lily pond. More recently, the moat border has been replanted with iris cultivars, trained specimen pears and Suffolk apple cultivars.

The park, rising to the east beyond the hall, is rather bald; but has recently been replanted with converging avenues of oak trees (grown from Melford acorns) in accordance with the estate survey of 1613; these follow the lines of the medieval pathways that once intersected the fields, and in time will forge a strong bond between the axes of the hall and its rural setting, as well as tempering the evil wind.

Mompesson House

The Close, Salisbury, Wiltshire

Cathedral Close, centre of Salisbury

Area ½ acre (0·2 ha)
Soil alkaline/loam with chalky subsoil
Altitude 150 ft (46 m)
Average rainfall 29 in (736 mm)
Average winter climate moderate to cold
Staff one, part-time

A glorious hollyhock.

There are few wall plants that could do justice to a façade such as Mompesson House presents to Choristers' Green, in the heart of Salisbury. Really there is only one, *Magnolia grandiflora*. Introduced from North America in 1734, its glossy foliage and cream, waterlily flowers are as bold and opulent as could be expected from any hardy evergreen, and it is no coincidence that it adorns so many of our grandest houses. By 1888, the pair at Mompesson had already reached the eaves; they have since been cut back to reveal more of the limestone front.

The house, built by Charles Mompesson in 1701, is as elegant inside as out. Major repairs were required by 1952, when it was purchased from the Church Commissioners by Denis Martineau, a London architect and connoisseur, but most of the original details survived intact and unaltered. The rear walled garden, however, Martineau had to set out anew, and since the late 1970s the Trust has modified and embellished his design. There has been no slavish adherence to the eighteenth century. The flavour is simply of an old-fashioned town garden, formally designed with a central lawn and a circuit of straight paths between rectangular flower-beds. On the right day, it is extremely beautiful.

I say on the right day because in winter it suffers from being in the permanent shade of the house, and is exceptionally cold and gloomy and is, sensibly, closed to visitors during these months. The rain shadows from the walls and buildings also cause problems, the shortage of moisture exacerbated by the chalky soil; the lawn had to be relaid following the severe drought of 1976. However, the garden in summer is well stocked with plants, imaginatively chosen and performing splendidly under the adverse conditions. In shady beds, directly beside

LEFT: Yellow roses, 'Rosemary Rose' and delphiniums in the border at Mompesson House.

175

the north-facing façade of the house, *Stachys byzantina* and lavenders provide unexpected pools of silver, in the company of hardy geraniums, veronicas and annual tobacco flowers. This theme is reinforced by a fine pyramidal specimen of the seldom-seen Silver Pear, *Pyrus × canescens*, growing in the south-west corner of the lawn; it was planted in 1977 to commemorate the Queen's Silver Jubilee.

Further streams of lavender flank the path running towards the stone cartouche, commissioned by Denis Martineau and bearing the Mompesson coat of arms. Old-fashioned and other Shrub roses, including 'Königin von Dänemark', 'Marie de Blois', 'Comte de Chambord' and 'Buff Beauty', contribute a mass of flowers at midsummer, while in spring, *Magnolia × soulangeana*, underplanted with Lily of the Valley and *Anemone blanda*, bears its pink-flushed chalices against the east-facing wall.

The north wall adjoins the cathedral close, but the intimacy of the garden is preserved by mophead acacias, clipped every few years to keep them within bounds. In front, the south-facing border presents a cheerful mix of daffodils, tulips and Canterbury Bells in spring, and hollyhocks, peonies, irises, mallows, columbines and delphiniums in summer, the whole tended in the cottage-garden style, with bulbs and annuals pushed freely into any gaps that appear. The small greenhouse nearby is crammed with pelargoniums, coleus and begonias for the house; on its exterior wall grows the jasmine-like *Trachelospermum asiaticum*.

The pergola to the east of the lawn provides a contrasting shady walk. Wisteria, evergreen *Clematis armandii*, winter-flowering *C. cirrhosa* var. *balearica*, *C.* 'Perle d'Azur' and honeysuckle, *Lonicera × americana*, give a succession of flowers; there is a striking disparity in leafing and flowering times between the plants of 'Perle d'Azur' at the sunny and shady ends. Fastigiate rosemary fills in the gaps at the base of the stone columns, and the interior glows with the lime-yellow foliage of golden philadelphus. On a warm summer afternoon, the scents are intoxicating. Pots of fuchsias, tender rhododendrons, bulbs and annuals, together with a fig, Judas Tree, scented viburnum and ornamental quince decorate the courtyard beyond. And viewed against the sun, through the windows of the garden-room teashop, the red leaves and black grapes of the Teinturier Vine are a sumptuous finale.

Monk's House

Rodmell, Lewes, East Sussex

4 miles south-east of Lewes in Rodmell village nr church

Area 1¾ acres (0·7 ha)
Soil alkaline/loam
Altitude 50 ft (15 m)
Average rainfall 35 in (889 mm)
Average winter climate mild
Staff maintained by tenant

'Back from a good week-end at Rodmell – a week-end of no talking, sinking at once into deep safe book reading; and then sleep: clear, transparent; with the May tree like a breaking wave outside; and all the garden green tunnels, mounds of green: and then to wake into the hot still day, and never a person to be seen, never an interruption; the place to ourselves: the long hours' (Virginia Woolf's diary, 1932).

Virginia Woolf and her husband Leonard bought Monk's House as a country retreat in 1919. A modest 'unpretending' building, clad in whitewashed weatherboard, and hidden down a lane at the edge of the village, it was to be a source of great happiness for many years. Leonard had fallen for the garden even before he became owner of the house. A cheerful assembly of low flint walls (the remnants of a piggery) and fruit trees, lawns and vegetable plot, it soon began to take on a bright and exotic air – Leonard's choice of plants no doubt influenced by his time in the Colonial Office in Ceylon. Today, after a period of decline, it is

Mixed planting and terracotta jars by the conservatory at Monk's House.

once again full of colour and character, although, because the garden has to be managed part-time by the tenants, more relaxed cottage gardening prevails.

Near the lane, a Holm Oak presides over a shady little Italian garden, complete with pond, the dark greens of yew and ivy, and Florentine ornaments. The main garden is on the sloping ground behind the house. A Chusan Palm greets you as you turn the corner, with, to the left, a lushly stocked conservatory, rudely flaunting the terracotta rear of a copy of Donatello's *David*. The frost-free half of the conservatory contains pelargoniums, fuchsias, clivias and other pot plants; the unheated section houses an old grapevine, datura, jasmine, camellia and tall pink crinums. From here the garden looks small and intimate, a pattern of brick paths, decorated with mill stones, punctuated by terracotta jars each containing a spiky yucca or agave, and bordered by cottage plantings of mock orange, geraniums and Feverfew; bold displays of fuchsia and osteospermum reflect the coastal climate. But as you explore, the site opens out. Another formal section is revealed, where coreopsis and cosmea, larkspur and gazania, gladioli and dahlias foam in summer, and in spring, wallflowers and tulips.

Bordering the walled gardens are quieter grassed areas, shaded by fruit and other ornamental trees and with a dew pond, made by Leonard. His and Virginia's ashes were scattered under the two elm trees that once stood in the hedge behind. The path from the southern walled garden leads out into the orchard and to the spire of St Peter's church. 'Our orchard is the very place to sit and talk for hours in', Virginia wrote. In spring, belts of crocuses and daffodil bloom here, and in summer, the long grass sways with wildflowers.

It is a contrast to the smooth sward maintained on the bowling green beyond. Now the garden's greatest surprise is sprung, for the ground drops and the landscape opens out to reveal a bald panorama of downs and water meadows. Virginia's writing-room, a weather-board outbuilding standing by the churchyard, looks over it, and the views were her greatest delight. At the bottom of the valley flows the River Ouse, into which Virginia stepped, terrified by her approaching madness and with her pockets weighed down with stones.

Montacute House

Montacute, Somerset

4 miles west of Yeovil on
south side of A3088

Area 12 acres (4·8 ha)
Soil alkaline/sandy silt loam,
   some clay
Altitude 250 ft (76 m)
Average rainfall 30 in (762 mm)
Average winter climate moderate
Staff three

A row of clipped yews marches
across the lawns towards one of
the pavilions at Montacute.

The Elizabethan mansion, ascending through three tiers of massive leaded windows, surmounted by soaring chimneys and high curved gables, dominates its site. Montacute was built of the same golden stone as nearby Tintinhull House for Sir Edward Phelips, at the turn of the seventeenth century. Its west front, which was added in 1785, was in fact a Tudor construction taken from another house, and is an edifice ornate with pillars and balustrades, statues, pinnacles and other carved details. Because the drive dips and rises, it looks deceptively close. In fact, it is a quarter of a mile from the wrought-iron gates to the door.

Such scale and ornament, designed to impress, is reflected also in the garden, where decorative walls and pavilions, lawns, trees and processions of trim Irish Yews (96 in all) make for a stately setting of green and gold courts, terraces and gravel walks. The framework is largely original, but the internal design was altered in the eighteenth century, and what you see today is the work of Ellen Helyar, who married into the Phelips family in 1845, and, with her able gardener, Mr Pridham (whom she brought with her from her family home, Coker Court), re-created and reinterpreted the Elizabethan style of gardening here. It is one of the many historic reconstructions prompted by the awakened Victorian interest in the architecture and gardening of the past.

The southern approach walk takes you past cauldrons of golden yew and variegated holly, a soaring Monterey Cypress and curious feathery evergreen tumps – in fact, giant redwoods transformed into multi-stemmed shrubs after their trunks were felled in the last war – and onward to the North Court, the grandest of the green enclosures. This is the site of the original Elizabethan garden; its shape and probably its raised walks dating from that period. Like many contemporary gardens, it once featured a mount, but this seems to have vanished by 1825 and is now replaced by a substantial balustraded lily pool, in a setting of neat lawns, broad gravel walks, seats and ornaments.

Flowers, formerly arranged by Ellen Phelips into an elaborately patterned parterre, are now largely confined to the fringes of the broad north terrace. *Yucca recurvifolia* and the richly fragrant *Daphne* × *burkwoodii* 'Somerset' grow by the upper walls, and below the terrace is a pair of borders filled with old-fashioned species and Hybrid Musk roses, including the incense-scented climbing Musk, *Rosa* 'Princesse de Nassau' (syn. *R. moschata* 'Autumnalis') – all simply underplanted with the bluish-leaved *Hosta fortunei* var. *hyacinthina*.

FAR RIGHT: Pink and purple
shrub roses fringing the north
terrace, with a view between the
topiary yews out into the park.

Purple smoke bush, clematis, achilleas, macleaya and coreopsis in the mixed borders of Montacute's East Court.

In May, the white blossom of the hybrid thorn trees, *Crataegus × lavallei*, stands out well against the high, contoured yew hedge; they were introduced by the Trust as a replacement for frost-damaged cypresses and as rounded shapes to contrast with the vertical Irish Yews. And there is further colour in and around the Orangery where standard fuchsias, jasmine and scented rhododendron bloom around a fern-covered fountain of stone and tufa.

The main flower garden is now within the East Court, presided over by the house's most decorative front and framed by balustraded, obelisk-capped walls and a romantic pair of pavilions. This was the former Tudor entrance court, and at that time you would have arrived through an outer court and through a gatehouse, and had a better prospect of the high façade, which is rather overpowering at close range. Golden euphorbias and achilleas, orange and red roses and dahlias, and numerous other hot-coloured perennials, in a scheme first devised by Phyllis Reiss of Tintinhull, now contribute to the summer kaleidoscope in this part of the garden. Claret-leaved vine and Smoke Bush, and an assortment of crimson and deep purple clematis cloak the walls behind. Acanthus and macleaya add some structural foliage, and evergreen magnolias, crambe, peonies, yuccas and the highly scented Rugosa rose, 'Blanc Double de Coubert', give some contrasting notes of cream and white. Flower gardens do not come more richly appointed.

Beyond the car-park – formerly the kitchen garden – a spacious lawn, shaded by blue and green cedars and a fine pair of Sweet Chestnuts, leads to an arcaded garden house and a hedged semi-circle of lawn (added this century), adorned with stone columns, yew topiaries and mirror beds of spiky yucca. Arizona Cypress, Weeping Silver Lime and Cut-leaved Beech grow nearby, with evergreen oaks, pines, koelreuteria and Judas Tree, underplanted with a succession of bulbs, to be found in a small adjunct of rough meadow.

Although the garden is formally severed from the village and park by its walls, hedges and railings, the raised walks allow you to survey the rolling countryside and the lines and scattered clumps of the nineteenth-century parkland oaks. This adds to the sense of space. From various parts of the garden, you also have a prospect of the wooded conical hill above the village and church – the *mons acutus*, which gives Montacute its name – and the folly tower erected on it in 1760.

Moseley Old Hall

Moseley Old Hall Lane, Fordhouses, Wolverhampton, Staffordshire

4 miles north of Wolverhampton, south of M54 between A449 and A460

Area 1 acre (0·4 ha)
Soil acid to neutral/varied
Altitude 250 ft (76 m)
Average rainfall 27 in (686 mm)
Average winter climate cold
Staff part-time contractor

From a distance, there is little to commend this property: a plain brick house set in undistinguished farmland. There are, however, surprises in store. Walk through the studded back door of the hall and you step back two centuries further than you expected; the nineteenth-century brickwork is merely cladding. Panelled and whitewashed rooms are revealed, with low ceilings and exposed timbers, heavy oak furniture, pewter and Royalist portraits. If you are reading the guidebook, an adventure unfolds simultaneously. For in 1651, the hall was a hiding place for Charles II after his defeat at the Battle of Worcester. He arrived, disguised as a woodcutter, and concealed himself two days later beneath a trapdoor in a bedroom cupboard while Parliamentarian troops passed by. He then escaped by night, disguised as a servant, to safety in France.

The King's Gate, standing between the Sweet Chestnut paddock and Nut Alley, marks his entry into the garden. But whether the present disposition of covered walks and orchards, roses and patterns of box resembles the garden he encountered, no one can say. For when the Trust took possession of the hall, the site was derelict. What you see is an educated piece of guesswork, a full-blown reconstruction of a small seventeenth-century garden, its design details drawn from contemporary sources and its plants those known to have been in cultivation before 1700. The red walls that surround the garden do it no favours, and on the wrong day, especially in late summer when flowers are few, the mood is very sober. But at rose and apple blossom time, or in autumn when the vines are turning, there are many features that will lodge in your memory.

Most celebrated of these is the Knot Garden. Executed in box, the simple geometric design

LEFT: The timber tunnel arbour of claret vines woven with *Clematis viticella* and *Clematis flammula* underplanted with Old English Lavender at Moseley Old Hall.

was copied from one laid out in Yorkshire in the 1640s by a Rev. Walter Stonehouse. In his original scheme, ornamental plants were grown inside the beds, but for ease of maintenance gravels have been used here; and the result is satisfyingly crisp. Like all knot gardens, it is best viewed from the upper windows of the house.

The covered walks provide some shade and a contrast in flavour. A succession of bulbs, including snowdrops and Winter Aconites, Snakeshead Fritillaries, colchicums and autumn cyclamen, accompany the hazels in the Nut Alley, while on the wall behind romps Shakespeare's Musk rose, *Rosa arvensis*. An arbour of hornbeam leads into the most beautiful passage of all, a tunnel of claret vines, *Vitis vinifera* 'Purpurea', *Clematis viticella* and *C. flammula* edged with Old English lavender. Constructed of oak, with arching sides as well as a vaulted roof, it is an absorbing structure in its own right. The design was taken from an illustration in Thomas Hill's *The Gardener's Labyrinth*, published in 1577. But with the sun shining through them, the dusky black vine leaves are transformed, and the interior of the tunnel acquires stained windows of ruby red. There is a lesson here in the placing of all purple-leaved plants.

The marriage of the utilitarian and ornamental sets the theme of the garden. The trees that line the central path all provide fruit for the house – medlar, Black Mulberry, quince and Morello Cherry. The cherries on the large, spreading Cornelian Dogwood, *Cornus mas*, would also have been stewed to make preserves. Herbs, used for cooking, medicine or strewing, fringe the house walls. And there are niches for bee-skeps beside the barn.

But from medieval times, gardeners took delight in growing plants simply for their

The Knot Garden with its standard box balls at Moseley.

flowers – sweet-scented roses and Eglantine against walls, for example, and wildflowers in meadow grass. Here, the apples and pears stand among narcissi and other spring and early summer perennials, and around the walls there is a varied cast of roses. Against the south façade of the house, above a bed of unimproved marigolds, sunflowers, sweet peas and other annuals, grows the true Musk rose, *Rosa moschata*, an ancient garden plant valued for its late-summer flowering.

There is a concentration of Shrub roses accompanying the tiny lawns and box topiaries in the front garden, reached from the main plot by a wrought-iron gate. The Jacobite rose, 'Alba Maxima', the Red Rose of Lancaster, *R. gallica* var. *officinalis*, and the Autumn Damask, *R. × damascena* var. *semperflorens*, are among the cast. A mixed array of cottage perennials adds to the colour and extends the season, including red and pink peonies, yellow daylilies, Madonna Lilies, Florentine Iris, Solomon's Seal and double pink *Saponaria officinalis* 'Rosea Plena', a herb long used in making soap.

Mottisfont Abbey

Mottisfont, nr Romsey, Hampshire

4½ miles north-west of Romsey, ¾ mile west of A3057

Area 25 acres (10ha)
Soil alkaline/thin loam over gravel
Altitude 110ft (33m)
Average rainfall 29in (737mm)
Average winter climate moderate
Staff three

Rosa 'Graham Thomas' at Mottisfont Abbey. The extensive rose collection at Mottisfont was assembled over many years by Graham Stuart Thomas, Gardens Consultant to the Trust.

Push open the green door of Mottisfont's walled garden at midsummer and you plunge into a sea of roses. Not the gaudy roses of today, but the pink and crimson roses of yesterday, eulogised by the classical poets, painted by the Dutch masters, assiduously collected by the Empress Josephine and hybridised by the nurserymen of nineteenth-century France: rounded, petal-packed, drenched in fragrance and giving, in the main, one bountiful, mid-June to early July performance. There is nothing to equal them.

The paths lead you along their ranks, past the Apothecary's Rose and Red Rose of Lancaster, *R. gallica* var. *officinalis*, and its pink-striped sport 'Rosa Mundi'; the Jacobite Rose, 'Alba Maxima', the White Rose of York, 'Alba Semi-plena' and the soft pink 'Great Maiden's Blush', known since the fifteenth century; past Damask roses, Cabbage roses, Moss roses and on to those carrying the inheritance of the Autumn Damask and, more importantly, of the

A white garden seat in the Walled Garden framed by *Rosa* 'Adélaïde d'Orléans'.

China roses, conferring the much desired ability to flower late or continuously: the short Portlands, the Bourbons, the Hybrid Perpetuals, the China roses themselves and their early Tea rose hybrids.

The collection was assembled over many years by the eminent rosarian and Gardens Consultant to the Trust, Graham Stuart Thomas, and brought here in 1972, when the garden became available. The formal design, echoing the original kitchen garden layout, is founded on four open plots of grass, framed by borders and an outer box-edged walk – a clever piece of geometry, in fact, since none of the walls was parallel or is the same length. The centrepiece is a circular lily pool, flanked by pillars of Irish Yew and with a low dome of the pink rose 'Raubritter' spilling into it, providing the enhancing note of asymmetry. It is to this that the sweep of yellow gravel carries the eye as you enter the garden. The borders either side of

185

the path, also planned by Graham Stuart Thomas and almost entirely herbaceous, are a lesson in planting design, demonstrating the virtue of a restricted palette, of orchestrating the colours in clear bands, of providing vertical shapes to complement the mounds, of repeating key subjects and of much else. They are among the most perfectly schemed borders I have come upon. In 1982, ten years after this garden was planted, the adjacent enclosure to the north became available, allowing a home for a further collection of old roses, acquired by Graham Stuart Thomas from the German National Rose Garden at Sangerhausen.

But the rose gardens are by no means Mottisfont's only attraction. The abbey itself, a grand and romantic medieval house remodelled in the Tudor and Georgian periods, lies low amid undulating parkland, sweeping lawns and gigantic plane, cedar, Sweet Chestnut and beech trees. The prize specimen is a twin-trunked London Plane (in reality, two trees melded together), over 130 feet (40 m) high, with a 40-foot (12-m) girth and with a canopy covering a third of an acre; it is possibly the largest tree in the country. But there are also fine old mulberry and crab apple trees; good specimens of hornbeam, walnut, Tulip Tree and the more upright bean tree, *Catalpa speciosa*; and a short-trunked oak, probably as old as the medieval abbey itself.

The topsoil here is dry and gravelly, but underneath there is water. A tributary of the famous trout river, the Test, flows just to the east of the house (you can walk along its banks the half mile to the hamlet of Oakley), fed by the adjacent spring, or font, that probably gives the abbey its name; Mottis – being derived from the Saxon *moot* meaning 'meeting-place'. The clear water rises into the deep pool at a rate of at least 200 gallons (909 litres) a minute, and is carried off by a stream, bordered by blue hostas and yellow *Primula florindae*.

Two noted designers have contributed effective formal details to this part of the garden, both commissioned by Mr and Mrs Gilbert Russell, who bought the property in 1934. Geoffrey Jellicoe introduced grass terraces, one bordered by a contrasting run of lavender, speared by clipped Irish Yews; an octagon of English Yew; and a connecting walk of pleached limes, underplanted with chionodoxa. It is a crisp and simple linear treatment, in his own words, 'muted to leave the existing ethos of place undisturbed'. A couple of years later, in 1938, Norah Lindsay set out a small parterre on the south side of the house, edged in lavender and box, and filled seasonally with bedding plants in a pattern of blue and cream for spring, and yellow and mauve for summer.

Later, Russell Page was asked to recommend shrubs for the garden. Some of these, with later additions, are grouped along the house walls – among them, *Schizophragma integrifolia* growing on the north-east corner, and, on the sheltered, sunny wall behind the parterre, quite tender plants like *Feijoa* (syn. *Acca*) *sellowiana*, *Hoheria lyallii*, *Ceanothus thyrsiflorus* and the climbing Tea rose 'Lady Hillingdon' picking up the apricot tints in the brick. Others, primarily for a late summer display, are massed in beds flanking the eighteenth-century Gothick summer-house; hypericums, fuchsias, hebes, potentillas and the Paperbark Maple, *Acer griseum*, are among those demonstrating their tolerance of the chalk.

Elsewhere, there is a collection of *Magnolia* × *soulangeana* varieties, underplanted with crocus and daffodils. And recently, the Trust has been enriching the area beyond the river with more bulbs and autumn-coloured shrubs, including Shrub roses and viburnums, to enhance the existing display from the red-stemmed dogwood. But none of these interrupts the peace of the garden, induced by the grass, the trees and the sound of bubbling water.

FAR RIGHT: Hybrid perpetual Rose 'Magna Charta' with campanulas and salvias at Mottisfont.

Mount Stewart

Newtownards, Co. Down

5 miles south-east of
Newtownards on A20
Portaferry road

Area 80 acres (32 ha)
Soil acid/brown earth
   overlying beach deposits
Altitude 0–80 ft (0–24 m)
Average rainfall 35 in (889 mm)
Average winter climate almost
   frost-free
Staff six

The Spanish Garden at Mount
Stewart, flanked by high arched
hedges of Leyland Cypress.

This is an extraordinary place, a flight of fancy on the grandest scale. It is a garden founded on rare and exotic plants, strange and mythical beasts, poetry and symbolism, and only the most sullen of visitors will be able to resist the dream-like state it induces, the moment you plunge into its 80 lushly wooded acres (32 ha). But, when its creator Edith, Marchioness of Londonderry, first visited her husband's family home, some years before he inherited in 1915, she thought 'the house and surroundings were the dampest, darkest and saddest place I had ever stayed in'. From 1921, the transformation began.

The hillside's south-facing aspect, its all-important sheltering woods, the influence of the adjacent salt-water lough, and above all its close proximity to the Irish Sea and the Gulf Stream create mild, humid, almost subtropical conditions. These, with the help of her gardening mentors, Sir John Ross of Rostrevor, Co. Down, and Sir Herbert Maxwell of Monreith, Scotland, she exploited to the full, joining them to an idiosyncratic design and a theatre of imagery, evoking family history and Irish legend.

The house opens exotically on to a view of New Zealand cabbage palms, and 100-foot (30-m) high Tasmanian gum trees *Eucalyptus globulus*, punctuating stone terraces, a grand sunken Italian parterre and, terminating the vista, a Spanish water parterre and tiled garden house. The quantity of architectural and horticultural detail is mind-boggling, and it takes a moment to adjust to it. The cast of plants on the upper terrace alone will provoke a good many gasps: fat clumps of spiky fascicularia, *Puya alpestris* and *Beschorneria yuccoides*, planted in 1922; soaring white and yellow Banksian Roses and *Rosa gigantea*; scarlet Lobster's Claw, *Clianthus puniceus*, above a hummock of China blue Chatham Island forget-me-not,

The Ladies' Walk stream, running through the bog garden, contains purple phormium, orange euphorbia, bluebells, primroses and ferns.

Myosotidium hortensia. Edgings of purple berberis, white heather, blue rue, golden thuja and silvery hebe, frame the herbaceous plants on the parterre below; and in the Spanish Garden, Leyland cypresses are clipped to make an open hedge of tight arches.

Already there are references and allusions in the design – among them coronets and a picture of George and the Dragon made in cobbles on the terrace. On the adjacent Dodo Terrace, the imagery is at its most playful. Here, cement statues of the Ark and various living, extinct or mythical creatures, including a dinosaur *Stegosaurus*, hedgehog, mermaid, frog and monkey, as well as four dodos, relate to the First World War and Lady Londonderry's Ark Club; members, drawn from the family, politics, the armed forces and other branches of the war effort, were given the Order of the Rainbow (the sign of hope) and an animal name.

189

A cement mermaid and harp on the Dodo Terrace at Mount Stewart. She is one of many exotic features to be found in this garden of rare plants and strange statuary.

Close by is the Mairi Garden, named after Lady Londonderry's daughter, Lady Mairi Vane-Tempest-Stewart (later Viscountess Bury), overlooked by a summer-house and dovecote, and designed in the shape of a Tudor rose. The nursery rhyme 'Mairi, Mairi, quite contrary', is illustrated with cockle shells, silver bells (campanulas) and Pretty Maids (*Saxifraga granulata* 'Flore Pleno'). Everywhere there are choice, tender and luxuriant plants, grouped for harmony of flower colour and contrast of shape and foliage: among them you will find *Melianthus major*, *Lapageria rosea*, *Camellia japonica* 'Akashigata' (syn. *C. j* 'Lady Clare'), *Fuchsia excorticata*, *Pittosporum eugenioides*, *Cupressus arizonica* (beautifully partnered with blue hydrangeas), *Olearia phlogopappa*, *Stipa arundinacea* (syn. *Apera arundinacea*), agapanthus and crinums.

To the west of the house, further rooms are revealed. The large Sunken Garden, divided from the terrace by great domes of clipped sweet bay (like those on the north Front Court, imported fully grown from Belgium) and based on a design sent by post by Gertrude Jekyll, is enclosed on three sides by a stone pergola, hung with vines, yellow and apricot roses (including another superb *R. gigantea*), and blue and violet clematis, ceanothus and solanum. Tender rarities join them, such as *Lardizabala biternata*, *Dendromecon rigida*, *Mutisia oligodon* and *Hakea sericea*; *H. ulicina* has grown against the south-facing wall since 1922. And borders of Azalea 'Coccineum Speciosum', flame red but peppered with orange and yellow-bloomed branches that have risen from the rootstocks, fuel the colour scheme. In summer, the herbaceous beds below flaunt electric blue delphiniums and hoops of imperial purple *Clematis × jackmanii*. Beyond is the famous garden of Irish symbolism, a hedged enclosure in the shape of a shamrock, containing a topiary Irish Harp, and, coloured in seasonal annuals, the Red Hand of Ulster. Other topiary is being restored.

This lush wooded backdrop, a patchwork of greens and an assortment of silhouettes from oaks and limes, pines and Wellingtonias, cypresses and eucalyptus, is highlighted in spring with flashes of colour from rhododendrons. I recall my first foray into this wood on a balmy afternoon in early May, walking through cool glades of emerald ferns and blue Himalayan poppies and, with each breath, tasting the scents of tender, white-flowered rhododendrons. At every turn, there is a plant to amaze or confound you: *Luma apiculata* (syn. *Myrtus luma*), *Rhododendron sinogrande*, *Gevuina avellana*, nothofagus, eucalyptus, magnolias, candelabra primulas, *Dryopteris affinis* (syn. *D. pseudomas*), tree ferns and giant lilies (Cardiocrinum).

There is more in the Memorial Glade, planted by Lady Mairi Bury after her mother's death in 1959: scarlet embothriums, yellow azaleas, orange-cupped narcissi, white lilacs, purple hydrangeas and *Prunus sargentii*. And among the towering conifers beyond, huge specimens of *Rhododendron arboreum* and *R. macabeanum* light up the drive with spring colour; later, the beacons are Handkerchief Tree, hydrangeas and white-flowered eucryphias, including the tender *E. cordifolia*.

As you return to the green woods and open lawns to the north of the house, you might easily assume that this dream sequence was now reaching its end. But you would be mistaken. A short walk up the hillside, and you find yourself looking across a 5-acre (2-ha) lake, excavated by the 3rd Marquess in the 1840s, fringed by water plants, a new cast of ornamental trees and shrubs (including some superb red rhododendrons such as half-hardy *R. elliottii* and *R. facetum* (syn. *R. eriogynum*), and, in the distance, the towers and walls of yet another formal garden. The larger part of the garden tour is yet to come.

The towers and walls belong to Tir Nan Og (Gaelic for 'The Land of the Ever Young'), the family burial ground built by Lord and Lady Londonderry in the 1920s. According to the legend, it is a great white stag that bears you to Heaven, and on the east side of the lake, you will glimpse it, between the trunks of trees, standing in a glade. The burial ground hillside is the sunniest and best-drained part of the garden, and an extensive range of Southern Hemisphere plants has been established here: among them, leptospermums, acacias, corokias, sophoras, callistemons, cassinias, hakeas, watsonias and kniphofias. This esoteric character is taken to extremes on Tir Nan Og's south wall, where the company includes such rarities as *Metrosideros umbellatus* (syn. *M. lucidus*), *Kennedia rubicunda*, *Vallea stipularis* and *Picconia excelsa*. Below are fine stands of echiums.

The eastern return route is through the Jubilee Avenue, planted in 1936 to mark the Silver Jubilee of King George V and Queen Mary. The patriotic theme of red, white and blue is achieved with embothriums, fuchsia, photinia and *Rosa moyesii*; cherries, philadelphus, rhododendrons and white hydrangeas; ceanothus, solanum, blue hydrangeas and *Eucalyptus globulus*. A streamside garden of primulas and complementary plants follows, decorated with ornaments brought back by Lord and Lady Londonderry from Japan. And then, once again, it is headlong into rhododendrons, fifteen undulating acres of hybrids and species leading you down to the house. In addition to the many with richly coloured flowers, there are choice forms grown for their scents, including tender *R. burmanicum*, *R. maddenii* and *R. johnstoneanum*; for their elephantine foliage, such as *R. sinogrande*, *R. magnificum*, *R. rex* subsp. *arizeleum* and *R. falconeri*; and for their fine bark, such as chocolate-hued *R. genestierianum*. This is a garden no one can afford to miss.

Nostell Priory

Doncaster Road, Nostell,
nr Wakefield, West Yorkshire

6 miles south-east of Wakefield
on A638 Doncaster road

Area 12 acres (4·8 ha)
Soil acid to neutral/clay
Altitude 200 ft (61 m)
Average rainfall 25 in (635 mm)
Average winter climate cold
Staff four

Behind this Palladian mansion, built for Sir Rowland Winn in about 1735 by the young James Paine and later modified by Robert Adam, the ground plunges into a self-contained landscape of lakes and trees. It is a welcome oasis at the edge of the Leeds/Wakefield conurbation, and a refresher for drivers as they cross the hump-backed bridge on the Doncaster road. Sir Rowland commissioned the famous gardener Stephen Switzer to prepare plans for this park, though little of it seems to remain, and his clump planting of trees was largely obscured by the introduction of rhododendrons, conifers and other exotics in the Victorian era. The more ornamental portion of the park is on the west side of the middle lake. Here the hiss of Cut-leaved Beeches and the scent of mock-orange and pine ushers you into the shadows, where the rhododendron belts are edged with foxglove, campion, comfrey and hosta. Snowdrops, daffodils and bluebells succeed each other in spring, and in early June, the shrubs of *Rosa* 'Paulii' are a mass of white.

Shortly, you find yourself in the Dell, following a curving path between neatly mown lawns and a grove of *Magnolia* × *soulangeana*. Beds of azaleas and Japanese maples are backed by the exposed rock face, and *Hydrangea anomala* subsp. *petiolaris* scrambles up a stone column. A rhododendron tunnel and stone arch bring you back to the lakeside, and you can view the bridge from under the branches of a splendid Cedar of Lebanon; the view enhanced in spring by massed bulbs reflecting in the water.

Nunnington Hall

Nunnington, York,
North Yorkshire

4½ miles south-east of
Helmsley

Area 8½ acres (3·4 ha)
Soil neutral/loam
Altitude 150 ft (46 m)
Average rainfall 25 in (635 mm)
Average winter climate moderate
Staff one

While an epic landscape of avenues, triumphal arches and obelisks was being fashioned by the Earl of Carlisle and Sir John Vanbrugh at nearby Castle Howard, a more modest formal garden was being perfected at Nunnington. Enough details remain, or have been restored, to give us an insight into the appearance of a country squire's garden of the late seventeenth and early eighteenth centuries. The sandstone house, part Elizabethan and part Stuart, is rather plain, but the assortment of roofs, chimneys and gables, in company with the sycamores, oaks and willows, gate pillars and hump-backed bridge over the river, makes a picturesque first impression. You approach the house across a wooden footbridge, and crunch across a gravel court enclosed by beech hedges. Robinias, aralia, *Hydrangea paniculata* 'Praecox', wall-trained Morello cherries, and, quite likely, displaying peacocks, draw your eye *en route* to the main, walled south garden.

A generous rectangle of grass, formalised into close-mown lawn and flanking squares of rough orchard, occupies the bulk of the space. The apple trees are all local varieties reintroduced by the Trust. For Ryedale, although a frosty valley with a short growing season, had a thriving industry in producing long-storing fruit for the sailing ships; 'Burr Knott', 'Cockpit', 'Gooseberry' and 'Dog's Snout' are among the idiosyncratic names.

Fruit, grown in the company of flowers, was a valued ingredient of gardens from the Elizabethan era onwards, and here pears are also trained on the surrounding walls, where they play host to a large collection of clematis. Beside the wall to the east of the house are glamorous displays of mainly pink, red and white Hybrid Tea and Floribunda roses, punctuated by standard 'Iceberg' roses and catmint in post-war style.

The hidden garden of tall and dwarf bearded irises is a pretty sight at midsummer, when the fringes of cottage pinks are also scenting the air. These colourful plantings reflect the gardening of Mrs Ronald Fife, who restored much of the hall in the 1920s and bequeathed it to the Trust on her death in 1952.

Nymans

Handcross, nr Haywards
Heath, West Sussex

4½ miles south of Crawley
on B2114

Area 30 acres (12 ha)
Soil acid/sandy loam
Altitude 500 ft (152 m)
Average rainfall 30 in (762 mm)
Average winter climate cold
Staff five

The wooded ridges and valleys of the Sussex Weald were in the eye of the great storm of October 1987, and the high plateau and slopes of Nymans, with their plantations of rare and wild-collected trees and shrubs, were hit by winds of 100 mph. Woods and shelter belts collapsed and more than 80 per cent of the garden's specimen trees were destroyed. Today, with the monumental clearance operation long completed and new plantings established and maturing, many of the scenes must resemble those of a hundred years previously, when the stockbroker Ludwig Messel was first alerted to the horticultural opportunities of the time, and, with his talented head gardener James Comber, began annexing the countryside.

This is particularly true in the pinetum below the entrance gate, where, but for a few remaining Giant and Dawn redwoods and other trees, the collection was flattened. You now look out on a sweeping panorama eastward to Crowborough ridge, with the foreground occupied by a cast of young conifers thrusting upward. As before, they are arranged in a horseshoe shape around the wide paddock. Fast-growing birch, larch, cherry and southern beech lend some temporary shelter, and clumps of white-plumed pampas grass provide some telling autumn contrast.

The Summer borders at
Nymans with cleome, cosmos,
snapdragons, canna and other
summer bedding, backed by
eupatorium, helianthus and
buddleja.

Those who knew Nymans before the storm will certainly regret the exchange of the
intimate, dappled, rather mysterious spaces for the present, more exposed hilltop, dotted
with trees looking thin-crowned and a little shell-shocked, but the redevelopment does have
its own excitement, and there is now a richer plant variety than at any time in its history.
Much was lost on the night of October 16th, but there was also much that could be salvaged.
The detailed records held in *The Woody Plant Catalogue* – a continuously updated listing of
the trees growing in the more important collections – gave the Trust the name and origin
of the fallen species. Propagation material was taken from the rarest specimens and those
with the most valuable genetic pedigrees, and dispatched to nurseries. The resulting plants,
together with those supplied by other tree collections and botanic gardens, and the spoils
of more recent plant-collecting expeditions, formed the basis for a replanting programme.
Along with the specimens left standing by the storm (and there are many – this was an over-
stocked garden), the groups of young trees and shrubs are now establishing themselves.

The collection spills over almost all the garden, but each area has its own mood. In the small
Tea Garden, redeveloped with buildings by the contemporary architect Robert Adam, there

are cheery plantings of pink and white cherries, yellow hybrid rhododendrons and 'Mariesii Perfecta' (syn. 'Blue Wave') hydrangeas give a succession of summer flowers; autumn colour comes from *Sorbus hupehensis* var. *obtusa* (syn. *S.h.* 'Rosea') and the Amur Cork Tree.

Meandering paths lead from the pinetum into a dappled plantation of large trees, rising from grass and shrubberies of camellia and rhododendron. Here there are fine specimens of Chinese *Davidia involucrata* var. *vilmoriniana*, *Meliosma veitchiorum* and *Styrax japonicus* 'Fargesii', as well as *Nothofagus menziesii* from New Zealand, and magnolias, *M.* × *veitchii* and melon-scented *M. hypoleuca*.

Magnolias are a Nymans speciality, and their pink and white waterlilies and goblets are major contributors to the long spring season. Excellent hybrids, derived from the shrubby species, have been raised here, and the lilac-pink *M.* × *loebneri* 'Leonard Messel' grows in this upper enclosure beside its parents, *M. kobus* and *M. stellata* 'Rosea'; nearby, you come upon *M.* 'James Comber' and *M.* 'Michael Rosse' (named after the 6th Earl of Rosse). But tree magnolias were also planted with abandon, and, happily, proved themselves fairly gale-proof. There are impressive plants of *M. campbellii*, its hybrid 'Charles Rafill', and *M. sargentiana* in the nearby Wall Garden – all producing their blooms on bare branches in spring – in addition to cultivars of *M.* × *soulangeana* and *M. liliiflora*, and the summer-flowering *M. sieboldii*. *Styrax hemsleyanus* and *S. obassia*, *Cornus kousa* (striking when bearing its red fruits and crimson autumn leaves, as well as when covered in white bracts in June), and August-flowering eucryphias – including the evergreen *E.* × *nymansensis* 'Nymansay' raised by James Comber – are also here as fine specimens.

But the big woody plants are not the only attractions in these northern sections of the garden. There are daffodils, erythroniums and Snakeshead Fritillaries in the grass; ground-cover plants fringing the shrubberies (including notable runs of the gentian-blue *Omphalodes cappadocica*); a walk of camellias; double border of lupins, delphiniums, poppies, peonies and daylilies (to tide the garden over the June gap between the spring- and summer-flowering shrubs); and, against the warm south-facing wall of the walled garden, a bed of Chilean plants – abutilon, *Solanum crispum* and *Lobelia tupa*, among them – in honour of Harold Comber, James's son, who collected plants in South America and Tasmania from the mid-1920s.

On the approach to the Wall Garden, you come to a formal garden of old Shrub roses, recently renovated and much extended by the Trust. They were the enthusiasm of Maud Messel, who began collecting them in the 1920s during their lull in fashion; many were given to her by the rosarians Ellen Willmott and Edward Bunyard, others she found in France, and the collection became an important repository. And inside the Wall Garden, there is that spectacular, much-photographed, pair of high-summer Edwardian borders, steeply tiered, kaleidoscopically coloured, and fuelled with a large proportion of annuals to ensure a long and continuous performance. They run either side of an Italian marble fountain, flanked by intricate yew topiaries, and in their structure and impact have changed little since they were installed by Ludwig Messel.

The house looms over the wall to the east. It was built in 1928 in the style of a late-medieval manor house by Col and Mrs Leonard Messel as a replacement for his father's Victorian villa but, in the winter of 1947, it caught fire. The standpipes were frozen and before the flames could be brought under control, the building was gutted, with the loss of almost all its contents, including a notable library of botanical books. So the storm was not Nymans' first

The dovecote at Nymans seen between clipped yew topiary.

disaster. The event was turned to advantage, however, for although its rear section was rebuilt, the remainder was left as a ruin, roofless, jagged-walled, and with its high, mullioned windows glassless and gaping. Thus the garden gained a wonderfully romantic centrepiece. It stands, clothed in roses, honeysuckle, clematis, wisteria and (of course) evergreen magnolia, with some suitably quaint Old English accompaniments – fat topiary hens brooding on the gravel, a circular dovecote and a flock of white doves.

There are further turn-of-the-century touches on and beside the lawns that lead off to the south and east: a living basket, woven with winter jasmine and filled with red hydrangeas; a sunken garden, where a Byzantine urn stands in a pattern of spring and summer bedding, backed by an Italian loggia and four slim cypresses (*Chamaecyparis lawsoniana* 'Grayswood Pillar'); and details inspired by Japan – a long wisteria pergola (rebuilt after being smashed by the great storm), a weeping hornbeam (replacing the Wych Elm that died) and stone lanterns acquired from the Japanese Exhibition of 1903. The sombre Cherry Laurel walk is a reminder of an earlier era.

Along the perimeter of the garden, colourful camellias, azaleas, *Rhododendron arboreum* and hydrangeas give way to landscaped ground of hillock and dell. The acid sand is well suited to heathers, and Ludwig Messel made a collection here – possibly the first heath garden in the country. They grow in the company of pieris, conifers and some of the plant-hunters' dwarf rhododendrons such as *RR. anthopogon* subsp. *hypenanthum, calostrotum, saluenense* and *cerasinum*, and blend into hot Mediterranean and Southern Hemisphere beds of cistus, phlomis, origanum and prostanthera. Beyond, the ground falls and rises to the South Downs.

Ormesby Hall

Ormesby, nr Middlesbrough, Cleveland

On B1380 in Ormesby village, 3 miles south-east of Middlesbrough

Area 5 acres (2 ha) within parkland
Soil alkaline/heavy clay
Altitude 155 ft (47 m)
Average rainfall 27 in (686 mm)
Average winter climate cold
Staff one, plus two trainees

The park and farm at Ormesby now form an island of greenery set in the suburbs and industrial development area of Middlesbrough, but the hall still stands soberly in its rise, surveying pasture and woodland belt. Designed in the fashionable Palladian style, it was built in the 1740s for Sir James Pennyman, whose family had lived here since the fifteenth century. The grand stable block that accompanies the house is used by the Cleveland Mounted Constabulary, and the hefty police horses can be seen grazing the park.

The garden is formal in design, with modest terraces of mixed Hybrid Tea roses and lavender, close-mown lawn and specimen trees. Beds of delphiniums, agapanthus and seasonal annuals add further colour, and the house walls are part-draped in climbing roses and wisteria. Scarlet *Tropaeolum speciosum*, infiltrating the yew structures above the main lawn, is a memorable feature. In contrast to this formality, a loop to the east of the croquet lawn takes you towards the church, where William Lawson, author of *A New Orchard & Garden* of 1618, was vicar from 1583 to 1635. The ash, beech and oak copse is fringed in spring with snowdrops, aconites, daffodils and primroses, and later with cow parsley and aruncus. And in the lower part of the west garden, you are led into a holly walk and along a shady ribbon border. Much of the garden's character comes from trees. Bolstered by evergreen Portugal Laurel, they give a sheltering frame to the exposed site, and within the garden give the rather thin composition some weight and substance. Limes, chestnuts, crab apples and walnut are among the company, and there is a fine sycamore and Purple Beech.

Osterley Park

Isleworth, Middlesex

North of Osterley London
Underground Station
(Piccadilly line); access from
Syon Lane, north side of Great
West Road (A4), or from
Thornbury Road

Area 142 acres (57·5 ha)
Soil varied, some gravel and
  some clay
Altitude 100ft (30m)
Average rainfall 24in (610mm)
Average winter climate moderate
Staff five

Osterley Park, viewed through a
veil of weeping willow, across
the frozen lake.

'It is a pleasant drive between sweet little villages and villas to this park . . .' wrote one visitor in the autumn of 1786. How things have changed. Osterley has been engulfed in London's western conurbation, Heathrow is only 5 miles (8km) to the south-west, and the M4 has amputated the northern section of the park. But there are still 140 acres (57ha) of oasis remaining, and it is a surprise and relief suddenly to be able to exchange the roads, housing and light industry for a landscape of meadows, trees and lakes.

The house itself is the park's principal ornament, standing in the centre of the flat parkland, and as you follow the circuit walk, it provides a series of eye-catchers between the trees. From the east, there are views also of the stable block, the legacy of Sir Thomas Gresham, Chancellor of the Exchequer to Elizabeth I, who built the first great house here in the mid-sixteenth century.

The character of the flowing landscape park changed radically during the nineteenth century, in response to the taste for heavier and more varied scenery, and in this century the tree planting has continued apace. By the 1980s, the grounds were short-staffed and in serious decline, and it was then that a major restoration project was initiated.

On the west side of the house, you now look out on to a section of park, girdled once again with iron railings according to the nineteenth-century plans. The meadow within is grazed by impressive but benign Limousin cattle, and kissing gates allow you to wander across. As well as the many isolated, scattered trees, including Black Walnut and Turkey Oak, there are fenced-in plantations, again comprising mixed trees such as Horse and Sweet Chestnut, oak and hornbeam, but all underplanted with hazel or ringed with hawthorn, reminiscent of eighteenth-century clumps. The trees in the adjacent pleasure ground gradually blend into a pinetum, with closely mown lawn lapping about them. Adam's garden house and the Doric temple, by an unknown architect, are presently being parted by the reintroduction of a Regency flower garden, with myriad paisley beds of Shrub roses, pinks, rosemary and sweet peas, trained up wooden pyramids. This is one of the first gardens in this style that the Trust has re-created.

Beyond the pinetum and meadow is the lazy wilderness walk that takes you through glades of Hungarian and other oaks, darkened by holly, rhododendron and Portugal Laurel, and fringed with foxgloves, campion and other wildflowers, to the lower lake. Beginning as a narrow river, the channel swells as it curves past the fine Cork Oak, cedars and other specimen trees south of the house, to conclude in a wide pool, elegantly decorated with waterlilies and a Chinese water pagoda.

Beyond the drive, the second lake leads off to the north-east corner of the park. The main eighteenth-century attraction here was the menagerie of exotic birds on the east bank, reached by a rope-drawn ferry. Now, it is the native species that provide the entertainment, the park being large and peaceful enough for grebes, jays, owls and many other birds that have been driven from the rest of London. There is even a small heronry on the lake's island, a stone's throw from the rumbling motorway.

Overbecks

Sharpitor, Salcombe, Devon

1½ miles south-west of Salcombe, signposted from Marlborough and Salcombe; single-track lanes

Area 6 acres (2·4 ha)
Soil slightly alkaline
Altitude 100 ft (30 m)
Average rainfall 40 in (1,016 mm)
Average winter climate mild
Staff two

FAR RIGHT: 'First Flight', a bronze statue of a young girl by Albert Bruce Joy, overlooks the garden at Overbecks with its exotic subtropical plantings.

200

'It is so warm and beautiful here. I grow Bananas, Oranges, and Pomegranates in the open garden, and have 3,000 palm trees, planted out in my woods and garden.' So Otto Overbeck wrote in a letter to friends in 1933. Here on the balmy Devon riviera, this subtropical mood is appropriate and achievable. The house, perched on a shelf of rock high above Salcombe estuary, looks down across a coastline spangled with white holiday villas and a broad channel of water bobbing with yachts. Summers are long and winters are usually very mild, and the hillside and hanging woods provide shelter from the wind. The garden was already well established when Overbeck bought it in 1928. The grey stone walls that break the site into an irregular series of small enclosures, banks and terrace walks, were set out by Edric Hopkins at the turn of the century, and the subsequent owners, Mr and Mrs George Medlicott Vereker, extended and embellished the plantings after 1913. Otto Overbeck followed their example, and the Trust, in its turn, continues to develop the garden actively.

In contrast to the more famous Devon gardens, the soil here is alkaline and fast-draining, so there is no springtime surge of camellias and rhododendrons. But below the formal statue garden is an unforgettable March sight: a hundred-year-old *Magnolia campbellii* holding its deep pink chalices against the sea. Soon afterwards, daffodils, anemones, primroses and the carmine-pink *Cyclamen repandum* appear in sheets on the rough grass banks. *C. hederifolium* follows in late summer. The slightly tender, evergreen climber *Holboellia latifolia* sends sugary scent over the flagpole wall, and *Clematis armandii* wafts vanilla along the stairways. Other spring highlights include the long-racemed *Wisteria floribunda* 'Multijuga', the South African tree heather, *Erica canaliculata*, Camphor Tree from the Far East, *Euphorbia mellifera* from Madeira and the startling young red foliage of *Euonymus lucidus* from the Himalayas.

In summer, the beds are packed with the rich colours and unfamiliar shapes of a vast array of tender and half-hardy border and bulbous perennials. By the house and its lawn, you come upon agapanthus, crocosmias, dahlias, crinums, cannas and, in early autumn, hedychiums, eucomis and amaryllis; *Lobelia tupa*, *Fuchsia splendens*, the curious shrubby *F. excorticata* and the Chatham Island Forget-me-not grow in the rare damp and shady corners. By this time, the formal Statue Garden is a riot of osteospermums and argyranthemums, salvias,

kniphofias, echiums, sunflowers and other chirpy annuals. Elsewhere, the colour is boosted by shrubs, including olearias and massed hydrangeas.

Structure and focal points are furnished as much by foliage as by the walls and castellated parapets and gate-posts. Phormiums, potted agaves and palm trees are ubiquitous, with additional spiky notes coming from cordyline, yucca, astelia, fascicularia and beschorneria. The lush tropical flavour of canna and hedychium is echoed by the giant paddles of the hardiest banana, *Musa basjoo*, and by the great trumpets of daturas. Italian and golden Monterey cypresses make arresting pillars, and the various pittosporums unusually coloured domes and cushions. And on the bank above the house lawn, the myrtle, *Luma apiculata*, creates a grove of cinnamon-suede trunks; like the Chusan Palm, echium and *Cornus capitata*, this species self-sows freely.

This is merely a taste of what is here. The paths lead you to one treasure after another, each strikingly partnered for maximum impact. In another setting, the variety might be excessive, but at Overbecks there is always the tempering harmony of sweeping sea views. This is not a grand or historically important property; the only inspiring feature of the house – a plain, modestly sized Edwardian villa – is the conservatory, where the old citrus trees spend the winter. (A new parterre now provides a summer home for the orange and lemon trees.) But the garden is a treat.

Oxburgh Hall

Oxborough, nr King's Lynn, Norfolk

7 miles south-west of Swaffham, on south side of Stoke Ferry road

Area 18½ acres (7·5 ha)
Soil alkaline–neutral/sandy, clay
Altitude 100 ft (30 m)
Average rainfall 25 in (635 mm)
Average winter climate cold
Staff two, plus two trainees

The moated hall rises from flat ground into a broad Norfolk sky. Built and fortified for Sir Edmund Bedingfield in about 1482, it was romanticised and remodelled for the 6th and 7th baronets in the mid-nineteenth century. The landscape has also been tamed, for the surrounding fields were marshland until drained and dyked in the late eighteenth century. Woods and belts of trees give some intimacy and shelter from the worst of the wind, and the warm red brickwork is cheery even on a grey day.

The garden's *pièce de résistance* lies beneath the hall's east front, an elaborately scrolled and patterned *parterre de compartiment* laid out by Sir Henry Paston Bedingfield, the 6th Baronet, and his wife Margaret, in about 1845. The design was taken from a garden they saw in Paris, and is very similar to one illustrated in *La Theorie et la pratique du jardinage*, published anonymously in 1709, by the French engraver and writer on the arts Antoine-Joseph Dezallier d'Argenville. Originally, the colour in such parterres was provided not by flowers but by gravels and other materials. Here, crushed chalk, black stone and painted cement were used, but in addition to massed annuals. It is remarkable that such a labour-intensive feature managed to survive for so many years, although it was in urgent need of attention by the time it came into the Trust's hands.

To reduce the amount of bedding required, blue rue and *Cineraria maritima* 'Silver Dust' have been added to some of the shapes, but each spring, the gardeners still plant out quantities of *Geranium* 'Paul Crampel', marigolds and ageratum – the violet-blue and yellow in the pattern being reversed each year, to ring a subtle change in appearance. Crushed stone, tightly cropped grass, yew globes and dwarf box edging complete the scheme, and the whole design is set off by lawn. Such a ground-hugging scheme preserves the sense of openness and isolation, for the hall stands alone in the smooth, empty plane of water, grass and gravel drives. Apart from the weeping willow on the south-west corner of the moat, the trees stand as a frame beyond the lawn, the tall oaks and beeches being joined by the favourite Victorian cedars and Wellingtonias. Beside the Gothic chapel, a path leads into the recently restored Victorian Wilderness. The lime avenue here is sheeted with bluebells in late spring, and the meandering paths on either side are bordered with snowdrops and daffodils.

Across the lawn from the parterre, a clipped yew hedge screens the long herbaceous border, where aconitum, lupins, delphiniums and irises rise behind a run of catmint, and the old wall is cloaked with clematis, roses and soft shrubs. For practical and economic reasons, the large Victorian kitchen garden behind, enclosed by castellated walls and turreted towers, has been converted by the Trust into orchard. Mulberries were the intended theme, but they suffered so badly from canker that they were eventually replaced with a collection of plums and gages, grown as half-standards. Medlars, quinces and pears are also part of the pattern, with sweet bays growing in pairs by the towers. At the north end is the working area, with a vegetable and cut-flower bed bordered by a picket fence. Sun-loving flowering and foliage shrubs bask against the potting-shed wall, on the site of the old peach and vinery houses. The scheme includes cistuses, romneya, potentilla, Trumpet Vine (*Campsis radicans*), woolly *Buddleja crispa*, ceanothus and the large-leaved vine, *Vitis coignetiae*.

From the space and formal order of these areas, you can follow the stream beyond the border of spring bulbs and summer shrubs, and walk across the wooden drawbridge that leads into My Lady's Wood. Now you are in the peaceful shadows of oak, beech and sycamore, among thickets of snowberry and carpets of snowdrops, winter aconites, violets and other wildflowers. The circular walk leads to a thatched summer-house, recently rebuilt as part of the wood's restoration. A second circular walk has been completed recently in woodland reacquired by the Trust, south of the hall.

The parterre at Oxburgh Hall seen in consecutive years. The gardeners bedding out in spring (LEFT) and the parterre in full bloom the previous summer (RIGHT).

Packwood House

Lapworth, Warwickshire

11 miles south-east of
Birmingham, 2 miles east
of Hockley Heath

Area 7 acres (2·8 ha)
Soil alkaline, heavy soil
Altitude 396 ft (120 m)
Average rainfall 27 in (686 mm)
Average winter climate cold
Staff two, plus one trainee

On rising ground to the south of this house is one of the great topiary gardens of Britain. Mystery surrounds its origins and theme, though by tradition it is a representation of the Sermon on the Mount, with The Master on the summit of the mound, the twelve Apostles and four Evangelists on the cross-walk below, and the lawn filled with the assembled Multitude. The 1723 plan may indicate some of these yews, but the Multitude does not appear to have been planted until the mid-nineteenth century. Whatever the true history, the topiaries are today an impressive sight. Leaning or bulging, cylindrical or conical, each is a character in the throng. Some now stand 50 feet (15 m) high, others are considerably less, either because they have a more taxing site or because they are replacements for earlier casualties.

The cutting is done with the aid of a hoist, though ladders are used in the more inaccessible areas of the Mount. The gardeners consider the clipping of The Master to be the ultimate test for any topiarist, for the ladder stands high at a 90 degree angle, secured by ropes.

In the remainder of the garden, the flavour is more domestic, set by the house, bristling with gables and tall chimneys, and by the formal pattern of walls, gazebos, gateways and flights of steps that accompanies it. It is a handsome assembly of mellow orange brickwork, rich in design detail. The development of the garden's rectangular enclosures was probably

LEFT: A weathered stone urn planted with houseleeks on the steps at Packwood, looking across red-hot pokers to the Sunk Garden.

RIGHT: The Yew Garden, known as the Sermon on the Mount, behind an undulating hedge of box.

205

begun after the Restoration by John Fetherston, whose father remodelled the existing timber-framed house. The raised terrace between the South Garden and the Yew Garden, affording a fine view of the lake and park, and the north-east gazebo, are attributed to him. They are both clearly depicted in a drawing of about 1756, as is the wall with its 30 recesses for bee-skeps.

The present appearance of this main South Garden, however, reflects the sensitive hand of Graham Baron Ash, who devoted much of his early life to the rescue and embellishment of a neglected Packwood, bought for him by his father, a wealthy industrialist and racehorse owner, in 1905. It was he who rebuilt the missing gazebos, installed the Sunk Garden in the lawn and set out the double borders on the raised terrace.

Herbaceous plants are the third prominent element at Packwood, adding delicacy and complementary colours to the composition of greens and orange brick. They are arranged with a remarkable lightness of touch, capturing that romantic, mingled and deliciously carefree quality that you see in Victorian watercolours of cottage gardens. The style was perfected by E.D. Lindup, one of the Trust's first head gardeners, and has been continued since. Asters, phlox, sedums, heleniums, delphiniums, dahlias, daylilies, monardas, geraniums, polygonums (persicarias), achilleas and gypsophila are all here, complemented by wisterias, figs, vines, clematis, ceanothus and climbing roses, and a host of spring and summer annuals and biennials. At one time, the Sunk Garden was planted solely with annuals, but now, to reduce labour, these are planted in pockets among perennials. There are very few structural foliage plants or bold eye-catchers in any of these many borders; everything here merges and intertwines.

A series of fine wrought-iron gates offers glimpses into the park and connects the various courts. The two quietest are to the west and north of Packwood House. The former, Fountain Court, is named after the strange plunge bath built here in 1680. The north court also contains a well, shaded by a young collection of lime trees; there is a good show of snowdrops here in late winter.

Peckover House

| North Brink, Wisbech, Cambridgeshire | On north bank of River Nene in Wisbech (B1441) | *Area* 2 acres (0·8 ha) *Soil* neutral/rich alluvial loam *Altitude* 100 ft (30 m) *Average rainfall* 15 in (381 mm) *Average winter climate* cold *Staff* three |

FAR RIGHT: A display of flowering pot plants inside the Orangery at Peckover House, including begonias, coleus, fuchsias and cyclamen.

A showcase of plants and a thrilling example of the Victorian gardenesque style, this spacious town garden is one of the Trust's lesser-known jewels. The first impression is of Georgian elegance – a square, russet-brick house, standing in a handsome residential row on the north bank of the River Nene. Behind it, you might expect a sober composition of grass, evergreens and gravel walks, and these are indeed the ingredients of the garden's eastern section.

The Ribbon Border at Peckover House, with bronze cordylines, cotton lavender, busy lizzies, thrift and London Pride.

But the lines of paths, croquet lawn and shrubberies surprise you by twisting and turning the moment they leave the house. The hollies, laurels, box and yew are joined by Victorian favourites such as spotted aucuba, golden privet and ferns; there is a wrought-iron seat with a fern design; and, as you walk on to the adjacent lawn, you suddenly come upon exotic specimens of Monkey Puzzle, California Redwood and Chusan Palm, a rustic summer-house, a circle cut in the grass for cannas and tall marigolds (in spring, with either winter pansies or wallflowers), ironwork enveloped in roses and a border where perennials, including thrift, saxifrages, blue grass, coreopsis and purple sand cherry, play parts in a permanent bedding scheme.

The scenes now unfolding show both the best and 'worst' aspects of the gardenesque style, the term first proposed in 1832 by the author J. C. Loudon, to mean planting designed to display the character of each plant and the art of the gardener. There are crisp juxtapositions of shape, foliage and flowers – cypress next to bergenia and ivy; palm with variegated holly, yew and *Viburnum davidii* – and space is provided for each plant to grow and parade itself well.

But there is also the frantic eclecticism that the style soon came to embody: a large and diverse plant collection, assembled in a startling variety and quantity of geometric and abstract beds, with no discernible theme uniting them. Here, mercifully, walls and hedges do provide some visual barriers. But it is all conducted with such great panache, and tended with such minute attention to detail, that critical faculties are readily suspended.

Little is known of the garden's history, and the Trust has taken its cue for the wholesale expansion of this gardenesque theme from the layout, mature planting and garden buildings inherited from the last of the house's Quaker owners, the Hon. Alexandrina Peckover. One of the biggest surprises is to discover that the garden is not confined to a strip directly behind the house, but runs westwards along the backs of half a dozen other properties in the row. Behind the first dividing brick wall, you find yourself in a small enclosure, where a pretty green and white pavilion looks upon an oval lawn and thyme-fringed waterlily pond. Beds of hydrangeas, peonies and lilies (excellent companions for a hearty soil), edged in sedum and liriope, complete the outer oval.

Through a gap in the hedge, a pair of double borders is revealed, segmented by short hedges and mixed in content. *Dianthus* 'Mrs Sinkins' runs either side of the gravel path, and iron supports holding climbing roses and clematis punctuate the groups of shrubs and perennials, which include white 'Iceberg' roses, hydrangeas, Guelder Rose, potentillas, Japanese anemones and agapanthus.

The brick-based glasshouse in which the vista terminates is grandly called the Orangery. Supported by many other exotic pot-plants, its centrepiece comprises three orange trees in glazed tubs; the plants are thought to be well over 300 years old, and are still bearing heavy crops of fruit. A neighbouring glasshouse contains half-hardy ferns, and another holds pelargoniums, begonias, carnations and other potplants for indoor decoration. More vibrant beds of roses and tender perennials give you a thirst for the refreshing greens and shadows of the westernmost enclosure. The mulberry, quince and other fruit trees are reminders that this was once the kitchen garden, but now they are united by grass. Rambler roses hang from the hollies, and, silhouetted against a curving hedge of golden privet, a bed of fiery reds and purples is a final, potent sample of what Betjamen called Victorian 'ghastly good taste'.

Penrhyn Castle

Bangor, Gwynedd

1½ miles east of Bangor
on A5122

Area 48 acres (19·4 ha)
Soil neutral/sandy and stony
Altitude 150 ft (46 m)
Average rainfall 43 in
   (1,092 mm)
Average winter climate mild
Staff three

'Got up to look at the glorious view of the splendid range of hills lit up by the sun, which has not entirely risen ... After breakfast I went out with Col. and Ly. L. Pennant, our children, & almost all the company & planted 2 trees in Albert's and my name ... The view on the sea with Pen Man Mear [Penmaenmawr] rising above it is very beautiful', wrote Queen Victoria in her journal, October, 1859. The tree the Queen planted, a Wellingtonia, is still standing, and with the many other exotic conifers and specimen trees added during the nineteenth century, continues to inject the sloping pleasure grounds with the flavour of that period. The views, south towards Snowdonia, east along the coastline and north across the Menai Strait to Anglesey and Puffin Island, remain spectacular. And, above and within the Walled Garden, there is the bonus of a treasure trove of rare plants.

The scene is, of course, dominated by the great mass of the castle built for G.H. Dawkins Pennant between 1822 and 1838, and considered the outstanding example of the short-lived Norman Revival. Its scale drops the jaw the moment it comes into view on the crest of the hill; picturesque Austrian Pines and croaking jackdaws add to the ambiance. Dawkins Pennant accompanied his building with extensive tree planting, and the collection was steadily augmented over the years. From 1880, it was entrusted to the distinguished Scottish forester and botanist Angus Duncan Webster (son of Prince Albert's head forester at Balmoral), who, over a period of thirteen years, added many new and untried species.

The walks lead past this wealth of trees – redwoods, Douglas Firs, Bishop and Scots Pines, evergreen and deciduous oaks, Caucasian and Noble Firs, sycamore, beeches, limes, ashes and self-sown strawberry trees (*Arbutus unedo*); tucked under the castle walls are some impressive Japanese maples and a reliably flowering foxglove tree (*Paulownia tomentosa*). Quantities of bulbs and wildflowers accompany the trees on the slopes. And as you explore the glades, you will come upon other features – the Gothic chapel to the former house, left as a romantic ruin; a heather slope; and a rhododendron walk – *R. arboreum, yunnanense, irroratum* and *decorum* are some of the highlights.

Descending this west side of the hill, through the plantations of evergreen broad-leaved shrubs, you sense you are moving into a warmer temperate zone. In the Walled Garden, you have arrived. For, with the benign influence of the Gulf Stream, the climate at Penrhyn is exceptionally mild and, given shelter from the wind, a very rarified vegetation can be staged.

Among the many surprises on the sunny walls are *Mutisia decurrens, Sophora japonica, Lomatia ferruginea, Clianthus puniceus* (Lobster Claw), lapageria, decumaria, *Camellia reticulata*, the florist's broom (*Cytisus racemosus*) and the Pot Jasmine (*Jasminum polyanthum*) – all shrubs and climbers from the world's softer climates. The very tender *Cordyline indivisa* is also here, together with *Pittosporum eugenioides* and huge-leaved *Magnolia macrophylla*. But this is no lush subtropical scene. The exotics are displayed in ordered fashion within a formal, period framework. Box-edged beds, lily ponds, fountains and loggia adorn the upper terrace, the whole composition remodelled from the original Victorian parterre by Lady Penrhyn in the 1930s. Formerly, the parterre would also have been a showpiece of complex exotic bedding, its planting supervised for many years by the noted head gardener, Walter Speed – one of the inaugural recipients of the Royal Horticultural Society's highest award, the Victoria Medal of Honour, in 1897; extensive fruit and vegetable gardens then complemented the flower garden, and Penrhyn had the reputation of being one of the best properties in the country for the training of young gardeners.

Below the upper terrace, the impressive collection of taller shrubs and trees is displayed on sloping lawns, divided into rectangles by the grid of gravel paths. Among the cast are *Drimys winteri*, *Davidia involucrata* (Handkerchief Tree), *Crinodendron hookerianum*, *Magnolia tripetala*, *Sciadopitys verticillata* (Japanese Umbrella Pine) along with a notable sequence of late summer eucryphias.

An ironwork pergola runs along the lowest terrace. This was reinstalled by the Trust and again plays host, according to precedent, to the dripping red flowers of *Fuchsia* 'Riccartonii' and the purple stars of *Clematis* 'Jackmanii Superba'. Accompanying it is one of the oldest specimens in Britain of *Metasequoia glyptostroboides* (Dawn Redwood), the Chinese conifer known only in fossilised form until rediscovered in the wild in 1941.

Dramatic contrast to this safe and steady formal layout is now revealed, for the garden drops abruptly into damp meadows and the scale changes. Rising from the grass are stupendous clumps of giant rhubarb, gunnera and tree ferns, New Zealand flax and bamboo, backed by Holm Oaks, whitebeams, eucalyptus and purple maples. The area was once a more intricate stream garden, again created by Lady Penrhyn in the 1930s, but the present scheme is perhaps more fitting — as a link with, and reminder of, the gigantic and slightly forbidding architectural spectacle on the hill above.

Petworth House

Petworth, West Sussex

At Petworth on A272

Area 30 acres (12 ha)
Soil acid/sandy loam and clay
Altitude 108–426 ft (33–130 m)
Average rainfall 32 in (813 mm)
Average winter climate moderate
Staff four

By 1751, the reputation of Lancelot 'Capability' Brown was established, and for the next 35 years, he would be the dominant force in English landscape gardening. The park at Petworth is arguably his finest remaining landscape, the scene surveyed by the magnificent, 320-foot (97-m) long, west façade of the house, created for the 6th 'Proud' Duke of Somerset in about 1690. The duke also created an important formal garden, almost certainly designed by the royal gardener George London. The park is a typical open and uncomplicated composition of grass, water and well-spaced specimens and clumps of trees, predominantly oak, beech and sycamore, concealing the bounds, outlining the contours and standing sentinel on the ridges. A large herd of fallow deer roams among them.

At the heart of the landscape is the serpentine lake, fashioned by Brown from an existing series of small fish-ponds. Willow, birch and poplar fringe the water and cover the lake's islands, accompanied by some fine stands of Swamp Cypress; the Trust has recently replanted the clump of trees Brown planned at the head of the water. The boathouse was added by the 3rd Earl of Egremont, who is also responsible for the urns and sculptures that punctuate the park. It was he who commissioned the atmospheric paintings of the landscape by J.M.W. Turner which hang in the house.

The Pleasure Grounds to the north of the house were devastated by the 1987 storm. The Trust has replaced the central original core of dense woodland as it was 180 years earlier, however, it will be many years before the new plantings restore the patterns of wood and glade. Yet there is much to see. Brown suggested the Doric temple and Ionic rotunda as eye-catchers, and enclosed the whole with a ha-ha. He also enriched the planting, drawing on many ornamental species of tree and shrub introduced from America and southern Europe during the previous century. Further phases of adventurous planting took place in the late

The Rotunda in the Pleasure Ground at Petworth, with a spring carpet of bluebells, and the expanding leaves of Japanese maples and yellow azaleas.

eighteenth, nineteenth and early twentieth centuries, and the tradition continues today under the guidance of the present Lady Egremont and the Trust.

The greensand seams, and the diversity of dry, damp, sunny and shady habitats, allow a remarkable rate of tree growth, and a far wider range of plants than would grow in the exposed ground of the park. You walk from plantations of Shrub roses and crataegus, crabs, rowans and wild pear, to banks of massed azaleas and rhododendrons and marshy stands of willows and dogwoods.

Elsewhere, cornus, arbutus, aesculus, hydrangeas and Japanese maples provide highlights between laurel and aucuba, Hungarian and American Oaks, Tulip Trees and the twisted trunks of Spanish Chestnuts. In early spring, the Pleasure Ground is flooded with Lent Lilies and primroses; later, there are bluebells, fritillaries and camassias: in short, colour and variety to complement the sublime expanses of landscape.

Plas Newydd

Llanfairpwll, Anglesey,
Gwynedd

East coast of Anglesey
on Menai Strait (A4080)

Area 40 acres (16ha)
Soil varied
Altitude 0–150ft (0–46m)
Average rainfall 44in
   (1,118mm)
Average winter climate mild
Staff four

With yachts coursing the tidal water below its sloping lawns, the mountains of Snowdonia rising behind the Vaynol woods on the far shore, and, to the east, Robert Stephenson's Britannia railway bridge cutting across the curve of the Strait, Plas Newydd has as fine a setting as any coastal property in Britain.

There is the further boon of a mild climate, announced immediately by the massive screens of the half-hardy New Zealand evergreen *Griselinia littoralis*, which flank your descent to the house. The summers here tend to be cool and sunny, the winters wet and windy, and given the sheltering woods, the site proves ideal for many woody plants from the warmer temperate regions of the world. The planting, however, is not in competition. The drifts of trees and shrubs are bold and harmonious, framing the views and providing expanses of green and islands of colour to echo the sinuous shapes of the landscape. The bones of this layout were set out by the leading landscape designer of the late eighteenth century, Humphry Repton, engaged by Henry, Earl of Uxbridge, as work on the house was nearing completion. His proposals are contained in one of his famous Red Books, dated 1798–9.

But much has happened since Repton's day. Lord Uxbridge's son, the celebrated Waterloo commander, the 1st Marquess of Anglesey, undertook a great deal of tree planting after 1815. Between the First and Second World Wars, the 6th Marquess added a range of conifers, specimen deciduous trees and ornamental shrubs, in particular rhododendrons and camellias. And the present Marquess continued to augment the collection through the 1950s and '60s. Since the transfer of ownership to the Trust this momentum has been maintained, with several major new features established. Within the historic framework, the garden thus reflects twentieth-century taste.

West of the house is the area known as the West Indies, a long and broad sweep of lawn fringed and broken by trees and shrubberies. In May, the shadows are lit with pastel-coloured azaleas and in summer with hydrangeas, whose blooms, indicating the increasing acidity, change from pink near the house to purple and intense sky blue and gentian as the garden flows deeper on to the greensand. *Magnolia × veitchii* 'Isca', *M. wilsonii*, *Prunus* 'Tai-Haku', and scarlet *Embothrium* 'Norquinco Valley' add further early highlights, with eucryphias and hoherias giving showy white flowers in July and August. The hybrid *Hoheria* 'Glory of Amlwch' is a speciality and seems to perform better here than in any other Trust garden – appropriately, since it originated at Anglesey. Unfortunately, another noted feature, the hedges of *Viburnum* 'Lanarth', have suffered from the spread of honey fungus in the grounds.

A small quarry dell, snaked with stone paths and stairways, adds to the adventure. Camellias, pink 'Donation' prominent among them, are massed here, with cherries, pieris and hedges of scented *Osmanthus delavayi* giving an April boost of colour. In the summer sunshine, it offers a cool and shady respite from the glare on sea and lawns. The garden's rarest tree, the tender Asian evergreen *Schima wallichii* var. *khasiana*, is found at this end of the garden; it produces its white flowers in autumn.

Following the line of the Long Walk, a double avenue of yew and *Chamaecyparis pisifera* 'Squarrosa' introduced as a windbreak in the 1930s, you arrive in the arboretum known as 'Australasia'. Planted in 1981 to replace the exhausted wartime orchard, this features a collection of eucalyptus and nothofagus grown among wildflowers and meadow grasses, with a fringe of Australasian shrubs. These are fast-growing trees and the Southern Hemisphere mood is already well established.

The most recent improvements have centred on the formal terraces east of the house. On the upper level, a trellis garden house with bubbling tufa fountain has been erected, marking the site of the former Edwardian conservatory. On the levels below, the Italianate flavour set by the 6th Marquess has been reinforced with the introduction of pools and water features, additional hedging and clipped evergreens. In high summer, there is a fine show of agapanthus on the top terrace.

Almost a mile's walk along the line of the strait brings you to a quite different garden, a wild and exotic rhododendron wood. The 6th Marquess began introducing choice species and hybrids here in the 1930s, including *RR. fortunei, thomsonii, praevernum,* 'Shilsonii', 'Nobleanum', 'Loderi King George' and *montroseanum*, which self-sows freely. But the collection has been steadily augmented by the present Lord Anglesey, who received 'thinnings' from Bodnant (qv), as a wedding gift from the 2nd Lord Aberconway. For three seasons, beginning in 1948, lorry-loads of rhododendrons arrived, accompanied by two gardeners to plant them. Many of Bodnant's famous scarlet *R. griersonianum* hybrids were among them. Large-leaved species, such as *RR. falconeri, macabeanum* and *sinogrande*, perform particularly well here at Plas Newydd, and the climate is also mild enough for scented conservatory varieties such as 'Lady Alice Fitzwilliam', 'Princess Alice' and 'Fragrantissimum'. Open only until the end of May, this isolated corner of the Plas Newydd gardens is a bonus for springtime visitors that should not be missed.

Plas-yn-Rhiw

Rhiw, Pwllheli, Gwynedd

12 miles west of Pwllheli on south coast road to Aberdaron

Area ¾ acre (0·3 ha)
Soil acid/light loam
Altitude 100 ft (30 m)
Average rainfall 40 in (1,016 mm)
Average winter climate frost-free—mild
Staff one full-time, one part-time

Atlantic rollers may sweep into Porth Neigl (Hell's Mouth Bay) below and the west wind may roar across the Lleyn Peninsula on which its sits, but Plas-yn-Rhiw seems to stay unruffled. Protected by hills and woods, the small granite house and its three-quarter-acre (0·3-ha) garden snuggle into the lower slope of Mynydd Rhiw, exposed only to the south and east. Thanks to the warming influences of the Gulf Stream, the climate is also mild, temperatures rarely dropping much below freezing.

It was their deep love for the Lleyn landscape, and a desire to protect it for future generations, which prompted the three Keating sisters, Honora, Lorna and Eileen, and their mother to buy Plas-yn-Rhiw and its 58 acres (23 ha) in 1938; later they purchased over 300 more with the express purpose of giving it to the Trust. They planted in time-honoured cottage-garden fashion, pushing bulbs in here and slips of shrubs there, gradually building up a very large and varied plant collection, traditional favourites rubbing shoulders with exotics, and everywhere ferns and wildflowers. Things were getting a little out of hand by 1981, when Lorna, the last Miss Keating, died, and the Trust began a programme of gentle restoration.

To explore Plas-yn-Rhiw, you still have to squeeze between box hedges down narrow grass passageways and duck under arching pink rhododendrons and carmine camellias to follow the curving stone and cobbled paths. And at each turn there is something to marvel at: great clumps of *Fuchsia magellanica*, its soft hazes of scarlet toning so well with the grey walls; an old pear tree and forsythia growing through the roof of the ruined dairy; or the superb *Magnolia campbellii* subsp. *mollicomata*, planted by the Keatings in 1947, silhouetted against the bay below.

View of the garden and path towards the house at Plas-yn-Rhiw.

The garden is also full of scented plants and on warm days they can infuse the air. Viburnums, philadelphus, azaleas, daphnes, jasmines and clethra all contribute sweetness, and from the pillars of the Victorian verandah the fragrance of 'Zephirine Drouhin' roses pervades the house. Forever drawing you away from the garden are the stupendous views, of the curve of Porth Neigl, of the Gwynedd mountains and even, on a clear day, down the full length of Cardigan Bay to St David's Head in South Wales.

Polesden Lacey

nr Dorking, Surrey

2 miles south of Great
Bookham, off the A246
Leatherhead–Guildford road

Area 30 acres (12ha)
Soil alkaline/some clay and
flint
Altitude 300–470ft (91–143m)
Average rainfall 30in (762mm)
Average winter climate cold
Staff five

A view of the astrolabe sundial
in the Lavender Garden at
Polesden Lacey.

From 1906, this was the home of the Hon. Mrs Ronald Greville, one of the most celebrated hostesses in the Marlborough House circle of Edward VII, and the mansion and gardens offer a delicious insight into the life of Edwardian high society. The present house, a yellow-washed and green-shuttered villa, was built in the 1820s, but enlarged and refurbished for the Grevilles, in the French Neo-classical style, by Mewis and Davis, the architects of the Ritz Hotel. Captain Greville died in 1908, and his plans for an equally grand scheme of parterres for the garden were never implemented. Instead, his wife enriched the planting within the inherited framework of avenues, formal walks, lawns and kitchen garden.

The setting is magnificent. The house stands just below the southernmost ridge of the North Downs, and the trees on the lower lawns frame sweeping views over the Mole Valley and across to the wooded crest of Ranmore Common. One of the garden's principal features is the panoramic Long Walk that stretches for a quarter of a mile eastward above the valley. This was begun in 1761, but considerably enlarged by the playwright Richard Brinsley Sheridan, who brought the property in 1797; it is the only remnant of his garden.

The chalk and sunny aspect make for a hot, dry hillside. Wildflowers do well among the hungry meadow grasses, and the open, mown lawns are stained purple by creeping thyme. But the site is well furnished with trees, and seams of richer, acid loam allow the chalk-tolerant beeches, oaks, maples and pines to be supplemented by Sweet Chestnut, Wellingtonia, Douglas Fir and other more fastidious species. The plantations were badly hit by the great storm of 1987, and to a lesser extent that of 1990, but new plantings are now maturing. Ornamental gardening is concentrated across the lawn to the west, except in the immediate vicinity of the house, which is hung with wisteria, yellow Banksian Rose and other climbers and wall shrubs, and fringed with box-edged borders of spring and summer bedding.

Here, in the nineteenth-century walled kitchen garden, is Mrs Greville's rose garden. Set out in a simple cross pattern, with long, box-edged, wooden pergolas, adjoining seams of 'Munstead' and deeper 'Hidcote' lavenders, walls draped in clematis and a water tower festooned in an old Chinese wisteria, it is a mass of pink, white and crimson during the summer months. A little earlier in the year, the same colours occur in the first of the yew enclosures beyond, containing double borders of peonies (succeeded by lilies). The other compartments

215

present collections of lavenders – and of bearded iris, a selection of early hybrids, some of which have been invigorated through laboratory propagation of virus-free tissue.

As in the house, there is fine classical ornament at every turn. A Venetian well-head stands at the junction of the rose garden paths, a discus thrower disports in the iris garden, and the theme is pursued throughout, where you come upon a Veronese font and a Roman sarcophagus as well as further well-heads, urns and statues, all adding luxury to the compositions.

To the west, the path leads past herbaceous borders to a winter garden, shaded by three large Persian Ironwood trees. Beyond, a thatched bridge leads over the sunken estate road to the Edwardian kitchen garden, now grassed over and patterned with limes, fruit trees and cherries. To the south runs the main herbaceous border, 450 feet (137 m) long and divided into four sections. The pastel colours rise into yellow climaxes of achilleas, daylilies and kniphofia, and spiky yuccas and blue-grey *Crambe maritima* contribute emphatic foliage to the corners. Agapanthus do particularly well in the hot, dry ground here, supreme among them a superb midnight blue form of the pendulous *A. inapertus*.

Below, colour comes from the shrubs and trees on and adjacent to the bank of Westmorland limestone that plunges into the Sunken Garden. Berberis, lilacs, hydrangeas and perovskia give a succession of flowers, beautifully complemented by pear trees with silver foliage (*Pyrus nivalis*), whitebeam, Smoke Bush, large-leaved *Viburnum rhytidophyllum* and a massive Pfitzer Juniper.

Mrs Greville died in 1942 and lies buried outside the Walled Garden, in an enclosure presided over by eighteenth-century French statues of the Four Seasons.

Powis Castle

Welshpool, Powys

At Welshpool, via either A483 Oswestry road, or A458 Shrewsbury road

Area 25 acres (10 ha)
Soil acid woodland area, otherwise neutral to alkaline/clay
Altitude 0–450 ft (0–137 m)
Average rainfall 32 in (813 mm)
Average winter climate cold
Staff seven

FAR RIGHT: Yew tumps overhanging the Terrace below the castle at Powis.

It will annoy visitors following behind you, but I recommend slowing the car as you come to the ornamental wrought-iron gates between park and the garden, on your way up the hill. Behind the railings, and from a platform of smooth grass, appointed with finely clipped topiaries, your eye is swept up over a canopy of mixed trees to a steep ridge in the middle distance. Mellow Baroque terraces, masked in shrubs and bordered by a gigantic hedge, ascend this in tiers towards the skyline. And here, seemingly among the clouds, is perched a massive fortress of red limestone – the medieval seat of Welsh princes and later the earls of Powis – crowned with battlements and lapped by domes of dark yew.

The appetite for exploration is whetted and there is no disappointment, for this is one of the Trust's richest flower gardens, with some of the most swashbuckling and sophisticated herbaceous planting to be seen anywhere in the country. The curving drive leads you on up the slopes, well wooded with oaks of such a size and quality that they were insisted upon by Admiral Rodney for his fighting ships. Groups of red and fallow deer can usually be glimpsed in the shadows.

You enter the garden just below the castle to be met by the reverse panorama: layers of herbaceous borders, topiaries, stairways and balustrades, descending to a 2½-acre (1-ha) lawn; north of it, a large formal garden of fruit trees and rose beds; and opposite, another lower ridge, encased in oaks and yews, and backed by the patchwork of fields, villages and hills of the English border countryside.

The grand terraces, incorporating an Orangery and Aviary, and an array of fine lead statuary from the workshop of the Flemish John van Nost, are a unique and remarkable legacy, having survived intact the destructive eighteenth-century taste for naturalistic land-scaping. Legend has it (there is not a shred of evidence) that 'Capability' Brown visited and recommended that they be returned to the natural rock from which they were quarried, and that this was, therefore, a narrow escape. Their exact history is something of a mystery. It seems most likely that they were designed by William Winde, the architect of the terrace at Cliveden (qv), and that construction began in the early 1680s, when William Herbert, the 1st Marquess of Powis, was at the height of his political career. The Glorious Revolution of 1688 sent the Herberts into exile with King James II, and work is then thought to have come to a standstill until after 1703, when the family returned. In its entourage was now a Frenchman by the name of Adrian Duval and he, perhaps under the continuing supervision of Winde, completed the design. This included an impressive Dutch water garden on the site of the Great Lawn below – dismantled by 1809.

The cue for the lavish overlay of flowers comes from Violet, wife of the 4th Earl, who, in 1911, set about transforming a 'gradually deteriorating' garden into 'one of the most beautiful, if not the most beautiful, in England and Wales'. However, the garden was once again in decline when it came to the Trust, and its present content – ever-changing and experimental in the spirit of Edwardian flower gardening – reflects the expertise of its head gardener and staff from the 1970s onwards.

The high, sheltering walls of the terraces, angled to the south-east, together with the comparatively mild climate, allow an adventurous range of shrubs and climbers. In late spring, deep blue ceanothus billow above the brick like thunderclouds, while against the Orangery, the buff-yellow roses, *Rosa banksiae* 'Lutea' and 'Gloire de Dijon', pick up tones in the sandstone frontispiece, in the company of orange eccremocarpus and white abutilon. Later, there are curtains of flowering clematis, cream waterlilies from *Magnolia grandiflora*, a waterfall of pale green from honey-scented *Itea ilicifolia* and scarlet showers from wall-trained *Phygelius capensis*; less showy curiosities like *Dregea sinensis*, *Rhodochiton atrosanguineus* and *Abutilon* 'Nabob' are to be discovered on every tier.

The display of tender perennials has been raised to the level of high art at Powis, where, with the backup of glasshouses, cuttings are grown on into bushy plants during the winter, brought into flower, hardened off and returned to the garden as early as April. Potfuls fill the pedimented niches in the upper terrace wall – the orange brick fringed with the compact form of silver artemisia, brought here in 1972 and subsequently named 'Powis Castle' – and punctuate almost every balustrade and stairway. Fuchsias, an Edwardian favourite, are a speciality, with both the petticoated hybrids and scarlet-tubed *FF. fulgens*, *boliviana* and dark-leaved 'Thalia' presented in old basketweave pots. Elsewhere, you come upon glorious salads made from the likes of glaucous-leaved melianthus, crimson-red cestrum, trailing yellow bidens, double red nasturtium, and the most sumptuous of all the pelargoniums, the damson, crimson-edged 'Lord Bute'.

Each terrace border has its theme. Drier conditions on the narrow Aviary Terrace have suggested plantings of sun-loving Mediterranean, Californian and Southern Hemisphere plants, including cistus, carpenteria, broom, lavender, iris and *Artemisia arborescens*. While the Aviary itself, its roof studded with lead urns and draped in Japanese wisteria, contains troughs

FAR RIGHT: *Clematis* 'Perle d'Azur' with euphorbia and agapanthus in one of the Powis borders.

ABOVE LEFT: A peacock at Powis backed by ceanothus.

ABOVE RIGHT: White *Argyranthemum foeniculaceum* with dahlias, fuchsias and milk thistles in a border at Powis.

of half-hardy, scented rhododendrons in the company of the giant-fronded chain fern and webs of Creeping Fig.

On the third terrace, the deep, heavy soil allows lush herbaceous planting, and either side of the Orangery, pairs of long, boxed-edged borders recede into the distance. They are at their peak in late summer, and because of the milder light and temperatures here, the plants have a freshness and length of season rarely met in more southerly gardens.

Behind a tortuously trunked, bronze-leaved Japanese maple, the tints are of violet, white and warm pink from perennials such as monkshood, cimicifugas, polygonums, asters and *Clematis* 'Jackmanii Superba', grown on balloon hoops; beyond the Orangery, the scene is of fire and brimstone, fuelled by orange crocosmias, yellow kniphofias, the vermilion hips of *Rosa moyesii* and *R.* × *highdownensis*, and a plume of golden cypress.

The seasons of the lowest terrace's borders straddle this display, with one border focused on the euphorbias, galegas, verbascums and other perennials of early summer; the other on the chrysanthemums, sedums and Japanese anemones of early autumn – at which time the leaves of *Acer japonicum*, amelanchiers and euonymus on the adjacent grass slope are beginning to ignite.

The yews are dramatic counterweights to this casual, ephemeral vegetation. The fourteen specimen 'tumps' that sit like jellies on the upper terrace, together with the stupendous, bulging hedge at the northern end, were probably planted in the 1720s, with darker Irish Yews planted as companions a hundred years later. The boxwood is hardly less impressive, and on emerging through a gap in the yew hedge, you meet a towering wall of it, running beside a sloping, serpentine walk. The smell is always intense.

This path leads down to the lower formal garden, made by the 4th Countess from the former kitchen garden. A long vine tunnel and lines of pyramidal apple trees are reminders of the earlier use – the latter including rare, old varieties like 'Mother' and 'Broad-Eyed Pippin', all set into silver and gold ground-cover plants, serving as permanent bedding. Beds of Floribunda and Hybrid Musk roses and other Edwardian favourites, including phlox, del-phiniums, campanulas and hollyhocks, stretch away from the half-timbered gardener's bothy.

At the opposite end of the Orangery terrace, you are enticed out of the formal garden past an exposed face of rock, the path curving eastwards towards the opposite ridge. Paperbark Maple, evergreen eucryphia, a tall Maidenhair Tree and shrimp-tinted *Acer pseudoplatanus* 'Brilliantissimum' are among the trees on this bank. Remarkably, the ridge itself is formed of acid sandstone, in contrast to the limestone of the Castle ridge, allowing the 3rd Earl to indulge in the Victorian taste for rhododendrons.

The paths lead you to an ice-house and a Ladies' Bath, both probably dating from the nineteenth century, and here and there, you are given tree-framed prospects out to Long Mountain and the Breidden Hills and back across the daffodil and wildflower paddock and Great Lawn to the castle and its terraces. Few properties can offer such a variety of vantage points, or views of such breathtaking scale and detail. This is a garden that draws the visitor back again and again – several times a year, in my case.

Prior Park

Bath, Avon

Ralph Allen Drive, Bath

Area 28 acres (11 ha)
Soil clay/loam
Altitude 295 ft (90 m)
Average rainfall 30 in (768 mm)
Average winter climate sheltered with frost pockets
Staff three, plus many volunteers

An intimate Arcadian valley just a mile from the centre of Bath, Prior Park came to the Trust in 1993 in an advanced state of decay, but in its design remarkably little-changed since the death of its creator, Ralph Allen, in 1764. Thanks to generous bequests and donations from the public, the major task of restoration is now well under way.

The 30 years of the park's development was a golden era in garden history, during which the new, 'natural' landscape style evolved from its early wooded, serpentine and allegorical phase to embrace the open, uncluttered panorama of lake and meadow. Allen responded, and his park both charts the changing fashion and preserves the work of some of the movement's most influential figures.

At the head of the combe stands the Palladian mansion, built by John Wood from the honey-coloured stone that Allen, a self-made businessman, was quarrying in Combe Down for Georgian Bath; it has been a school since 1867. Below, the meadow sweeps down to a magnificent Palladian bridge and a chain of three ponds appearing as a curving lake, the whole prospect framed by woods. Beyond are the hills and skyline of Bath.

It is in the west woods that the oldest features of the garden are to be found. Here you come upon the Wilderness of the 1730s, attributable to Alexander Pope, one of the most persuasive advocates of the style – heavily overcast by branches, dense with evergreen shrubbery, punctuated by black ponds, and with the remnants of many of its architectural surprises, including grotto and cascades. Sadly, features that have vanished include a Serpentine River and a Sham Bridge at its head. In time, the Trust intends to replace them, but the clearance of scrub and the uncovering and remaking of paths are the current priority.

In the valley, the restoration has begun with the dredging of the silted upper pond and the repair of the Palladian bridge. This main vista was refashioned several times. It began, in 1734, as a quite formal landscape, with a triangular lawn, circular basin of water and straight-edged woods. In the 1750s, it was greatly extended down into the combe, the woods were made to billow down the banks, the lower lakes were created by damming the stream and, in 1755, the Palladian bridge was built.

After 1759, the naturalisation process was concluded, the circular basin, with its accompanying cascade and plantations being removed to provide the present uninterrupted sweep of meadow. The leading landscape gardener was now 'Capability' Brown, and it was he who made the final alterations for Allen in the few years before his death.

The circuit of the park takes you around the meadow and down to the water by way of the eastern woods. As you descend, the lake is gradually revealed as three ponds standing at different levels. Another dam was made under the bridge, so that the water gushed through the arches. The architect of this masterpiece, one of only three Palladian bridges to survive in Britain (the earlier examples being at Stowe (qv) and Wilton), is unknown, but it was built by Allen's clerk of works Richard Jones, and the stone brought down via a new driveway to the north-west, with a Chinese gate at its entrance. From the bridge, you have the equally impressive view back up the combe. Until 1921, this took in not only the mansion but also the Gothic Temple of 1753, perched on the edge of the Wilderness: another of the many missing or broken pieces of the jigsaw that the Trust is slowly reassembling.

Rievaulx

Rievaulx, Helmsley,
North Yorkshire

2½ miles north-west of
Helmsley on B1257

Area 62 acres (25 ha)
Soil alkaline, light soil
Altitude 591 ft (180 m)
Average rainfall 27–31 in
  (700–800 mm)
Average winter climate cold,
  exposed
Staff two (who cover three
  properties)

This serpentine grass walk, high on a wooded escarpment at the head of Ryedale, is one of the most beautiful products of the Picturesque phase of English landscape gardening. As at Studley Royal (qv), 30 miles (48 km) away, the composition combines natural beauty with a suitably atmospheric eye-catcher – the majestic ruins of the great Cistercian abbey of Rievaulx, founded in 1131. The terrace's story really begins across the combe at Duncombe Park, where, sometime after 1713, Thomas Duncombe II broke from the French-inspired practice of designing wooded *allées* along straight axes, and commissioned instead a hillside ride that followed the natural contours of the terrain and curved in a crescent.

Some 40 years later, Duncombe's son, Thomas Duncombe III, conceived this second terrace above the abbey. Superficially similar in shape to that at Duncombe, and also with Ionic and Doric temples at either end, the Rievaulx Terrace is, however, devoid of all its predecessor's residual formality. Undulating woods replace the hedges and linear plantations, and the walk meanders in a succession of curves, not enclosed by trees but revealing, through gaps in the woods, a series of superb views of the landscape – the abbey, the arched bridge over the river and the green patchwork of the Hambleton Hills and Rye Valley. Piles of dressed masonry found in the combe suggest that Thomas Duncombe III was planning a viaduct to connect the two terraces but, alas, it was never built.

Beech is the principal tree of the terrace's backdrop, supported by a range of other hardwoods including, unexpectedly, variegated sycamore. Further diversity is found on the woodland floor – the cast including Martagon Lilies, Dog's Mercury, columbines, Lords and Ladies and the parasitic pink toothwort – and on the rough grassy bank on the other side of the terrace, where there are rich communities of primroses, cowslips, oxlips, Early Purple Orchids, Bird's Foot Trefoil, hawkbits, clovers and many others, giving carpets of colour through spring and summer. Who dares claim the eighteenth-century landscape garden is devoid of flowers?

Rowallane

Saintfield, Ballynahinch,
Co. Down

11 miles south-east of Belfast,
1 mile south of Saintfield, west
of the Downpatrick road (A7)

Area 52 acres (21 ha)
Soil acid/loam
Altitude 200 ft (61 m)
Average rainfall 36 in (914 mm)
Average winter climate mild
Staff four

Candelabra primulas in the rock garden at Rowallane.

The land at Rowallane, Hugh Armytage Moore was told, was 'not fit to graze a goat'. This is rough drumlin country. The fields are boxed small by dry-stone walls and sheltering hedgerows and stands of gorse and massive outcrops of rock break from the grass. But the rainfall is moderately high, the summers cool and the winters comparatively mild. From 1903, Moore began planting, and his legacy is a large plantsman's garden of striking scenic beauty and distinctive character. In parts of the grounds, a foundation of trees and walls had already been set out by his uncle, the Rev. John Moore, who bought the property in 1860. The long entrance drive, now richly coloured by immense arboreal rhododendrons, already had its close fringes of deciduous trees and its sinuous grassy glades shaded by specimen conifers. The stone seats and arresting cairns of giant's marbles were also in place, complementing the exposed rock.

Behind the modest, apricot-painted farmhouse, is the Rev. Moore's pleasure ground, a broad sweep of lawn and arboretum, featuring a pond and a circular stone dais, from which he is reputed to have delivered some of his sermons; this looks less odd now that it is the base for the iron bandstand from Newcastle promenade which was given to the Trust, in a derelict state, in 1985.

Many trees have been added here over the past hundred years, but those planted by Rev. Moore still set the quiet mood. Monterey, Scots, Bishop and Umbrella Pine, redwood, Wellingtonia, cypresses, multi-stemmed Western Red Cedar, Douglas Fir, podocarpus, cunninghamia and *Fitzroya cupressoides* are among the many fine conifers framed by the beech trees.

The adjacent walled garden was also built by the Rev. Moore, but although it retains its formal kitchen garden pattern of gravel paths, its planting is now very different. In place of some of the vegetable beds, Hugh Armytage Moore introduced borders of choice perennials, shaded by ornamental trees, and this theme has been seized and developed in red-blooded fashion by the Trust. The moist climate allows wonderfully lush plantings. Drifts of Himalayan poppies, in particular the scintillating turquoise-blue *Meconopsis × sheldonii* 'Slieve Donard', course between lime-green hostas and bronze and tropical-leaved rodgersias. Species peonies are displayed in variety, followed by primulas, daylilies, astilbes and magnificent belts of giant Himalayan lilies. A National Collection of penstemons, alongside phloxes and the Japanese *Kirengeshoma palmata* with its soft yellow shuttlecocks, provide colour in late summer.

Low blocks of ornamental grasses, libertias, violas and dwarf rhododendrons give contrasting flavours, while above and behind, ornamental trees, taller shrubs and climbers are providing backdrops, evergreen structure and, in many parts, a dappled, woodland atmosphere. Cherries and spring- and summer-flowering magnolias are prominent, including forms of *M. × veitchii* introduced, in the early part of the twentieth century by the Veitch nursery in Exeter, from which Hugh Armytage Moore obtained plants.

Rhododendron cinnabarinum in many guises, *R. hanceanum* and the superb *R. shilsonii*, with blood-red flowers and cinnamon bark peeling to reveal purplish branches, are highlights among the shrubs, with *Hoheria lyallii* (which self-sows freely) and eucryphias giving later blossom. The compact form of *Viburnum plicatum*, raised from seed at Rostrevor but distributed from here and named 'Rowallane', grows in the centre of a small paved area, designed in the shape of a Celtic cross. The recently restored walls – unique in having projecting pierced tiles incorporated, through which supporting wires for climbing plants may be threaded – shelter the New Zealand Kowhai, *Sophora tetraptera*, *Acradenia frankliniae* from Tasmania and the conservatory *R.* 'Lady Alice Fitzwilliam'.

The outer walled garden, formerly Hugh Armytage Moore's nursery area, springs further surprises: a Handkerchief Tree, *Davidia involucrata* var. *vilmoriniana*; *Helwingia japonica*, curious for producing its pale green flowers on the upper surface of the leaves; and a cream-variegated form of *Azara microphylla*. The unusual *Hydrangea aspera* subsp. *strigosa* is included in the large collection of hydrangeas, partnered with colchiums, and here also is the original plant of the popular garden japonica, *Chaenomeles × superba* 'Rowallane'. Crinums, watsonias, species dahlias and dieramas add some exotic herbaceous interest.

The rest of the ground the garden now covers consisted, in 1903, of rock-strewn fields. Gradually, as his experience and enthusiasm grew, Hugh Armytage Moore annexed them. But he did no taming, levelling or ploughing. He kept the dry-stone walls, the gorse and the spongy turf, made a feature of the rock and had his planting follow the undulating rhythm of the land. The result is an extraordinarily heady mix of the wild and the exotic, and a succession of images that could belong to no other garden. Wildflower management here is outstanding.

The fields retain their age-old names. From the Haggard, or stackyard (a remarkable sight in July when the falling cotton seeds of *Populus lasiocarpa maximowiczii* envelop it in a local blizzard), a gate leads first into the Spring Ground, long valued for its early-warming, southerly orientation. In spring, you are greeted by swathes of flowers. The foreground ridge is heavily planted with daffodils, including many old Irish cultivars; they are succeeded by colonies of Devil's Bit Scabious and other wildflowers.

FAR RIGHT: Fragrant yellow deciduous azaleas wedged between purple Japanese azaleas and larger rhododendrons at Rowallane.

224

The view down the bank, framed by pine, beech and oak, is punctuated by eruptions of rhododendrons. Large hybrids such as white 'Dr Stocker' and 'Loderi King George' give way to stands of sun-loving azaleas and pink and purplish Triflorum species. Red Kirishima azalea, *R.* × *obtusum* and the scented yellow *R. luteum* are prominent, the latter in its traditional garden partnership with wild bluebells. The white variety of *Magnolia campbellii* and summer-flowering *M. wilsonii* also grow here. Like many of the trees and shrubs in the garden, they have associations with the great plant-hunters of the early twentieth century. Moore corresponded with E.H. Wilson and George Forrest, and grew many of their introductions as they became available through Irish and English nurseries.

More rhododendrons, this time in the company of Bird Cherry and specimen trees such as Dawyck Beech, stewartias and deliciously fragrant *Malus toringo* subsp. *sargentii*, entice you through the New Ground to the famous rock garden. Here, Moore exposed a gigantic outcrop of grey whinstone, smoothed and striated by glaciers, and imported cartloads of soil to make beds around it. The rock, gravel and grass paths curl and plunge past heathers, low conifers and an array of choice alpines, among which daphnes and runs of silver-leaved celmisias are memorable incidents. Mats of mouse plant, *Arisarum proboscideum*, lie at the bottom. There are rhododendrons everywhere. The rock fringes and streamsides are home to

A fine hybrid of Himalayan blue poppy *Meconopsis sheldonii* 'Slieve Donard'.

Rhododendron orbiculare, R. baileyi, the aromatic *R. glaucophyllum* and hybrids such as 'Yellow-hammer' and 'Blue Tit'. In sheltered corners grow the tender *R. virgatum* and lily-scented 'Countess of Haddington'. A fine pieris, from Forrest's seed, gives a spectacular show, as does the thicket of *Mahonia japonica* Bealei group and the collection of streamside perennials, which includes *Primula* 'Rowallane Rose'.

Wooded enclosures lie ahead. Once planted as wind shelter for the grazing stock, this matrix of forest trees is equally important for the protection of the garden. A young shelter-belt of beech is gradually replacing the felled larches on Trio Hill above the rock garden; among them are fine groups of embothrium, berberis and *Enkianthus campanulatus*, this last delivering sensational autumn tints. Scots Pine and beech form the mainstay of the plantations on the slopes running west towards the entrance drive.

In these lower woods and glades, the contrast between the wild and the ornamental is at its most potent. For as you cross the bumpy terrain, past tree heathers, pieris and still more rhododendrons, between specimen maples, southern beeches, paulownia, davidia, sorbus, birch, chestnut and eucalyptus, you skirt the low boundary walls, over which you see land similarly contoured and compartmented, but empty. This is what Hugh Armytage Moore began with; behind you is what he made of it.

Rufford Old Hall

Rufford, nr Ormskirk, Lancashire	7 miles north of Ormskirk, in village of Rufford on east side of A59	*Area* 14 acres (5·7 ha) *Soil* acid/sandy loam *Altitude* 26 ft (8 m) *Average rainfall* 32 in (813 mm) *Average winter climate* cold *Staff* one

A brick, red sandstone and black-and-white timbered Tudor house, framed by massed rhododendrons and azaleas in full bloom, is a heady sight. This is the moment, in late spring, to see early Victorian taste displayed at Rufford in glorious potency; at other times, the garden takes on a quieter, complementary role. The site is narrow and rectangular, wedged between canal and main road, but a tranquil, rural mood is struck the moment you enter the curving drive. Drifting into woodland to the north, Turkey Oaks, sycamores, beeches, limes, Sweet Chestnut and Silver Willows shade the rough grass, in which appears a succession of bulbs and wildflowers through spring and early summer. There are good stands of osmunda fern and pampas grass and, near the house, a venerable weeping ash.

The first rhododendrons are here in island beds. Their variety and rich colour greatly appealed to Victorian gardeners, and the continual introduction of new species and home-bred hybrids kept appetites sharp. The acid, sandy soil at Rufford is well suited to them. On this west side of the garden, there are some gorgeous reds, including 'Britannia', 'Fusilier' and 'Bagshot Ruby', and the inclusion of yellow *R. wardii* and the scented azalea, *R. luteum*, in close proximity, satisfies the Victorian taste for contrast. Accompanying hydrangeas and berried hollies give continuity of bloom into the summer and autumn.

South of the house, some of the rhododendrons and azaleas are marshalled into a pair of long, open, formal borders, lapped by lawn and divided by a gravel path. Here, the yellows of azaleas associate with the pinks and purples of 'Mrs Davies Evans' and 'Praecox'. Other trees and shrubs – among them laburnum, *Rosa multiflora* and *Magnolia kobus* – fuel the scheme and extend its season, with the help of bulbs, lilies and perennials such as geraniums, sedums, rudbeckias and daylilies, including the pale yellow variety 'Lady Fermor-Hesketh', which was introduced in 1924 and raised by Amos Perry. Bold clumps of blue and variegated hostas are a feature of the shadier parts of the garden's shrubberies. In the West Border, they partner weigela, philadelphus, viburnum, enkianthus, pieris and the summer-flowering shrub chestnut, *Aesculus parviflora*, and, with these, supply some lively autumn tints.

Set against this exotic woodland flora are ingredients more familiarly associated with such a domestic rural setting. White and mauve wisterias drape the high wall of the estate yard, beside beds of Floribunda and Bourbon roses and mounds of lavender. Quirky topiaries punctuate the lawns, most notable being the pair of squirrels at the head of the main vista. And in the south-west section of the garden is a small orchard, featuring old northern varieties of apple such as 'Keswick Codlin', 'Duke of Devonshire' and 'Lord Suffield'. Beyond and between the box-lined 'Lovers Walk' is a small paddock, home to Jacob sheep. Plans are afoot to reintroduce grazing into the area beyond the main garden, bordering the beech walk which leads to the village church. Beside the canal, *Rhododendron ponticum* thickets have been thinned to make a pleasant walk, between pine, yew and thorn, southwards to the meadow.

St Michael's Mount

Marazion, nr Penzance, Cornwall

½ mile south of A394 at Marazion, access by foot at low tide, or by ferry at high tide during the summer

Area 10 acres (4 ha)
Soil acid/loam
Altitude 15–250 ft (5–76 m)
Average rainfall 35–40 in (889–1,016 mm)
Average winter climate frost-free–mild
Staff three

Fortress, priory and family home welded together, this assembly of granite walls and towers perched on its rocky islet off the Cornish coast is one of the most romantic sights in Britain. The garden has an equally powerful vein of fantasy.

Wind is the enemy here, and bold ridges of pines (*P. radiata*, *P. muricata* and *P. thunbergii*), sycamore and Holm Oak have been planted for protection, nursed and buttressed by shrubberies of salt-tolerant escallonia, olearia, hebe, tamarisk, griselinia, *Rosa rugosa* and *R. virginiana*, fuchsia and Sea Buckthorn. In the lee of these, a succession of colourful plantings is revealed as you make the long ascent up the stairway from harbour to castle. In the sunnier areas, you see brooms, cordylines, brachyglottis and tree lupins; on the cooler slopes, fuchsias, hydrangeas, camellias and the tougher rhododendrons.

Anticipation mounts as you climb, and on reaching the summit terraces and rock garden, and looking over the southern slopes, you find some really adventurous gardening, allowed by the sun, excellent drainage and absence of frost. Plantings of tender aloes, kniphofias and agapanthus contrast with the massive rock outcrops, and along the maze of stony paths you meet callistemons, aeoniums, mesembryanthemums, pelargoniums, fascicularias, *Sparmannia africana*, *Brugmansia chlorantha* (syn. *Datura chlorantha*), *Medicago arborea* and many other exotics usually to be seen only under glass. These outcrops, largely native igneous rock, provide the right environment.

Saltram

Plympton, Plymouth, Devon

2 miles west of Plympton,
3½ east of Plymouth city centre

Area 20 acres (8ha)
Soil acid/sandy loam
Altitude 100ft (30m)
Average rainfall 40in
  (1,016mm)
Average winter climate mild
Staff two, plus one trainee

BELOW LEFT: Trachelospermum
frames a statue in the Orangery
at Saltram.

BELOW RIGHT: Snowdrops
brighten the late winter
woodlands.

The sweeping views must have played a large part in persuading John and Lady Catherine Parker to move to Saltram from their estate at Boringdon, north of Plymouth, in the 1740s. Encompassing the estuary, the citadel, tiers of hills and the woods of Mount Edgcumbe, the panorama answered perfectly their fashionable aspiration for an elegant and undulating land-scape in which to create a private arcadia.

Sadly, the outside world has since encroached upon the idyll. Housing estates and light industry now fringe the estate, and the park is bisected by the noisy Plympton bypass. Many of the open views, once carefully framed by trees, have had to be closed to make screens and shelterbelts. Nevertheless, the grand classical façades of Lady Catherine's house, the stucco now washed a creamy-grey, continues to instil a civilised atmosphere through the grounds, the mood reinforced by smooth lawns, trim gravel walks and handsome garden buildings.

The pattern and content of the present enclosed garden derive from the following century, when formality returned to favour and a tradition of plantsmanship was established – in spite of the shallow stony soil and windy site. Shrub borders and spacious tree-studded lawns flow along the long, flat ridge west of the house, and the paths take you back and forth along parallel lines. The lowest walk is a long, vaulted avenue of sheltering limes, coloured with a succession of bulbs and wildflowers, from snowdrops and old varieties of daffodil to prim-roses, bluebells and cow parsley, before being mown in early July; in August, cushions of *Cyclamen hederifolium* appear between the boles.

On the adjacent lawn, impressive Monterey and Stone Pines, *Pinus radiata* and *P. pinea*, are indicative of the soft, maritime climate, while Chusan Palm, *Trachycarpus fortunei*, strikes an exotic note. The balmy flavour intensifies as you walk back along the middle glade and pine

tree paths where numerous stands of half-hardy shrubs are revealed, including the cinnamon-trunked myrtle, *Luma apiculata*, *Olearia × macrodonta*, *Itea ilicifolia*, *Hoheria* 'Glory of Amlwch', *Feijoa sellowiana*, *Drimys lanceolata* and loquat. Sober-leaved evergreens, in particular large, old rhododendrons and camellias, are the backbone of the shrubberies. Along the North Path, you find them in the company of ferns and other evergreen shrubs such as *Osmanthus delavayi* and the rarified *Michelia doltsopa*, *Drimys winteri*, *Umbellularia californica* and *Viburnum odoratissimum*.

In spring, the warm, coconut fragrance of double-flowered gorse infuses the air around the castle, the octagonal belvedere that is the conclusion of each walk running west. The approach is darkly lined with bergenia, rhododendron, skimmia and Cherry Laurel, and from it, there is still an attractive prospect of the river. The northernmost path, the Melancholy Walk, leads between more dark evergreens to another vantage point, Fanny's Bower. Named after the diarist Fanny Burney, who visited Saltram in 1789 as part of the entourage of George III, this classical temple has now had its view up the valley carefully edited to remove the worst of the city sprawl.

The Mediterranean flavour is strong in this north-east section of the garden. Large-leaved loquat, Chusan Palm, yucca and Italian Cypress surround the oval pond, and, in summer, pots of oranges and lemons are set out on the gravel. According to long-standing tradition, they are put out on Oak Apple Day (29 May) and taken in on Tavistock Goose Fair Day, the second Wednesday in October. They spend the winter in the white Doric orangery that commands the vista across the West Lawn; partly destroyed by fire in 1932, this was restored by the Trust in 1961.

Scotney Castle

Lamberhurst, Tunbridge Wells, Kent

1 mile south of Lamberhurst on A21

Area 8 acres (3·2ha)
Soil neutral/sand, clay
Altitude 250ft (76m)
Average rainfall 36in (914mm)
Average winter climate moderate–cold
Staff four

FAR RIGHT: Scotney Castle viewed across azaleas, rhododendrons and Weeping Silver Pear.

'Bless'd too is he who, midst his tufted trees,
Some ruin'd castle's lofty towers sees
Nodding o'er the stream that glides below.'

In 1836, twelve years after the death of Richard Payne Knight, landscape gardener and the author of these lines, this same romantic vision began to take shape here. His friend the cultured creator of Scotney, Edward Hussey, was determined to take full advantage of the scenic potential of his site, and in that year he invited here W. S. Gilpin, the noted designer and nephew of the originator of the Picturesque style, William Gilpin. The 'picture' was to be fashioned in its entirety, with Anthony Salvin preparing plans for a new house, which was to command views across the ridge of hills to Goudhurst and down into the Bewl Valley. The impulse for the entire composition lay below: a handsome medieval 'castle', its surviving tower reflecting in a lake-like moat. Really a fortified manor, with sixteenth- and seventeenth-century additions, the castle was considered too cold and damp for habitation by the family, and Hussey had the walls selectively demolished, to leave the present fairytale ruin. Gilpin's work centred on the terrace beside the new house, but the treatment of the entire valley landscape, with its planted quarry, sinuous sweeps of shrubbery and strikingly shaped trees dramatically sited, was clearly a red-blooded realisation of his and Knight's precepts.

A haze of bluebells in woodland at Scotney Castle.

Today, we see a post-1987 landscape, for the storm of that October ripped out large numbers of the great limes, beeches, oaks and yews that gave the slopes their billowing curves, together with most of the Cedar of Lebanon, Scots Pines, incense cedars and Lawson Cypresses that furnished the dashing horizontals and verticals between them. There has, however, been much clearance and replanting, with fast-growing species, such as Leyland Cypress, installed as temporary accents, to be felled when the slower, long-term trees make their presence felt.

But from the bastion, you still look out on a scene of breathtaking beauty, with the large numbers of deciduous trees and flowering shrubs ensuring a spectacular seasonal cycle. Bold and harmonious banks of shrubs, especially rhododendrons, were expressly welcomed by the advocates of the Picturesque landscape. But for the array and succession of colour, much is owed to subsequent plantings by Christopher Hussey, the architectural historian, who, with his wife Betty, tended his grandfather's creation from 1952 until his death in 1970. Betty Hussey still has a considerable influence at Scotney.

Early in the year, waves of primroses and daffodils succeed the snowdrops, and large specimens of *Magnolia stellata* bloom in the quarry. In late spring, it is the turn of the massed *R. ponticum* hybrids and the scented azaleas, in shades of yellow, cream and orange. Wildflowers abound. In June, the pink bells open on impressive mounds of *Kalmia latifolia*, to be succeeded in late summer by hydrangeas and, in the quarry, hardy fuchsias and willow gentians. In autumn, the valley is filled with the mellow tints and flame highlights of leaves, furnished by Japanese maples, rhus, parrotia, liquidambar, nyssa and stands of Royal Fern.

The more domestic gardening is focused in the vicinity of the new house and bastion, where Climbing, Shrub and Floribunda roses tumble about a Venetian font, and also in the forecourt of the castle, where Christopher Hussey set out a formal pattern of beds around the Venetian well-head installed by his aunt; its present scheme of herbs was designed by Lanning Roper, who became Mrs Hussey's garden adviser after her husband's death. Herbaceous and bedding plants fill the adjoining border, and roses, vines and wisteria explore the ruined walls.

The lake itself is strewn with waterlilies and fringed with marsh plants, including a memorable sweep of the white Candelabra primula 'Postford White'. A reclining figure in bronze by Henry Moore, given by the sculptor in tribute to Christopher Hussey, occupies this same isthmus. This is a powerfully atmospheric place.

Sheffield Park Garden

Uckfield, East Sussex

4 miles south-east of Lewes, off former A275 (now unclassified)

Area 120 acres (48·6ha)
Soil acid/heavy clay
Altitude 300ft (91m)
Average rainfall 35in (889mm)
Average winter climate moderate
Staff five

The reflections in the water of coloured leaves, soaring conifers, balustraded bridges, cascades and the towers and pinnacles of the Gothick mansion give Sheffield Park an unmistakable sense of place. The axes of the garden are the four lakes, which are strung down the southerly slope below the house in an inverted 'T' formation. This is an ornamental landscape of dazzling scale and richness, planted above all for the drama of shape, trees, rhododendrons and autumn foliage, and encompassing over a hundred acres of meadow, marsh, woodland and glade.

The estate belonged to the Earls of Sheffield until it was purchased in 1909 by Arthur Soames, a Lincolnshire brewer, who had coveted the park since visiting it twenty years earlier. It was then that the rich overlay was applied. Scarlet oaks, Japanese maples, nyssas and amelanchiers were woven around the lakesides in the boldest drifts, complemented by new stands of giant conifers and seams of rhododendrons. But plant variety was always secondary to landscape impact, and Soames barely indulged in the new Chinese and South American introductions then being welcomed into other great woodland gardens.

These carefully conceived pictorial scenes were ravaged by the great storm of October 1987. Shelterbelts were devastated, ornamental trees brought down by the dozen and much of the 30 years' creative work of renewal and expansion carried out by the Trust undone. But the core of the garden survived largely intact, the native oaks were high-pruned and have

LEFT: Japanese maples and pampas grass beside the Middle Lake at Sheffield Park.

regenerated splendidly and the replanting has continued apace. Only those visitors acquainted with the previous landscape will now sense the loss.

The circuit of the park follows lazy figures of eight, and if all the tributary paths and glades are explored, and periodic pauses taken to savour the views, it lasts the best part of a day. No season is disappointing. In spring, the park wakes to camellias and a grass sward spangled with bulbs. You walk down banks sheeted with wild Lent Lilies, *Narcissus pseudonarcissus*, and as the many old hybrid daffodils succeed them, there are the warm tints of amelanchiers and maples among the expanding greenery, and the scents of osmanthus on the air.

May brings the first great climax of colour, with pink and white dogwoods and the many thickets of rhododendrons and azaleas flowering in an ocean of bluebells. The palette is subtly graded, with the softer tones predominating through stands of tall, fragrant Loderi rhododendrons and other whites and pastels. Crimson, pink and purple Hardy Hybrids are grouped around the upper lake, and the more vibrant orange and gold Exbury azaleas (superb against Copper Beech), intense carmine and rose evergreen Kurume azaleas and electrifying violet-blue rhododendron hybrids (partnered with creams and lime-yellows) are gathered in their own glades. Nevertheless, the zany group of 'Hino-mayo' azaleas, clipped tight in late autumn and looking uncannily like a flock of brilliant pink sheep, is guaranteed to have eyes on stalks.

By now, the Purple Beeches and maples are reflecting sumptuously in the lakes, and the emerald leaves of the other deciduous trees have thrown the huge Wellingtonias, redwoods, pines and cedars into deep relief. Every path has its quiet interludes, from sparkling glades

BELOW LEFT: *Hydrangea* 'Blue Wave' at Sheffield Park.

BELOW RIGHT: Brewer's Weeping Spruce in fresh young growth.

The stone Top Bridge, flanked by maples and rhododendrons, reflected in the First Lake at Sheffield Park.

of beech and birch (the cream trunks looking well among the bluebells), to exotic and solemn groves of hardy Chusan Palms, cypresses and hemlocks. But among these trees, the connoisseur will find rarities galore, including *Athrotaxis × laxifolia* from Tasmania, *Pinus montezumae* from Mexico and *Fagus engleriana* from China.

One of the Trust's policies, as in many other woodland gardens, has been to enrich the summer display and, accordingly, an extensive collection of the late-flowering Ghent azaleas has been assembled (now the National Collection), and hydrangeas, lacecaps in particular, have been planted in quantity. There are no formal beds of herbaceous plants at Sheffield Park, but the lakes are edged in moisture-loving species and have their rafts of waterlilies. In 1979, the banks of the stream, west of the lowest lake, were also enriched, including a colony of giant Himalayan lilies, *Cardiocrinum giganteum*, which begin opening their white, crimson-stained trumpets from eight-foot stems in June.

The advent of the park's second climax is heralded by the red tints on Spindle Trees and *Prunus sargentii* (the only ornamental cherry grown). By mid-October, the landscape is alight. At ground level, fires break out among azaleas, fothergillas, enkianthus, blueberry and berberis, the flames rising through amelanchier, parrotia, Japanese maples, *Acer circinatum* and *A. maximowiczianum* (syn. *nikoense*), to engulf the American oaks, the celebrated grove of Tupelos (*Nyssa sylvatica*), and, a little later, the liquidambars. Simultaneously, the numerous birches have turned to butter yellow, the columns of deciduous conifers (taxodium and metasequoia) to orange-brown, and the native trees to copper and russet. Added to all this are plumes of white pampas grass, sky-blue streaks of autumn gentians (linear beds of *Gentiana sino-ornata* – another quirky touch), complementary domes and spires of evergreens, the lakes and James Wyatt's fantasy architecture.

In spite of its exotic content, the park is a tranquil place to stroll, the underlying mood set by the expanses of grass and water, the native trees and wildflowers. Beyond the third lake, the exotics melt away almost entirely as you follow the Trust's new walk that takes you, via rustic bridges of hornbeam, across a marsh. Native sedges and bog plants grow here between thickets of alder and willow, and it is the haunt of kingfishers, grebe, marsh tits and several species of duck. The cricket field beyond, the scene of the first Test Match against the Australians in 1884, is also tended as a wildflower reserve and has a large population of Spotted Orchids.

Shugborough

Milford, nr Stafford

6 miles east of Stafford on A513

Area 22 acres (9 ha)
Soil acid/sandy loam
Altitude 100 ft (30 m)
Average rainfall 27 in (686 mm)
Average winter climate cold
Staff three

The capture of a Spanish treasure galleon in 1743 brought a fortune in prize money to Captain George Anson RN, later Admiral Lord Anson, and with this wealth, the fashionable improvements to the family estate at Shugborough, already being wrought by his older, bachelor brother Thomas, took on a new breadth and scale.

Entering the park through the belt of woodland beside the Stafford road, you immediately taste the second phase of Thomas Anson's work, as to left and right three classical monuments appear in quick succession: on one side, the Lanthorn of Demosthenes, a cylindrical building with Corinthian columns, capped by a decorative tripod; on the other, mounted on a knoll, a Triumphal Arch, adorned with busts of Admiral and Lady Anson; and beyond, the Tower of the Winds, a slim octagon with windows and pedimented porches. The monuments are no longer part of a picturesque landscape. Following a disastrous flood of 1795, which swept away many of Anson's garden features, John Webb, a pupil of William Emes, was engaged to remodel the park, and with agriculture now the prime interest, its character altered. Trees, planted in great numbers in the 1820s and afterwards, have also affected the views.

The setting is mellow and pastoral – flat, low-lying ground at the confluence of the rivers Sow and Trent (an attractive packhorse bridge crosses at the join), with the wild expanse of Cannock Chase rising behind. The drive curves towards the east façade of the mansion, remodelled by Samuel Wyatt around the turn of the nineteenth century and rather ghostly in its milk-grey, ashlar-like cladding.

There are some notable wisterias on the adjacent coach-house, and in the midden yard you will find the celebrated edible blue-flowered pea, *Lathyrus nervosus*, brought from Patagonia by Captain Anson's cook and known as Lord Anson's Blue Pea. But the gardens lie behind and to the sides of the house, and it is here that you encounter Thomas Anson's earlier, more eclectic structures, absorbed into a nineteenth-century layout of formal lawns and flower schemes, and gently meandering pleasure grounds, all strung along an arm of the River Sow, which flows directly below the house. To the south, on the site of Anson's shrubbery, is the loop of the Ladies' Walk, leading between oak, beech and lime trees (including a particularly fine Weeping Silver Lime), past banks of ornamental shrubs and on to open lawn beside the water, where massed daffodils are followed by a riverside fringe of meadowsweet, lythrum and other wildflowers.

Rhododendron ponticum is very much at home on the estate's sandy acid soil, but in the pleasure grounds, wherever the soil is moist enough, it is gradually being replaced by a range of Hardy Hybrids. Brooms, species roses, escallonia, snowberry, osmanthus and the late-flowering buckeye, *Aesculus parviflora*, are among the supporting cast along the Ladies' Walk. Around the lawns and glades to the north of the house, the colour is boosted by fiery plantings of Ghent azaleas and a lavish new herbaceous border, and here you will also come upon an impressive Weeping Silver Holly and a Common Yew of gigantic proportions, noted in 1898 as being one of the most remarkable in the country, and shading an acre of ground.

As you arrive in front of the house, the mood becomes strongly Victorian. A series of terraced lawns, set out by W.A. Nesfield in about 1855, replaces Anson's bowling green, and glowing cones of golden yew process down them towards the river, contrasting with the Purple Beech and plum woven into the backdrop of trees. This provocative yellow and purple contrast, much favoured at the time, has been intensified by beds of the canary-coloured Floribunda rose 'Bright Smile' and seams of 'Hidcote' lavender. Purple pansies and petunias are grown in the stone troughs and urns. Close by, a rose garden in more delicate late nineteenth-century style has been reconstructed by the Trust. This takes the form of a pattern of small formal beds and ironwork arches arranged around a sundial, and sporting the pink, white, crimson and purple flower colours of the period – but again, against the challenging backdrop of golden yew.

Beside the river, directly below the house, you pick up the first in the remaining series of garden buildings belonging to Anson's early phase of Rococo landscaping. Here stands the fragment of a ruin, with a rubble crag and the remains of a Coadestone druid attached. And at the turn of the river is the Chinese House, a white pavilion reflecting elegantly in the water. It was the first building Anson erected, in about 1747, and an early example of the new taste for Chinoiserie. It is set off by a red iron bridge, and planting of an oriental flavour, including bamboo, stephanandra, berberis and Pagoda Tree enriches the flavour. The scarlet lacquered stems of dogwood and the smoky plume of a Swamp Cypress (albeit an American conifer) add to the atmosphere.

On an island between the rivers, a dark yew and laurel tunnel brings you to a curious monument sporting carved goat's heads and surmounted by a cat, probably commemorating the Corsican goats and rare breed of Persian cat kept by Thomas Anson. And returning to the main, curving gravel path, you encounter the Shepherd's Monument. A cryptic sequence of letters runs along its base, but the centrepiece is a marble tablet depicting a pastoral scene by Poussin and inscribed with a phrase that resonated in many an eighteenth-century landowner, 'Et in Arcadia ego'.

Sissinghurst Castle

Sissinghurst, nr Cranbrook, Kent

2 miles north-east of Cranbrook, 1 mile east of Sissinghurst village (A262)

Area 6 acres (2·4ha)
Soil neutral/clay
Altitude 200ft (61m)
Average rainfall 29in (737mm)
Average winter climate moderate
Staff seven, plus one trainee

The sudden view of the twin-turreted tower, rising from the open farmland, always brings a surge of anticipation. The garden's reputation, reinforced by talented head gardeners, sails before it, and anyone who has been here knows that it is not exaggerated. The Trust, which must cope with the wear and congestion caused by the excessive numbers of pilgrims, discourages publicity and has introduced timed tickets, but still people return in their droves, again and again. Over fifteen years, I have been one of them.

'To Vita Sackville-West, who made this garden,' reads the tablet under the Tower. Vita saw the castle for the first time in April 1930. 'I fell in love; love at first sight. I saw what might be made of it. It was Sleeping Beauty's Castle; but a castle running away into sordidness and squalor; a garden crying out for rescue.' An aerial photograph of July 1932 shows the site cleared and the gardens laid out in front of the South Cottage and Priest's House. By May 1938, when Sissinghurst opened to the pubic for the first time, all the bones of the garden were in place and the new plantings maturing.

Her husband, Harold Nicolson, was responsible for the pattern of the design. A diplomat, biographer, journalist and politician, he was also, according to Vita, an 'architect manqué',

NEAR RIGHT: Azaleas, hostas and bluebells fringing the Moat Walk at Sissinghurst Castle.

FAR RIGHT: Shuttlecock ferns partnering euphorbias in the Nut Walk.

239

delighting in the pleasures of 'square-ruled paper . . . stakes and string'. They decided upon a formal, emphatic structure: '. . . long, axial walks, running north and south, east and west, usually with terminal points such as a statue or an archway or a pair of sentinel poplars, and the more intimate surprise of small geometrical gardens opening off them, rather as the rooms of an enormous house would open off the arterial corridors,' wrote Vita. Comparisons with Hidcote Manor (qv) are perhaps inevitable, though there is no evidence that Harold or Vita visited it before laying out their garden. The principal ingredient that distinguishes Sissinghurst from Hidcote, however, is the romance. At Sissinghurst are the ancient buildings, the moat, and above all the fairytale tower, the garden's centrepiece, built shortly before Queen Elizabeth I's visit in 1573; visible from most parts of the site, it lifts the eye from the enclosed spaces, and, from its roof, you have the opportunity of a bird's-eye view of the garden.

Then there is the all-pervading character of Vita herself. Her writing room in the Tower is much as she left it, a Cape Primrose or other flowering pot-plant on the table, and visitors intrigued by her intricate private life or under the spell of her writing can come to probe or to pay homage.

The tour begins in the courtyard, where Irish Yews process from the entrance arch to the tower, between pads of tightly mown lawn. As at Hidcote, the mood of the beds and garden rooms is set by a clearly defined colour scheme. Here, there are plants echoing the salmon and copper tones of the brick: chaenomeles, evergreen magnolia with its suede-backed leaves, climbing roses like 'Gloire de Dijon' and apple-scented 'Paul Transon', and, in late summer, the burnished foliage and glowing hips of *Rosa moyesii* 'Geranium'. But there are also contrasting notes: in spring, the great bushes of rosemary, billowing a rich shade of blue at the foot of the tower (the variety, 'Sissinghurst Blue', occurred here as a seedling); in summer, *Solanum crispum* 'Glasnevin', casting a lilac veil over the east wall. And then there are the troughs and Italian pots: the former simply filled with trailing blue *Euphorbia myrsinites* or white osteospermums, and the latter perhaps with violas or purple petunias. (In the main, plants at Sissinghurst are not blended into salads, but displayed as individuals, in generous groups, and with partners that show off their shape and habit.)

All this intensifies in the deep, south-facing border, where purple, violet-blue, mauve-pink and magenta perennials and climbers are assembled. Thundery and brooding, it is my least favourite scheme, and I itch to weave in some cracks of sunlight, some lemon yellow, or at least some lime green. But the plant arrangement is masterly, with purple vine and clematis like 'Perle d'Azur' and 'Ville de Lyon' cloaking the wall behind, and a well-matched succession of middle and foreground flowers from tulips, wallflowers and dwarf irises to black-eyed *Geranium psilostemon*, platycodon (the campanula-like balloon flower), lythrum, asters and, a long-serving ingredient, the white-flecked, crimson dahlia, 'Edinburgh'.

At midsummer, there is only one way to turn, to the Rose Garden, now awash with the petal-packed, scent-drenched flowers of the old-fashioned Shrub varieties that were Vita's passion. For her, they were infused with the romance of legend, poetry and the East – with the bazaars of Constantinople, where one afternoon, 'the rugs and carpets of Isfahan and Bokhara and Samarcand were unrolled in their dim but sumptuous colouring and richness of texture for our slow delight'.

Irises, peonies, violas, pinks and alliums spread a Persian carpet beneath them, and on the curved wall at the west end of the garden there is that much-photographed curtain of

LEFT: A view of the Tower from the Cottage Garden in late summer.

241

Clematis 'Perle d'Azur'; this feat is achieved by regular training and tying-in of shoots through the spring and summer months. Plantings of Rugosa roses, single-flowered Hybrid Teas and Hybrid Musks extend the rose season beyond mid-July, and in autumn there is a second flush from many others. Japanese anemones, sedums, caterpillar-like pennisetum grasses, caryopteris, lavatera and felt-leaved *Hydrangea aspera* Villosa Group are then in full bloom.

Much of the late summer colour comes from tender perennials – plants that must be propagated annually by cuttings and overwintered under glass. Vita would have known few of the many varieties now used here to take over from the biennial wallflowers, honesty and foxgloves. Their greatest concentration is in the adjacent Cottage Garden – from spring to autumn, a cauldron of oranges, yellows and tropical reds. Wallflowers, tulips, irises, daylilies, euphorbias, helianthemums and coloured grasses fire up the garden earlier in the year, and then, from midsummer, it is the turn of Mexican salvias, argyranthemums, leonotis, cannas, dahlias and the sheets of the daisy-like arctotis hybrids, grown under the brick walls of the cottage. The contents of the verdigris laundry copper in the centre of the garden usually turn from crimson-red (the tulip 'Couleur Cardinal') to apricot-orange (*Mimulus aurantiacus*).

Roses are ubiquitous partners. Together with figs and vines, Sissinghurst's old walls seemed to Vita to cry out for them: 'I planted them recklessly, and have never regretted it.' Here, the glowing red 'Parkdirektor Riggers' partners orange honeysuckle, and, from the cottage wall, 'Madame Alfred Carrière' gives soft white backlighting.

Below, a strip of lawn runs down to the moat, flanked on one side by a bank of deciduous azaleas – as fiery in their autumn leaf tints as they are in their flowers – and an old plantation of Kentish cobnuts. For some years, there was a famous carpet of coloured polyanthus under the nuts, but as often happens when one plant is bedded in the same spot year after year, the soil became exhausted and the plants sickened. Now, the richest spring surprise is sprung in the pleached lime walk, where primroses, anemones, muscari, species tulips, narcissi and a host of other bulbs are planted in mixed colours and assorted groups at the base of the trunks, to the accompaniment of alpine clematis spilling from Italian oil jars. This was Harold Nicolson's personal garden, and his diaries record the many happy hours spent planning and improving the display each year, aided by visits to the Royal Horticultural Society's spring shows at Vincent Square.

Herbs, with their historical and poetic associations, were assured a home at Sissinghurst. They are formally arranged in their own enclosure, around a camomile seat and a lion-guarded bowl of red houseleeks, and with rugs of prostrate thymes laid at the entrance: patterned pink, white and crimson in summer, these are perhaps my favourite single feature, but, like so much of Sissinghurst's planting, do depend on a very high level of maintenance – intricate hand-weeding and frequent renewal of plants.

From here, you walk past the moat wall, hung with white wisteria and lapped, from August to October, with the lavender daisies of *Aster × frikartii* 'Mönch', and into the orchard. This area, bordered on two sides by water, is the garden's only open and expansive compartment, and provides a welcome interlude. In spring, gold, citron, cream and white daffodils, in separate but interlocking drifts, appear *en masse* under the apple and cherry trees. And in summer, there are wildflowers in the grass and Rambler roses foaming in the branches.

Returning to the walls and hedges, there is still much to see. There is the Tower Lawn, with

PREVIOUS PAGE: A lead cast of a statue by Rosandic in the White Garden among the flowers and leaves of Weeping Silver Pear, phlox, argyranthumum, artemisia and *Crambe maritima*.

ABOVE LEFT: Apricot foxgloves taking up the tints of purple elder in the Rose Garden at Sissinghurst.

ABOVE RIGHT: Phygelius, egyngium and kniphofia backed by *Berberis* 'Rose Glow'.

its 'Albertine' roses and a shady sunken garden (formerly an unsuccessful pond) with blue poppies and scarlet fuchsia. And there is the most famous compartment of all.

'I am trying to make a grey, green and white garden,' wrote Vita in one of her weekly gardening articles for the *Observer* in January 1950. The idea transported her readers, and the garden itself has prompted countless imitations. The images hardly need describing: Regale Lilies, white delphiniums, irises, eremerus, galtonias and onopordum thistles rising above cushions of artemisia and hosta; a Weeping Silver Pear (the original fell in the great storm of October 1987; the present one is a replacement) sheltering the lead statue of a virgin; an ironwork bower spun in the white Rambler rose, *R. mulliganii*; the Priest's House sheeted in *R.* 'Madame Alfred Carrière' and *R. laerigata* 'Cooperi'. The colour range embraces every crisp tint and tone, with every plant sited for maximum impact of shape, height and leaf size.

'It may be a terrible failure,' added Vita with her customary modesty. 'All the same, I cannot help hoping that the great ghostly barn owl will sweep silently across the pale garden next summer in the twilight, that I am now planting under the first flakes of snow.' Whether or not it is twilight when you leave Sissinghurst, I recommend this enclosure as your departing image. It is a sorbet after the feast of colour and the most magical part of a magical garden. 245

Sizergh Castle

nr Kendal, Cumbria

3½ miles south of Kendal,
north-west of interchange
A590/A591

Area 16 acres (6·5 ha)
Soil neutral/shallow loam
overlying limestone
Altitude 200 ft (61 m)
Average rainfall 50 in
(1,270 mm)
Average winter climate mild–
moderate
Staff two

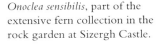

Onoclea sensibilis, part of the
extensive fern collection in the
rock garden at Sizergh Castle.

Just to the east of the castle's fourteenth-century pele-tower is one of the most impressive rock
gardens in the Trust's hands. Built in 1926 by the noted Ambleside firm of T.R. Hayes &
Sons, it is a quarter-acre bowl of rough limestone terraces, contained within a dell and
watered by streams, pools and falls fed from the natural lake above. Originally more open,
the garden now has a fringe of sizeable conifers, including Bhutan, Arolla and Mountain
pines, maples and other ornamental trees, creating a quieter, leafier, more secret world
within. On the lower banks, many of the dwarfer conifers, which punctuate the various
meandering walks with numerous green and purple Japanese cut-leaved maples, have been
allowed to mature into magnificent specimens.

The semi-prostrate Caucasian Fir, golden Westfelton Yew and weeping hemlock are
among the most memorable, but every path brings you past curiosities in the form of
miniature Norway Spruce, Noble Fir, junipers and chamaecyparis, interspersed with taller
gems such as the Japanese Umbrella Pine, *Sciadopitys verticillata*, and the rare glaucous blue
form of the Japanese White Pine, *Pinus parviflora* 'Glauca'. A number of larger outsized
conifers have been selectively felled to make room for them, to expose the contours of the
bowl and to let in the sun. But as the high-altitude alpines have been shaded and elbowed out,

the bowl has become filled with an alternative cast, appreciative of moisture and dappled light. The prime sources of flower colour are no longer the rock plants but the woodland geraniums and the bog and aquatic plants along the watercourses. Cool and moist, the dell has also become a paradise for ferns ranging from Shield and Sword ferns (Polystichum), bladder ferns (Cystopteris), delicate maidenhairs (Adiantum) to elegant forms of the royal fern, including the miniature *Osmunda regalis gracilis*. Sizergh can now boast one of the finest collections in the country.

Part of the success of the rock garden is that it is a locally inspired feature. This is limestone country and Sizergh's 1,500-acre (607-ha) estate encompasses screes, cliffs and pavements, as well as panoramic views of the distant Lakeland fells. (The walks also take in some fine tracts of ancient woodland, in which the red squirrel is still resident.) These habitats are rich in wildflowers, and there is a taste of this abundance on the bank west of the castle and in the meadow below the rock garden, where the wild Lent Lily, *Narcissus pseudonarcissus*, is followed by a kaleidoscope of local species, including early Purple, Twayblade and Butterfly Orchids, Meadow Geranium, Ladies' Smock, quaking grass, vetches and ox-eye daisies – the colours augmented by orange-tipped butterflies and much other insect life.

Elsewhere, natural themes are pursued with more decorative plants. The thin shady grass above the rock garden is lit in spring with crocus, scillas, Dog's Tooth Violets and double white anemones, to the accompaniment of the white Mount Fuji Cherry, *Prunus* 'Shirotae'; formerly an orchard, this leads into the old kitchen garden, whose walls are now the backdrop to a varied summer display of herbaceous plants, arranged for foliage contrast and a progressively stronger sequence of colours.

And to the west of the house, you walk into an area of grassy glades, shaded by magnolias, Handkerchief Tree and more flowering cherries, where Shrub roses like 'Cerise Bouquet', 'Macrantha' and the red-thorned *Rosa sericea* subsp. *omeiensis* grow among carpeting geraniums (and the local green hellebore, *Helleborus viridis*), and where the drifts of daffodils are succeeded by lime-tolerant lilies like *Lilium martagon*, *henryi* and *pardalinum* and belts of white colchicums.

The castle itself, built originally as defence against the marauding Scots and the home of the Strickland family for over 750 years, rises above the garden lake. A curtain of Boston Ivy, green in summer and scarlet in autumn, softens the massive, grey edifice, and 'Brown Turkey' figs and an array of other shrubs and climbers covers the long garden wall adjacent – among them, *Escallonia* 'Iveyi', *Ceanothus* 'Percy Picton' and the Moroccan Broom, *Cytisus battandieri*; a cast that indicates the gentle (but wet) maritime climate. Below the terrace lawn, a second grass terrace, formerly an elaborate Dutch parterre, runs between a summer-house and flights of stone steps, the second stairway descending to a bastion over the garden lake, created from the former moat. Much of this is the work of T. R. Hayes.

Everywhere, the walls, balustrades and paving are decorated with plants: fuchsias, honeysuckle, *Clematis montana* and various dianthus and other alpines making cushions between the stones. The mauve *Erinus alpinus* colonises the castle's own stairway, and the pink and white daisies of *Erigeron karvinskianus* has seeded high into the wall cervices. These details play against the grander scenery: the still sheet of water, in which the castle and fringe of Manna Ash, willow, sumach and weeping hornbeam are reflected; the rolling parkland, with its fine walnuts and field maples; and beyond, the looming Howgill hills.

Snowshill Manor

nr Broadway, Gloucestershire

3 miles south-west of
Broadway, turning off the A44

Area 2 acres (0·8 ha)
Soil neutral–lime/light loam
Altitude 750 ft (228 m)
Average rainfall 26 in (660 mm)
Average winter climate very cold
Staff one

A bronze waterspout in the garden at Snowshill Manor.

From the mid-nineteenth century, the honey-coloured villages of the Cotswold hills — unspoilt, harmonious, rich in vernacular detail and an alluring antidote to the growing Victorian industrialisation — became an idyll and inspiration to a succession of painters, illustrators, craftsmen and other adherents to the Arts and Crafts creed. Charles Wade, an architect, artist and woodworker, and a tireless collector of curios, saw a *Country Life* advertisement for the sale of Snowshill Manor in 1919.

His legacy is one of the most extraordinary houses in the country, and the garden, anchored to the steeply sloping hillside below, is no less absorbing: a gold and green patchwork of intimate walled courts, narrow corridors, terraces, ponds and rustic outbuildings, idiosyncratically ornamented and sensitively planted. In spring and summer, a lively mix of cottage flowers, dispersed in repeated stands down the long, outer path, injects a swathe of bright colour across the mellow composition: tulips, Oriental poppies, lupins, foxgloves, veronica, lime-green alchemilla and purple sage are among the company, backed by specimen common elders beyond the fence. With white doves disporting on the roof of the medieval dovecote, the tops of clematis and roses visible beyond, and the fresh greens of the countryside all about, this is traditional England at its picture-postcard best.

All parts of the garden have their flower-filled moments. Here and there, you will come upon mixed beds of hellebores and Japanese anemones (an excellent, long-lasting partnership for part shade), peonies, phloxes, lavender, acanthus, thalictrum and viola; steps fringed with red valerian; grass strewn with daffodils; and walls hung with roses. Wade found blue, mauve and purple toned best with the stone and these he allowed to predominate, with secondary use of salmons and creams, and sparing use of reds and yellows. Orange was banished.

But this is emphatically an architect's garden. 'A garden is an extension of the house, a series of outdoor rooms,' Wade wrote, echoing contemporary philosophy. 'The plan is much more important than the flowers in it. Walls, steps and alley ways give a permanent setting, so that it is pleasant and orderly in both summer and winter.' Each room has its rustic details and

LEFT: Oriental poppies, campanulas, penstemons and purple sage in the double borders leading to the Dovecote at Snowshill Manor.

249

crafted ornament: gate-piers, troughs and cisterns carrying the sound of water, a gilded armillary sundial crowning a stone column, a Venetian well-head, a bellcote with figures of St George and the Dragon, a shrine for a Madonna on the byre roof and a wall-mounted astrological dial. These last, like all the garden's wooden furniture, are painted in Wade's preferred shade of turquoise-flushed French blue, which, as with his favoured slice of the floral spectrum, he found the most satisfactory foil to stone and grass.

Beyond the walls and tiled roofs, there is the sweeping contrast of the Cotswold landscape. Though independent of it, the garden nestles into it as comfortably and organically as does the village, and any sense of claustrophobia engendered by the passages and small, introspective rooms is dispelled by the open views offered by others.

Areas of rough grass, native trees, hedgerow shrubbery and wildflowers also create a bond. Common ivy, ferns, boxwood and ash are among the garden flora, and a dark tunnel of Guelder Rose, *Viburnum opulus* (a replacement for the aged elders planted by Wade), leads from the byre at the head of Well Court; scillas, Snakeshead Fritillaries and primroses spangle the ground here in spring, followed by the pink and white Turk's caps of Martagon Lilies. This all adds to the rustic mood, and in sympathy, the Trust maintains the garden entirely on organic principles.

Speke Hall

The Walk, Speke, Liverpool

On north bank of the Mersey, 8 miles south-east of Liverpool centre, 1 mile south of A561, on west side of Liverpool airport

Area 35 acres (14ha)
Soil mainly acid/thin layer of loam over sand
Altitude 100ft (30m)
Average rainfall 32in (813mm)
Average winter climate cold
Staff three

In a landscape littered with industrial buildings, busy roads, security fences and airport runways, Speke offers seclusion and oxygen. Woods and fields provide an immediate welcome, and around the perimeter of the grounds, trees have been judiciously sited to block ugliness and frame desirable views of the adjacent Mersey estuary and the distant Welsh hills. To the south, a horseshoe-shaped soil mound, or bund, muffles the noise of aircraft. Thus soothed, you can take in the wonder of the hall. A mesmerising expanse of black and white timberwork, sandwiched between mellow roof tiles and a base of red sandstone, it is one of the finest surviving Tudor manorhouses in England; it was built, on the site of an earlier house for the Norris family, who were prominent landowners in the area.

A stone bridge leads across the moat – both sections of which were drained by the mid-nineteenth century – and into a warren of panelled rooms, filled with heavily decorated oak furniture and dimly lit through leaded and stained-glass windows. Contributing to the atmospheric gloom are the two yew trees in the cobbled courtyard, known as Adam and Eve. They were first referred to in the eighteenth century, but are reputedly as old as the present hall; surgery has recently been necessary to repair and rejuvenate them.

The present garden layout was established after 1855, when, after a long period of neglect, the hall was inherited by the twenty-year-old Richard Watt and a programme of restoration and embellishment began. This was continued from 1867 by Frederick Leyland, who became the tenant after Watt's sudden death, and from 1878 by Watt's daughter Adelaide. Since the Trust assumed direct control of Speke from Merseyside County Council in 1986, it has undertaken a further phase of major improvements in the late Victorian 'Old English' idiom, and a varied garden is once again emerging.

The most delicate planting is found in the small, low-walled enclosure outside the Great

Parlour, where a pretty scheme of Floribunda and Shrub roses has been established, centred on the small-flowered varieties 'White Pet', rose-pink 'The Fairy' and apricot-pink 'Peek A Boo', grown as bushes and half-standards. The design was inspired by old photographs and realised in 1985. The colouring echoes that of the moat border, where the marriage of white and warm pink roses, phlox, hydrangeas and Japanese anemones and damson-purple cotinus and berberis, with the sandstone and timberwork of the house, is a lesson in good planting; even the tones of the leaded windows are repeated – in the white-flecked, grape-purple flowerheads of acanthus.

The sandy soil is well suited to rhododendrons, and these were planted in large numbers in the second half of the nineteenth century. Azaleas and pink and white Hardy Hybrids are the main feature of the North Lawn border, growing in the company of yucca, pampas grass, heather, pine, laburnum and crataegus. Rhododendrons are also prominent in the new wood and water dell, a significant addition to the garden developed by the Trust from 1987 out of derelict land. A stone tunnel leads into it, and ferns, primulas and other perennials flank the bubbling watercourse. With the fresh green foliage and autumn tints of azaleas, these provide light and colour to contrast with the blocks of sombre evergreen rhododendrons, yews and laurels that will, in time, re-create the shadowy, Gothic passages that delighted the Victorians.

Springhill

Moneymore, Magherafelt,
Co. Londonderry

1 mile from Moneymore on
the B18 Coagh road

Area 45 acres (18ha)
Soil acid/light soil
Altitude 100ft (30m)
Average rainfall 35in (889mm)
Average winter climate cold–
 very cold
Staff one

Touches of formality and grandeur are here heavily diluted by unpretentious domesticity and mellow landscape. White-washed walls, slate roofs and the matching pair of low, plain, roughly plastered staff houses counter the impact of the long, straight entrance drive and the late seventeenth-century elegance and symmetry of Springhill's façade. While in the garden, you are lured away from the mountain views into a sequence of service yards, small walled enclosures, shrubberies and copses.

Around the house, the stonework is only lightly ornamented with plants, but the white walls make a striking backdrop for the foliage of bay trees and the cinnamon trunks of the half-hardy myrtle, *Luma apiculata*. East of the forecourt, flower colour comes into play. Lines of columnar rowan, *Sorbus aucuparia* 'Fastigiata' and slender Irish Juniper, *Juniperus communis* 'Hibernica', have been introduced by the Trust to set an underlying formal pattern; the Bleach Green border has also been given a crisp blue and yellow colour scheme; and in the walled herb garden, marjoram, mint, rue and sage are grown in slate-edged squares around the camomile lawn.

But otherwise the plantings are relaxed, with mosses, *Erinus alpinus* and ferns colonising between the climbing roses and clematis. Wallflowers, Martagon Lilies, *Viola cornuta*, colchicums and Willow Gentian flower in succession between the junipers, while in the walled flower garden, there is a lusher mood from hostas, globe flower, Solomon's Seal, Bistort, daylilies, *Ligularia przewalskii* and *Lobelia* 'Tania' – the mood prompted by the moist climate and heavy soil. Of the cast of roses the most famous is the old, and sadly rather sickly, specimen of the McCartney Rose, *R. bracteata*. Lord McCartney brought this superb species home to Co. Antrim from China, where he was Ambassador in about 1793, and is said to have planted the original one himself here against the barn wall.

'At Springhill are the finest trees in this county,' wrote G. V. Sampson in his 1802 *Statistical Survey of the County of Londonderry*. Subsequent phases of planting have ensured the estate remains well stocked, and the sloping ground gives you varied vantage points from which to survey them. Mature oaks, Horse Chestnuts, beeches, sycamores, *Pinus radiata* and *Taxus baccata* are among those prominent around the house and garden, while more recent additions include an avenue of red-fruited sycamores, *Acer pseudoplatanus* 'Erythrocarpum', and a collection of unusual birches. The beech walk to the rear of the house, established by Springhill's builder William Conyngham, was replanted in 1984 after the original trees developed beech bark disease. But the yews in the woods are probably a vestige of the ancient forest of Glenconkeyne which used to extend to Loch Neagh. Yellow azaleas, hybrid rhododendrons and bluebells furnish contrasting swathes of colour in spring, and in summer there are hoherias and blue hydrangeas.

Standen

East Grinstead, West Sussex

2 miles south of East Grinstead, signposted from B2110

Area 12 acres (4·8 ha)
Soil slightly acid/greensand
Altitude 200 ft (61 m)
Average rainfall 27 in (686 mm)
Average winter climate moderate
Staff one

A paving stone pathway meanders through a blur of bluebells in a woodland walk at Standen.

This quirky assembly of tile-hung, weatherboard and warm brick and stone walls, high chimneys, gables and prospect tower is a product of the late nineteenth-century revival of unpretentious, vernacular styles of architecture, built using local materials and traditional skills. Its architect, Philip Webb, was one of the pioneers of this Arts and Crafts movement and a close associate of William Morris, whose wallpapers and textiles enrich the house's interior. The buildings are set into wooded hillside, and in autumn when the trees turn copper, red and russet, the harmony is remarkable. The views are far-reaching, south and south-east across the Medway valley to the ridges of Ashdown Forest, the pastoral middle ground enhanced more recently by the creation of Weir Wood reservoir. Exposed faces of sandstone beside the winding entrance drive and in the quarry, from which the stone for the house was excavated, add to the picturesque qualities.

Massed rhododendrons between the Croquet Lawn and the house at Standen.

The garden, created by Margaret Beale (whose gardening diaries survive) largely comprises a series of asymmetrical, tree-fringed lawns, undulating shrubberies and intricate tapestries of ground-cover plants, and rolls down the steep hill at right angles to the house. Highlights of the planting include the textures and colours bordering the meandering gravel paths above the house, and filling the adjacent quarry, the garden's finest feature. Here, the shrubs and woodland perennials have been encouraged to mingle and interlace, giving an atmospheric setting for the chimneys and rooftops, and adding to the rugged drama of the precipitous quarry sides plunging into water, which can be viewed from all angles.

In May, the banks are awash with the colour and scent of azaleas and bluebells, and at other times there are flowers from camellias, magnolias, bergenias, epimediums, heathers, brooms, geraniums, montbretia and polygonum. But mostly the interest centres on the leaf patterns. 253

A large collection of ferns and some discreet variegation from weigela, osmanthus and ground elder, adds to the spring and summer variety, and in autumn, the tints of the azaleas are joined by enkianthus, Japanese maples, birches, liquidambar and osmunda ferns.

There are many more discoveries to be made lower down the slopes: Tulip Tree, Monterey Pine and *Prunus sargentii*, glades of Hardy Hybrid rhododendrons, scented pockets of azaleas and clethra and banks of bamboo. Bulbs and wildflowers are encouraged in the grass and woodland fringes; there are orchids in the lawns, Hoop Petticoat Daffodils in the quarry and sheets of bluebells under the trees.

Formal walks and compartments, complemented by retaining walls and garden buildings, contrast with these wilder reaches. The Top Walk leads to an azalea-lined terrace and gazebo, from which there is a panorama out towards Crowborough Beacon. And below, a second terrace walk, flanked by box, catmint, pinks, trailing rosemary and bulbs, leads to the summer-house. Here, in the vicinity of the main house, cottage plants and country-house borders come into play. Runs of lavender, trellis hung with rose and clematis, and a pastel-coloured herbaceous border punctuated with the spring-flowering evergreen *Osmanthus delavayi*, add to the domestic mood; yellow and white Banksian roses grow on the house walls. The old vegetable garden lower down the slope has recently been planted as a rose garden; Rugosa roses, Scotch Briar and apple-scented Sweetbriar provide the flowers and hips, in the company of catmint and formalising lines of Irish Junipers. A fact that never fails to astonish and encourage visitors is that all this is able to be maintained by a single gardener.

Stourhead

Stourton, Warminster,
Wiltshire

At Stourton, off B3092,
3 miles north-west of Mere
(A303)

Area 93 acres (37·6 ha)
Soil acid/greensand
Altitude 700 ft (213 m)
Average rainfall 40–44 in
 (1,016–1,118 mm)
Average winter climate moderate
Staff six

Here we have probably the most bewitching and beautiful of this country's landscape gardens, an eighteenth-century arcadia of hills and hanging beechwoods, water and classical architecture, but dashingly overlaid with a later collection of exotic broadleaved trees, conifers and richly coloured rhododendrons. A few purists baulk at the combination, but they are in the minority. The balance, however, is fine, and the Trust has been working to recapture more of the flavour of the earlier phase, by reopening vistas and reordering the planting, eliminating disjointed patches of colour and strong contrasts in favour of gentle harmonies and smooth transitions.

The valley landscape is the work of various members of the Hoare family, beginning in the early 1740s, with Henry Hoare II, son of the founder of Hoare's Bank. Motivated by the new-born idea of garden-making not as an exercise in geometry but as a branch of landscape painting, and freshly returned from a three-year tour of Italy, he set about creating a poetic landscape inspired by the Roman Campagna – scenes from the much-admired era of peace and artistic accomplishment under Augustus, alluding allegorically in part to the epic journey of Aeneas. Hoare's architectural advisor was Henry Flitcroft, an associate of William Kent, the new landscape movement's leading designer, and the scenes are very much in his style. It was his grandson, Richard Colt Hoare, who, responding to the current influx of new plants from America and Asia Minor, introduced *Rhododendron ponticum*, Cherry Laurel and the Tulip Tree into the landscape, and the exotic planting continued in the late nineteenth and early twentieth centuries, under the direction of Sir Henry Hoare.

ABOVE LEFT: A view of the Temple of Apollo at Stourhead in spring.

ABOVE RIGHT: The Temple of Flora seen through the golden tints of beech trees in autumn.

The valley is tucked between folds of chalk downland and divorced from the grand Palladian villa, which stands back on the ridge to the north. One way of entering is to bypass the house by walking immediately downhill from the car park and arrive at the lakeside through the little estate village of Stourton, with its inn, church and row of cottages. The more dramatic approach, however, is to descend the wooded hillside across the lawn from the house, and have the first surprises sprung from above.

A line of ancient Sweet Chestnuts, a vestige of an earlier avenue to Stourton Castle, flanks part of the curving driveway to the mansion, and to the left are the old stable yard and walled kitchen gardens, currently being renovated by the Trust and planted with a simplified arrangement of fruit trees, borders and hedges. Ahead looms the house, designed by Colen Campbell for Henry Hoare I, but with a later portico and flanking pavilions; the backdrop is of tree belts and open countryside carrying the eye across the edge of Salisbury Plain.

Opposite the south front, across a lawn lined with rows of beech trees, Edwardian-style shrubberies of purple, red and white rhododendrons – hybrids such as 'Britannia', 'Mrs Charles E. Pearson' and 'Loder's White' – colour the way, and there is a particularly good ice-house concealed down a laurel passage. Specimens of Japanese Varnish Tree, *Rhus verniciflua*, *Ligustrum chenaultii*, liquidambar and pampas grass encourage you to roam the lawn edges.

Magnificent Tulip Trees mark the beginning of the valley landscape. First, there is a view down to the village church, past Sweet Chestnuts and Himalayan Whitebeam, and then you enter the wood, the path winding downhill between the beech and oak and the rough carpets

255

PREVIOUS PAGE: Stourhead in early evening light, with the Stone Bridge and the Pantheon beyond.

The River God seen from inside the Grotto at Stourhead.

of ferns, grasses and wildflowers – the browns and greens seasonally washed with snowdrops, bluebells and the native yellow Lent Lily, *Narcissus pseudonarcissus*. An obelisk, surmounted by a gilded solar disc, is the focal point for Richard Colt Hoare's broad, straight Fir Walk, now regenerated with young Western Hemlocks. Cherry Laurel, kept low by annual pruning, gives a glossy evergreen understorey to the woods, with the more interesting rhododendrons appearing in loose drifts: Ghent azaleas and large-leaved Himalayan species; cool-coloured Hardy Hybrids like 'Blue Peter', 'Cynthia' and 'Nobleanum Venustum'; and fragrant yellow azaleas, the flowering sequence beginning early with 'Christmas Cheer' and *R. barbatum*, and continuing into high summer with *R. auriculatum* and 'Polar Bear'.

Between the trees, two of the garden buildings suddenly appear – first, the Temple of Apollo, a pale cylinder with domed roof and Corinthian columns, perched on its hill across the valley, and then, on the far bank of the lake, the portico and rotunda of the Pantheon. No sooner glimpsed, than lost. Enveloped by the wood, you continue down to the valley floor, where a more ornamental cast of trees again takes over from the beech and oak – handsome flowering species like halesia, Handkerchief Tree, Italian Maple (*Acer opalus*) and tree magnolias, including a champion *M. campbellii* subsp. *mollicomata* and *M. heptapetala*; conifers like Macedonian Pine, cryptomeria, Dawn Redwood and Noble Fir.

This assortment of exotics, backed by the hanging woods, extends around the lakeside. There are the evergreen rockets of Wellingtonias and thujas (an immense, broad-skirted specimen awaits across the water); the elegant uprights of Tulip Trees, punctuating the banks and rising from the central island; a number of purple beech trees; blasts of springtime rhododendron colour; and an exciting autumn panorama of red Japanese maples, American oaks and russet cypresses. Inside this rich canvas, you follow the circuit walk from one poetic building to the next, passing from sunlight to shadow. The reflections in the water add greatly to the composition, not only of the main lake but of the flanking pools – to the west, a lily lake, with a view beyond, up Six Wells Valley, where the River Stour rises; to the east, Turner's Paddock Lake, fed by a cascade and married with trees.

The path leads through a tunnel of yew, under a rustic stone arch, and into one of the most impressive of English grottoes, dank and gloomy but alive to the sound of water splashing from the natural springs; a nymph sleeps above the cascade, and from the opening in the lakeside wall, there is a view across the water to the village church and arched bridge, framed in limes and Sugar Maples. A river god in the adjacent cave points in the direction of the Pantheon, and you leave by way of a rustic stairway, edged in Hart's Tongue Fern. Now you come to the old Watch Cottage, here before the garden was laid out, but Gothicised by Richard Colt Hoare in 1806 and with a good Japanese maple, *Acer palmatum* 'Osakazuki', beside it. From here, an array of features is visible – the Temple of Apollo on its mount, the slim and skeletal sculpture of the Bristol High Cross in the village; and, on the opposite bank, the pediment and Doric columns of the Temple of Flora.

A statue of Hercules and other classical figures stand inside the rotunda of the Pantheon, and thence it is around the edge of the lake, and on to the temples of Apollo and Flora, from where you obtain the equally glorious reverse views of the lake, trees and architectural ornament. These vistas are as close to perfection as any artist gardener can compose, and, thanks to their exotic plant content, they pass through a breathtaking sequence of colours. This is a landscape to visit at every season.

Stowe Landscape Gardens

Buckingham,
Buckinghamshire

3 miles north-west of
Buckingham via Stowe
Avenue, off A422
Buckingham/Banbury road

Area 350 acres (141·6ha)
Soil alkaline/clay and gravel
Altitude 394ft (120m)
Average rainfall 26in (660mm)
Average winter climate cold
Staff four

'The visitor should prepare to be impressed,' writes John Martin Robinson in the Stowe guidebook. This is one of England's foremost landscape gardens. The grandeur is announced at the entrance lodges, where you are met by drives charting a long, straight course across the undulating, wooded ridges of the Buckinghamshire countryside. On the Oxford side, there is the picturesque composition of an arched bridge across a small lake, with a domed pavilion set into trees on the hill behind. At the Buckingham entrance, the scale is more heroic – 1½ miles (3·6km) of beech and chestnut avenue, carrying you to a triumphal Corinthian arch, the landscape's crowning monument.

Through this arch, you look across the valley into a 400-acre (161·2-ha) garden, flowing down the south-facing slopes, watered by a string of lakes and centred on a magnificent

BELOW LEFT: The Palladian Bridge at Stowe seen through the Doric Arch during restoration of the gardens.

BELOW RIGHT: The Congreve Monument.

Palladian mansion, now Stowe School (only open to the public in the summer holidays). This stupendous composition is the work of the socially and politically ambitious Temple-Grenville family, beginning with General Sir Richard Temple, later Viscount Cobham, who, funded by his marriage in 1715 to a wealthy heiress, Anne Halsey, set about transforming his father's small terraced garden in splendid style. This was a momentous period in landscape design, with the pendulum about to swing towards more natural and less formal composition. Stowe would not only reflect but pioneer the change in taste, with many of the leading architects, designers and sculptors employed here.

The early phase was executed by the royal gardener, Charles Bridgeman, and adorned with buildings designed by Sir John Vanbrugh, the architect of Blenheim and Castle Howard. Very little of this layout remains today, for it was gradually dismantled in the 1740s, and then, in the 1750s, finally converted by Cobham's nephew, Earl Temple, into the more confidently sweeping style of the time, in harmony with the later parts of the landscape.

The main garden axis, below the house's majestic south façade, is now broad and open. Where once the eye would have been channelled over an elaborate parterre, between an avenue of poplars, and across an octagonal pond, there is empty lawn, informal flanks of forest trees, and a seemingly natural pool of water, strewn with the native white waterlily.

Beyond, Earl Temple pushed apart Vanbrugh's pavilions, giving the present grand vista into the park, terminated by his masterstroke, the Corinthian Arch. To the west of the house, Vanbrugh's domed rotunda, once the centre of radiating gravel walks, is similarly now set in an informal wooded glade.

Bridgeman's principal legacy is the ha-ha. This French device of a sunken ditch, giving gardens protection from grazing animals yet allowing them to merge uninterrupted with the countryside had a decisive impact on the development of the landscape garden. Stowe was the first English property in which it was used extensively. The runs were constructed like military fortifications and punctuated by projecting bastions, and on the south-west and south-east corners, these are adorned with monuments, a Palladian Temple of Venus and a Tuscan Temple of Friendship added by Earl Temple and now a ruin, following a fire in the nineteenth century.

The second phase of the garden's development under Lord Cobham took place from 1734 and is centred in a narrow dell, a little to the east – once occupied by Stowe village and its public road, of which only the fourteenth-century church remains. Garden design was now being compared to landscape painting, with landowners beginning to yearn for the sort of pastoral landscapes depicted by Claude Lorraine and Salvator Rosa. The pioneer of this Picturesque style was William Kent, who was engaged by Lord Cobham to create these Elysian Fields (the Romans' mythological paradise) here at Stowe. It is the most intimate portion of the garden.

Access, as in the myth, is across the serpentine River Styx, spouting from a grotto and created by damming the existing stream (the upper dam being the Shell Bridge). You enter into bright glades, fringed by trees and filled with monuments, but presided over, on the west bank, by the Temple of Ancient Virtue, an Ionic rotunda erected in 1736, and on the east, by the Temple of British Worthies, a curved screen in which the busts of distinguished men of action and of contemplation are displayed in niches (along with that of one woman, Queen Elizabeth I). The cast ranges from King Alfred and Walter Raleigh to William Shakespeare

LEFT: A view across the lake to the Temple of Venus before its restoration.

261

The Palladian Bridge with a glimpse of the Gothic Temple beyond.

and Isaac Newton, and includes Cobham's friend, the poet and influential landscape theorist Alexander Pope – all Whig heroes. This was one of the first monuments intended to be 'read' by visitors, who would have noticed the pointed omission of Catholic priests. Exploring the Arcadian landscape was intended to be as much an exercise for the mind as for the feet. Here at Stowe, there are not only classical and literary references to pick up, but also the family's strongly held beliefs and prejudices often conveyed with satire.

At the base of the Elysian Fields, you are enticed further east, across Hawkwell Field, which rolls down to another naturalistic stretch of water, spanned by one of the garden's best-known monuments, the Palladian Bridge by James Gibbs. Lord Cobham began developing this area in the late 1730s as ornamental pasture, combining classical decoration with agricultural use; it was an early example of the *ferme ornée*, and is still grazed today. Presiding over the scene, on a ridge far to the north, stands the Queen's Temple, a Corinthian temple built as a summer-house for Lady Cobham, and on the same axis, halfway to the water and flanked by young and old cedar trees, the Gothic Temple, a monument to the 'Liberty of our Ancestors'.

The last part of the garden to be completed – but the first the visitor comes to on the tour, which confusingly presents the garden almost in its reverse order of development – was the Grecian Valley, north-east of the house. A carefully contoured sweep of hay meadow – full of wildflowers, including massed cowslips – and framed by broad and muscular banks of deciduous trees, cedars and pines, this marks the arrival of a more open and bold style of naturalistic landscaping. It was begun in 1746, by which time Lord Cobham's head gardener was none other than the young 'Capability' Brown.

The Grecian Valley contains one of the most impressive of Stowe's monuments. This is the Ionic Temple, completed by Earl Temple with the addition of a magnificent carved pediment, showing Britannia receiving the tribute of the world; it was transferred here from the Palladian bridge, structures being moved about the garden like chess pieces. Named the Temple of Concord and Victory in line with Earl Temple's development of the garden on still grander lines, it embraces not only national but imperial achievements.

Stowe is the most complex of English gardens, and for the full account of its conception, development and meaning, you should turn to John Martin Robinson's book *Temples of Delight*. But no deep understanding is needed in order to appreciate its beauty – the open meadows, the lofty plantations of beech, lime, oak and chestnut with their yew, holly, Cherry Laurel and box understorey, the waterside fringes of alder and ash, and the golden architecture. It presents a succession of magnificent landscape pictures, changing in response to every phase of light and season.

Only after the Second World War, when the study of garden history grew, did Stowe School begin to realise the landscape's true significance and of the scale of the rescue work demanded. Repairs were tentatively begun, gathering momentum in the 1960s with assistance from the Trust. But the scale of the declining landscape and the sheer quantity of crumbling buildings was alarming. In 1989, a major appeal was launched. Numerous individuals and public and private bodies have contributed subsequently, a comprehensive historical survey has been commissioned, and lake by lake, plantation by plantation, and temple by temple, the work has proceeded, involving archaeology, dredging, skilled stonemasonry and the planting of thousands of trees. It has been one of the most ambitious restoration projects ever undertaken.

Tatton Park

Knutsford, Cheshire

3½ miles north of Knutsford,
4 miles south of Altrincham;
signposted from junction 19
of M6 and junction 7 of M56

Area 60 acres (24·3 ha)
Soil acid/sand
Altitude 197 ft (60 m)
Average rainfall 28 in (711 mm)
Average winter climate cold
Staff thirteen

'A grand domain of great verdure, and with a noble lake; these are the charms: the per contra, no inequality of ground; the timber of neither stature nor girth', wrote the diarist Lord Torrington in 1790. The terrain is certainly fairly flat. The estate lies at the northern end of the Cheshire plain, amid pastureland and meres. The trees, however, have become one of the chief assets. Before, and in the decades after Lord Torrington's visit, a considerable number were planted as clumps and woods, and these, with their replacements, now bring shape and texture to the setting; an extensive arboretum has also grown up beside the house. Herds of red and fallow deer graze the meadows, together with sheep; and there is further animation from the boats coursing the lake – sailing being one of many recreational activities for which the park is available to the public.

A varied landscape thus presents itself, much in the style of Humphry Repton, who paid a visit here in 1791 and prepared one of his Red Books of proposals the following year, though, in fact, it owes more to one John Webb, a pupil of William Emes, who worked here in the second decade of the nineteenth century, and to planting by the 1st and 2nd Lords Egerton in the 1870s and 1880s.

Surveying the scene is an imposing Neo-classical mansion of pinkish-grey sandstone, built by Samuel Wyatt and his nephew Lewis Wyatt, between 1790 and 1812. And to accompany it are gardens: the full panoply of parterre and croquet lawn, herbaceous borders and topiary, glasshouses and aviaries, shrubberies, water gardens and pinetum, which would provide a string of diversions for the leisured Victorian and Edwardian family and their guests.

Directly below the portico, terraced lawns flow down to the Italian Garden, constructed in the 1880s and restored by the Trust a hundred years later, with the aid of old photographs. Grass, gravel, box and bedding (polyanthus and forget-me-nots, followed by armeria, ager-atum and the single, mauve-pink 'Marie José' dahlia, in adherence to precedent), provide the pattern, which is sculpted around marble vases and a Neptune fountain.

The decorative glasshouses stand to the west. The Orangery, built by Lewis Wyatt in 1818, has been impressively renovated and replanted, and is stocked with oranges and lemons. Formerly, these would have been stood outside on the terrace for summer, but now they are permanent inhabitants accompanied by clivias, passion flowers and mimosa. Many other gardens have a conservatory on this scale, but none has as impressive a fernery. Dating from the 1850s, its architect was probably Joseph Paxton, the designer of the Crystal Palace and the conservatory at Chatsworth. The speciality is the Australian tree ferns collected on his travels by Captain Charles Randle Egerton RN, the brother of the 1st Lord Egerton.

The path curves under their crowns – mesmerising traceries of emerald, as you look through them towards the roof glass – passing a dry-stone wall studded with maidenhairs and

cymbotiums, while the enormous fronds of the chain fern, *Woodwardia radicans*, brush against your legs. The connecting conservatory, also rebuilt, is now a traditional riot of colour. Beyond are further flower gardens: a long L-shaped border, colour-coded within buttresses of yew, and backed by walls densely clothed in climbers and shrubs (including the rare *Magnolia cordata*, which gives a good show of yellow flowers in summer); a garden partially restored in the sinuous and curious gardenesque style of the early nineteenth century, where specimen plants are shown off as individuals in small beds; and a walled enclosure of Edwardian pastel roses and scented plants set beside a pool. Topiary yews, a fountain, a shady pergola and trellis arbour, and a castellated sheep-watcher's tower, dating from before 1750, add further incident.

By now, the rich variety of trees and shrubs in the garden will have impressed themselves on you. The view from the house towards the distant hills beyond Congleton encompasses fine evergreen and Turkey Oaks and Cedar of Lebanon, and, in the dell below, high conifers, beeches and Sweet Chestnuts (the twisted deeply fissured trunks are a memorable motif). Around the lawns of the flower gardens, you will have come upon Handkerchief Tree, *Malus hupehensis*, *Magnolia hypoleuca*, large-leaved *Emmenopterys henryi*, Kentucky Coffee Tree (*Gymnocladus dioica*), blue-podded *Descaisnea fargesii* and choice conifers such as Brewer's Weeping Spruce, Korean Fir and the red-coned Chinese spruce, *Picea likiangensis*.

These are a taste of what awaits in the arboretum's many acres of grassy and pool-side glades. The cast is arranged fairly erratically, and often very closely packed, but it is an interesting catalogue of what will thrive in a cold northern climate, and there are also some magnificent specimens, not least among the conifer collection.

The pinetum was well established by 1795, though the oldest of the present plants date mostly from the late nineteenth and early twentieth centuries. In addition to the extensive range of tall American and Far Eastern species, such as *Pinus jeffreyi*, *P. wallichiana*, *Abies recurvata* var. *ernestii* and *Picea likiangensis purpurea*, there are contrasting plumes from Sawara Cypresses (*Chamaecyparis pisifera*) and cryptomeria, dawn redwoods grouped in a glade, and Swamp Cypresses (*Taxodium distichum*) beside a stretch of water. Among deciduous trees, there are cherries and parrotia, styrax and halesia, a very tall Bay Willow (*Salix pentandra*) and a prickly curiosity in the form of *Kalopanax pictus* (syn. *K. septemlobus*) whose maple-like leaves are among the last to drop in autumn.

In summer, the glades are predominantly green, but in spring, there are blasts of colour from massed rhododendrons. The collection was built up by the last Lord Egerton in the 1940s, during his enforced confinement in Britain away from his beloved estate in Kenya – the walls of the Tenants' Hall are covered with the heads of game that crossed his path, and at one point in the garden tour you come upon a heather-thatched African hut.

En route, you encounter two surprising vestiges of an earlier layout. One, tucked into shrubbery, is a small beech maze, a rare feature that was established here before 1795 and said to be the same plan as at Hampton Court. The other, splicing the arboretum into two parts, is an avenue predominantly of beech. Known as the Broad Walk, it dates from the 1730s, and in the 1820s the family installed a grand monument at its head, inspired by that to Lysicrates, the chorus or storyteller, in ancient Athens. This marks the boundary of the garden, from where you can look out over the park.

I have left the jewel in Tatton's crown until last. The opening of Japan to foreigners in

Tree ferns above clivias and chain fern *Woodwardia radicans* in the Fernery at Tatton Park.

the late nineteenth century brought a fascination with all things Japanese, culminating in the Japan Exhibition of 1905. Five years later, the 3rd Lord Egerton embarked on a Japanese garden in one of the dells at Tatton. It is probably the finest in the country. A fusion of the various styles of classical garden, it has a still, dark pool as its centre, fed by four streams that flow over cascades, under flat bridges, past stone lanterns and key rocks (including a mound of white stones representing Mount Fuji), and between a carefully placed cast of plants, including maples, bamboo, water iris, cherry, pine and particularly fine specimens of *Picea pungens glauca*. Cranes and other mythically charged animals are met on the way, and the centrepiece, standing on the Master's island, is a thatched tea-house. Beyond the arched bridge a Shinto temple, brought from Japan, adorns the island on the adjacent lake – made for Lady Charlotte Egerton, wife of the 1st Baron, out of disused clay pits. These Japanese features are heavy with a symbolism that passes most of us by, but the craftsmanship and tranquillity of the setting are there for all to savour. A Japanese gardener may well have supervised the original work.

So, there are large and varied gardens at Tatton, not all elegant or well composed, but full of interest and reflecting the enthusiasms of many generations of the Egerton family, who lived here from 1598 for more than 350 years.

267

Tintinhull House

Tintinhull, nr Yeovil,
Somerset

5 miles north-west of Yeovil,
½ mile south of A303

Area 1 acre (0·4 ha)
Soil neutral/loam over marl
  clay
Altitude 100 ft (30 m)
Average rainfall 30 in (762 mm)
Average winter climate moderate
Staff one

Rows of maturing onions in the kitchen garden at Tintinhull.

The west front of Tintinhull House, part-hidden by a high wall at the edge of the village, is as dreamy a façade as you are likely to come upon. Compact, symmetrical, built of a warm and welcoming honey-coloured stone (quarried at nearby Ham Hill), and adorned with pediment and pilasters, mullioned windows and carved scrolls, it is the picture of early eighteenth-century elegance. The lines and proportions of the manor have been extended to create an equally exceptional garden: an open and varied sequence of rooms, or courts, formally set out over the more or less flat terrain, and decorated with a varied but discerningly chosen range of plants. 'Nothing is out of place, and the result is a garden that is the embodiment of peace', wrote the cottage gardener Margery Fish.

From the sitting-room door, a long straight path, flanked by low domes of clipped box, invites you west through three enclosures. The first, Eagle Court (named after the pair of birds mounted on its gate-piers), is the oldest part of the garden, dating from the eighteenth century, with the stone paving added, and the further enclosures formally connected and shaped, sometime after 1905, probably by Dr S. J. M. Price, a churchman of private means who was then the tenant.

But the planting, the design of the larger courts and the character of the present garden is the inspiration of Phyllis Reiss, who, with her husband Capt. F. E. Reiss, came to live here in 1933, having already made a garden near Cheltenham – not far from Hidcote, to which Tintinhull owes more than a passing acknowledgement. She had an ordered and distinctive approach. 'Her special gift', wrote the garden designer Lanning Roper, was 'for selecting and placing plants to create an effect . . . If a plant is distinguished in form and texture it is used boldly and often repeated, this making a unity of design . . .'.

Within the parameters of colour and mood set by Mrs Reiss, the Trust, until recently in partnership with its former tenants, the garden writer Penelope Hobhouse and her husband Professor John Malins, has continued to experiment and rejuvenate. As at Hidcote, there is an exciting tension between the plants and their trim and emphatic framework. The design is very firm, with the new courts running parallel with the old, and bound together with strong east-west and north-south axes in the form of stone paths, terraces and channelled views leading to a seat or other ornament.

Thus, from the central old court, a gateway offers a prospect down the length of a rectangular waterlily pool to a stone loggia; this garden was made from the old tennis court in

1947, and the loggia erected by Mrs Reiss in memory of her nephew who was killed in the Second World War. And from the Fountain Garden beyond, the eye is led between rivers of catmint (or, in spring, white daffodils) down the centre of her Kitchen Garden, to a farm gate and then out into a Somerset cider orchard. Often, the symmetry is reinforced in the planting. Rosemary, white *Clematis montana*, lavender, tall verbena, corylopsis and evergreen *Choisya ternata* are repeated either side of the Eagle Court's terrace steps, for example, and Chanticleer pears and beds of the Apothecary's Rose, *Rosa gallica* var. *officinalis* (underplanted with scillas and the tall Gravetye cultivar of the Summer Snowflake, *Leucojum aestivum*), either side of the southern entrance to the Kitchen Garden.

A clump of yellow flag iris stands in each corner of the waterlily pool; Japanese honeysuckles, grown on metal frames, process either side of one of the Kitchen Garden walks; and a pair of white-tiered *Cornus controversa* 'Variegata' (introduced by the Trust, and perhaps a

A view from the Fountain Garden towards the west front of the house, with topiary of clipped box lining the stone path.

A hot planting of lilies, crocosmia, phygelius and *Lysimachia ciliata* 'Purpurea' in the Pool Garden at Tintinhull.

touch too flashy for Tintinhull) preside over the extension to the Fountain Garden, nicely teamed with Willow Gentians and blue foliage.

But everywhere, there is the contrasting exuberance: hellebores and Japanese anemones filtering between evergreen *Itea ilicifolia* and *Mahonia lomariifolia*, oak-leaved hydrangea and mock orange, in a north-facing bed; a haze of sky-blue love-in-a-mist amid a kaleidoscope of bearded irises; or (my favourite scheme) an undulating blend of blue ceanothus, lime-green euphorbia, lilac abutilon, white clematis and the lemon rose 'Helen Knight'. As at Hidcote, colour is the medium that orders the mixed cast of plants. The beds around the circular pool in the Fountain Garden have a crisp white theme, founded on the flowers of honesty, campanulas, delphiniums, roses, agapanthus and anemones, and set off by silvery foliage and a dark backdrop of yew hedges.

The large north-eastern court has a border of smouldering crimson and bronze-red leaves, provided by fennel, elder, various berberis and the young growth of Bush roses, partnered with the magenta-red flowers of *Rosa* 'Zéphirine Drouhin' and 'Rosemary Rose', the yellow of the dogwood *Cornus alba* 'Spaethii', and the blues of veronica and rue; a more subdued, old-world mood than the red borders at Hidcote, with their brilliant scarlets and oranges.

And flanking the rectangular waterlily pool is a contrasting pair of schemes, one with the soft, feminine tones of pink phlox and penstemon, violet-blue campanula, salvia and aster, and the other with the more potent, advancing shades of blood-red 'Frensham' roses and dahlias, yellow achilleas, verbascum and coreopsis – but subtly and harmonised by the presence of white and silver in the form of artemisias, crambe, romneya and *Clematis recta*.

Because most of the garden is seen from the upstairs windows of the house, Mrs Reiss planned the borders for an all-year display, and wherever possible, bulbs, annuals and biennials are used to give each piece of ground a second season of colour. Thus, snowdrops, winter aconites, anemones, chionodoxas and scillas are ubiquitous (the blues particularly striking beneath plants whose young leaves are in shades of red); tulips, daffodils, wallflowers and forget-me-nots appear in advance of roses; pink and white cyclamen after the spring magnolias. And there is an additional boost from pots, notably around the waterlily pool, where white or yellow tulips perform ahead of grey-leaved marguerites. Later, the loggia steps and terraces are home to potted oleander, salvias, heliotrope, francoa and *Lilium regale*.

In every enclosure, large and small, there is a sense of space and tranquillity, an impression fostered by the central uncluttered expanses of lawn or water. The terraces are generous, appointed with steps wide and shallow to 'emphasise the change of level on what is a relatively flat site', as Lanning Roper observed. And the trees are also of an unexpected scale: there are just a handful to lift the eye and draw in the sky, including yew, cedars (young replacements are installed now) and Holm Oak, *Quercus ilex* – all evergreen and nicely in period with the house.

All this, together with the various subdivisions and wealth of detail, makes it very hard to believe that the entire composition encompasses an acre – as many writers before me have commented. The ideas and lessons here for all owners of small gardens are legion.

Trelissick

Feock, nr Truro, Cornwall

4 miles south of Truro, on both sides of B3289

Area 25 acres (10ha)
Soil acid/loam
Altitude 100ft (30m)
Average rainfall 40in (1,016mm)
Average winter climate frost-free–mild
Staff four

Cornish gardens spring many surprises, but the apparitions at Trelissick take some beating. Detached from the Neo-classical mansion, the grounds are on an intimate scale, a tranquil composition of plunging lawns, specimen trees, shady paths and stream-fed dell framed by woods and the expected masses of rhododendrons and camellias. There are occasional glimpses of the River Fal below, a ribbon of light between the tree-clad banks. But as you emerge from the shrub walks to the north, the jaw drops. For the water near the river mouth is deep, and at anchor on the garden's boundary is likely to be a substantial cargo ship. Like the land approaches to the Suez Canal, where great tankers suddenly appear, gliding between folds of empty desert, not only their size, but their very presence is a shock.

It would be more appropriate if the ships were galleons, for this is a country of creeks and secret coves, of smugglers' legend and historical romance. The house commands an excellent view of Carrick Roads and beyond to Falmouth Bay. And the road that bisects the garden drops to the King Harry Ferry, connecting Truro with the isolated Roseland Peninsula. The garden acquired its present richness after 1937, when the estate became the home of Mr and Mrs Ronald Copeland. Since 1955, the Trust has developed the grounds considerably in response to various losses from drought, frost and storm, by extending the shrubberies and tree collection into Carcadden, the land across the Ferry road, as well as boosting the post-spring displays.

271

Entering the garden beside the walls of the old kitchen garden, you plunge immediately into flowers. In spring, violet abutilon, Chinese and Japanese wisterias accompany clove-scented *Viburnum × juddii*, while in summer, hot-coloured cannas, dahlias, hedychiums and heliotrope are backed by scented *Trachelospermum jasminoides* and evergreen *Magnolia grandiflora* 'Galissonière'. There is also a collection of figs further on near the shop.

The climate, though not quite as benevolent as at Glendurgan or Trengwainton (qqv), is mild and moist, and the shrub display that draws you into the woodland walks begins early. Brazen stands of 'Cornish Red' rhododendrons, and the blood-red form of *R. arboreum* give way to groves of *Camellia japonica* and *C. × williamsii* in their many red, pink and white cultivars. There are splashes from blush-pink *Rhododendron sutchuenense* and red *R. thomsonii*, the pink *R. williamsianum* cultivars and other Cornish hybrids like 'Penjerrick' and 'Beauty of Tremough'. And so the succession continues, with appearances from evergreen azaleas, violet-blue *R. augustinii* hybrids, scented white 'Avalanche', purple *R. concinnum*, orange and red *R. cinnabarinum* varieties, scented deciduous azaleas, numerous Hardy Hybrids and a large collection of blood-scarlet rhododendrons from early 'Little Bert' and 'Earl of Athlone' to 'May Day' and 'Romany Chai', and the Trelissick speciality 'Gwilt-King'. The more tender varieties grow on the sides of the dell, on the far side of the main lawn. Australian tree ferns inevitably steal the show here, but the collection of the white, lily-scented Maddenii rhododendrons is bewitching. The shelter and moisture is also enjoyed by large-leaved species, such as the rose-tinted form of *R. rex* subsp. *arizelum* and by the beautiful sulphur-yellow hybrid 'Mary Swaythling'.

The bog garden below is at its most brilliant in early summer, when awash with variously coloured Candelabra primulas, but earlier it is lit by the yellow flares of Skunk Cabbage in spring, and, later in the summer, by lemon-scented *Primula florindae* and astilbes. The accompanying fern and hosta leaves are as large and lush as you will see anywhere.

Hydrangeas, extensively planted by the Copelands, have been still further exploited by the Trust, so that now the banks of spring shrub colour have their match in summer and autumn. A walk of blue and white hydrangeas, overhung with cherries and the snowdrop tree, *Halesia carolina*, skirts the dell, and more white varieties, grown near eucryphias and orange kniphofias, illuminate the view over the river to the Gothick mansion of Tregothnan. Hydrangeas are also massed in Carcadden. This young arboretum, reached by a new bridge – the original of which was part of the system of carriage rides set out in the early nineteenth century – is a former orchard and nursery, and was brought into the garden in the 1960s. Magnolias and viburnums, as well as rhododendrons, camellias and cherries, now feature here, together with a range of unusual trees and larger shrubs, including two fine plants of the Chilean Hazel, *Gevuina avellana*.

Much of the garden's attraction comes from the vistas, across from one side of the plant-filled valley to the other, along the undulating lawns and meandering paths, and, of course, down over the River Fal and the estuary. Daffodils, anemones and countless wildflowers carpet these views in spring and summer, and the mixed deciduous and evergreen trees provide an ever-changing frame: the highlights including *Acer pseudoplatanus* 'Brilliantissimum' in the south border, *Acer platanoides* 'Cucullatum' in Carcadden and, most memorably, C.D. Gilbert's Japanese Cedar, *Cryptomeria japonica*, stretching its many limbs in the centre of the main lawn.

LEFT: The Dell at Trelissick with tree ferns, rhododendrons, echiums and a bare-branched dogwood.

Trengwainton

nr Penzance, Cornwall

2 miles north-west of
Penzance, ½ mile west of
Heamoor on Penzance–
Morvah road (B3312)

Area 25 acres (10ha)
Soil acid/loam over granite
Altitude 246–394ft (75–120m)
Average rainfall 46in
  (1,168mm)
Average winter climate mild–
  moderate
Staff four

The south-west corner of the Cornish peninsula enjoys the mildest climate in Britain, and in some of the dappled glades and old walled enclosures at Trengwainton, you feel you could be in some subtropical garden. The long summers, high rainfall and moist sea air promote fast, lush growth, mosses and lichens, and the soft winters allow trees, shrubs and climbers from the world's warmer regions to flourish. The exotic flavour is appropriate, for its was wealth from his family's Jamaican sugar plantation that enabled Sir Rose Price to lay the foundations of the garden in the early nineteenth century. It was he who built, in about 1820, the series of small walled compartments close to the entrance lodge, of great interest to garden historians for their sizeable, raised brick vegetable beds, specially angled to take full advantage of the winter sun; though known to have existed elsewhere, these are thought to be the only survivors. The southernmost compartments are now mysterious and jungly plantsman's plots, with wild ferns running through the grey granite walls, primroses and anemones spreading around the skirts of shrubs, and old, spring-flowering tree magnolias, *M × veitchii* and forms of *M. campbellii*, shading a mossy carpet patterned with scented plants, and areas of finely mown grass.

The microclimates here suit a mouth-watering range of tender trees and shrubs. *Eucryphia milliganii* from Tasmania, *E. moorei* from Australia, *Michelia doltsopa* from China and the Himalayas, *Schima argentea* (syn. *S. wallichii noronhae superba*) from Sichuan and *Weinmannia trichosperma* from Chile have all grown into fine specimens, as have hardier Asian species such as *Styrax hemsleyanus*, *S. japonicus* and *Stewartia sinensis*, appreciative of the additional warmth, shelter and moisture.

Tender rhododendrons abound, among them the Formosan azalea, *R. oldhamii*, and numerous white-flowered, lily-scented species and hybrids of the Maddenii Series. The soaring biennial *Echium pininana*, from the Canary Islands, is a luxurious sight, as is *Geranium palmatum* from Madeira and the Chatham Island Forget-me-not, *Myosotidium hortensia*. The abundance of broad-leaved evergreens and scarcity of conifers contributes much to the balmy flavour of the gardens, but a few Southern Hemisphere coniferous species add exotic notes, among them *Podocarpus salignus* from Chile and *Athrotaxis selaginoides* from Tasmania.

Trengwainton began sampling such treasures after 1925, when Lt. Col. Edward Bolitho inherited. The foundation for his collection of rhododendron species was Frank Kingdon-Ward's 1927–8 plant-hunting expedition to north-east Assam and the Mishmi Hills in Upper Burma, in which he was offered shares by G.H. Johnstone of Trewithen and Lawrence Johnston of Hidcote (qv).

A number of species, including *RR. macabeanum, elliottii* and *cinnabarinum* subsp. *Xanthocodon* Cocatenans Group, flowered here for the first time in the British Isles. Over a long spring season, their flower trusses colour the woodland fringes and grassy glades, through which the curving drive and its parallel long walk climb towards the house following the old carriage drive. At the height of the display, strong patches of magenta and pink Kirishima and Kurume azaleas draw the eye through the softer rose tones of *RR. schlippenbachii* and *vaseyi*, the violets of 'Penheale Blue' and 'Saint Breward', and a great many other handsome selections, some bred here and most growing in the company of daffodils or wildflowers.

The scents are rich and heavy, from deciduous azaleas and tender rhododendrons such as *RR. johnstoneanum* and 'Lady Alice Fitzwilliam'. And in the shadows and moist troughs, you come upon the elephantine foliage of *RR. grande, magnificum, falconeri* (layers from the

original specimen dating from the 1880s), and, of course, *R. macabeanum*. Camellias are also here in quantity, massed into *allées* and scattered in drifts; and, later in summer, the drive and woodland walks are flushed blue and white with hydrangeas. Shortly after beginning the walk up the hill, you hear the sound of water. The hills are laced with underground springs, and the stream beside the drive is fringed with lysichitons, candelabra primulas, astilbes, polygonums, arum lilies, hydrangeas and crocosmias. This contrasts with the jungle mood recaptured in the shady, sheltered pockets between the trees and rhododendron thickets, where wooden bridges cross the water and the mossy streamside banks support self-sporing colonies of Australian tree ferns; the open zones of bamboos, grasses and phormiums give a special theme to the Jubilee Garden.

In front of the Victorian house, the trees give way to falling lawns and a stunning view of St Michael's Mount (qv) rising from the sea. The garden's chief threat – the wind – may also become apparent. The westerlies can be savage, and without Sir Rose Price's extensive tree planting to protect the slope, little ornamental gardening could have been attempted. The shelterbelts need continual management, and much restoration has been necessary following the severe gales of January 1990; Leyland Cypress and Italian Alder have been used to provide quick temporary cover between the young beech, sycamore, ash, Holm and Turkey oaks, together with hedges of holly and thorn to give a low buffer.

Even here, at the summit of the garden, there is a wealth of exotics to defend. The house is clothed in such shrubs as the New Zealand Lobster Claw, *Clianthus puniceus*, *Berberidopsis corallina* from Chile and *Dendromecon rigida* from California. And in the adjacent walks, there are still more tree magnolias, including splendid specimens of *M. sargentiana* var. *robusta*, *M.* 'Charles Raffill' and *M. delavayi*, still more rhododendrons, including the deliciously scented *R. taggianum* and still more camellias. New and little-known plants continue to be sampled and tested for hardiness at Trengwainton, ensuring that the collection retains its pioneering flavour and can always spring exotic surprises, even on the experts.

Trerice

nr Newquay, Cornwall

3 miles south-east of Newquay, via A392 and A3058

Area 6 acres (2·4 ha)
Soil neutral–alkaline/sandy loam
Altitude 100 ft (30 m)
Average rainfall 37 in (940 mm)
Average winter climate moderate
Staff one

This is bald, windswept, coastal countryside. High hedges flank the winding lanes that lead here, and the house is tucked into the hillside, sheltered by belts of pale-trunked sycamore, beech and other tenacious trees. It is an ancient but unexpected property, a rare survivor from the Elizabethan era. The garden is a far cry from the exotic woodlands of the south coast. It is small and intimate, comprising a series of formal terraces and grass banks, enclosed by walls and hedges. Of its early design, little is known. A painting of 1818 depicts the ground east and north of the house in a rough state, but photographs taken before 1915 show a neat Dutch garden to the south, with small borders, paths and Standard roses. By 1969, when the Trust assumed control, it had again fallen into neglect, and a programme of restoration and re-planting began.

There has been no attempt to create a period piece. Rather, formal touches combine with orchard, copse and meadow to make a tranquil, timeless setting for the house. On the sloping land to the south, old varieties of apple, pear, plum, damson, gage and medlar grow, in quincunx pattern, in the grass. Blue and cream comfreys are among the spring highlights

Shafts of early morning sun filtering through the orchard trees at Trerice.

in the beds leading up to the house, and at the top, over a hedge of scented *Osmanthus × burkwoodii*, you come upon a garden of predominantly white flowers.

Like most of Trerice's beds, these are at their most colourful in summer, when the bronze phormiums are foils for cistus, anaphalis, osteospermum, mallow, 'Iceberg' roses and many other shrubs and perennials. By contrast, the borders in the Front Court are richly coloured in gold and purple leaves and flowers, the cast including philadelphus, berberis, potentillas, *Clematis × jackmanii* and *C. tibetana* subsp. *vernayi*. The bowling alley above has a permanent bedding scheme of *Geranium tuberosum* and muscari, which bloom in spring and disappear in summer, paired with the hardy fuchsia 'Chillerton Beauty', hebe and prostanthera. From the top meadow, strewn with daffodils in spring, there are views over the house and countryside, with Newquay, though not the sea, visible between the trees. The descent takes you past beds of seaside shrubs – olearias, escallonias, hebes and senecios – to the house's back cobbled court, where ceanothus, wisteria and the tender South American *Araujia sericofera* clothe the walls; this last, a scented climber that sets sticky traps for pollinating moths and holds them over-night by their proboscies, is known as the cruel plant.

For gardeners, one of the most absorbing corners of Trerice is the hayloft adjoining the Great Barn – another rarity in Cornwall. Here, the Trust has assembled a selection of many different types of lawnmower, some unearthed in its various properties, others gifts from manufacturers and private individuals – particularly David Halford – giving a unique, and occasionally hilarious, insight into the history of lawn care, a peculiarly British obsession.

Uppark

South Harting, Petersfield,
Hampshire

5 miles south-east of Petersfield
on B2146, 1½ miles south of
South Harting

Area 54 acres (21·8 ha)
Soil alkaline/brown earth,
   chalk
Altitude 492 ft (150 m)
Average rainfall 37 in (940 mm)
Average winter climate cold
Staff one

Uppark has suffered more than its fair share of calamity this past decade. In October 1987, and again in January 1990, its garden, park and woods were devastated by gales. In August 1989, when the restoration of the house was nearing completion and while the roof was being releaded, the building caught fire and was severely damaged. But the house has been painstakingly reconstructed, plaster wall by ceiling, door hinge by bracket, and looks uncannily unchanged; the scars suffered by the garden from the building works are gone; trees are growing up to re-create the former wooded setting; and the Trust's programme of improvements for the garden is well advanced.

Its position, high on the South Downs, with a view between flanking hills, to a distant band of sea, is the chief delight. The house stands proud in this landscape, an elegant Dutch-style building with steeply pitched roof, pediment and red-brick walls, dressed in pale stone. It was built in about 1690 for Lord Grey of Warke, later 1st Earl of Tankerville, and in the mid-eighteenth century was given its supporting pair of large brick outbuildings, a stable block and kitchen/laundry range (later becoming the orangery), each with a clock-tower. Your first sight is of its rear, north façade and portico, at the head of a short drive, informally bordered by grass glades and groups of free-growing yew and other evergreens. Clearly, this is not a 1690s setting. The early, rather larger, formal gardens, which seem to have had terrace walks, courts, orchards and a bowling green, had mostly disappeared by about 1730, in favour of parkland sweeping to the house walls. The present rear garden of sinuous lawns, meandering gravel paths and shrubberies evolved afterwards.

The north drive and portico are the work of Humphry Repton who advised over a long period and, in 1810, produced one of his celebrated Red Books of proposals and sketches. He probably also designed the iron gratings in the light wells over the intriguing underground service passages in the rear forecourt which link the house to the kitchen, laundry and stables; the upstairs/downstairs world here was experienced at close hand by the young H.G. Wells, whose mother was housekeeper for 12 years until being dismissed for incompetence in 1892.

Some of the accompanying planting is extremely fine. The beauty is not so much from seasonal colour, though there are displays from an assortment of shrubs such as Guelder Rose, hydrangea, lilac and escallonia, and from the Bush roses grouped in the small, late-Victorian garden west of the drive; also from the eruptions of spring bulbs and chalkland wildflowers, including a colony of Ladies' Tresses orchids below the stables. Rather, it comes more from the crisp contrasts of texture and form between the many evergreen plants and their companions. So you find broad-leaved *Viburnum tinus* and *V. davidii* set against the hazier foliage of yew and Japanese maple; laurel and bergenia with cotoneaster, juniper and Deodar Cedar; spotted aucuba, choisya and Gladwin Iris rising from banks and belts of ground-hugging ivy. Added to this are touches of variegation from holly, rhamnus and kerria; exotic surprises from aralia; and, here and there, bursts of scent.

Repton commented on the 'atmosphere of sweets'. 'I may truely say that in no place have I ever seen such accurate attention given to olfactory joy as at Uppark – every window has its Orange Tree or Tube roses – and admits perfume from the surrounding beds of Mignionette and Heliotrope.' Now, it comes from the various osmanthus, philadelphus and mahonias; honeysuckle in the garden behind the Orangery; lavender in front of the Orangery; and soapwort, *Saponaria officinalis*, near the summer-house – introduced by Lady Meade-Featherstonhaugh for use in cleaning the curtains and upholstery.

Upton House

Banbury, Warwickshire

On A422, 7 miles north-west of Banbury, 12 miles south-east of Stratford-upon-Avon

Area 37 acres (15 ha)
Soil neutral/iron-sandstone
Altitude 693 ft (211 m)
Average rainfall 27 in (686 mm)
Average winter climate cold
Staff five

BELOW LEFT: The late seventeenth-century Banqueting House at Upton, with the leaves of *Ligularia* 'Desdemona' in the Bog Garden in the foreground.

BELOW RIGHT: The Cherry Garden at Upton House awash with blossom; among the trees are *Prunus jamasakura* 'Kanzan' and *Prunus avium* 'Plena'.

Upton stages one of the great *coups de théâtre* of English gardening. The opening scene is sober, even austere. The house, a wide, plain and symmetrical building, constructed of the local honey-brown Hornton sandstone, stands at the head of a straight drive, enclosed by tall beech and Scots Pine, holly and yew. Its core was built by Sir Rushout Cullen, the son of a London merchant, in 1695; its additions date from the late 1920s, when the estate was brought by the 2nd Viscount Bearsted, the noted art collector and philanthropist.

The garden front is cheerier. There are roses, wisteria, Virginia Creeper and the grey-leaved 'Dusty Miller' Vine (*Vitis vinifera* 'Incana') on the walls, and a pretty assortment of plants fringing and spilling over the flagged terrace: yellow, blue and silver schemes to complement the stone, including the Hybrid Scots Briar rose 'Williams' Double Yellow', primrose bedding, catmint, iris, artemisias and dianthus – the groups spiced by the rich pink

The Aster border in evening light, early autumn.

of the Rambler rose 'Albertine', and the crimson of an uncommon Floribunda rose 'Moulin Rouge'. Opposite, a broad platform of lawn, framed on one side by yews and on the other by eighteenth-century Cedars of Lebanon, sweeps to a ha-ha, beyond which the land climbs up a hillside, dotted with sheep and clumps of trees. It is a gentle and pleasing scene. Some visitors may look out upon it and turn back. On my first visit, I nearly did, but luckily decided to continue to the lawn edge.

As you peer over, the contents spring up at you like a jack-in-the-box. A valley is revealed, the nearside bank tamed by terraces of flowering shrubs and perennials, double herbaceous borders running down to a Copper Beech tree, a garden of roses, sloping yew hedges, a grand Italianate stairway, a large fruit and vegetable garden and, at the bottom, a rectangular lake. There is another lake off to the left, appointed with a porticoed pavilion, and to the right, a curious plantation of pink and white cherry trees around a rectangular lawn, backed by a wood of beech, ash and sycamore. A complete garden landscape is hidden here. The parterre walls, like the yews above, are contemporary with the older part of the house, and it seems that for three centuries the slope has been providing fruit and vegetables for the household.

Angled to the south, the plots absorb all the available warmth, and they are still managed intensively, with greenhouses used to raise seedlings and cloches to protect young plants. The gamut of vegetables, grown on a four-year rotation, runs from french beans and brussels sprouts to kohlrabi and onions (which grow especially well here). Falling rows of salad crops, asparagus beds, blocks of soft fruit and apple trees complete the scene.

But while this productive section remains as the centrepiece, and a reminder of the priorities in the late seventeenth- and early eighteenth-century garden, the remainder of the slope has been developed for purely ornamental purposes. This was undertaken for Lord and Lady Bearsted by their architect, Percy Morley Horder, and the garden designer Kitty Lloyd-Jones. With the construction of the stone stairway, the Baroque grandeur of the house was extended into the composition. The flights descend elegantly either side of a crown of wisteria, and at the base, where once the greenhouses stood, you come to the formal rose garden with beds of assorted Hybrid Tea roses around a statue of Pan; her Ladyship's paved garden composed of silver stachys and cool pastel perennials, with a standard wisteria as its centrepiece; and a garden of blue flowers, woven around *Hibiscus syriacus* 'Oiseau Bleu' (syn. *H.s.* 'Blue Bird'), and framed again by double yellow Hybrid Scots Briar roses.

Soft and carefully focused associations of colour distinguish the planting here on the terraces, with blue and yellow, alone or in partnership, as a principal motif. There are many memorable passages: Dutch lavender, punctuated by rosemaries, running beside the upper grass walk, accompanied by ceanothus, romneya and laburnum; a wave of creamy, iris-like *Sisyrinchium striatum*, beneath outcrops of red valerian and purple aubrieta; and fine displays from the apricot Tea rose 'Lady Hillingdon Climbing', the buff Noisette rose 'Rêve d'Or', *Lonicera etrusca*, golden fremontodendron and, in autumn, from the leaves and berries of numerous berberis.

The Mediterranean and Californian flavour of these upper borders is in response to the sunny, dry conditions, but where the light and soil changes, you meet a different cast. On the cool, shady side of the vegetable garden's brick wall, for example, a National Collection of asters has been assembled: not the mildew-prone *Novi-belgii* hybrids, the true Michaelmas daisies, but the various cultivars of the taller, smaller-flowered *A. ericoides* and *A. cordifolius*, which include so many desirable garden plants, interspersed with varieties of short, starry *A. amellus*. They are at their peak in early October. As you reach the lake, water sets a new theme. For this is one of a chain of six former fish- or stewponds, formalised by Sir Rushout Cullen, but dating back to medieval times when the land was held by the Church; the water, fed from a spring on top of Edgehill, collects first in the Monk's Well, south-west of the house, passes through the stewponds and flows eventually into the Thames. The lake you see from the lawn above is part of this, and was given its irregular shape and temple in 1775, when the property was owned by the banker Robert Child.

The cherry plantation's sunken lawn is now explained, for as you arrive through the nuttery (another essential in the productive garden), you realise that it too, together with the other, water-filled depression now revealed – bordered by rushes and trees, including an impressive hornbeam – is part of the sequence.

Upton's second big surprise is now sprung. For beyond this pond, yet another garden of distinctive character opens up – a water garden of meandering grass paths and sinuous pools, presided over by a Dutch-style banqueting house, now looming between the trees. The building, like the formal framework of the gardens, dates back to the late seventeenth century, but the area was re-landscaped and planted in the 1930s, by which time the stewponds here had become an overgrown marsh. Lush marginal plantings of hostas, rodgersias, ligularias and rheums contrast with the more elegant foliage of ferns, kirengeshoma and the multi-stemmed Katsura Trees (*Cercidiphyllum japonicum*), and there are strong flashes of colour from lysichiton, primulas, irises and the conspicuous, surface-feeding shoals of Golden Orfe now living in the water.

This is by no means a complete catalogue of the garden's horticultural attractions. There is Lady Bearsted's limestone rock garden beside the swimming-pool on the main lawn; the secret herb garden; the orchard with its damsons, medlars and greengages; and the Wilderness, where Queen Anne's Lace and campion follow the daffodils and bluebells. All has now been brought to a very high standard of cultivation and display.

The Vyne

Sherborne St John,
Basingstoke, Hampshire

4 miles north of Basingstoke
between Bramley and
Sherborne St John

Area 12 acres (4·9 ha)
Soil neutral/clay
Altitude 200 ft (61 m)
Average rainfall 30 in (762 mm)
Average winter climate moderate
Staff one

This composition of spacious pleasure grounds and crisp, clear colours fills a quiet hollow just a few miles from Basingstoke. The house was built for William Sandys, later Lord Chamberlain to Henry VIII, in the early part of the sixteenth century, and modified by Chaloner Chute, Speaker of the House of Commons, after 1653. It is a wide and welcoming building of rose-red brickwork, dressed in stone and decorated with purple header-bricks in diamond pattern (diapering), and when you walk around to the north-facing garden front, it springs the surprise of a white Palladian portico – the earliest known example to adorn an English country house.

The low-lying position makes for a lush, green setting. Towering limes together with an old Horse Chestnut and ancient oak, shade the entrance lawns (flooded with daffodils in spring), and on the north side, a vast expanse of close-mown grass rolls gently down to a lake, flanked by cedars, walnuts, Scots Pines and other trees. You can see carp basking in the water, and there is much other wildlife besides, including kingfishers, which often dart over the wilderness pool beyond the weir. A circular walk takes you across two bridges at either end of the lake (the brick piers are the remains of a fine Victorian bridge which replaced a Chinese-Gothic structure put up by John Chute in the eighteenth century) and passes through Morgaston Wood, full of bluebells in the spring.

The other, more ornamental, wilderness area was developed by Sir Charles Chute in about 1907, following the woodland and meadow gardening ideas of the writer William Robinson. Here, snowdrops, daffodils, anemones and Snakeshead Fritillaries are naturalised in the grass, accompanied by clumps of perennials, such as asters, crambe and the autumn-flowering scented *Clerodendrum trichotomum*. These areas are in contrast to the architectural and more formal touches that John Chute incorporated, or which were reinstated or added in the Victorian and Edwardian eras, when the grounds were reshaped and replanted. These include the gravel walk in front of the house, the narrow avenue of Red-twigged Limes dating from 1884, and, at its head, the splendid domed brick pavilion, in the shape of a Greek cross, dating from the 1650s. One of two erected (John Chute demolished the other in 1756), it was probably designed by John Webb, a pupil of Inigo Jones. Standing next to it is one of the oldest oak trees in Hampshire. Nearby, beside the Chapel, you also come upon two evergreen *Phillyrea latifolia*, with ancient, twisted trunks.

In summer, the most colourful area of the garden is the small enclosure beside the house's west front. Here, backed by a yew hedge, is a colourful herbaceous border planted in the 1960s, where violet-blues, purples, pinks, carmines and whites (catmint, *Campanula lactiflora*, acanthus, phlox, sedum, Japanese anemone and others) melt into a scheme of yellows, apricots, creams and scarlets (ligularia, daylilies, macleaya, crocosmia) – all finely associated for height and foliage contrast. I caught this border at its peak in July and it has lodged in my memory as one of the best formal herbaceous schemes I have come across in Trust gardens. Opposite, beds of the pinky-red Bush rose 'Comte de Chambord' lead to the door, which is flanked by a pair of purple vines grown on frames. These are a reference to the house, thought to have been named after 'Vin Domus', or 'House of Wine', in Roman times.

Waddesdon Manor

Waddesdon, nr Aylesbury, Buckinghamshire

6 miles north-west of Aylesbury, on A41, 11 miles south-east of Bicester

Area 165 acres (67 ha)
Soil alkaline/clay, sand
Altitude 250 ft (76 m)
Average rainfall 34 in (864 mm)
Average winter climate cold
Staff seven

Baron Ferdinand de Rothschild rejected the initial design for his country house as being rather too ambitious. His French architect, Gabriel-Hippolyte Destailleur, told him he would regret his decision, commenting that 'one always builds too small'. 'He prophesied truly', said the Baron. 'After I had lived in the house for a while I was compelled to add one wing and then another . . .' The manor is revealed at the end of a double avenue of oaks (gradually being replanted with the Turkey Oak, *Quercus cerris*, which does better on the shallow limestone soil than our native species). It is a fantastic sight: a broad expanse of Loire château perched on a cold, windy Buckinghamshire hill, bristling with conical towers, high-pitched pavilions, spires and ornament. Accompanying it is sweeping parkland with swirling belts of beech, lime, Horse Chestnut and other trees – many of which were planted in a semi-mature state, coming to their sites by teams of Percheron horses, specially imported from Normandy.

The tree collection was considerably enriched by Miss Alice de Rothschild after Baron Ferdinand's death in 1898, and is characterised now by its sumptuous stands of specimen exotics, arranged, species by species, for landscape impact. Unfortunately, there were comparatively few subsequent introductions in the years after her death, with the result that a major programme of replacement planting for the future has been required of the Trust, supported and funded by Lord Rothschild. Horse Chestnut, Silver Lime and Austrian Pine are among those you pass as you ascend the curving drive from the village, and at the head of the oak avenue, Weeping Limes drench the air with summer scent around the grand fountain of Triton and Nereids riding on sea monsters.

Coloured-leaved trees, much favoured in the late-Victorian garden, are prominent here on the approach as elsewhere, with blue Atlas Cedar, and Purple Beech and Norway Maple (*Acer plantanoides* 'Schwedleri') used as highlights among the tapestry of greens. Golden yew and the golden Lawson Cypress 'Stewartii' supply the yellow through the grounds. But the trees are just one element in this composition, which was planned as a series of varied and impressive entertainments for the family and their weekend guests.

The changes in terrain provide some drama, not just the contrast of the levelled areas and the falling hillside, but also the more picturesque additions, in particular the eruptions of rock

283

The Dairy Garden at
Waddesdon in a photograph
taken in 1898, showing Baron
Ferdinand's planting, with
fountains, topiary specimens,
statuary and rose arbours.
On the right is the buttery, on
the left the dairy, and at the
end the cowman's cottage.

to the west of the oak avenue. These seem natural but, in fact, were made up of stone removed during the creation of the plateau on which the house is built, and are layered with artificial stone, brick and concrete. They were built by the noted rockwork specialists, Pulham & Sons, and, until the smell became too offensive, their caves were used as shelter by Baron Ferdinand's flock of mountain sheep. Further down the hill, you come upon a deep gulley (excavated for part of the railway track installed to transport materials for building the house) spanned by a bridge and with its steep sides planted as a rock garden, with hardy shrubs and ground covers. The grass here is full of bluebells and primroses, an echo of the great sloping meadow of wildflowers and daffodils, planted by Mr and Mrs James de Rothschild as a memorial to Miss Alice, further to the south.

The contrasts of artful gardening and natural landscape, man-made eye-catchers and plant forms, play throughout the grounds. In another area, you come upon a summer pergola, hung with the pink rose 'Compassion' and *Clematis* 'Perle d'Azur' and dripping with baskets of fuchsia and geranium. And below Pulham's rustic rockwork is the most splendid structure of all: a magnificent Rococo ironwork aviary, each compartment housing an assortment of exotic birds. The raucous calls, including those of the dashing white Rothschild's Mynah from Bali, can be heard deep into the park, and on my first visit here, years ago, there was the astonishing sight of macaws flying free over the trees; this policy had to be discontinued because of the damage they inflicted on plants.

The grandest piece of formal gardening, however, is to be found to the south of the house. Here, below the terrace, is the great parterre, designed by the Baron and the arena where he could demonstrate to his guests his gardeners' mastery over plants. With an ornate fountain displaying Pluto and Persephone as their centrepiece, and a stone balustrade and clipped hedges of green and golden yew as their frame, the beds heave with many thousands of tulips, summer annuals and tropical dot plants. Across the parterre, there is a panoramic view, past the pink-candled chestnuts, down into the Vale of Aylesbury and towards the Rothschild pavilion at Eythrope, near Upper Winchendon, to which Baron Ferdinand would conduct his guests in a procession of landaus on a Sunday afternoon. In the morning, they would have toured Waddesdon's series of show glasshouses, rose, rock and water gardens, all formerly attached to the 7-acre (2·8-ha) kitchen garden, which is outside the Trust's boundary.

It was a sumptuous world, and present-day Waddesdon offers more than a taste – not least in the manor's interiors, which are one of the treasure chests of Europe.

Wakehurst Place

Ardingly, Haywards Heath, West Sussex

1½ miles north-west of Ardingly, on B2028

Area 180 acres (73 ha)
Soil acid–neutral/sandy, clay
Altitude 200–500 ft (61–152 m)
Average rainfall 35 in (889 mm)
Average winter climate moderate
Staff 33, under administration of Royal Botanic Gardens, Kew

The setting for this mind-boggling collection of trees and shrubs is the unspoilt countryside of the Sussex Weald, with its rolling hills and tracts of ancient woodland. The gardens spill down grassy and rocky slopes below a high plateau, on which stands the Elizabethan mansion, built for Sir Edward Culpeper and restored by the Edwardian architect Sir Aston Webb.

The tall redwoods, formal lawns and small garden lake and rockery that accompany it are part of the nineteenth-century legacy, but it was in 1903 that the exotic planting began in earnest. Then the estate was bought by Gerald Loder, later Lord Wakehurst, who, following his brother Sir Edmund at nearby Leonardslee and his nephew Giles at The High Beeches, began tapping into the stream of new trees and shrubs now becoming available from the Americas, the Far East and Australasia.

In 1965, the garden came, by way of a 99-year lease from the National Trust, to the Royal Botanic Gardens, Kew, whose influence now shows in the stricter rationalising policy of grouping plants by geographic region and habitat, so that one has a sense of walking through the world's temperate woodlands, among fairly natural associations of leaf and flower. The great storm of 1987, which tore through Wakehurst with the loss of around 20,000 trees, has accelerated this shift in display in various parts of the grounds, including near the house, where sheltered and shady woodland beds were converted overnight into a sunny, exposed hilltop. Replanted with dwarf rhododendrons, junipers and potentillas, and with a copse of birch, rowan and maples behind, this now gives a taste of the subalpine heathland and scrub of eastern Asia.

Such innovations interplay with the more ornamental features. Here, around the upper lawns, there are displays of autumn colour, comprising parrotia, *Euonymus alatus* and pampas grass, and a curiously effective, almost monochrome planting on a rock bank, consisting of mounds of bronze-purple Japanese maples and creeping *Persicaria vacciniifolia* in copper and pale pink.

Another area has been planted for winter, presenting witch-hazels and other flowering shrubs in an optically challenging cartoonscape of tinted-leaved heathers, conifers and white-trunked birches. This is preparation for the more expansive display of heathers further to the west, where they merge with botanical collections of shrubs from Tasmania, mainland

Australia and New Zealand, including hebes, phormiums, ozothamnus, leptospermums, prostantheras and telopea. There are also more formal elements. To the west are walled gardens, one with yew hedges and a fountain, and the other filled with silver-leaved and pastel-flowered shrubs, including lavenders, cistus, ballota, ceanothus and Shrub roses; the walls of both enclosures sheltering many interesting climbers, including a noted specimen of the Chilean Coral Plant, *Berberidopsis corallina*. Outside, there is a border devoted to bulbs and other monocotyledons, featuring some ravishing ginger lilies (Hedychiums).

But as you walk away from the house, the traces of formality quickly melt away. Trees and shrubs, especially rhododendrons, are all around the lawns, in informal stands and belts – specimens such as white-tiered *Cornus alternifolia* 'Argentea' and golden cypresses, and rarities like *Aesculus wilsonii*, aromatic *Zanthoxylum ailanthoides* and, in the pinetum (80 per cent of which was destroyed by the great storm), *Picea farreri* and *Keteleeria davidiana*. Suddenly, beyond the lake, the ground drops away, and from the semi-circular balustrade of the viewing bastion, you find yourself looking down into a steep glen, known as the Slips, the entrance to one of the two planted valleys that ring the house like a horseshoe. In autumn, there is a memorable cascade of the bicoloured knotweed (with pink and crimson spikes) *Persicaria affinis* 'Superba', directly below, swirling around the rocks, and with its tints picked up further down by other knotweed species and the umbrella-shaped leaves of darmera.

A stream flows down, falling over ledges, and feeding into pools of various sizes, again bordered by a rich array of moisture-loving perennials including blue poppies, osmunda fern, arisaemas, and, in well-manured ground, a spectacular colony of the giant Himalayan lily, *Cardiocrinum giganteum*. Magnolias and nyssas thrive on the grassy banks, joined by a range of unusual but extremely garden-worthy species such as *Stewartia pseudocamellia*, *Trochodendron aralioides* and *Maytenus boaria*. Curving paths, short flights of steps and small bridges over the water beckon this way and that, with ever more dells opening up, some densely covered with established vegetation, others freshly planted in the wake of the storm, and all framed by native oaks and beeches and soaring North American conifers – the Western Hemlocks and Douglas Firs, in particular, have reached a notable size and, in the shelter of the valley, managed to survive the 1987 gales.

To the west, a massive outcrop of weathered, grey sandstone is the centrepiece for a wilder and more rugged Himalayan scene, comprising curtains of *Persicaria vacciniifolia* and extensive thickets of *Berberis wilsoniae* rolling down the slope, while among the moister pockets and shadier banks, you wander among extensive plantings of the larger-leaved rhododendrons, such as *RR. fulvum, rex* and the Loderi Group. Here, as elsewhere, views are continually revealed, with the glimmer of Ardingly reservoir in the middle distance.

The estate is as rich in native as in exotic flora – including rare mosses, liverworts and lichens, and the native filmy fern, *Hymenophyllum tunbrigiense* – and in line with Kew's involvement with plant conservation worldwide, an extensive sweep of meadows, woods and wetlands is now managed as a nature reserve. The public is admitted only by permit, but you get an idea of its content to the south of the garden's lower lake, where an area of swamp, surrounded by woods, has been made accessible by means of a raised wooden walkway, enabling you to pass between plantations of basket willows, through reed beds, and over watermint and other aquatics, looking down at fish and dragonflies; grebe are usually present, and occasionally you catch a glimpse of a kingfisher. It is a complete change in mood.

A view of Wakehurst Place from across Mansion pond.

Beside Westwood Lake, rhododendrons and other Asian exotics again reappear, and in autumn, there is another bonfire of coloured leaves, this time from American species such as *Cotinus obovatus*, *Acer rubrum*, *Oxydendrum arboreum* and liquidambar.

The walk back up the western valley takes you through further American forest types, including atmospheric groves of Douglas Fir and Wellingtonia; a belt of high Arctic species; slopes of Mediterranean pines, oaks and arbutus; a Southern Hemisphere wood of nothofagus (a National Collection) and eucalyptus; and plantings made up of the world's birches (another National Collection). Bluebells and Lent Lilies carpet the banks in spring. This is one of the Trust's largest gardens, and a full day is never long enough.

287

Wallington

Cambo, Morpeth,
Northumberland

12 miles west of Morpeth
(B6343), 6 miles north-west
of Belsay (A696)

Area 65 acres (26·3 ha)
Soil neutral–acid/medium
  loam
Altitude 500 ft (152 m)
Average rainfall 33 in (838 mm)
Average winter climate
  moderate–cold
Staff five, plus three trainees

FAR RIGHT: The walled garden
at Wallington in early spring,
with its terraced borders,
conservatory and Owl House.

288

The moorland road from Hexham to Rothbury and Cragside runs through the heart of the Wallington estate, crossing the River Wansbeck over the stone-balustraded bridge, designed by James Paine in 1755, and then climbing the wooded hill, to skirt the eastern front of the Palladian mansion. Four griffins' heads, embedded in the lawn, grin at you as you pass. Sir Walter Calverley Blackett embarked on the creation of his Georgian idyll sometime in the mid-1730s, helped principally by a 'Mr Joyce', and possibly later in the 1760s by 'Capability' Brown, whose childhood home was only a mile away.

So, you arrive at Wallington to a taste of the eighteenth century. Either side of the house are the remnants of Sir Walter's elaborately designed plantations: dark walks, straight and serpentine, leading between the beeches, oaks, limes and sycamores, and their laurel and yew understorey, to open pools colonised by waterlily, iris, great water dock and many other native species. Red squirrels still live in these woods, and there is a rich birdlife, including nuthatch, wood warbler and pied flycatcher.

From the house, there is the contrast of sweeping views across the ha-ha, down into the parkland and up over the rolling Northumbrian hills towards Hadrian's Wall and the distant Shaftoe Crags. Urns draw the eye east and west across open lawn, the west view taking you down an avenue of Red-twigged Limes, planted by the Trust. But there are also more colourful touches, added in Victorian and more recent times: mixed shrubberies of golden yew, golden lonicera, red-purple plum and bronze-purple sloe (*Prunus spinosa* 'Purpurea'); the Bourbon rose 'Madame Isaac Pereire' successfully trained as a climber up the south front of the house, in the company of other roses, sage, rosemary and fuchsia; and, where the entrance drive curves into the clock-tower courtyard, an unexpectedly pretty midsummer partnership of deep violet *Campanula lactiflora*, rich red valerian, moonlight-yellow tree lupin and white philadelphus (backed by purple sloe).

All this is an appetiser for what awaits in the Walled Garden, half a mile to the east. The route takes you through the wood, past prospects of Sir Walter's triumphal archway (he had it repositioned here in an upper field, as a folly, after it proved too narrow for coaches to pass through); alongside his handsome, recently restored Portico House, built into the north wall of the original kitchen garden; and then, at the head of the easternmost wilderness pond, you walk through a modest blue gate, crowned by a small statue of Neptune.

The surprise is sprung. Ahead are stone terraces and curving stairways, lawns and hedges, ponds and rockeries, conservatory and pavilion, ornamental trees and border after border of flowering shrubs, herbaceous plants, roses and bulbs; all backed by views of parkland and woods. The walls and central, erect pavilion (the Owl House, formerly the Head Gardener's dwelling) were built by Sir Walter to enclose his new kitchen garden, but the internal design is largely the work of Sir George Otto Trevelyan, who inherited in 1886 and gardened here enthusiastically until his death in 1928, at the age of 90. The planting, on the other hand, is almost entirely the work of the Trust, which took over a garden weedy, overgrown and in structural disrepair.

There is a wealth of detail to investigate. Lead figures of Scaramouche, folk dancers, a Roman soldier and gladiator, a Greek goddess and others, parade along the brick, fern-flecked wall of the eighteenth-century upper terrace, facing inwards (unlike those at Powis Castle) on to a summer border of pastel-tinted Hybrid Musk roses and the almost single-flowered, richly scented 'Souvenir de St Anne's' (a sport of the popular Bourbon rose

Fuchsias, abutilons and other flowering plants in the conservatory at Wallington.

'Souvenir de la Malmaison'), accompanied by alliums, eryngiums and a froth of white valerian; pampas grass gives the Edwardian centrepiece and *Rosa glauca* (well teamed with black-eyed, magenta *Geranium psilostemon*) terminates the view in a haze of purplish grey.

The colour schemes are loose, but there is an underlying theme to most of the borders. In front of the conservatory, purple Smoke Bushes billow over hot plantings of yellow, orange and scarlet. Metal arches of cream honeysuckle (*Lonicera caprifolium*) and *Clematis* 'Perle d'Azur' (an echo of the fruit tunnels of the original garden) span beds of blue irises and rue, yellow loosestrife and marjoram. White Martagon Lilies partner golden yews; salmon alstroemerias, violet campanulas. The wide lower, north-facing, border is graded from soft to strong colours.

Elsewhere, the planting is dictated more by the nature of the habitat. Dwarf conifers, brooms, potentillas and hebes are grouped along the rocky beds beside the paths and stream. While the damp western fringe of the garden supports large and lush colonies of hostas, water irises and ligularias, accompanied by a comprehensive range (a National Collection) of elders.

When bad weather threatens, there is Sir George's conservatory for shelter. The very highest standards of cultivation underpin this splendid Edwardian scene, where pink and red flowers are arrayed against white-painted timberwork and furniture, marble busts and stone-slabbed floor. Pelargoniums and begonias, interspersed with palms, ferns and trailing ivy, fill the display bench with colour, while huge fuchsias, including an 85-year-old specimen of 'Rose of Castile Improved' (pruned back to its trunk and main branches in late winter), cascade from the central pillars. Scent is provided by *Heliotropium arborescens* and a huge lemon verbena, said to pre-date the house.

The Weir

Swainshill, nr Hereford,
Hereford and Worcester

5 miles west of Hereford
on A438

Area 10 acres (4 ha)
Soil alkaline/sand
Altitude 200 ft (61 m)
Average rainfall 30 in (762 mm)
Average winter climate moderate
Staff one, plus one part-time

A picturesque curve of the River Wye, and an accompanying patchwork of fields and woods stretching away towards the Black Mountains, provide the setting for this individual garden of trees and wildflowers. It extends over 11 acres (4·4 ha) of high, steep riverbank – with its plain, whitewashed villa, now a retirement home, perched above – and you cover them by a network of meandering and plunging paths, stairways and adventurous bridges. The sense of exploration is heightened by the pockets of more formal gardening that reveal themselves between the trees: clipped tumps of yew, box and laurel hedges bordering the river, and a rock garden of Cheddar limestone, spangled with pools and shaded by Japanese maples and exclamatory Irish Junipers. In summer, when the tracts of rough grass and flowers around them are high, the whole place takes on an abandoned air, while the bulbs and wildflowers are given time to seed and die back naturally.

The paths and early plantings are largely the work of R. C. Parr, a Manchester banker who bought the property as a fishing lodge in 1922 – assisted, from 1942, by his companion, Victor Morris. Parr's most colourful legacy is the surge of bulbs. Sheets of snowdrops, chionodoxas, scillas, daffodils and bluebells appear in bold succession under the trees, to be followed by patches of Snakeshead Fritillaries, blue camassias, Martagon Lilies, and, in late summer, cyclamen and colchicums. This is a display that continues to be augmented by the Trust's gardeners, who instal a minimum of 2,000 bulbs each autumn with the aid of a long-handled, step-on planter.

But it is the range of wildflowers that is most remarkable. The poor, alkaline soil enables a wide variety of species to compete with the grasses, and as well as dry, sunny slopes and shady woodland, there is damp ground and waterside. This is, therefore, a rich and diverse preserve, all the more precious for being set inside a wide, 'improved', arable landscape. Primroses and thick carpets of violets appear with the bulbs early in the year, and as the summer advances, the sunny banks are stained and scented with crosswort, thyme, marjoram, vetches, yarrow, wild carrot, scabious and ox-eye daisies. Purple loosestrife, figwort, eupatorium and Himalayan Balsam colonise the river's edge. And in the more heavily shaded woodland, the bluebells and wild garlic are followed by swathes of pink campion.

At every turn, something catches your eye, whether it be drifts of Twayblade orchid and quaking grass, or eruptions of parasitic toothwort, blooming in late spring along the surface-feeding roots of the poplars. At the end of July, when the growth is becoming rank, the garden is cut by rotary mower, and it then enters a period of green calm until the first autumn leaf tints appear in late September.

A late autumn view to the Tall Pavilion at Westbury Court, over the box parterre.

Westbury Court

Westbury-on-Severn,
Gloucestershire

9 miles south-west of
Gloucester on A48

Area 5 acres (2 ha)
Soil alkaline/alluvial silt, clay
Altitude 20 ft (6 m)
Average rainfall 27 in (686 mm)
Average winter climate moderate
Staff one

Seventeenth-century espaliered
pears at Westbury Court.

The Tall Pavilion offers an elevated vantage point of this handsomely appointed walled garden. The view is of tranquil canals, mown lawns, neat hedges and topiaries, white-painted benches, flashes of flower colour and fruits espaliered against mellow brick. Little seems to have ruffled the scene for 300 years. In fact, when Westbury Court came to the Trust in 1967, it was in an advanced state of dereliction.

Enthusiasm for the major restoration project sprang from the garden's rarity. Very few formal gardens in Britain survived the long era of naturalistic landscaping of the eighteenth century, and among them, Westbury Court was the only example to show a Dutch-style layout from the reign of William of Orange. The low-lying meadows bordering the River Severn make an ideal site for a water garden, but it may also have been the influence of his Dutch neighbour, Catherine Boevey of Flaxley Abbey, that prompted Maynard Colchester to embark on its construction. He began in 1696, with the excavation of the Long Canal, and work continued apace until his death in 1715. The garden was then embellished and altered by his nephew, Maynard Colchester II.

Within the walls, the parallel lines of yew hedges create a series of rectangular, framed vistas down the waterways and lawns, with the topiaries, flowering and pot-plants conveying the Dutch absorption and expertise in the art and craft of horticulture. Some of the hedges themselves sprout yew cones and spheres of holly, while balls and cones of box feature in the flower-filled 'cut-parterre' beyond the T-shaped canal. A quincunx of standard trees and clipped evergreens surrounds it, including domes of *Phillyrea angustifolia*, umbrellas of Portugal Laurel, and thorns sporting nests of mistletoe (established by pressing the ripe berries into the cracks of branches in late winter).

The espaliered fruit trees, reminders of the garden's important productive role, contribute to the formal patterns. Evocatively named varieties, these were all in cultivation before 1700, and include the apples 'Calville Blanc d'Hiver', 'Catshead' and 'Court Pendu Plat'; the pears

'Beurré Brown', 'Forelle' and 'Bellisime d'Hiver'; and the plums 'Red Magnum Bonum' and 'Catalonia '. Peaches, apricots and Morello cherries are also here.

In spring, bulbs make a patchwork of colour between them. The mid-seventeenth century saw the height of 'tulipomania' in Holland, when freakish tulips exchanged hands for vast sums, and although those famous varieties no longer exist, the selection of species and cultivars here evokes that period. Daffodils, anemones, muscari, ranunculus and Crown Imperials accompany them.

In the small walled enclosure beside the gazebo is a collection of the border perennials grown at the time. Campanulas, astrantia, hellebores, veratrums and meadow sages are among the cast filling the box-edged beds, and at midsummer they are showered with the scented blooms of old Shrub and Climbing roses. A small collection of dianthus is grown outside the walls, in beds specially raised and gritted.

The garden is essentially intimate and introspective, but framed views of the countryside are given by the two ironwork grilles, or *clairvoyées*, in the north wall – one, surmounted by stone pineapples, made in 1704, and the other, capped by vases, made after 1715. There are some fine trees in the neighbouring fields, including, to the south, a line of rare native Black Poplars. A recently planted avenue of Barland pears, willow and alder shade the glades beyond the canalised stream, which forms the garden's eastern boundary. And within the formal garden itself stands a superb Tulip Tree and a stupendous evergreen oak, presumed to pre-date the Dutch layout and thought to be one of the largest and oldest specimens in Britain.

West Wycombe Park

Venus' Temple at West Wycombe Park in spring.

West Wycombe, Buckinghamshire	At west end of West Wycombe, south of the A40 Oxford road	*Area* 46 acres (18·6 ha) *Soil* alkaline *Altitude* 250 ft (76 m) *Average rainfall* 30 in (762 mm) *Average winter climate* cold *Staff* part-time only

The red-blooded passion for life and art held by Sir Francis Dashwood, politician, antiquarian, connoisseur, practical joker, party-giver, founder member of the Society of Dilettanti and of the notorious Hellfire Club, is behind the creation of this Elysian landscape. The mansion, sitting on rising ground and commanding northerly views down its own wooded Chiltern combe and up to Church Hill opposite, was remodelled by Dashwood over a period of 45 years, from 1735 – by which time he had spent the best part of eleven years on successive cultural tours through Europe and Asia Minor – until his death in 1781.

The combe was landscaped over the same long period. By 1752, the first phase had produced a semi-formal composition, combining straight-edged plantations and avenues with serpentine walks and an irregularly shaped lake, made by damming the River Wye. From 1770, there was a fresh impetus, as Dashwood responded to the current taste for a

A view over the Cascade to the house.

parkland of more sweeping views and flowing contours. Although this phase – probably directed throughout by Thomas Cook, a pupil of 'Capability' Brown – did much to soften the earlier formality, many of the Baroque and Rococo elements were retained and absorbed, leaving the evolution of the garden clearly exposed.

Little has disturbed the scene since, although a programme of restoration and replanting was much needed by the middle of this century and has been conducted by the Trust and the 11th Baronet, with assistance from the Historic Buildings Council. The circuit of the park unfolds a succession of composed views and architectural surprises. From the north front of the house, you look down the greensward to the lake, where, on the largest of three islands, a colonnaded music temple by Nicholas Revett shines against the trees. On the hill to the west, above the plantation screening West Wycombe village, stands St Lawrence's Church, topped with its gilded sphere.

Past the Palladian east portico, the double colonnades of the south front, the great stone and flintwork arch of the Temple of Apollo, blue cedars and banks of shrubs, you walk up the slope to find the Round Temple suddenly revealed, a circular dovecote designed by Revett in about 1775. From here the dog-leg ha-ha draws you between open pastureland above, and dark, straight-edged plantations of deciduous trees below, to the Temple of the Winds, a flint and stuccoed wonder, built *c.*1759 and one of the earliest reproductions of an ancient classical monument in the country. The old entrance drive now takes you down to the lakeside and cascade. The early garden's impressive rock arch and accompanying River God were replaced by 1781 with the present simplified structure of piers and reclining nymphs, but the water still gushes over the knobbed steps into the stream. Across the lake, the view is more tranquil, the eye channelled between the islands and down the Broad Walk opposite, the only survivor of the two great avenues shown on the 1752 survey.

Daphne's Temple and Kitty's Lodge mark the original entrance to the park, and from here, you skirt the top end of the lake and enter the woods where, by means of little bridges crossing sinuous streams, you pass the eighteenth-century Temple of Venus, cross the Broad Walk, and return to the mansion. But *en route*, the mind must be allowed to wander, conjuring up visions of the many Bacchanalian feasts, musical spectacles and other lavish entertainments the park has witnessed.

Wightwick Manor

Wightwick Bank,
Wolverhampton,
West Midlands

3 miles west of
Wolverhampton, up
Wightwick Bank (A454)

Area 17 acres (7 ha)
Soil acid/varied, clay-
   sandstone outcrops
Altitude 250 ft (76 m)
Average rainfall 27 in (686 mm)
Average winter climate cold
Staff two

Nostalgia for a more romantic past was a natural accompaniment to the nineteenth-century's relentless industrialisation and urban sprawl. Beside the old manor and malt-house at Wightwick, the paint and varnish manufacturer Theodore Mander commissioned Edward Ould to build a neo-Tudor mansion, with feudal great hall, spiral brick chimneys and elaborately patterned black-and-white timbered walls. For the garden, Mander called upon Alfred Parsons, who, as well as being an accomplished landscape painter and illustrator, was a practised designer of gardens in the 'old-fashioned' style.

The formal compartments, clipped yew hedges, cottage-garden flowers, topiary peacocks and roses arrived at Wightwick between 1887 and 1906, in which year the famous Thomas Mawson of Windermere strengthened and embellished the patterns with beds, hedges and topiaries, and bonded house and garden by means of a broad, stone-flagged terrace, steps and oak balustrade. Parsons' and Mawson's yews have now swelled into massive cylinders and high screens, and they are an imposing presence both in the rose garden, where they complement beds of summer perennials, 'Iceberg' and golden roses and a rustic arbour, and on the lawn below the terrace, where they process to the southern boundary.

Here, the fringes of colour include a curious assortment of shrubs and perennials known as the 'Poets' Gardens', in which all the plants gleaned as cuttings or divisions from the gardens of William Morris, Tennyson, Dickens, Shelley and the artist Charles Kempe, who gave the house a number of its decorative features.

In late spring, the two large ponds, recently cleaned by the Trust and restocked with trout and carp, reflect the rich colours of massed rhododendrons; wildflowers bloom on the banks, while the air is stirred with the scents of bluebells and yellow azaleas. Mixed deciduous trees provide the backdrop, and their varied autumn tints follow the summer greens; Maidenhair Tree and Red Oak are among the highlights. Such tranquil pockets make the garden a haven for kingfishers, jays, woodpeckers and other wildlife. The adjacent paddocks add to the country flavour, and on the other side of the house, there are further productive areas including a hazel coppice, a second orchard and, over the road spanned by a copy of the 'Mathematical' bridge at Queens' College, Cambridge, a former fruit garden, now cleaned and replanted with early spring bulbs. With limes, beeches and other great trees all about, it is easy to forget you are in the Wolverhampton suburbs.

Wimpole Hall

Arrington, nr Royston,
Hertfordshire

8 miles south-west of
Cambridge (A603), 6 miles
north of Royston, (A14)

Area 60 acres (24·3 ha)
Soil alkaline/clay
Altitude 100ft (30m)
Average rainfall 23 in (584mm)
Average winter climate moderate
Staff two

A ridge of chalk meets the Cambridgeshire plain to the north and west of Wimpole Hall, giving sudden views of rising woods and grassland, the scene picturesquely animated by flocks of rare antelope-like sheep and herds of hefty (but docile) huge-horned cattle. The approach, however, is across level ground, from which the red-brick Georgian façade ascends imposingly. This is the county's grandest country house, and it is fitting that its park should have been moulded by some of the most famous names in landscape gardening.

A 2-mile (3·2-km) long, double avenue slices across the flat farmland opposite the south front. Sadly, the original elm trees here, and in the older west avenue, fell victim to Dutch Elm disease in the 1970s, but, in a major, phased planting project, the Trust has now replaced them with young limes, some propagated from ancient trees in the park.

From the mid-eighteenth century the landscaping at Wimpole was essentially directed along more 'natural' lines. The first phase was conducted for the 1st Earl of Hardwicke by Robert Greening, advised by the garden architect Sanderson Miller. It was Miller who produced the design for the Gothic Tower that serves as the distant eye-catcher from the hall's north front, though it was not built until 1774, and then in a modified form. The broad sweeps of hilly pasture and the clumps and tiers of trees that frame this folly have also been moulded by later designers. For ten years from the mid-1760s, the park was in the hands of 'Capability' Brown, and from 1790, his pupil William Emes. As you walk across the park towards the tower, you will come upon the lakes Brown created from the former fish-ponds and enhanced with islands and a Chinese bridge. The lakes are being cleared and restored.

The last great name in this extraordinary roll of designers is Humphry Repton, who came here in 1801. He planned a new approach to the hall from the Cambridge road, filled out Brown's tree clumps, and set out the present pattern of neat lawns and paths, exclaiming that 'It is called natural, but to me it has ever seemed unnatural that a palace shall rise immediately out of sheep pasture'.

Decorative gardening is confined to areas immediately beside the hall and to the pleasure grounds to the east. Box-edged Dutch gardens between the wings of the house are the work of the Trust, and are simplified versions of the parterres created in the Victorian period. Further colour comes from the shrub garden, to the west of the house, recently established on the site of the Victorian conservatory.

The most arresting seasonal flower show is from daffodils. These were the passion of Elsie Bambridge, daughter of Rudyard Kipling, who, with her husband Capt. George Bambridge, made a start on the formidable task of restoring the house and grounds after their long decline since the turn of the century. The collection includes many that have long disappeared from the nursery lists – among them, 'Bath's Flame', 'John Evelyn' and 'Mrs Barclay'.

A view of the Gothic Tower from the Saloon window at Wimpole Hall.

Trees, however, are Wimpole's chief glory, and while the native oaks, beeches, limes and ashes give the artful backdrop, ornamental varieties, planted over the past two centuries, enhance the foreground. Manna Ash, Copper Beeches and Indian Bean Trees are highlights in the formal areas, and in the pleasure grounds, the meandering path to the walled garden takes you past cherries, crab apples and a range of American species, including good specimens of redwood, Black Walnut and Cornelian Dogwood. There has been much replanting here in the wake of the storm of October 1987, and the new cast includes a generous percentage of conifers, which have proved surprisingly tolerant of the heavy, alkaline soil. Western Red Cedar, Spanish Fir, Incense Cedar and Serbian Spruce are among the species added.

Winkworth Arboretum

Hascombe Road, Godalming, Surrey

Near Hascombe, 2 miles south-east of Godalming on east side of B2130

Area 110 acres (44·5 ha)
Soil acid–neutral/sandy
Altitude 200–350 ft (61–106 m)
Average rainfall 30 in (762 mm)
Average winter climate cold–very cold
Staff three

Sun through the leaves of a Japanese maple in Winkworth Arboretum.

Autumn colour is Winkworth's chief glory, and as the surrounding countryside assumes its mellow wash of russet, copper and gold, its steep hillside takes on the more potent livery of Chinese mountains and New England forests. Wilfrid Fox, a skin specialist and amateur arborist, began clearing the brambles and bracken in 1938, working mainly alone but with the help of friends and neighbours at weekends.

The oak and bluebell wood beside the lower lake, he left largely undisturbed, but for a flash of Japanese maples. The wet ground is still colonised by Tussock Grass and native marsh plants, and the banks part-fringed by tangled stands of elder, alder and young elm. The hillside, too, remains rough and unmanicured, the exotics having been planted among native trees in a natural carpet of grasses, ferns, bracken, primroses, Stitchwort, wild garlic and other flowers. So there is still a sense of wilderness, and often the only sounds are from birds – among them, the hammering of woodpeckers and the screams of water rail. The stream goes on to fill the lake at Bramley House, where the influential Edwardian gardener Gertrude Jekyll spent her childhood.

Elsewhere, you find yourself in a plantsman's domain. Near the hilltop entrance is a glade planted for winter, with cherry, camellias, early rhododendrons, scented witch-hazels, and *Symplocos paniculata*, with ultramarine-blue berries. Further on, you are drawn by the exposed trunks of birches, snakebark and paperbark maples; the stands of Scots Pine, Blue Cedar, Serbian Spruce and other conifers rising from the orange bracken; and the traceries of branches against the silver lakes and the sheep-grazed hillside opposite.

Spring sees the tints of expanding leaves and blossom on cherries, dogwoods and magnolias, the last massed in the shelter of a plantation of coppiced hazel. The flight of over 100 steps, leading down to the old boathouse, Dr Fox fringed with evergreen Japanese azaleas to make a May cascade of carmine, pink and white. Elsewhere, there are white handkerchiefs on davidia, musk-scented vases on *Magnolia tripetala* and clouds of young white leaves on the collection of whitebeams. Thickets of the yellow deciduous azalea, *Rhododendron luteum*, drown the bluebell glades with honeysuckle fragrance. A little later, snowbells hang from styrax and melon-scented waterlilies open on *Magnolia obovata*. Hydrangeas then give a blue and white flush to the shadows, and, in August, the massive evergreen columns of *Eucryphia × nymansensis* 'Nymansay', planted by the Trust to guard the memorial to Dr Fox above the escarpment, open their white saucers.

Autumn tints on the banks above the lake.

Mountain ashes were among Dr Fox's favourite trees, and a large collection grows on the slope above the upper lake. The berries ripen in succession from August onwards. The dazzling orange and scarlet fruits on species such as *Sorbus commixta, S. pohuashanensis, S. esserteauana* and on *S. aucuparia* 'Rossica Major' from Kiev, standing beside the water, are vulnerable to birds, of course; though Dr Fox noted that berries on the foreign species tend not to be consumed as voraciously as on forms of the native rowan. However, trees with amber-yellow berries, such as 'Joseph Rock', and with pink or white berries, such as *SS. vilmorinii, hupehensis* and *cashmiriana*, often persist well into winter.

The peak period for autumn leaf colour is mid- to late October, though some trees, notably *Prunus sargentii* and its fiery clone 'Rancho', begin much earlier, while others, such as liquidambar, *Acer carpinifolium* and the shrubby *Photinia villosa* can delay until November. Japanese and other maples, amelanchier, sumachs (including the unusual *Rhus trichocarpa*) and *Enkianthus perulatus* give streaks of orange-scarlet, and fothergilla and deciduous azaleas bands of crimson. Rich reds come from the fastigiate Red Maple, *Acer rubrum* 'Columnare', *Oxydendrum arboreum, Viburnum cassinoides* and the compact ash, *Fraxinus angustifolia* subsp. *oxycarpa* 'Raywood'; bright yellows from *Acer cappadocicum, A. platanoides* and the Cherry Birch,

Betula lenta; and orange-browns from the many kinds of oak found here at Winkworth.

There are arresting views from all angles. In one spot on the upper path, you look down at a bank of Red Maple, *Acer rubrum*, dashingly partnered with the flame and yellow of *A. rufinerve* and *A. pensylvanicum*, and the blue of cedar and Bhutan Pine; the whole scheme silhouetted against the lake. While from the lakeside you look up at slopes of parrotias and Japanese maples, and walk past good stands of *Nyssa syvlatica* and *Cercidiphyllum japonicum*, the latter – on the right day – infusing the air with caramel scent from falling pink- and parchment-coloured leaves.

The Trust has recently purchased Badger's Rake, Dr Fox's house and grounds, to the west of the site, adding another 8 acres (3·2ha) of planting opportunities to the 99 acres (40ha) already covered by arboretum and oak wood.

Wordsworth House

Main Street, Cockermouth, Cumbria

Main Street, Cockermouth

Area ½ acre (0·2ha)
Soil acid/loam
Altitude 149ft (45m)
Average rainfall 50in
  (1,270mm)
Average winter climate moderate
Staff one, plus one part-time

'When having left his Mountains, to the Towers
Of Cockermouth that beauteous River came
Behind my Father's House he pass'd, close by
Along the margin of our Terrace Walk.
He was a Playmate whom we dearly lov'd.'

William Wordsworth was born in this town house in 1770 and lived here until the age of thirteen, when his father died. It is a plain, institutional-looking building, only slightly cheered by the terracotta wash on the walls, but the rooms are handsomely furnished and the small walled garden is acquiring some period charm, as the Trust's restoration advances – the layout based on sparse records of the original design. Trim gravel paths now replace the broken concrete paving, the borders that skirt the central rectangle of lawn are contained by sharp-edged box hedges and punctuated by trained apple trees, and white-painted Georgian seats mark the corners.

Colour is provided by the favourite cottage-garden flowers of the time: red and pink peonies, honesty, columbines, violas, bellflowers, lilies, monkshood, Cabbage roses, bluebells and, appropriately, the Poet's Daffodil, *Narcissus poeticus*. A long-established pink *Clematis montana* (a Victorian introduction) cloaks part of the wall, which has been planted mainly with northern varieties of apple and pear, trained as cordons; 'Greenup's Pippin' has been used for the free-standing specimens. Food production was, for many centuries, the most important duty of a garden, and in the smaller walled enclosure adjacent, the Trust has taken the opportunity to re-create a vegetable and herb garden, which will become part of the garden circuit in future years.

There is a good view of the main garden from the landing window, a vantage point that also reveals how much the lines of the layout are askew from those of the house; the lawn is mown on the diagonal to disguise this. The celebrated Terrace Walk overlooking the river, where Wordsworth played with his sister Dorothy, marks the end of the garden. The scene beyond is less pastoral than in the poet's day, but trees screen the less attractive aspects, and there is still a good sweep of grass, woods and water.

	Orangery	Conservatory	Bridge	Statuary	Ornaments	Fountain/pool	Formal water	Moat	Natural water	Terrace	Raised walk	Ha-ha	Mount	Ice house	Walled garden	Temple	Garden house	Dovecote	Grotto	Folly	Rock garden	Great trees	Pleaching	Avenue	Hedges	Maze	Topiary	Knot garden	Parterre	Formal beds	Borders	Rose garden	Rhododendrons	Woodland garden	Naturalised bulbs	Notable shrubs	Bog or water plants	Herb beds or garden	Fruit and vegetables
ACORN BANK		●							●		●			●								●		●	●					●	●		●	●				●	●
ANGLESEY ABBEY			●	●					●							●						●	●	●						●	●					●			
ANTONY HOUSE			●	●					●	●								●				●	●	●	●		●	●		●	●					●			
APPRENTICE HOUSE																								●												●		●	●
ARDRESS HOUSE														●																	●	●		●					
THE ARGORY		●		●					●		●																			●	●								
ARLINGTON COURT	●			●	●				●	●									●	●	●									●	●					●			
ASCOTT			●	●	●	●				●												●		●	●		●			●	●	●				●			
ATTINGHAM PARK		●							●			●	●									●																	
BADDESLEY CLINTON		●						●	●		●			●													●			●	●							●	●
BARRINGTON COURT		●		●	●	●		●														●	●	●						●	●					●		●	●
BASILDON PARK				●						●												●													●	●	●		
BATEMAN'S				●					●												●			●						●	●			●		●		●	●
BELTON HOUSE	●			●	●	●	●		●	●		●		●		●						●		●	●	●				●	●			●					
BENINGBROUGH HALL		●		●											●							●		●	●					●	●			●					
BENTHALL HALL				●					●									●			●	●					●			●			●			●			
BERRINGTON HALL									●						●																		●						
BIDDULPH GRANGE		●		●												●					●	●		●							●		●	●	●	●			
BLICKLING HALL	●	●	●	●	●				●	●		●			●							●		●	●					●	●			●	●	●			
BODNANT		●	●	●	●				●	●						●						●		●	●						●		●	●	●	●			
BUCKLAND ABBEY															●							●					●			●								●	
BUSCOT PARK			●	●	●	●	●	●							●							●	●	●						●	●			●					
CALKE ABBEY	●														●																●								
CANONS ASHBY				●						●					●							●		●			●			●	●								
CASTLE DROGO										●																				●	●	●		●		●	●		
CASTLE WARD			●		●	●		●	●				●	●	●			●	●	●	●	●			●					●	●			●	●				
CHARLECOTE PARK	●			●					●		●											●		●						●	●								
CHARTWELL		●	●	●		●			●	●				●		●						●								●	●	●		●	●	●			
CHIRK CASTLE			●	●	●					●							●				●	●		●						●	●		●	●	●	●			
CLANDON PARK			●	●	●				●							●	●		●			●	●	●		●				●	●								
CLAREMONT				●					●	●		●				●			●	●	●	●		●										●					
CLEVEDON COURT						●				●												●														●		●	
CLIVEDEN		●	●	●	●	●	●		●	●						●	●		●			●		●		●				●	●			●					
CLUMBER PARK		●	●	●		●			●	●						●	●	●	●			●		●						●	●			●	●			●	●
COLETON FISHACRE			●	●					●	●					●							●		●						●			●	●	●	●	●		

Garden Specialities

	Orangery	Conservatory	Bridge	Statuary	Ornaments	Fountain/pool	Formal water	Moat	Natural water	Terrace	Raised walk	Ha-ha	Mount	Ice house	Walled garden	Temple	Garden house	Dovecote	Grotto	Folly	Rock garden	Great trees	Pleaching	Avenue	Hedges	Maze	Topiary	Knot garden	Parterre	Formal beds	Borders	Rose garden	Rhododendrons	Woodland garden	Naturalised bulbs	Notable shrubs	Bog or water plants	Herb beds or garden	Fruit and vegetables
COTEHELE						•			•	•				•	•	•	•		•		•			•	•		•			•	•		•	•	•	•			
THE COURTS		•	•	•	•	•	•		•	•						•					•	•		•			•			•	•				•	•			•
CRAGSIDE HOUSE				•			•		•	•									•	•											•					•			
CROFT CASTLE									•	•		•								•											•					•			
DUDMASTON					•				•	•							•				•												•			•			
DUNHAM MASSEY	•		•					•	•	•			•	•														•	•			•		•					
DUNSTER CASTLE		•	•			•			•	•																							•			•			
DYRHAM PARK	•			•	•				•	•																					•								
EAST RIDDLESDEN HALL									•						•						•												•	•				•	•
EMMETTS GARDEN						•														•													•						
ERDDIG						•	•									•		•					•	•	•				•	•	•					•			
FARNBOROUGH HALL					•				•	•	•	•		•		•				•				•	•						•								
FELBRIGG HALL	•	•			•	•						•												•							•		•			•			
FENTON HOUSE				•	•	•								•										•	•					•	•		•					•	•
FLORENCE COURT			•						•		•		•	•		•					•											•	•	•	•				
FOUNTAINS ABBEY AND STUDLEY ROYAL			•	•	•				•	•	•	•		•		•			•	•	•			•											•				
GAWTHORPE HALL					•				•	•																	•				•								
GLENDURGAN			•						•												•					•							•	•	•	•	•		
GREAT CHALFIELD MANOR						•		•	•	•						•								•		•		•	•	•				•					
GREYS COURT			•		•	•			•		•		•	•							•				•		•			•	•					•			•
GUNBY HALL		•			•				•	•					•	•					•			•						•	•					•	•	•	•
HAM HOUSE	•		•	•					•					•								•	•	•		•		•	•	•	•		•	•					•
HANBURY HALL	•		•	•			•				•		•								•			•						•			•					•	•
HARDWICK HALL			•	•	•									•		•					•			•						•					•	•		•	•
HARDY'S COTTAGE																					•				•	•				•				•				•	
HARE HILL GARDEN								•						•																			•	•					
HATCHLANDS PARK			•	•					•	•			•		•						•						•		•					•					
HIDCOTE MANOR			•	•	•				•		•			•		•				•	•	•		•		•				•	•					•	•		
HILL TOP																															•								•
HINTON AMPNER			•			•			•		•												•	•		•				•	•					•	•		
HUGHENDEN MANOR			•	•					•		•																			•	•					•			
ICKWORTH	•		•		•				•	•	•					•					•			•	•					•	•	•			•	•	•		
IGHTAM MOTE		•		•	•		•	•										•						•						•					•	•		•	•
KEDLESTON HALL	•								•					•							•												•	•	•	•		•	•

303

Garden Specialities

	Orangery	Conservatory	Bridge	Statuary	Ornaments	Fountain/pool	Formal water	Moat	Natural water	Terrace	Raised walk	Ha-ha	Mount	Ice house	Walled garden	Temple	Garden house	Dovecote	Grotto	Folly	Rock garden	Great trees	Pleaching	Avenue	Hedges	Maze	Topiary	Knot garden	Parterre	Formal beds	Borders	Rose garden	Rhododendrons	Woodland garden	Naturalised bulbs	Notable shrubs	Bog or water plants	Herb beds or garden	Fruit and vegetables
KILLERTON			•		•					•		•		•			•				•	•		•					•		•		•	•	•	•			
KINGSTON LACY					•					•		•									•	•	•						•		•		•	•	•				
KNIGHTSHAYES GARDENS		•		•	•	•	•								•						•			•	•				•	•		•		•		•			
KNOLE				•	•	•				•				•	•	•										•	•				•	•	•		•	•		•	•
LACOCK ABBEY				•	•		•		•	•	•			•								•													•				
LAMB HOUSE					•																	•									•								
LANHYDROCK					•				•	•					•						•			•	•						•		•		•	•			
LITTLE MORETON HALL		•					•					•									•				•				•									•	•
LYME PARK	•		•		•	•				•	•								•					•					•		•	•	•	•	•	•		•	
LYTES CARY MANOR			•	•	•	•					•	•					•						•		•				•		•		•		•			•
MELFORD HALL			•		•	•				•	•	•											•		•				•		•		•		•	•		•	
MOMPESSON HOUSE														•																	•								
MONK'S HOUSE		•			•																•				•						•			•		•			
MONTACUTE HOUSE	•				•	•					•			•	•			•			•	•	•	•	•				•		•		•			•			
MOSELEY OLD HALL														•							•			•	•	•	•		•	•		•			•				
MOTTISFONT ABBEY		•	•	•	•	•			•	•				•	•						•	•	•	•					•	•	•	•		•	•	•			
MOUNT STEWART		•	•	•	•					•					•				•		•								•		•		•	•	•	•			
NOSTELL PRIORY	•	•								•					•						•			•					•		•	•	•		•				
NUNNINGTON HALL		•					•		•					•							•			•				•	•	•	•		•	•	•			•
NYMANS			•	•	•				•			•		•							•				•				•		•		•	•	•	•			
ORMESBY HALL					•				•					•							•				•				•		•		•	•		•			
OSTERLEY PARK									•				•		•						•			•					•		•	•	•			•			
OVERBECKS		•		•	•					•											•								•		•		•	•		•			
OXBURGH HALL		•					•	•		•				•							•			•					•	•	•		•			•			
PACKWOOD			•	•	•		•	•	•		•			•		•								•					•		•								
PECKOVER HOUSE	•	•		•	•	•				•					•						•				•				•		•				•			•
PENRHYN CASTLE				•			•	•						•							•				•				•				•		•			
PETWORTH HOUSE				•	•					•					•			•			•			•					•		•				•			
PLAS NEWYDD				•	•				•	•		•			•						•			•					•		•		•	•	•	•			
PLAS-YN-RHIW									•												•										•		•		•			
POLESDEN LACEY			•	•	•				•		•										•	•		•	•				•		•		•	•	•			
POWIS CASTLE	•		•	•	•				•	•			•								•	•			•				•		•		•	•	•	•			
PRIOR PARK			•		•	•					•													•									•		•			
RIEVAULX																•																							

304

Garden Specialities

Garden	Orangery	Conservatory	Bridge	Statuary	Ornaments	Fountain/pool	Formal water	Moat	Natural water	Terrace	Raised walk	Ha-ha	Mount	Ice house	Walled garden	Temple	Garden house	Dovecote	Grotto	Folly	Rock garden	Great trees	Pleaching	Avenue	Hedges	Maze	Topiary	Knot garden	Parterre	Formal beds	Borders	Rose garden	Rhododendrons	Woodland garden	Naturalised bulbs	Notable shrubs	Bog or water plants	Herb beds or garden	Fruit and vegetables
ROWALLANE GARDEN					●				●						●		●			●	●	●									●	●	●	●	●	●	●		
RUFFORD OLD HALL				●						●																													
ST MICHAEL'S MOUNT										●						●								●								●			●	●			●
SALTRAM	●			●	●	●						●				●														●		●		●	●				
SCOTNEY CASTLE		●	●	●			●	●	●	●				●																			●	●	●	●			
SHEFFIELD PARK		●																															●	●	●	●			
SHUGBOROUGH		●			●	●			●	●						●					●										●	●	●		●	●			
SISSINGHURST		●		●	●					●																					●	●	●		●	●		●	
SIZERGH CASTLE		●																		●	●										●	●				●		●	
SNOWSHILL MANOR				●			●			●	●	●					●		●								●		●								●	●	
SPEKE HALL		●									●	●									●										●	●				●			
SPRINGHILL														●		●		●			●										●				●				
STANDEN		●				●														●	●			●							●								●
STOURHEAD			●	●	●			●	●							●			●	●	●										●	●			●	●			
STOWE LANDSCAPE GARDENS			●	●	●	●		●								●		●	●	●											●	●			●				
TATTON PARK	●			●	●	●			●						●	●					●			●	●		●		●	●	●		●	●	●				
TINTINHULL HOUSE																								●			●				●	●			●			●	
TRELISSICK		●												●							●										●		●	●	●				
TRENGWAINTON									●	●						●				●	●	●									●		●	●	●	●			
TRERICE										●					●										●						●								●
UPPARK					●				●	●		●									●										●	●			●				
UPTON HOUSE		●				●									●	●					●	●									●	●		●		●			
THE VYNE	●							●						●							●										●				●				
WADDESDON MANOR			●	●	●									●									●	●			●		●						●	●			
WAKEHURST PLACE GARDEN			●	●	●			●							●						●			●							●	●		●	●	●	●		
WALLINGTON		●	●	●	●				●	●	●			●			●				●			●	●						●	●							●
THE WEIR			●						●	●	●					●				●	●												●	●		●			
WESTBURY COURT			●			●										●											●		●		●								●
WEST WYCOMBE PARK			●	●	●				●	●		●				●		●					●	●											●				
WIGHTWICK MANOR			●	●					●							●					●				●						●	●	●	●	●	●		●	●
WIMPOLE HALL		●		●					●			●									●			●			●	●		●			●	●					
WINKWORTH ARBORETUM																					●			●									●	●	●	●			
WORDSWORTH HOUSE									●					●						●	●										●							●	●

305

Other Gardens

ALFRISTON CLERGY HOUSE
The Tye, Alfriston, Polegate
Sussex BN26 5TL

ASHDOWN HOUSE
Lambourn, Newbury
Oxfordshire RG16 7RE

AVEBURY MANOR
GARDEN
nr Marlborough
Wiltshire SN8 1RF

CASTLE COOLE
Enniskillen
Co. Fermanagh BT74 6JX

CHERRYBURN
Station Bank, Mickley
Stocksfield
Northumberland NE43 7DB

CLAYDON HOUSE
Middle Claydon
nr Buckingham
Buckinghamshire MK18 2EY

COLBY WOODLAND
GARDEN
Colby Bothy, Amroth
Narberth
Pembrokeshire SA67 8PP

COMPTON CASTLE
Marldon, Paignton
Devon TQ3 1TA

COUGHTON COURT
nr Alcester
Warwickshire B49 5JA

DERRYMORE HOUSE
Bessbrook, Newry
Co. Down

DINEFWR PARK
Llandeilo
Dyfed SA19 6RT

DORNEYWOOD GARDEN
Dorneywood, Burnham
Buckinghamshire SL1 8PY

DOWNHILL CASTLE
Bishop's Gate
42 Mussenden Road
Castlerock, Coleraine
Co. Londonderry BT51 4RP

FELL FOOT PARK
Newby Bridge, Ulverston
Cumbria LA12 8NN

GIBSIDE
nr Rowlands Gill
Burnopfield
Newcastle-upon-Tyne
Tyne & Wear NE16 6BG

GODDARDS
27 Tadcaster Road
Dringhouses, York
Yorkshire YO2 2QGT

GRANTHAM HOUSE
Castlegate, Grantham
Lincolnshire NG31 6SS

THE GREYFRIARS
Friar Street, Worcester
Worcestershire WR1 2LZ

ILAM HALL
COUNTRY PARK
Ilam, Ashbourne
Derbyshire DE6 2AZ

LAVENHAM GUILDHALL
Market Place, Lavenham
Sudbury
Derbyshire CO10 9QZ

LEITH HILL
nr Coldharbour
Surrey

LINDISFARNE CASTLE
Holy Island
Berwick-upon-Tweed
Northumberland TD15 2SH

*LINDSEY HOUSE
99–100 Cheyne Walk
London SW10

LITTLE CLARENDON
Dinton, Salisbury
Wiltshire SP3 5OZ

LLANERCHAERON
nr Aberaeron
Dyfed SA48 8DG

LYVEDEN NEW BIELD
nr Oundle
Peterborough
Northamptonshire PE8 5AT

MORDEN HALL PARK
Morden Hall Road
Morden
London SM4 5DJ

*MORVILLE HALL
nr Bridgnorth
Shropshire WV16 5BN

MOTTISTONE MANOR
GARDEN
Bookings and enquiries to
the Gardener, Manor Cottage,
Hoxall Lane, Mottistone
Isle of Wight PO30 4ED

MOUNT GRACE PRIORY
Osmotherley, Northallerton
North Yorkshire DL6 3JG

MR STRAW'S HOUSE
7 Blyth Grove, Worksop
Nottinghamshire S81 0JG

NEWARK PARK
Ozleworth
Wotton-under-Edge
Gloucestershire GL12 7PZ

OAKHURST COTTAGE
Hambledon, nr Godalming
Surrey

OWLETTS
Cobham, Gravesend
Kent DA12 3AP

PAYCOCKE'S
West Street, Coggeshall
Colchester
Essex CO6 1NS

PRINCES RISBOROUGH
MANOR HOUSE
Princes Risborough
Buckinghamshire HP17 9AW

QUEBEC HOUSE
Westerham
Kent TN16 1TD

ST JOHN'S JERUSALEM
Sutton-at-Hone, Dartford
Kent DA4 9HQ

SHAW'S CORNER
Ayot St Lawrence, nr Welwyn
Hertfordshire AL6 9BX

SHERINGHAM PARK
Warden: Gardener's Cottage
Sheringham Park
Upper Sheringham
Norfolk NR26 8TB

SMALLHYTHE PLACE
Smallhythe, Tenterden
Kent TN30 7NG

SPRIVERS GARDEN
Horsmonden
Kent TN12 8DR

STAGSHAW GARDEN
Ambleside
Cumbria LA22 0HE

STONEACRE
Otham, Maidstone
Kent ME15 8RS

STYAL COUNTRY PARK
Estate Office, 7 Oak Cottages
Styal, Wilmslow
Cheshire SK9 4JQ

SUDBURY HALL
Sudbury, Ashbourne
Derbyshire DE6 5HT

TOWNEND
Troutbeck, Windermere
Cumbria LA23 1LB

TREASURER'S HOUSE
Chapter House Street, York
Yorkshire YO1 2JD

TUDOR MERCHANT'S HOUSE
Quay Hill, Tenby
Pembrokeshire SA70 7BX

WASHINGTON OLD HALL
The Avenue, Washington Village
Tyne & Wear NE38 7LE

WEST GREEN GARDEN
Hartley Wintney, Basingstoke
Hampshire RG27 8JB

WESTWOOD MANOR
Bradford-on-Avon
Wiltshire BA15 2AF

*open by written appointment only

Bibliography

The National Trust's detailed guides to individual properties and gardens have been the prime source of reference. In addition, I have had access to a vast store of information on file in Cirencester, including Gardens Advisers' reports and observations, management plans, park and garden surveys by Katie Fretwell, John Phibbs and others, entries in the *Woody Plant Catalogue* compiled by Michael Lear, and articles from journals and magazines past and present, most especially from *Country Life* by John Cornforth, Arthur Hellyer, Christopher Hussey, Gervase Jackson-Stops, John Sales and others. All has been grist to the mill.

A great many books have helped me understand better the evolution of British gardens, and of certain gardens in particular. The following were principal references:

Brown, Jane, *The English Garden in Our Time* (Antique Collectors' Club, 1986)
Brown, Jane, *Sissinghurst, Portrait of a Garden* (NT/Weidenfeld & Nicolson, 1990)
Brown, Jane, *Vita's Other World* (Viking, 1985)
Clarke, Ethne, *Hidcote, the Making of a Garden* (Michael Joseph, 1989)
Elliott, Brent, *Victorian Gardens* (Batsford, 1986)
Greeves, Lydia and Michael Trinick, *The National Trust Guide* (NT, 1989)
Hayden, Peter, *Biddulph Grange: a Victorian Garden Rediscovered* (NT/George Philip)
Jacques, David, *Georgian Gardens, the Reign of Nature* (Batsford, 1983)
Jellicoe, Geoffrey and Susan, *The Landscape of Man* (Thames and Hudson, 1975)
Jellicoe, Sir Geoffrey, Susan Jellicoe, Patrick Goode and Michael Lancaster, *The Oxford Companion to Gardens* (OUP, 1986)
Nicholson, Shirley, *Nymans, the Story of a Sussex Garden* (NT/Alan Sutton, 1992)
Ottewill, David, *The Edwardian Garden* (Yale University Press, 1989)
Plumptre, George, *British Gardens* (Collins, 1985)
Robinson, John Martin, *Temples of Delight, Stowe Landscape Gardens* (NT/George Philip, 1990)
Scott-James, Anne, *Sissinghurst, the Making of a Garden* (Michael Joseph, 1975)
Strong, Roy, *The Renaissance Garden in England* (1979)
Stroud, Dorothy, *Capability Brown* (Faber & Faber, 1975)
Stroud, Dorothy, *Humphry Repton* (1962)
Stuart, David, *Georgian Gardens* (Robert Hale, 1979)
Stuart, David, *The Garden Triumphant, a Victorian Legacy* (Viking, 1988)
Thomas, Graham Stuart, *Gardens of the National Trust* (NT/Weidenfeld & Nicolson, 1979)
Turner, Tom, *English Garden Design* (Antique Collectors' Club, 1986)
Woodbridge, Kenneth, *The Stourhead Landscape* (NT guide, 1971)

Plant Index

General Index

Author's Acknowledgements

Katherine Lambert undertook the monumental task of reading files and collating research at the National Trust's office in Cirencester, while I waltzed around the gardens. I am deeply indebted to her.

Margaret Willes, the National Trust's publisher, kept faith as deadlines passed, and without the enthusiasm and encouragement over five years by her editor, Sarah-Jane Forder, I would never have made it. Marilyn Inglis edited the final text and Gail Engert designed the book. Jane Royston, Pamela Jones and Marie Miller, successively, organised my garden visits, and back home, Georgina Salvin and Caroline Nesbitt stemmed the tide of paper. My literary agent, Anthony Goff, has been a much valued sounding board and advocate.

John Sales, the National Trust's Chief Gardens Adviser, his colleagues at Cirencester, the regional managers and representatives, and, in many cases, the donor families are among those I have turned to for information and comment, and all have been immensely supportive. Tony Lord and Oliver Garnett have scrutinised the text for botanical, historical and other errors. And not least, I must thank the Head Gardeners and Gardeners in Charge, whose guided tours have been one of this project's principal pleasures.

Picture Acknowledgements

The author and publishers are grateful to the *Country Life* Picture Library for permission to reproduce the photographs on pages 64, 76, 162 and 284. All the remaining illustrations are taken from the National Trust Photographic Library and are by the following photographers:

Matthew Antrobus 68, 70-71, 74, 118; Oliver Benn 111; Michael C. Brown 287; Neil Campbell-Sharp 24, 29, 30, 31 (left and right), 32, 66, 67, 86, 87, 88 (left and right), 91, 92, 94, 100, 101, 102, 137, 146, 149, 150, 155, 157, 175, 178, 179, 180, 184, 185, 187, 229 (left), 268, 269, 270, back cover; Don Carr 73 (right); Nick Carter 58, 59; Vera Collingwood 26, 60, 81, 82, 123, 124, 294; Joe Cornish 96, 117, 190-92, 214; Eric Crichton 136, 177; Mark Fiennes 37, 41; Jerry Harpur 6, 85 (left and right), 95, 106, 121, 165 (right), 188, 189, 223, 225, 226, 259 (left and right), 260; Derek Harris 19, 20, 62, 152, 165 (left), 207, 264-5, 267, 290; Christopher Hill 192; E.M. Kirk 217; Andrew Lawson 90, 140, 142, 143, 239 (left and right), 240, 242-3, 245 (left and right); Marianne Majerus 112; Rob Matheson 203 (left and right), 215, 289; Nick Meers front cover, 13, 16, 17, 36, 49, 50-51, 53, 99, 120, 132, 141, 166, 170, 171, 173, 182, 183, 198, 229 (right), 236, 248, 249, 255 (left and right), 256-7, 258, 272, 275; Kevin J. Richardson 54, 56; Stephen Robson half title page, frontispiece, 14, 15 (left and right), 34 (top and bottom), 35, 114, 125, 125-6, 128, 130, 131, 145, 148, 159, 161, 195, 197, 204, 205, 208, 219, 220 (right), 231, 232, 252, 253, 277, 279, (left and right), 280, 292, 299, 300; Ian Shaw 8, 39, 40, 43, 44, 45 (left and right), 47, 55 (left and right), 73 (left), 78, 83, 153, 199, 220 (left), 234, 295; Robert Thrift 246; Rupert Truman 104, 108, 173, 211, 262; Andreas von Einsiedel 298; Charlie Waite 235 (left and right); Mike Warren 169; Mike Williams 21 (left and right), 63, 134, 156, 293; George Wright 201.